D1222806

GOD AND ATHEISM

A Philosophical Approach to the Problem of God

by

Bernardino M. Bonansea, O.F.M.

The Catholic University of America Press

Washington, D.C. 20064

Imprimi potest: Matthew M. De Benedictis, O.F.M., *Commissary of the Holy Land*

Nihil obstat: Michael D. Meilach, O.F.M., *Censor deputatus*

Imprimatur: John F. Donoghue, *Vicar General of the Archdiocese of Washington*
January 23, 1979

Library of Congress Cataloging in Publication Data

Bonansea, Bernardino M.
  God and atheism.

  Bibliography
  Includes index.
  1. God—Proof—History of doctrines.   I. Title.
BT102.B55   212   78-12064
ISBN 0-8132-0549-2

INTRODUCTION

God continues to be at the center of much discussion not only among philosophers and theologians but also among people who may be less professionally competent but are equally interested in the subject. More and more men and women of all walks of life seem to realize that "the God issue" is of vital concern to them and that its outcome has an impact on the entire course and direction of their lives. It makes a difference, in fact, for a person whether he acknowledges or denies the existence of a supreme Being on whom he depends and to whom he is ultimately accountable. This issue involves the fundamental problem of the purpose and destiny of human life, a problem that, in Blondel's words, every man must inevitably face. Moreover, each man's solution, right or wrong, will be carried out in his own actions.[1] The meaning of life, concurs Camus, is "the most urgent of questions."[2]

It is true that there are still many people who do not seem to attach great importance to the question of God's existence, and for all practical purposes they live as though "the God issue" did not affect their lives in any appreciable way. Whether the claim of these "practical atheists" is a genuine one, or whether by their own admission they have already solved the problem of God's existence in the negative, is not our concern. The truth of the matter is that no rational being worthy of the name, and especially no well-educated person, can live his entire life without ever giving thought to the meaning and purpose of his existence and raising at least implicitly the question of the existence of some sort of superior and transcendent Being. As Socrates taught many centuries ago, an unexamined life is not worth living.

Admittedly, in recent years the discussion about God has taken a new turn and not necessarily for the better. There is a growing conviction in certain philosophical circles that the traditional notion of God as a provident creator of the universe has outlived its usefulness. In a world where so much evil is perpetrated and where so many innocent people suffer for no apparent reason, it is hard to conceive how an omnipotent and supremely good Being could allow such a situation to develop or be in any way responsible for it. On the other hand, it is claimed in some scientific sectors that "the God hypothesis" is unnecessary today, since science and technology have superseded it. The great achievements in the scientific and technological fields seem to lend support to this view and confirm the

---

[1]Maurice Blondel, *L'action* (1893); (reprint; Paris: Presses Universitaires de France, 1950), pp. vii–viii.

[2]Albert Camus, *The Myth of Sisyphus* (New York: Random House "Vintage Books," 1955), p. 4.

opinion of those who foresee the possibility that science will unlock all the secrets of man and the universe quite independently of a hypothetical God. Finally, the notion of a God who would determine man's conduct by a set of laws and restrictions that curtail man's deep-rooted tendency toward freedom and independence is far from meeting with the favor of those left-wing existentialists for whom freedom is an absolute not to be tampered with. If man is free, or rather, if man is freedom itself, then God cannot exist. The very notion of man as a free being excludes the possibility of a Being who is held to be his creator and the supreme arbiter of his life and death.

These views, in addition to the widespread theory that all talk about God is meaningless because it lacks the support of empirical evidence, have greatly contributed to present-day confusion in the field of natural theology. They also seem to be a challenge to traditional theistic belief. This may explain why so much literature is being produced today in an attempt to solve what has come to be known as "the problem of God." In a way, God has always been a problem for man, and especially for a philosopher, who in his inquiry is guided by reason alone. God's existence is indeed not a self-evident truth, and hence it must be demonstrated. But lately this problem has become more acute and has acquired a new dimension, inasmuch as scholars of different persuasions have challenged not only the existence of God but also the very possibility of any rational approach to the issue itself.[3] Moreover, attempts are made in various sectors to replace belief in God and religion with purely naturalistic and materialistic ideologies, so that today we are confronted not merely with certain isolated atheistic doctrines but with truly and unequivocally antitheistic systems of philosophy.[4] These systems have become more disturbing

---

[3]God was discussed in the past, especially in the Middle Ages, but never as a problem in the sense that we use the term today. God's existence was taken for granted, and the discussion centered mostly on his nature and operations. Thus Thomas Aquinas devotes a single question of his massive *Summa theologiae* to the existence of God, and only one article to its actual demonstration. And even in that article he only sets forth those arguments which, as he points out elsewhere, had been used by both philosophers and Catholic teachers to prove that God exists. (Cf. *Summa contra gentiles,* Book I, ch. 13.) It is true that John Duns Scotus wrote the treatise *De primo principio,* which is essentially a complex and fully developed proof of God's existence, but in medieval philosophical literature Scotus' treatise is an exception rather than the rule. Hence it is incorrect for Bishop Robinson to say that "traditional Christian theology has been based upon the proofs for the existence of God" and "the presupposition of these proofs, psychologically if not logically, is that God might or might not exist." Cf. John A. T. Robinson, *Honest to God* (Philadelphia: The Westminster Press, 1963), p. 29. For a survey of the problem of God in the history of philosophy see this writer's article, "Existence of God in Philosophy," *New Catholic Encyclopedia,* VI, 547-52.

[4]In the words of Jacques Maritain, contemporary atheism is both absolute and positive, for it truly denies the existence of God and it is an authentic antitheism "demanding to be lived in full by man and to change the face of the earth." *The Range of Reason* (New York: Scribner's Sons, 1952), p. 104.

because they present themselves as the authentic interpretation of the feelings and aspirations of contemporary man and as the embodiment of those scientific and technical values which, in the eyes of many people, constitute present-day civilization. The fact that political regimes have been at work for years in an all-out effort to de-Christianize the masses has, moreover, compounded the difficulty of the problem. It has converted what used to be considered a phenomenon among the elite into a mass phenomenon that involves a large segment of humanity and the populations of entire countries.[5]

In view of this situation, a reconsideration of the whole problem of God's existence within the context of classic and modern philosophy is needed. To provide this is the purpose of the present volume.

Our study will begin with a critical analysis of the principal atheistic trends of thought in modern and contemporary times, with a view to showing their weaknesses and deficiencies, and even their manifest contradictions. Thinkers to be considered include Marx (as understood in today's Soviet Russia), Feuerbach, Freud, Nietzsche, Sartre, and Camus. Certain naturalistic interpretations of religion in the fields of anthropology, sociology, and psychology will also be discussed, along with the views of those intellectuals who deny God either in the name of science or because of their inability to reconcile the notion of an infinitely good and merciful Being with the existence of so much evil in the world.

The second part of our study will be of a more constructive nature and may, in many respects, be considered as the answer to the problems raised in the first part. In it, we shall examine the classic theistic arguments developed by such great minds as Augustine, Anselm, Thomas Aquinas, and Duns Scotus, as well as Maurice Blondel's original approach to God, for the purpose of exploring their value as rational proofs of God's existence. The ideological and ontological arguments will be studied in their original sources and within the context of other pertinent works by their proponents. The history of the controversy aroused by them will also be traced from the time of the arguments' first appearance to the present day. The presentation will be followed in each case by our personal evaluation, which itself may be the object of controversy but is offered with what we hope is perfect honesty and objectivity.

The five ways of St. Thomas, held by many as the simplest and most

---

[5]The observation of a contemporary writer on the particular features of nineteenth-century atheism is even more applicable to present-day atheism. "Atheism, remarked Robespierre, is aristocratic; and because he hated aristocrats, he hated atheists also. However, during the course of the nineteenth century, from being aristocratic and intellectual, atheism became democratic and political." Jean Lacroix, *The Meaning of Modern Atheism*, trans. Garret Barden, S.J. (New York: The Macmillan Company, 1966), p. 18.

effective arguments for God's existence, will be presented in a new and original interpretation by a distinguished Thomist, who has kindly allowed us to publish his study in an English version especially prepared for this volume. The reader will find in Louis Charlier's penetrating analysis of the five ways many insights which may escape the attention even of a professional philosopher. In the author's view, the theological context in which the five ways have been developed does not detract in any way from their effectiveness as true and genuine metaphysical arguments for the existence of God, and that despite the incidental elements of an outmoded physics assumed by Aquinas. Charlier's interpretation of the five ways has been made possible because of his vast and thorough knowledge of St. Thomas' works, from which he generously quotes in his extensive and highly stimulating study.

The Scotistic proof for God's existence will be presented on the basis of the critical edition of the *Ordinatio,* Scotus' major work, but with due consideration of other pertinent works, especially the *De primo principio.* Since Scotus is the only medieval thinker to have devoted a whole treatise to the question of God's existence, it is felt that his proof should receive extensive treatment. This we will do in a special chapter, in which an attempt will be made to present Scotus' intellectual ascent to God as clearly and effectively as possible, following carefully the steps of his stringent dialectic. A comparison between Scotus' approach to God and the preceding theistic arguments will conclude the essay on Scotus' proof.[6]

To give this study a modern flavor, it will be fitting to discuss, in addition to the classic theistic arguments of medieval philosophy, the approach to God of Maurice Blondel, a contemporary original thinker who has not as yet received the credit he deserves, especially in the English-speaking world. By using the method of immanence and the dialectic of action, thought, and being, Blondel arrives at God as the "unique necessary" Being that can fully satisfy man's inner aspirations and is at the same time the answer to the crucial problem of human destiny. It is this latter problem, compounded by the atmosphere of religious indifference found among his masters and schoolmates at Paris, that spurred Blondel to seek new avenues in his quest for a solution that might be helpful to twentieth-century man. His exploration, marking the beginning of a new trend in philosophy, is worth studying, especially because of the positive results it has produced and the increasing number of Blondelian scholars it has inspired.

---

[6]In an Appendix, a simplified version of the theistic proof will be presented which, in a new and somewhat original formulation, attempts to reach God by a series of inferential judgments from the most fundamental facts of our experience, i.e., our own existence and the existence of the world around us.

The second part of our study concludes with a reflection on the nature, value, and limitations of a theistic proof, in which attention is called to the important but often overlooked distinction between the value of an argument and conviction of its value. Attention is also called to some persisting misunderstandings surrounding the theistic proof, while at the same time the relation between reason and faith in man's ascent to God is briefly discussed. As an argument *ab absurdo,* the inconsistencies and contradictions involved in two large philosophical movements today, atheistic existentialism and dialectical materialism, are carefully pointed out, to emphasize the rational character of the theistic position. This conclusion will be confirmed by the ensuing discussion of the various forms of modern and contemporary agnosticism, where special attention will be given to the movement known as logical positivism.

The third and last part of our study is concerned with the relationship between God and the universe and the impact of science on philosophy with regard to the question of the origin of the world. The first chapter will explore the reasons advanced by St. Bonaventure for the impossibility of creation from eternity, as against the opposite view of other medieval philosophers, and especially that of Thomas Aquinas. The controversy has significance for this study since, if Bonaventure's thesis is accepted, the world is bound to have had a beginning, and any purely materialistic or atheistic doctrine would prove to be faulty.

This thesis will be strengthened in the final chapter, where the doctrine of creation is confronted with the findings of positive science. After clarifying the notion of creation on strictly philosophical grounds, it will be shown that science, far from disproving the creationist theory, tends to support it. The results of this inquiry will help dispel the notion of any possible conflict between science and philosophy—and even theology, for that matter—and facilitate mutual cooperation between scientists and philosophers in their unrestrained yet justified ambition to unlock the secrets of the universe.

Although some sections of the book have already appeared in philosophical journals and scholarly works, they have for the most part been revised, developed, or updated for the purpose of this publication. A partially annotated bibliography has also been added to each chapter. We are confident that this volume, containing the results of many years of teaching at the Catholic University of America, as well as at St. John's University, N.Y., and Villanova University, Pa., will be of some help to both professors and students of philosophy. For one thing, they will find in it the most extensive treatment of the ideological, ontological, and Scotistic arguments for God's existence ever to appear in English in a single volume, along with an original and penetrating analysis of St. Thomas' five ways. Hopefully, the critical evaluation of the various forms of modern and contemporary atheism that serves as an introduction to our study, will help to enhance the value of the approach to God that has its foundation in Greek philosophy and has been accepted and variously developed by some of the greatest minds from the early Middle Ages down to the present time.

BIBLIOGRAPHY

This bibliography and that of the following chapters (with the exception of chapter 6) include only the sources used in the preparation of the text and those referred to in the Notes.

Blondel, Maurice. *L'action (1893)*: reprint. Paris: Presses Universitaires de France, 1950.

Bonansea, Bernardino M. "Existence of God in Philosophy," *New Catholic Encyclopedia,* VI, 547–52.

Camus, Albert. *The Myth of Sisyphus*. New York: Random House "Vintage Books," 1955.

Lacroix, Jean. *The Meaning of Modern Atheism*. Trans. by Garret Barden, S.J. New York: The Macmillan Company, 1966.

Maritain, Jacques. *The Range of Reason.* New York: Scribner's Sons, 1952.

Robinson, John A. *Honest to God.* Philadelphia: The Westminster Press, 1963.

ACKNOWLEDGMENTS

We would like to express our grateful acknowledgment to the following publishers and agencies for permission to reprint some of the material of this book, as will be indicated in the proper place in each case:

Herder and Company, Vienna, Austria; Casterman, Tournai, Belgium (copyright by Éditions Casterman and Father Charlier); G. P. Putnam's Sons, N.Y. (copyright by John Clover Monsma); Alba House, Staten Island, N.Y.; The American Catholic Philosophical Association; The Franciscan Institute, St. Bonaventure, N.Y.; and especially, The Catholic University of America Press.

We are grateful also to the following publishers for permission to quote from their copyrighted books and articles, as cited in their proper place:

Harper & Row Publishers, Inc., New York, N.Y.; Random House, Inc., and Alfred A. Knopf, Inc., New York, N.Y.; Regnery/Gateway, Inc., South Bend, Indiana; The New American Library, Inc., New York, N.Y.; New Directions Publishing Corporation, New York, N.Y.; Philosophical Library, Inc., New York, N.Y.; Encyclopaedia Britannica, Inc., and The Great Ideas Today, Chicago, Ill.; Open Court Publishing Company, La Salle, Ill.; Doubleday and Company, Inc., Garden City, N.Y.; Franciscan Herald Press, Chicago, Ill.; The Catholic University of America, Washington, D.C.

We wish also to extend our sincere thanks to the American Catholic Philosophical Association for a substantial subsidy for the publication of this book, which was made available by the De Rance Foundation, Milwaukee, Wisconsin. The recommendations by Dr. Jude P. Dougherty, of The Catholic University of America, and Dr. James Collins, of St. Louis University, were particularly helpful in obtaining the requested grant.

We are likewise deeply indebted to the following colleagues and members of the academic community for their valuable comments and suggestions, which have helped considerably to improve both the style and the text of the manuscript: the Rt. Rev. Msgr. John K. Ryan, former Dean of the School of Philosophy at The Catholic University of America; Dr. Allan B. Wolter, O.F.M., Professor of Philosophy at the same university; Dr. John M. Quinn, O.S.A., and Dr. Theodore J. Kondoleon, of Villanova University; and especially, Dr. Michael D. Meilach, O.F.M., of Siena College, Loudonville, N.Y., who has done an excellent job in editing the manuscript at the request of The Catholic University of America Press.

Finally, we would like to express our gratitude to Dr. David J. McGonagle, Executive Assistant to the Vice President of The Catholic University of America, for his favorable reception of the manuscript and his successful handling of the publication procedures, as well as to Mrs. Mitzi Jones and Miss Marian E. Goode for their secretarial and managerial assistance.

B. M. BONANSEA

The Catholic University of America
Washington, D.C.

TABLE OF CONTENTS

PART ONE

ATHEISM: CHALLENGE TO THEISM?

CHAPTER I

A CRITICAL STUDY
OF MODERN AND CONTEMPORARY ATHEISM

The problem of God's existence can be approached in two ways: positively, by expounding the reasons advanced by theists to support their affirmation, and negatively, by showing the weakness of the arguments used by atheists to justify their negation. Each approach complements the other. But whereas the first approach, if proved philosophically sound, is in itself sufficient to guarantee the truth of God's existence, the second approach, although in itself not absolutely conclusive, can be developed in such a way as to build up a strong argument for the theistic position. In this chapter we shall use the second approach in an attempt to show that the atheistic stance is not only philosophically untenable but also fraught with contradictions.

I. THE DENIAL OF GOD

To know who is really an atheist, we must first agree on what is meant by the "God" whose existence an atheist denies. For this purpose we do not need a comprehensive concept of God arrived at by strictly philosophical reasoning and including all the attributes that are usually ascribed to such a Being. This comprehensive concept is the conclusion, not the starting point, of a discussion about God's existence. What is needed is a nominal definition of God, that is, a concept of God that is found historically at the root of most religions, even though extraneous elements may have been mingled with it in the mind or imagination of believers.

What is that concept whose basic elements are usually associated with the term God in the mind of most believers? Philosophers are not of one accord on this point. Thus, at the beginning of his treatise on God, Van Steenberghen takes as his nominal definition of God the idea of a "provident creator of the universe." This definition he presents as an improvement upon the one found in the Larousse dictionary, where God is defined as a "Supreme Being, creator and preserver of the universe." His own definition, Van Steenberghen claims, corresponds to the idea of God commonly held by the great monotheistic religions and shared by all societies that have come under their influence.[1]

---

[1] Cf. Fernand Van Steenberghen, *Hidden God*, trans. Theodore Crowley, O.F.M. (St. Louis, Mo.: Herder, 1966), p. 37.

Gilson's definition of God as a starting point for his essay on atheism is more comprehensive. It includes the following elements: (1) a transcendent being, (2) who is necessary, and (3) is the cause of whatever else exists.[2] Delanglade assumes as his initial definition of God a more fully elaborated notion which, in his words, has been accepted by Christian tradition. He defines God as "a personal Being, distinct from the world and ourselves, on whom both the world and ourselves depend for our existence."[3]

We can perhaps synthesize the content of these definitions and describe God as "a transcendent being on whom the world depends both for its existence and its conservation." The elements of this definition, it is true, are not always understood in exactly the same way by all believers. Thus in some religions the notion of transcendence is vague and confused, and so too the concept of the world's dependence on God. But all religions seem to agree that God is to be conceived as a superior and extremely powerful Being on whom all other beings depend for their existence and, at least implicitly, for their conservation in existence.

Having established this fundamental concept of God, it will now be possible to classify as atheists all those who refuse to admit the existence of the being so conceived. Although this sounds logical on a theoretical level, it is not so easy in concrete cases to pinpoint an atheist, simply because his concept of God is not always clear. This difficulty has been pointed out by Lalande in his classic philosophical dictionary. There he defines atheism as "the doctrine that consists in denying the existence of God," but then he immediately remarks that the definition of the term "atheism" can be only a verbal one, for the content of the idea of atheism varies according to the different conceptions of God and of his mode of existing.[4]

In his extensive work on modern atheism, Fabro seems to agree with Lalande, inasmuch as he speaks of three stages or levels with regard to the concept of God: the popular-mythical, the philosophical-speculative, and the revealed-personal. Since the denial of God can take place at each of these levels, Fabro rightly observes that the judgments concerning the particular kind of atheism involved cannot always be the same.[5]

---

[2]Cf. Etienne Gilson, "The Idea of God and the Difficulties of Atheism," in *The Great Ideas Today*, eds. R. M. Hutchins and M. J. Adler (Chicago: Encyclopaedia Britannica, 1969), p. 239.

[3]Cf. Jean Delanglade, S.J., *Le problème De Dieu* (Paris: Aubier, 1960), p. 16.

[4]Cf. André Lalande, *Vocabulaire technique et critique de la philosophie* (Paris: Presses Universitaires de France, 1960), p. 89.

[5]Cf. Cornelio Fabro, *God in Exile*, trans. and ed. Arthur Gibson (Westminster, Md.: The Newman Press, 1968), p. 70. In his work Fabro takes the notion of atheism in a rather broad sense so as to include any philosophical system that denies the *true* God of Christian religion. Whether a philosopher denies God explicitly or does so simply by defending a

In the introduction to *L'ateismo contemporaneo,* a massive four-volume work which is unquestionably the most comprehensive study of atheism ever to appear in any language, the editor-in-chief, Giulio Girardi, takes issue with Lalande's statement that the definition of the term "atheism" can be only a verbal one. He emphasizes the point that the definition in question involves most profound problems and must be related to the notions of God and religion, which are far from being merely verbal definitions. In his approach to the problem, Girardi makes the traditional distinction between practical and theoretical atheism and defines the latter as a doctrine according to which the existence of God cannot be affirmed with certitude, either because it is denied (assertive or dogmatic atheism), or because the problem is declared insoluble (agnostic atheism) or meaningless (semantic atheism).[6]

From the foregoing survey, it becomes clear that just as there is no agreement among authors as to the initial definition of God, so there is not just one view concerning the meaning of atheism. For practical purposes we shall consider as atheist anyone who denies the existence of the God whose concept has been accepted as a working definition for our study and has the support of most religions throughout history. Its application to individual philosophers and systems of philosophy will be made with due consideration of the factors that have emerged from the preceding discussion and on the basis of objective evidence established by a careful analysis of pertinent sources.

An observation is in order. By discussing at some length the meaning of atheism and the related notion of God whose existence the atheist denies, we have wished to avoid the error of including among atheists many persons who claim to deny God but do so only because their concept of God is either inadequate or completely distorted. They are what Maritain calls pseudo-atheists. Such persons may be convinced that they do not believe in God, but in fact they unconsciously believe in him. The God whose existence they deny is not really God but a very different being.[7] They confuse God with an imaginary entity which seems to them either to be incapable of existence or to entail unacceptable consequences with regard to nature or humanity.[8] In the pages to follow we shall be concerned

---

theory that leads logically to the denial of the God of Christianity, is irrelevant to the effect of Fabro's classification. See for example his discussion of the atheism of the Cartesian *Cogito* (pp. 91 ff.), of Spinoza's metaphysics (pp. 120 ff.), of Leibniz' and Wolff's dynamism (pp. 502 ff.), and the section on the "Theology of Atheism" (pp. 971-1038) where Barth, Bultmann, Tillich, Bonhoeffer, and John A. T. Robinson are considered.

[6]Cf. *L'ateismo contemporaneo,* ed. by the Facoltà della Pontificia Università Salesiana di Roma (Turin: Società Editrice Internazionale, 1967-1969), I, 8-17.

[7]*The Range of Reason,* p. 97.

[8]*Ibid.,* p. 83.

solely with real atheists, or, more specifically, with those atheists who deny the existence of the real God as known by reason or faith or both. Real or positive atheists, as they are sometimes called, are distinct from both practical atheists, whose denial of God is a way of life rather than a philosophical position, and from negative atheists, i.e., those people who are simply unaware of God's existence.[9] Certain authors make a further distinction among positive atheists. Those who attempt to justify the denial of God with arguments of their own making are described as dogmatic atheists; on the other hand, those who simply deny any value to all theistic arguments are called agnostic. This subdistinction may help classify certain philosophers whose position on God's existence is not altogether clear but who at the same time defend a theory that quite obviously leads toward atheism.

With these distinctions drawn, we shall now proceed to study the various forms of modern and contemporary atheism beginning with what has been termed, although very improperly, scientific atheism.

II.   SCIENTIFIC ATHEISM AND CONTEMPORARY MARXIST PHILOSOPHY

In a study of the origin and tragedy of the modern denial of God, Hans Pfeil speaks of three kinds of atheism: intellectual, emotional, and volitive, each of which corresponds to a rebellion against God by one of man's

---

[9]There is some discussion among historians, as well as philosophers and theologians, concerning the existence of negative atheists. Following a solid opinion, it can be said that no man who enjoys the full use of reason and has attained to intellectual maturity, can for a long period of time, and especially for his entire life, be completely ignorant of any concept of a superior being upon whom man and the world depend. A mature man may perhaps for some time remain in ignorance about the existence of a being superior to himself, but he cannot persevere in this ignorance for a long time. If it is a question of an adult person living in a society with other adults, he will soon come to hear about God. History seems to prove in effect that even those referred to as uncivilized peoples have some notion of a superior being. If we imagine an adult cut off from all social contact, it is quite probable that he will be led by his intellect to the recognition of a superior being as the author of nature, or that he will at least suspect the possibility of such a being.

If the question is asked whether it is possible for *any individual man* to pass his whole life in ignorance of the existence of the *true* God, namely, of a superior being on whom man depends and to whom he is responsible for his actions, then the answer seems to be in the affirmative. Likewise, it is quite possible that some men who have been exposed to the idea of a true God, as explained above, may refrain from making any definite judgment about his existence. As to the responsibility, and hence culpability, of such ignorance, contemporary authors are not of one opinion. The whole question concerns the possibility or less of an invincible ignorance with regard to the existence of God. Some recent authors, following Cardinal Billot, admit the possibility of such ignorance. Cf. Maurice R. Holloway, S.J., *An Introduction to Natural Theology* (New York: Appleton-Century-Crofts, 1959), pp. 472-74.

powers. Intellectual atheism is a rebellion of the understanding and maintains that all reality and all events can be traced to causes within the
world. Hence the existence of a superior and transcendent Being becomes
superfluous. Emotional atheism is a rebellion of feeling. Its followers
believe that the existence of the many evils in the world is sufficient to rule
out the existence of God. Finally, volitive atheism is a rebellion of the will.
It claims that the existence of God amounts to the denial of the independence of the world, and especially of man's freedom and self-develop-
ment.[10] As far as the origin and nature of intellectual atheism is concerned, John Courtney Murray seems to agree with Pfeil when he writes
that "the modern godless man is characterized by his will to understand
and explain the world without God."[11] Jean Lacroix is of the same opinion. Speaking of a certain trend within modern science that would
replace philosophy and theology with a purely scientific explanation of the
world, he writes:

> The scientist does not contemplate the intelligibility of God; he creates
> the intelligibility of the world. This method of knowing, because of its
> honesty and rigor, tends to scorn all other methods, especially philo-
> sophical reflection and religious faith, which appear vague, subjective,
> even dishonest.[12]

The theory that science has done away with God is a conviction of
atheistic scientists themselves. In the course of a week of discussion
among intellectuals in France in 1965, several scientists made this point
very clear. Here are some excerpts from their communications. Laurent
Schwartz states:

> Neither God nor any dogma exists in scientific research.... Today
> science, whether for a believer or an unbeliever, explains nothing
> through God. Somehow or other God is placed outside the scientific
> explanation, in a world apart.[13]

This statement, although coming from a professed atheist, does not
amount necessarily to a denial of the existence of God, but Schwartz'
stress on the independence and autonomy of science points in that direction. Edgar Morin says even more emphatically: "For me...the question

---

[10]Cf. Hans Pfeil, "The Modern Denial of God: Its Origin and Tragedy," *Philosophy
Today*, 3 (1959), 19-26.
[11]Cf. Murray's article, "On the Structure of the Problem of God," *Theological Studies*,
23 (1962), 19.
[12]Lacroix, *op. cit.*, p. 27.
[13]Cf. *Dieu aujourd'hui*, "Semaine des intellectuels catholiques" (Paris: Desclée de
Brouwer, 1965), p. 15.

of God...is something that has been surpassed,"[14] while Roger Ikor affirms:

> ...in the last fifty years science seems to have been able to offer not merely partial explanations but a cosmic explanation. We know the structure of the universe in the same way we know the most intimate structure of matter....What role does God play in this reality which has been so well explained? None whatsoever. Everything happens as if the universe and man in the universe functioned simply through natural laws and had no need of God, either for their existence or for their coming into existence....
> I do not say that science proves that God does not exist. I say only that science has expelled God from the universe.[15]

In 1967, Nobel Prize winner Jacques Monod opened his course in molecular biology at the Collège de France by proclaiming his atheistic conviction. In so doing, he asserted that one of the greatest achievements of science is to have shown that man has emerged by chance from the material universe. He quoted approvingly Democritus' statement: "All that exists is the result of chance and necessity." Two years later, in an interview with Pierre-Henri Simon, a member of the French Academy of the Sciences and a believer, Monod confirmed his previously expounded theory on the origin of man and added: "The viewpoint that I endorse on this subject is by no means a mere personal opinion. It is the viewpoint of almost all modern biologists."[16] Monod's contention may be an exaggeration. The fact remains, however, that today many scientists, both in France and in other countries, have reached the conclusion that "the God hypothesis" is no longer necessary, since science and technology have displaced it. If this is true in the Western countries with their centuries-old tradition of Christianity and religious belief, it is much more so in those countries that are under the influence of Marxist philosophy, which is essentially and explicitly antitheistic. In it we find a perfect example of what "scientific" atheism is supposed to be.

To this effect, we shall turn to a fairly recent work, written by a Russian philosopher and printed in the Union of Soviet Socialist Republics, which purports to present "a popular outline" of Marxist philosophy. The fact that the work has been issued in an English version and had already a third revised edition in 1968 is indicative not only of the popularity of the

---

[14]*Ibid.*, p. 21.
[15]*Ibid.*, p. 53.
[16]Quoted in *Dieu pour l'homme d'aujourd'hui* by Jacques Duquesne (Paris: Grasset, 1970), p. 217.

work itself in Communist Russia but also of its "orthodoxy" from the point of view of contemporary Marxist ideology.[17]

In his opening chapter, the author asks what is the fundamental question of philosophy, and before providing his answer he states almost as a matter of fact that the material objects of our experience and the phenomena occurring in the world around us are the only objective reality. What exists in the mind of man and comes within the sphere of his mental activity, such as thoughts, sensations, and emotions, belongs to the realm of the ideal and the spiritual. Hence, since the material and the spiritual in the stated sense comprehend all the phenomena of our experience, the fundamental issue in philosophy is to determine the nature of the relationship between the spiritual and the material: "It is the character of this connection, the relation of thought to being, i.e., of the spiritual to the material, that constitutes the fundamental question of philosophy."[18]

The issue concerning the relationship between thought and being is fundamental, the author says, not only because the material and the spiritual are the only phenomena occurring in the world, but also because upon the solution of this issue depends the solution of all other problems in philosophy.

Since there is nothing else in the world outside the material and the spiritual, it is impossible to create a philosophical system, i.e., draw a picture of the world as a whole, without attempting to settle the fundamental question of philosophy.[19]

Having stated what he holds to be the fundamental question of philosophy, the author next suggests that the issue takes on two distinct aspects: first, what is primary, matter or consciousness?, and second, is the world knowable? Those who maintain that matter is primary and that consciousness derives from matter are called materialists; those who hold the opposite view are called idealists. The idealists may be subjective or objective, depending on whether the world is said to be "created by the consciousness of the individual," or whether it is said to be "created by some kind of an objective consciousness existing outside man."

---

[17]See *Marxist Philosophy* by V. Afanasyev, (3d ed. rev.; Moscow: Progress Publishers, 1968). As indicated on the copyright page, the book was translated from the Russian by Leo Lempert and edited by the late George Hanna. To make sure that Afanasyev's work reflects the teaching of contemporary Russian philosophy, we have checked its positions against those of an official textbook published by the Academy of Sciences of the Soviet Union in 1958 and edited by F. V. Konstantinov under the title, *Osnovy marksistskoj filosofii*. The principal theses of this textbook, which had an original edition of 750,000 copies, are summarized by J. M. Bochenski in *Soviet Russian Dialectical Materialism* (Dordrecht, Holland: D. Reidel Publishing Co., 1963), Appendix II, pp. 161–67.

[18]*Ibid.*, p. 10.

[19]*Ibid.*

If we give sufficient thought to this fundamental question, it will not be difficult to see that only two, diametrically opposed approaches are possible—either matter or consciousness must be taken as primary. This is the reason why two basic trends, materialism and idealism, long ago arose in philosophy.[20]

As for the other aspect of the question, namely, whether the world is knowable, the materialists answer it in the affirmative and hold at the same time that such knowledge is genuine and authentic; the idealists, on the other hand, deny the knowability of the world and claim that all man knows is his own thoughts (subjective idealists) or a universal spirit (objective idealists). From such a contrast it is obvious, the author comments, that "materialism in its contemporary Marxist-Leninist form is a progressive, scientific world outlook" and far superior to idealism, "which runs counter to science and is bound up with religion." The antireligious nature of Marxist philosophy is therefore a foregone conclusion.

Materialism is incompatible with religion; in a world where there is nothing else except matter in motion there is no room for a god.... Materialism, as a rule, has been and remains the world outlook of the advanced classes of society.[21]

Let us pause for a moment and comment briefly on the above statements. On what grounds, we may ask, does the author of *Marxist Philosophy* assume that the only objective reality is constituted by material objects? In making this statement the departing point of his inquiry, he evidently assumes either that its truth is self-evident or that it has been demonstrated beyond any doubt. In the case under consideration neither of these assumptions is valid.

But even if we were to grant the truth of the author's assertion, why should the relationship between being—material being in this case—and thought be considered as the fundamental issue in philosophy? Is not the question of the existence of material being, and in fact, of any being, more important than the consequent issue of its relationship to our mind? "Why are there beings, why is there anything at all, rather than nothing?" This, as Heidegger rightly affirms, is the first question of philosophy because it is the most far reaching, the deepest, and the most fundamental of all questions.[22]

Nor is that all. Assuming that the fundamental question of philosophy is the problem of the relationship between matter and thought, we may

---

[20]*Ibid.*

[21]*Ibid.*, p. 11.

[22]Cf. Martin Heidegger, *An Introduction to Metaphysics*, trans. Ralph Manheim (Garden City, N.Y.: Doubleday "Anchor Books," 1961), pp. 1–3.

still ask why only two alternative solutions to this problem are possible, namely, either that matter comes first and thought afterwards, or that thought comes first and matter afterwards? What about the other alternative, namely, that both matter and thought exist at one and the same time? This, at least, is a possibility to which no thought is being given by the author of *Marxist Philosophy*. Moreover, a professional philosopher, and in fact any person with but a superficial knowledge of the history of philosophy, should be aware of the existence of the philosophical system that assigns due importance to both matter and thought and is thus able to avoid the two extremes of complete materialism and absolute idealism. Although this dualistic system has been in existence almost from the birth of philosophy, the author of *Marxist Philosophy* does not have a single word about it. His wish to show the superiority of a godless materialism over monistic idealism seems to have led him to ignore completely a third and more balanced view of reality.

We shall now proceed with our analysis. Having settled the fundamental problem of philosophy by asserting the primacy of matter over thought, Afanasyev goes on to state that the way to study matter as the source of all reality is the dialectic method. This, in his words, is "the only scientific method" inasmuch as "dialectics sees the source of motion and development in the internal contradictions inherent in objects and phenomena."[23] Hence Marxist philosophy, which is both materialistic and dialectical, is called "dialectic materialism." Afanasyev describes it as follows:

> Dialectic materialism is a science which, on the basis of the correct solution of the fundamental question of philosophy, reveals the most general, dialectical laws governing the development of the material world—the ways for its cognition and revolutionary transformation.[24]

Following two long chapters in which the historical background of Marxist philosophy is presented, Afanasyev takes up the concept of matter as a philosophical category and quotes Lenin's definition of it from his treatise, *Materialism and Empirio-Criticism:* "Matter is a philosophical category denoting the objective reality which is given to man by his sensations, and which is copied, photographed and reflected by our sensations, while existing independently of them."[25] As Afanasyev points out, this definition of matter marks not only the fundamental difference between dialectical materialism and idealism, but "it also has deep atheistic mean-

---

[23]*Marxist Philosophy*, p. 14.
[24]*Ibid.*, p. 17.
[25]Lenin, *Collected Works* (Moscow: Foreign Languages Publishing House, 1960—), vol. 14, p. 130. See Afanasyev, *op. cit.*, p. 54.

ing, for it undermines the religious fable that god is the creator of the world."[26] The atheistic character of Marxist philosophy could not be made more explicit. Quite consistently, then, Afanasyev draws the logical consequences from the Marxist-Leninist concept of reality by saying that matter is eternal and infinite, uncreatable and indestructible; it is also the inner and final cause of everything that exists.[27] In fact, if there is no creator or outside agent responsible for its existence, matter must possess all these properties, unless one wants to say that matter has come into existence from nothing or that it can go out of existence for no reason whatsoever. Such suppositions contradict the notion of a self-existent and therefore necessary being. Nor can any limit be ascribed to matter so conceived, for any limitation would have to come from matter itself. This again contradicts the notion of a self-existent reality. Indeed, the source and principle of existence cannot be the source and principle of its limitation in existence.

We are therefore in perfect agreement with Afanasyev when he describes the attributes that follow necessarily upon the notion of a self-existent being. But nowhere in his work can we find a proof that the being in question must be a purely material being or what he terms the philosophical category of matter, unless we take as proof his gratuitous and naive assertion that matter is the only objective reality because that is all we see around us. Furthermore when Afanasyev tells us categorically that "scientific progress and all man's practical experience conclusively prove that matter...is infinite and eternal,"[28] we may seriously question his sincerity. How in the world has a scientist, whose investigation is guided by a strictly empirical method, ever been able to verify and "conclusively prove" the eternity and infinite nature of matter? As we read statements like the one above mentioned, we have the impression of being the victims of an illusion or a joke. But we must not forget the warning of Engels that, once we admit that the universe is limited and has a temporal duration, we are bound to accept the notion of a creator, which a Marxist philosophy must reject a priori.[29]

Matter, we are further told by Afanasyev, is not something static; it is in constant motion. Indeed, it is through motion that matter manifests

---

[26] *Ibid.*, p. 55.

[27] *Ibid.*

[28] *Ibid.*

[29] Richard T. De George writes in this connection: "[Soviet] philosophers, following Engels, claimed that space and time were objective and that the universe was infinite. Any admission of a finite universe, according to Engels, entailed the assumption of a creator or prime mover or God, which he rejected a priori. Consequently in arguing against the German philosopher Dühring, he argued for the infinity of the universe." *The New Marxism* (New York: Pegasus, 1968), p. 122.

itself to us. Motion is so intimately connected with matter that it becomes its inseparable attribute and "a form of its existence." In Engels' words: *"Motion is the mode of existence of matter.* Never anywhere has there been matter without motion, nor can there be."[30] If we substitute energy for motion we see little originality in Engels' understanding of motion, which can be brought into agreement with the definition of all modern manuals of physics. But in Marxist philosophy motion has a much wider meaning. In addition to being absolute and eternal like matter itself, and hence uncreatable and indestructible—and this always on the basis of scientific evidence!—motion is held to include all changes and all processes going on in the universe "from the simplest mechanical displacement to such an extremely complex process as human thinking."[31] It is to Engels' credit, we are told, that for the first time a scientific classification of the forms of motion in matter has been given which goes from mechanical, physical, chemical, and biological motion to the higher forms of social and intellectual life. The latest achievements of science, observes Afanasyev, have nevertheless considerably enriched our knowledge of the various forms of motion.[32]

Since motion is responsible for all changes in matter, and matter is supposedly the only objective reality, it is only logical to infer that human consciousness is but one form of the evolution of matter. This is precisely what the author of *Marxist Philosophy* attempts to show in a special chapter devoted to the study of the relationship between matter and consciousness. Appealing, as usual, to scientific evidence to back up his statements, Afanasyev affirms that "contemporary science has proved that consciousness—which includes man's thoughts and emotions, will and character, sensations, ideas, views, etc.—is a product of the prolonged evolution of matter." Not of any kind of matter, however, but only of such highly organized matter as is the human brain. Consciousness can therefore be defined as "a special property of highly organized matter, the brain, by which it reflects material reality."[33]

A materialistic interpretation of reality and knowledge is thus complete. Even the most distinct feature of man's life and activity, his power to abstract, reason, reflect and thus transcend the limits of all material boundaries, is simply reduced to an advanced stage in the evolutionary process of an all-powerful matter. The brain, which is the organ of thinking—a necessary and indispensable organ to be sure, but an organ never-

---

[30]Quoted in Afanasyev, *op. cit.*, p. 61, from Friedrich Engels, *Anti-Dühring: Herr Eugen Dühring's Revolution in Science* (Moscow: Progress Publishers, 1959), p. 68.

[31]*Ibid.*, pp. 62–63.

[32]*Ibid.*, pp. 63–64.

[33]*Ibid.*, pp. 71–73.

theless—becomes the cause itself of thinking. That is not all. The most mysterious aspect of this process of evolution is that non-thinking and therefore unintelligent matter can organize itself in such a way as to produce, by virtue of blind mechanical forces—for life itself is held to be the product of evolution—an organ whose complexity and efficiency has been the object of perpetual wonder to scientists of all times. Needless to say, logic is not the strong point of dialectical materialism.

A more complete discussion of how Marxist philosophy explains the origin of man and his intellectual activity from inanimate matter would demand a treatment of the three laws of dialectical materialism, which are offered as the key to the understanding of the whole theory. Because of the limits of this study, we shall confine ourselves to some general observations which, in our estimation, are sufficient to invalidate the reasoning behind the three laws in question. The second and principal law of dialectical materialism is "the law of transformation of quantity into quality." This law aims to explain how in the course of evolution new qualities suddenly appear which represent the transition from a lower to a superior being.[34] These "qualitative" changes are held to explain the transition from inorganic matter to life, sensation, and consciousness, just as water—this is the analogy used to illustrate the point—changes suddenly its state and becomes steam when boiled at 100 °C. The rationale behind this law is that the distinction between the various orders of beings, such as man, lower animals, and stone, is purely accidental or "qualitative," since all beings are essentially the product of matter and motion. The analogy of boiling water is significative.

But can we really say that the difference between man and a cabbage or a stone—to take some extremes in the order of being—is merely a difference in quality? Should we not rather acknowledge more realistically that since the beings in question have entirely different natures, they are also essentially, and not merely qualitatively, different among themselves? The answer should be obvious. Moreover, the analogy of water is completely misleading. Water and steam, although qualitatively different, are essentially the same as far as their chemical composition is concerned. Further, if left to itself, water will never change its state one way or the other. If a change takes place, it is because of a cause outside itself which

---

[34]The first law is "the law of the unity of contraries," which purports to explain the source of movement in the material world from the conflict of the elements that make up matter and conditions all development. The third law is "the law of the negation of negation," whose purpose is to show how in the course of development, when something new appears, the connection with the old is still preserved. Thus the fruit is the negation of the plant, which in turn is the negation of the seed, and both seed and plant are somehow preserved in the fruit. Cf. Afanasyev, *op. cit.*, pp. 93–128.

brings forth the change, such as heat that turns water into steam. Hence the analogy is self-defeating and so also is the second law of dialectical materialism which the analogy is supposed to illustrate.

In conclusion, it can be said that any attempt on the part of a dialectical materialist to explain the world without God is bound to run into contradictions.[35] The same holds true with regard to those philosophers who, following Hume, Comte, and the positivistic school in general, adopt the empirical method of investigation and rely exclusively on scientific and experimental data. Even while they defend their position, they make in fact statements concerning the limits and value of knowledge which are essentially metaphysical. By doing so, they directly contradict their system. Science can provide the philosopher with valuable information on the physical structure and laws of the universe, but it can never answer the questions of why and how the universe came into existence, what is its ultimate purpose, and why it is directed by the existing physical laws rather than others.[36] These questions transcend all empirical data and can be answered only by a philosopher on the basis of certain fundamental principles of reason that go beyond empirical evidence and stand or fall with reason itself. A philosopher will argue in effect from the nature of being to its ultimate causes and principles, and more specifically, from the contingent nature of the universe to its necessary and transcendent cause—God. To hold the contrary is to accept the consequences we have pointed out in connection with dialectical materialism which, by excluding God a priori, is forced to attribute to the universe those same characteristics that classic philosophy has long proved to be exclusive properties of the divine nature. Briefly, it is forced to accept the absurd.

III.   FEUERBACH'S HUMANISTIC ATHEISM
AND SOME
NATURALISTIC INTERPRETATIONS OF RELIGION

Whereas scientific atheism denies God and deifies the world, humanistic atheism denies God by deifying man. Humanistic atheism has taken

---

[35]For a detailed list of such contradictions see chapter VII of this volume.

[36]As a contemporary writer points out, "there are not and there cannot be 'scientific proofs' of the existence of God," just as "there cannot be 'scientific proofs' of the falsity of the affirmation of God." (Cf. Delanglade, *op. cit.*, pp. 58–60.) This amounts to saying that science can neither prove nor disprove the existence of God, unless it renounces the empirical method of verification which is proper to it. It is true that a scientist is also a man and often makes statements that reflect his attitude toward God as a total human being rather than as a scientist as such. However, in this case his statements carry only the weight proper to affirmations which are beyond his particular field of competence and they should not be given an importance they do not deserve.

different forms in the course of history, but in each case man becomes not
only the arbiter of his own destiny but also the norm and epitome of all
values and, to a certain extent, the embodiment of all reality. Thus in the
nineteenth-century naturalistic humanism of Feuerbach, whose influence
on the contemporary naturalistic movement in the United States is far
from negligible, man is "the true *ens realissimum*," while God is a mere
abstraction, a projection of the human mind. "There is no distinction,"
writes Feuerbach, "between the predicates of the divine and human nature, and, consequently, no distinction between the divine and human
subject."[37] In his doctrine human nature, whose constitutive elements are
reason, will, and affection, becomes the object of religion, and theology becomes anthropology. But can we still speak of religion in an atheistic conception of reality? To this question Feuerbach answers that "atheism is
the secret of religion itself," for "religion..., in its essence, believes in
nothing else than the truth and divinity of human nature."[38] Religion, he
further states, is self-consciousness, that is, "the consciousness which man
has of his own, not finite and limited, but infinite nature," since "consciousness is essentially infinite in its nature."[39] This is so because human
nature, once it is purified and freed from the limits of the individual man
and made the object of man's understanding, becomes, as it were, a distinct being and assumes all the characteristics of the divine being with
which it is to be identified.[40]

Accordingly, the measure of God is the measure of my understanding.
"If thou conceivest God as limited, thy understanding is limited; if thou
conceivest God as unlimited, thy understanding is unlimited."[41] In the
ultimate analysis, "the understanding is the *ens realissimum*, the most
real being of the old onto-theology."[42] It is the self-subsistent and
independent being, for in thinking of human nature the understanding
thinks of itself, and, since to think is to exist, it also exists in and by itself.
Furthermore, the understanding is infinite and necessary like human
nature itself, for, on the one hand, nothing can stand in its way and limit
it, and, on the other hand, the understanding has within itself the reason
for its own existence.[43]

Where does the world fit into such a scheme? Is there still room for an
objective world existing apart from human nature or its understanding of

---

[37]Cf. Ludwig Feuerbach, *The Essence of Christianity*, trans. George Eliot (New York:
"Harper Torchbooks," 1957), Preface by the author, p. xxxvii.

[38]*Ibid.*, p. xxxvi.

[39]*Ibid.*, pp. 2–3.

[40]*Ibid.*, pp. 12–14.

[41]*Ibid.*, p. 39.

[42]*Ibid.*, p. 38.

[43]*Ibid.*, pp. 39–42.

it? Moreover, where does the world come from? Arguing from the principle that something becomes the object of man's understanding only inasmuch as it is a manifestation of human nature,[44] Feuerbach answers
that the world exists out of necessity, and that its necessity derives from
reason.[45] Hence reason or self-consciousness is the origin of the world,[46]
while creation is a product of the will, but only as this is considered in its
function as an imaginary and purely subjective power. Creation out of
nothing, Feuerbach explains, means simply the nothingness of the world,
inasmuch as the will, which has called the world into existence, can, at
least potentially, call it back again into nothing. "The existence of the
world is therefore a momentary, arbitrary, unreliable, i.e., unreal existence."[47]

The humanization of God is thus complete. Creation itself, which
traditional theology ascribes to God as his exclusive operation, becomes
an action of man who, for all practical purposes, has taken the place of
God. Even the mystery of the Incarnation is explained by Feuerbach in
purely humanistic terms, for God was already human before he became
man: "The idea of the Incarnation is nothing more than the human form
of a God, who already in his nature, in the profoundest depths of his soul,
is a merciful and therefore a human God."[48]

There is no reason to go further in the exposition of what Karl Barth
has called an attempt to displace traditional theology with a theory that at
best is a platitude.[49] What we wish to point out is the contradictions to
which Feuerbach's anthropological approach to God and religion has
given rise. By identifying God with human nature and conceiving religion
as man's awareness of the infinity of his nature, Feuerbach can hardly
escape the charge of depriving the concept of God of its ontological foundation and making it a pure fiction of the mind. As a contemporary critic
puts it, "Feuerbach's God was all too human and, as such, was suspected
by many of being the illusion of illusions."[50] In fact, what is for Feuerbach
human nature with its asserted characteristic of infinity, except a concept

---

[44]"Whatever kind of object...we are at any time conscious of, we are always at the same
time conscious of our own nature." *Ibid.*, p. 6.

[45]"Thus the world is only necessary out of itself and through itself. But the necessity of
the world is the necessity of reason...as the sum of all realities." *Ibid.*, p. 43.

[46]*Ibid.*, p. 81.

[47]*Ibid.*, p. 101.

[48]*Ibid.*, p. 51.

[49]"Feuerbach worked with an energy surpassed by few contemporaries of his stamp,
precisely in order to displace theology." *Ibid.*, Introductory Essay, p. x. "Of course, his
[Feuerbach's] theory is a platitude." *Ibid.*, p. xxvii.

[50]Cf. Vincent P. Miceli, *The Gods of Atheism* (New Rochelle, N.Y.: Arlington House,
1971), p. 38.

of the mind or an abstraction which as such has no concrete correspondent in reality? This is brought out particularly in his materialistic conception of philosophy which he proposes as a direct counterpart to Hegel's idealism. In his words,

> I hold *that* alone to be an object which has an existence beyond one's brain.... In the sphere of strictly theoretical philosophy, I attach myself, in direct opposition to the Hegelian philosophy, only to realism, to materialism in the sense above indicated.[51]

If the only objective reality is material reality—a concept that, as we have seen, was later taken up by Marxist philosophy—and human nature as something distinct from man, the *ens realissimum*, is not a concrete being, then not only does God become an illusion but religion too, at least as it is traditionally conceived, loses all its meaning and value. After all, who is willing to worship an abstraction? Worse still, who is willing to worship another man or the human species as his own God, since in Feuerbach's view *Homo homini Deus est*?[52] Henri de Lubac rightly observes in this connection:

> Be it noted...that Feuerbach does not say, as Max Stirner was soon to say, *Ego mihi deus*. He believes that the human essence, with its prerogatives which call for worship, is not inherent in the individual considered in isolation, but only in the community, in the generic being (*Gattungswesen*).[53]

Commenting on Feuerbach's anthropological approach to religion, and especially on his conception of man as "the beginning, the middle, and the end of religion," Barth remarks: "We have heard something quite extraordinary, almost nauseatingly, trivial."[54] We are inclined to agree with the illustrious Protestant theologian, whom H. Richard Niebuhr commends for having shown the outcome of every theology that begins with man's subjective states.[55] Feuerbach's efforts to build up a system of reality from the mere rationalization about the states of one's own consciousness—and a sensible consciousness at that—leaves all the basic problems of philosophy unsolved, including the reality of one's own consciousness. As James Collins remarks, philosophy becomes for Feuerbach

---

[51]*Ibid.*, p. xxxiv.

[52]*Ibid.*, p. 159.

[53]Cf. *The Drama of Atheist Humanism*, trans. Edith M. Riley (New York: Sheed and Ward, 1950), p. 10.

[54]Feuerbach, *op. cit.*, Introductory Essay, p. xix.

[55]*Ibid.*, Foreword, p. viii.

a monologue of reason, discoursing about man's own nature and not about the author of nature, the infinite and independent God.[56]

We have singled out Feuerbach as a representative of that branch of humanistic atheism which denies the God of traditional theology because of the radical subjectivism with which he approaches the problem of God's existence. Another reason for our choice has been, in addition to Feuerbach's influence on modern and contemporary philosophy, the realization that in his system one can clearly see the absurd consequences to which such a subjectivistic approach can lead. The case is not quite the same with some other thinkers who, unlike Feuerbach, may not be directly concerned with the denial of the existence of a transcendent Being, but who nevertheless conduct their studies of God and religion from a purely naturalistic standpoint and draw conclusions similar to those of Feuerbach. We refer here to certain interpretations of religion that have become fashionable in the fields of anthropology, sociology, and psychology and that have strong atheistic connotations. A brief survey of these theories is the object of our immediate concern.

In the field of anthropology attempts have been made to show that the religious beliefs and practices of advanced societies are nothing but the natural development of religious forms and superstitions found among primitive peoples. Religion, in other words, is subject to the same law of evolution that, in the view of these anthropologists, has determined man's biological and intellectual development through the course of history. There is no agreement, however, among anthropologists as to the nature of those primitive superstitions, and various theories have been advanced in this respect. To mention a few, Edward Burnett Tylor (1832-1917), who is credited by Paul Radin with the creation of modern anthropology practically from its foundations,[57] advanced the theory of "animism" or belief in spiritual beings, i.e., spirits and souls, to account for natural phenomena such as life and death, health and disease, sleep and dreams. James George Frazer (1854-1941) believed that primitive religion was essentially "magic," while the French anthropologist Salomon Reinach (1856-1932) thought of religion as a natural phenomenon derived from irrational taboos of primitive societies.

Emile Durkheim (1858-1917), a prominent member of the French sociological school, developed the theory that religion is essentially a social phenomenon that must be studied in the light of sociological laws. The religious fact is not something that arises from the inner needs of the indi-

---

[56]Cf. *God in Modern Philosophy* (Chicago, Ill.: Regnery, 1959), p. 246.

[57]Cf. Introduction to Edward Burnett Tylor's *The Origins of Culture* (New York: "Harper Torchbooks," 1958), p. ix.

vidual, but rather an imposition upon the individual from the outside, i.e., the collectivity or the impelling force of the social environment. Divinity, according to this view, is but the idealization of society. The social phenomenon determining the origin of religion among primitive peoples is what Durkheim called "totemism" or belief in a clan's relationship to a specific "totem" or animal. The totem soon became the symbol of the clan and was considered as sacred. Durkheim's theory is not only a sociological interpretation of religion but it is also part of that philosophical approach to religion that goes under the name of sociological positivism. The sociological and philosophical character of Durkheim's theory is described by G. Michelet in the following points. First, religion is social in its origin, for it descends from the collectivity to the individuals. Secondly, religion is social in its contents, for it magnifies the collective life in its representations of the sacred. Thirdly, religion is social in its end, for it leads the individual to subordinate his innate egoism to the collective ends. Religion, in other words, is the apotheosis of society.[58]

In contrast to the sociological theory, the psychological school maintains that religion is an outgrowth of the individual rather than of society. Like the preceding naturalistic interpretations, however, it excludes any transcendent element from religion. Thus William James (1842-1910), a leader in religious psychology, claims that religious phenomena are due to psychic elements which, at a certain moment, spring from the region of the subconscious into consciousness. Applying his pragmatic principle to religion, James maintains in *The Will to Believe* (1897) that the truth of religion does not depend on abstract metaphysical thinking but rests on the answer to the question of whether religious belief has any practical value for man's concrete life. Elaborating further on this notion, James writes in *The Varieties of Religious Experience:*

> This thoroughly 'pragmatic' view of religion has usually been taken as a matter of course by common men. They have interpolated divine miracles into the field of nature, they have built a heaven out beyond the grave. It is only transcendentalist metaphysicians who think that, without adding any concrete details to Nature, or subtracting any, but by simply calling it the expression of absolute spirit, you make it more divine just as it stands. I believe the pragmatic way of taking religion to be the deeper way.[59]

Despite his emphasis on the pragmatic nature of religion, James defends himself against the charge of atheism and affirms that "on

---

[58]Cf. G. Michelet, "La religion," *Dictionnaire apologétique de la foi catholique,* IV, 862-63.

[59]William James, *The Varieties of Religious Experience* (New York: Collier Books, 1961), p. 401.

pragmatic principles, if the hypothesis of God works satisfactorily in the widest sense of the word, it is true."[60] However, he insists that his pragmatic type of theism, which he presents as standing between the two extremes of crude naturalism and transcendental absolutism, is perhaps best suited to a person who is "neither tough nor tender in an extreme and radical sense, but mixed up as most of us are."[61]

Sigmund Freud (1856-1939), the well-known father of psychoanalysis "who went through his life from beginning to end as a natural atheist,"[62] accepted the idea that totemism was the first form of religion from which all other religions have developed. In *Totem and Taboo* (1913) he gave an interpretation of religion in line with his own psychoanalytical theory of the Oedipus complex. Thus the totem became the first father-surrogate and God the sublimated father-image of later date. Freud expounded his analysis of religion in *The Future of an Illusion* (1927), where he describes how religious ideas have sprung from man's radical helplessness and need for security. The religious man is like a child who seeks the protection of his father. When he realizes that his helplessness will continue throughout adult life, "he creates for himself the gods whom he dreads, whom he seeks to propitiate, and whom he nevertheless entrusts with his own protection."[63] Thus religion is both an illusion and a neurosis. An illusion, Freud explains, is not the same as an error and therefore need not be false, that is, unrealizable or incompatible with reality. However, since the chances of its realization are extremely slim, they may for practical purposes be completely disregarded. "Thus we call a belief an illusion when a wish-fulfillment is a prominent factor in its motivation, and in doing so we disregard its relations to reality, just as the illusion itself sets no store by verification."[64] A psychologist, adds Freud, who strives to review the development of mankind in accord with his own analysis of the mental development of an individual from childhood to manhood, sees religion as a childhood neurosis and assumes that mankind will be able to overcome this neurotic phase in the same way that children grow out of other similar neuroses.[65]

In one of his latest works, *Moses and Monotheism* (1939), Freud attempts to find a confirmation of his theory in the biblical account of

---

[60]Cf. William James, *Pragmatism* (8th printing; Cleveland and New York: The World Publishing Company "Meridian Books," 1961), p. 192.

[61]*Ibid.*, p. 193.

[62]Cf. Ernest Jones, *The Life and Works of Sigmund Freud* (New York: Basic Books, 1957), III, 376.

[63]*The Future of an Illusion*, trans. W. D. Robson-Scott (Garden City, N.Y.: Doubleday "Anchor Books," 1964), p. 35.

[64]*Ibid.*, p. 49.

[65]*Ibid.*, pp. 70-71.

Moses, whom he wrongly assumes to have been murdered by the Hebrews during their wanderings in the desert. The Jewish race, Freud argues, tried but unsuccessfully to suppress the memory of the crime which developed into a national neurosis and led, under the influence of the prophets, to the re-establishment of the monotheistic religion first introduced by Moses. Christianity, too, is given by Freud a psychoanalytical interpretation. The Christian God is nothing but a glorified image of the human father conceived along the line of the theory expounded in *Totem and Taboo*. The death of Christ is made to fit into the theory and presented as an atonement by the Son for the ancient crime against the Father, whose historical origin goes back to the alleged story of the murdering of Moses. Obviously Freud did not adhere to a strictly scientific method in making generalizations and drawing conclusions that were not warranted by the material at hand. When he took a pattern from what he thought to be the most primitive people, the aborigines of Australia, and made it into a law that would apply to all peoples and at all times, he also violated one of the most fundamental principles of scientific research. Yet he did not seem to be bothered by such "scruples" as long as he could fit the "facts" into his preconceived theory, which reflects a completely materialistic view of life.

Another psychologist who showed concern with the problem of the origin of religion is Carl Gustav Jung (1875–1961). The son of a Protestant minister, he gave up all religious practices and became a leader in analytical psychology, a term that he coined in preference to Freud's psychoanalysis. Three phases or periods can be distinguished in the development of Jung's approach to religion. In the first period, he conceives religion as a sublimation of infantile sexuality along Freudian lines. This period came to an end with the publication of *The Psychology of the Unconscious* in 1912. In the second period, Jung still associates religion with libido but enlarges the concept of libido to encompass every psychic tendency in man. In the third period, Jung makes known the results of his studies on religious symbolism, which are contained in a series of lectures delivered at Yale University in 1937 and were published the year after in the book, *Psychology and Religion*. The symbol is the central element of Jung's analytic psychology. A symbol is not merely a sign or allegory; it is the expression of an archetype in a concrete situation. Jung's definition of "archetype" is not easy to grasp, because he seems to have shifted from one concept to another. His latest position indicates that by archetype he means an energic center of the collective unconscious which manifests itself in an individual form.

The archetype is not something static, but rather a dynamic disposition which tends toward its actualization. As Jung states, there is no way of explaining the origin of archetypes except by saying that they are residues of the experiences reported by mankind.[66] The transition of an archetype from the collective unconscious to the conscious is not clearly perceived by the individual who realizes only the archetype's dynamism, but the resultant interaction emerges into a symbol. This term, according to Jung, best indicates a reality relatively unknown in itself but recognized as present because of its dynamism. The symbol covers the entire psychic production from dream to fantasy and to spontaneous drawing. To confine ourselves to examples within the religious area, Jung sees in the Mother Church a symbol that helps the transition from the mother at the infantile level to the Church at an adult level. Likewise, the Cross is a symbol of divine love in the sense that it is seen as an expression of a mystic and transcendent reality which manifests itself through it in the most significant way.

Jung recognizes the fact that religion, especially Christianity, has played an important role in the shaping of Western civilization, but he denies any objective truth to it. Since he rightly felt that the existence of God as a transcendent Being cannot be established on empirical grounds, and he shared, on the other hand, Kant's critical attitude toward metaphysics, his position on God and religion is not very clear. Indications are that, despite his sympathetic attitude toward religion, Jung was not particularly concerned with proving either its truth or its falsity.[67]

The foregoing naturalistic doctrines do not by any means represent all the theories of religion in the fields of anthropology, sociology, and psychology. Indeed, there are many experts in those fields who flatly disagree with them. Thus in a series of lectures that Professor E. E. Evans-Pritchard delivered at the University College of Wales, Aberystwyth, in the spring of 1962, he stated quite frankly that most of what had been written in the past and was still being taught in colleges and universities about animism, totemism, magic, and so forth, has been shown to be erroneous or at least dubious. He also expressed his amazement that so much could have been written by men of supposedly great learning and ability which appears to be contrary even to common sense. He further remarked that

---

[66]Cf. Carl Gustav Jung, *Psychology and Religion* (New Haven, Conn.: Yale University Press, 1938), pp. 63–64.

[67]For a cautious view of Jung's attitude toward religion see Agostino Gemelli, O.F.M., M.D., *Psychoanalysis Today* (New York: Kenedy and Sons, 1955), pp. 87–109. Thomas McPherson writes in this connection: "Jung is generally considered more sympathetic to religion than Freud, and so indeed he is—that is, as far as intention goes. But Jung may be a more dangerous ally than Freud an enemy, and those Christian writers who have attempted the difficult task of Christianizing Freud may be wiser than those who have gratefully taken over large pieces of Jung. The view of religion as 'neither true nor false,' or as 'true only in a special sense' (symbolically true, psychologically true), has shortcomings." Cf. *The Philosophy of Religion* (Princeton, N.J.: Van Nostrand Company, 1965), pp. 173-74.

none of the anthropologists whose theories about primitive religion have been most influential had ever been near a primitive people. This is indeed a serious indictment against men of the stature of Tylor, Frazer, Durkheim, and other well-known anthropologists, but the charge seems to be justified. Moreover, if we consider the fact that most of the authors whose theories have been presented in this chapter were either agnostics or atheists at the time of their writing and, as Evans suggests, sought and thought they found in primitive religions a weapon to be used with deadly effect against Christianity, then we realize how cautious one must be in evaluating their theories of religion.[68]

One might have hoped that in the sixteen years since Professor Evans' lectures the situation would have somewhat improved. But unfortunately this does not seem to be the case. As Professor Edward Norbeck of Rice University has stated recently, modern anthropologists—and we may say modern psychologists as well—are not so much concerned with the problem of the origin of religion as their predecessors, but they still regard religion as a creation of man that has arisen from man's experience of daily life and serves for him various functions.[69] There seems to be no question that many anthropologists and psychologists today still consider religion to be a purely natural phenomenon and refuse to see any supernatural element in it. It is because of this widespread attitude among scientific and scholarly circles that the following observations are in order.

First of all, it must be admitted that ethnological and psychological studies of religion have contributed a great deal of information on the way religion affected certain primitive peoples and their social life, as well as their reaction to specific phenomena of nature which they were unable to explain. Those studies have also helped determine the origin and nature of certain superstitious practices and patterns of abnormal behavior which are a travesty of religion rather than genuine expressions of religious belief. To this extent the studies in question are useful and even necessary for a better understanding of the mentality of the peoples concerned.

Having granted that much, we cannot help seeing how these positive aspects of an ethnological and empirical approach to religion are often offset by so many negative points, as previously indicated, that the value of such studies becomes questionable. What is particularly distressing is the matter-of-factness with which certain ethnologists and psychologists draw general conclusions from the study of a particular group or class of

[68]Cf. E. E. Evans-Pritchard, *Theories of Primitive Religion* (Oxford: Clarendon Press, 1965), pp. 1–15.

[69]Cf. Norbeck's article, "Anthropological Views of Religion," in *Religion in Philosophical and Cultural Perspective*, ed. J. Clayton Feaver and William Horosz (Princeton, N.J.: Van Nostrand, 1967), p. 419.

peoples, as though all men, no matter what their ethnic and cultural background, ought to fit into that same, unique mold.

Furthermore, we may ask, why is so much emphasis placed on the study of the religious phenomenon among primitive peoples and little or no attention paid to the experience of highly qualified religious persons who are known for their learning, the strength of their convictions, and their untainted moral conduct? How, writes a contemporary author, can we compare the intensity and purity, the clarity and force of introspection with which the religious fact is presented to us in a primitive man and in men like St. Augustine, St. Thomas Aquinas, and St. Theresa—and, we may add, St. Bonaventure, St. Catherine of Siena, and St. John of the Cross? These men and women were both great saints and great theologians or mystics. They wrote about religion not merely because they had heard of it, but because of their personal experience. Hence they have at least the same right to be heard as the savages, the preferred source of information for modern and contemporary anthropologists.[70] There are undoubtedly advantages in the study of the religious experience of persons of high moral character and great intellectual ability because of the accuracy and reliability of its results. Such investigations ought to compare most favorably against the uncertain and often biased products of ethnological studies.

We must add that there is a fundamental and radical weakness in all the empirical approaches to religion that we have thus far discussed. It is the conviction, if not sheer prejudice, of both anthropologists and psychologists, that religion and religious experience are purely natural phenomena that can be explained in scientific terms with no reference to either philosophy or theology. Religion, they seem to argue, begins and ends with man, and any notion of a transcendent Being is not only outside their field of competence—a perfectly valid concession on their part— but has no ontological truth-value whatsoever. This conclusion is not only faulty, but it is not even warranted by their own premises, for, whether they admit it or not, it is a metaphysical conclusion. Thus we are confronted here with a new form of scientism which is quite similar to the one discussed in the preceding section and is properly called naturalism or psychologism, whichever may be the case.

Naturalism, it has been observed—and the same observation holds true for psychologism—is liable to severe criticism because "it involves us in a gigantic one-sided abstraction. It takes a segment of experience—the

---

[70]Cf. José Todoli, O.P., *Filosofía de la religion* (Madrid: Editorial Gredos, 1955), pp. 8-9, where he quotes from J. Graneris, *La religion en la historia de las religiones* (Buenos Aires: Editorial Excelsa, 1946), p. 71.

segment which is amenable to measurement and quantitative analysis—and represents it as the entire reality."[71] The criticism we have leveled against Feuerbach's naturalistic interpretation of religion can also, and perhaps even more so, be leveled against the exponents of naturalism and psychologism whose theories have been examined. Despite their differences, they are of one accord in defending some form or other of humanism, inasmuch as their explanation of religion and the religious phenomenon is restricted to man alone. Exponents of these theories need not be professed atheists. Indeed, some of them would most probably resent such appellation. But that is due to the fact that in practical life men are often better than their own theories. A contemporary critic rightly says of humanistic atheism:

> No humanistic doctrine will ever explain the religious phenomenon, because there is something in it that surpasses man. If religion is the principle of unity in man's activities, it is because it transcends all that is human. In the religious act, as Max Scheler said, man comes in contact with a Good, a Truth, and a Being that are beyond all good, all truth, and all being.[72]

The empirical approach to religion, we may conclude, is only one way, and not the most important one, to the understanding of the complex and somewhat mysterious religious phenomenon. A complete study of religion must include an analysis of the metaphysical foundation of that phenomenon and of the nature of the transcendent Reality with which man believes himself to be in communion.

IV. THE MORAL ATHEISM OF NIETZSCHE THE PROPHET OF THE "DEATH OF GOD"

The theories thus far considered involve the denial of God either because of an exaggerated notion of the power of science and therefore of the world as the sole object of scientific investigation, or because of an overemphasis on man and his creative power. In the first case we have what we have called scientific atheism, while in the second case we are confronted with humanistic atheism. There is a third theory that is close to humanistic atheism and for this reason it is often listed under the same heading. However, since the atheistic nature of this theory is due mainly to its conception of morality, it seems appropriate to classify it as moral atheism. This is the system of Friedrich Nietzsche (1844-1900), the prophet of

[71]Cf. John Macquarrie, *Twentieth-Century Religious Thought* (New York: Harper and Row, 1963), p. 112.

[72]Cf. Paul Ortegat, S.J., *Philosophie de la religion* (Paris: Vrin, 1948), I, 59.

"the death of God": an expression that has become fashionable among certain radical theologians today but for reasons other than those of Nietzsche. In keeping with the nature of this study, we shall present the basic features of Nietzsche's thought, not so much because of its intrinsic value, as because of the influence it has had on subsequent thinkers up to the present day.[73]

Nietzsche's first proclamation of the death of God is contained in a passage of *Joyful Wisdom*, where he portrays a madman who on a bright morning ran into the market-place with a lighted lantern and began to cry out: "I seek God! I seek God!" As the people in the market started laughing at such strange behavior, the madman jumped into their midst and called out: "Where is God gone? I mean to tell you! We have killed him—you and I! We are all his murderers!...God is dead! God remains dead! And we have killed him!"[74] The death of God is also the opening theme of Nietzsche's best known and perhaps most important work, *Thus Spoke Zarathustra*, in which the substance of his entire philosophy is contained.

Obviously the expression that God is dead cannot be taken literally, because, as has been rightly observed, immortality has always been associated with the concept of God—even, e.g., by the Greek philosophers. Nietzsche, who had been raised in a deeply Christian environment and had devoted some of his early years to training for the Lutheran ministry, could not ignore that fact. What he actually means is that the God of traditional religion, and especially the God of Christianity, as the arbiter of good and evil, the defender of the weak and the humble, does not exist. If he did, he would be defending a morality of decadence against which man must rebel with all his power. In his autobiographical essay, *Ecce Homo*, Nietzsche writes:

> I am the first immoralist: that makes me the annihilator *par excellence*.... Fundamentally, my term *immoralist* involves two negations. For one, I negate a type of man that has so far been considered supreme: the good, the benevolent, the beneficient. And then I negate a type of morality that has become prevalent and predominant as morality itself—the morality of decadence, or, more concretely, *Christian* morality.[75]

---

[73]In his lecture, "Man Before the Death of God," delivered at Loyola University in New Orleans on March 25, 1965, Gabriel Marcel said of Nietzsche: "Without a doubt, there can be no greater mistake than to say Nietzsche belongs to the past, for it is the contrary that is true. Even, and above all, for those who regard themselves as his opponents, Nietzsche is the most modern of the moderns." Quoted by Miceli, *op cit.*, p. 79.

[74]*Joyful Wisdom*, trans. Thomas Common (New York: Frederick Ungar Publishing Co., 1960), no. 125, pp. 167-68.

[75]Cf. "Ecce Homo," in *Basic Writings of Nietzsche*, trans. and ed. Walter Kaufmann (New York: The Modern Library, 1968), pp. 783-84.

Thus the God whose existence Nietzsche denies is a *moral* God, as he himself asserted in one of his notes.[76]

If God does not exist, then man has to take his place and a new set of values must be established. This is the task Nietzsche sets before himself. "*Revaluation of all values*: that is my formula for an act of supreme self-examination on the part of humanity, become flesh and genius in me."[77] How is Nietzsche going to carry out this revaluation? Schopenhauer, following the idealistic trend in philosophy started by Kant and developed by Fichte, Schelling, and Hegel, had taught that the world is only an idea of the human mind and that the entire realm of phenomena, including the human body, is nothing but objectified will. Nietzsche went further in this idealism and proclaimed that man creates all values. Such is the basic idea that he propounds in *The Will to Power*, whose subtitle, as originally conceived by its author, was *Attempt at Revaluation of All Values*.[78] In his reassessment of all values, man will have to react against the accepted valuations of his own time and go "beyond" the good and evil of conventional morality. He will establish himself as a Superman. Zarathustra, speaking for Nietzsche, says:

> Once upon a time we said 'God' when we looked at distant seas, but I taught you to say 'Superman.' God is a surmise but I want your surmises to reach no farther than your creative will can reach. Can you *create* a god?—Then be silent about all gods! But you could create the Superman.[79]

But who is this Superman? Nietzsche does not give us a strict definition of the Superman; rather he speaks of the different functions man has to perform to attain to that ideal state. The Superman must affirm his superiority over the ordinary man, for "man is something that must be mastered." The ordinary man is to the Superman what the ape is to man himself. More specifically, "man is a rope, stretched between beast and Superman—a rope across an abyss."

To dispel any doubt about the purely earthly function of the Superman, Nietzsche tells us through Zarathustra that "the Superman is the aim of the earth" and makes an earnest request to "his brothers" to remain true to the earth and avoid the "poisonous" teaching of any celestial

---

[76]Cf. note entitled "The refutation of God" in Nietzsche, *Also Sprach Zarathustra*, French trans. by G. Bianquis (23d ed.; Paris: Gallimard, 1950), Appendix, 62, p. 310. Quoted in Gilson, *art. cit.*, p. 242, n. 3.

[77]"Ecce Homo," in *Basic Writings*, p. 782.

[78]Cf. Friedrich Nietzsche, *The Will to Power*, trans. Walter Kaufmann and R. J. Hollingdale (New York: Random House "Vintage Books," 1968), Editor's Introduction, p. xvii.

[79]Cf. Friedrich Nietzsche, *Thus Spoke Zarathustra*, trans. Marianne Cowan (Chicago: Regnery "A Gateway Edition," 1957), p. 84.

hopes. The soul will be dead before the body, and we need not fear that anything will happen to us, for "there is no devil and no hell."[80] The soul is in effect only a part of the body, and consequently we should love the body more than the soul.[81] It becomes obvious, then, that the ideal of chastity as conceived by Christian religion loses all its value and may have to be discouraged. Chastity, says Nietzsche, may be a virtue for some people, but for many others it is almost a vice. Women after all are only inferior human beings—Nietzsche compares them to cats and cows—and men should be able to use them for their own satisfaction.[82] Along with chastity, all other values of the Christian religion must be revaluated. Thus the concept that all men are equal must be superseded by the doctrine of a master and slave morality. The slave pretends to conquer his master by his servility, but since he is incapable of positive action, his will to power is almost nil. The slave can do neither good nor evil; the master, on the contrary, having the capacity to do evil, has also the power to do good. Within this perspective even truth becomes an aspect of the will to power, for truth can be discovered only by a free spirit that, in willing, goes beyond truth and falsity, just as it goes beyond good and evil.[83]

If the will to power, as impersonated in the Superman, involves a continuous struggle for the creation of new values, we may ask whether this creative process will ever come to an end. Or, to put it another way, will the Superman ever be able to achieve the goal of his moral revolution? Nietzsche provides the answer to this question in Part III of *Thus Spoke Zarathustra* and in certain other works by advancing the idea of eternal recurrence. Life, as it appears now, will return again and again in the future, just as it did in the past, in a self-perpetuating cycle. "Alas, man forever returns! Little man forever returns!...Even the greatest: all-too-small!"[84] In a world where "everything goes and everything returns," "everything dies and everything blossoms anew,"[85] the Superman too will be part of this everlasting flow. In a sense his work will never be finished, for his life never comes to an absolute end. His ability to impose some sort of stability upon this continuously changing world, or, to use Nietzsche's expression, "to impose upon becoming the character of being," manifests his supreme will to power.[86] Thus the theory of eternal recurrence aims to bridge the gap between being and becoming and avoid at the same time the concepts of a transcendent God and of pantheism. Moreover, by advo-

---

[80]*Ibid.*, pp. 4-12 passim.
[81]*Ibid.*, p. 30.
[82]*Ibid.*, pp. 52-65.
[83]*Ibid.*, pp. 93-117.
[84]*Ibid.*, p. 226.
[85]*Ibid.*, p. 224.
[86]Friedrich Nietzsche, *The Will to Power*, no. 617, p. 330.

cating the idea of an eternal return, Nietzsche provides man with a substitute for the doctrine of personal immortality as found in the Christian religion and gives him the assurance, or illusion, of a never-ending life. The eternal recurrence, it is worth noting, is not the effect of law, design, or purpose; it is rather the result of chance and audacity. "Over all things is spread the sky of accident, the sky of innocence, the sky of randomness, the sky of audacity." There might be, Nietzsche says, some seed of wisdom scattered here and there, but for all practical purposes all things "dance on the feet of chance." Briefly, eternal recurrence is a blind process that involves no intelligibility: "With all things only one thing is impossible—rationality."[87]

As we have followed through Nietzsche's gradual destruction of all traditional values and the affirmation of the Superman as the embodiment of will to power, we have often wondered how seriously his thought should be taken. When a commentator called *Thus Spoke Zarathustra* "destructive nonsense,"[88] he may have exaggerated the negative aspects of Nietzsche's work, but he undoubtedly expressed the natural reaction of many of its readers. The last part of the book, with its vulgar and blasphemous parodies of Christianity, supports that impression. Nietzsche himself seems to have had doubts about the value of what he termed "the most profound book" of world literature,[89] since he subtitled it "A Book for All and No One." In his autobiography he wonders if perhaps he is merely a buffoon.[90] Whatever the case, a man who devotes a major portion of his autobiography to explaining "why he is so wise and so clever," "why he writes such good books," and in the section "Why I Am a Destiny," signed "Dionysus versus the Crucified," states that history will henceforth be divided into two periods, one before and one after him, such a man, we may say, cannot help but raise serious doubts about the soundness of his judgment. This is especially true in light of his later insanity and the fact that embarrassing statements similar to those contained in his later works, such as *Ecce Homo* and *The Antichrist,* are already found in letters dated early in his career, and even in his school years.[91] Nietzsche's insanity throughout the last twelve years of his life did not prevent a growing interest in his thought. As a result of his widely publicized illness, his

---

[87]*Thus Spoke Zarathustra,* pp. 169–170.

[88]Cf. Crane Brinton, *Nietzsche* (Cambridge, Mass.: Harvard University Press, 1941), p. 63. To be exact, the author attributes this comment to "a limited critic whose values have not been properly transvalued." *Ibid.*

[89]Cf. "The Twilight of the Idols," IX, 51, in *The Complete Works of Friedrich Nietzsche,* ed. Oscar Levy (New York: Macmillan, 1911), XVI, 111.

[90]"Ecce Homo," in *Basic Writings,* p. 782.

[91]Cf. Walter Kaufmann, *Nietzsche* (New York: The World Publishing Company "Meridian Books," 1959), p. 56.

reputation began to spread and his books, which the publishers had first found difficult to sell, were suddenly in great demand. It may be added that the intellectual climate of the late nineteenth and early twentieth centuries contributed to Nietzsche's popularity, whose decline coincided with a more objective study of the man and his work. Since our concern in this essay is Nietzsche's attitude toward God, we shall limit our observations to this particular aspect of his thought.

The first thing that strikes an analyst of Nietzsche's approach to God is his initial assumption that belief in a creator and ruler of man and the universe is groundless and even harmful because it runs counter to man's creative power. "This will of mine lured me away from God and all the gods; what would there be to create, if gods existed!"[92] The very thought of God, or of any being superior to man, should be dismissed altogether on the ground that man cannot accept his inferiority and inability to match or cope with such a being. "If there were gods, how could I stand not being one! *Therefore* there are no gods."[93] Moreover, the idea of the Superman as the incarnation of the will to power is to have the effect of freeing man of all his worries and belief in a supreme Being. In the words of Zarathustra, "The beauty of the Superman came to me as a shadow. Oh, my brother—what do I care now for—gods!"[94] Thus, as one commentator puts it, at the root of Nietzsche's rejection of God there is just one thing: his supreme, absolute individualism.

> For Nietzsche to think is to create and the measure of thought is man alone. For him there can be no knowledge as mental reproduction and comprehension of a reality other than the self. Hence, as far as faith in God is concerned, there is only one problem: Could you *create* a god? But God must fall, for, as the primary source of all creation, he is in direct antithesis to the Nietzschean individualism.[95]

This interpretation of Nietzsche's rejection of God is shared by another contemporary author who sees Nietzsche's atheism as the unfolding of the principle of immanentism. This principle can be traced ultimately to Descartes' *Cogito* but becomes more evident in the idealism of Hegel and his followers.

> This Nietzschean thought develops not in deductive form but rather in the form of an analysis of the drama of the modern mind which has condemned itself to self-motion and self-structuring, to positing the denial of God as the basis for the assertion of man.[96]

---

[92]*Thus Spoke Zarathustra*, p. 86.
[93]*Ibid.*, p. 85.
[94]*Ibid.*, p. 86.
[95]Cf. Georg Siegmund, "Friedrich Nietzsche," in *L'ateismo contemporaneo*, II, 284-85.
[96]Fabro, *op. cit.*, p. 873.

Just as an exaggerated concept of the self, or, in Nietzschean terminology, *hybris* or pride, is at the root of Nietzsche's atheism, so the theory of eternal recurrence is its logical consequence. Since faith in man must replace faith in God, belief in man's earthly return must likewise replace the Christian belief in personal immortality. The theory of eternal return is, however, the weakest point in Nietzsche's system. It is not only purely gratuitous, for neither he nor anyone else has ever been able to demonstrate it, but it also flatly contradicts his doctrine of the Superman. Indeed, how can man freely determine his course of action, his creativity through will to power, and at the same time be subject to an eternal, self-perpetuating cycle of natural events whose only principle is the principle of determinism? The difficulty is compounded by Nietzsche's firm belief in fate or *amor fati*, which is precisely the opposite of what man's self-determination is meant to be.

While the arbitrariness and internal contradictions of the theory of eternal recurrence have made it the target of Nietzsche's critics and embarrassed even his admirers, the notion of a world in which accident and chance reign supreme is equally groundless and inconsistent. Yet, all things considered, these objections to the Nietzschean system are by far outweighed by the disastrous and catastrophic consequences to which an arbitrary will to power as man's only norm of morality would lead if put into effect. This theory is so repugnant to man's social nature and instinctive drive for love and compassion, and so much opposed to everything Christian civilization stands for, that, if one took it seriously, he might be inclined to agree with Nietzsche's self-characterization as "the most terrible human being that has existed so far."[97] It must be said, however, somewhat in Nietzsche's defense, that the concept of God against which he rebelled all his life was not the Catholic concept but the concept of the Lutheran church, with its emphasis on God's absolute control over man and the consequent impairment of man's free will. If Nietzsche had had an accurate concept of the Christian God, which allows for man's free activity within the limits of the divine moral law, perhaps he would not have been so bitter in his attacks against Christianity.

Before concluding our appraisal of Nietzsche's atheism, we must raise a final issue whose solution may throw some light on Nietzsche's whole approach to God. Was Nietzsche really convinced of the nonexistence of God, and if so, was his conviction the result of truly philosophical reasoning or merely the effect of an emotional state of mind determined by factors other than those of an intellectual order? This issue deserves special consideration in the case of Nietzsche because of his persistent attacks on

---

[97]"Ecce Homo," in *Basic Writings.* p. 783.

belief in God and the ridicule and contempt he showed for Christianity. In an attempt to find an answer to this question, we shall turn to Nietzsche's works, especially his autobiography.

Despite Nietzsche's categorical denial of God's existence, there is no indication whatsoever in his writings that he ever took upon himself the trouble of critically analyzing any of the classic theistic arguments. In the words of an able scholar, Nietzsche never faced objectively the problem of the possibility of man's knowledge of God. Involved from his very early writings in the philosophical movement known as transcendental idealism, he fell victim to the prevailing agnosticism of his time and never fully recovered from it. The question of whether there could be an extramental reality corresponding to the concept of God in traditional philosophy and theology never seems to have occurred to his mind; or, if it did occur, there is no evidence that he ever gave any serious thought to it. At the age of twenty-four he wrote an incomplete essay entitled *Theology after Kant*, where he mentions the teleological argument for the existence of God. But far from engaging in a discussion of it, he simply states that the finality of the organic world and the regularity of law in the inorganic world are attributed by our mind to nature. Thus the suppression of a true teleology leads to the denial of the transcendent mind or superior *ratio* of classic philosophy. Ignorance of the fact that Nietzsche never tackled seriously the problem of God's existence has perhaps led many writers to exaggerate his importance and originality.[98]

Nietzsche's lack of interest in a philosophical discussion of God's existence and related problems of natural theology can be documented with statements from his own autobiography. He writes: " 'God,' 'immortality of the soul,' 'redemption,' 'beyond'—without exception, concepts to which I never devoted any attention, or time; not even as a child. Perhaps I have never been childlike enough for them?"[99] This admission supports the view of those critics who question the value and significance of Nietzsche's statements on God and religion. The admission becomes even more relevant as we learn from the same context that what was uppermost in Nietzsche's mind to the point of displacing his interest in God, the immortality of the soul, and other similar questions, was a very human and materialistic concern. "I am much more interested," he asserts, "in a question on which the 'salvation of humanity' depends far more than on any theologians' curio: the question of *nutrition* ."[100] Commenting on this passage, Gilson observes very effectively: "Food is surely important, but cooking is not a problem comparable in importance to that of the ex-

[98]Cf. Siegmund, *art. cit.*, p. 283.
[99]"Ecce Homo," in *Basic Writings*, p. 692.
[100]*Ibid.*, p. 693.

istence of God. That Nietzsche thinks it is, or pretends that it is, shows what little interest he has in the question."[101]

If Nietzsche was not interested in a question of such magnitude and of such far-reaching consequences as that of God's existence, then we may ask, why did he display such a strong anti-theistic attitude in his writings? Why did he show so much bitterness and concern in denouncing religious belief and in counteracting it with the idea of the death of God? What is, in other words, the "rational" basis for his denial of God? None! This is what Nietzsche himself tells us: "I do not by any means know atheism as a result; even less as an event: it is a matter of course with me, from instinct."[102] Thus Nietzsche's rejection of God is due to an instinctive feeling, if we may use such a term, rather than to intellectual reasoning. This acknowledgment, while extremely helpful in determining the nature of Nietzsche's disbelief in God, makes it clear that his atheistic position has no philosophical value. No instinct of the nonexistence of a transcendent Being can ever be justified rationally, for instinct is something purely subjective and impervious to any philosophical proof.

One may go further in the analysis of Nietzsche's disbelief and question even his "instinctive" knowledge of the nonexistence of God. If he was really convinced that God did not exist, why did he go to so much trouble to deny the existence of a nonentity, a fiction of the mind? Fictional beings after all should not worry a man so down-to-earth as Nietzsche, whose principal concern was good food and proper diet. Perhaps in Nietzsche's mind the existence of God was still a possibility to be reckoned with, and, despite his repeated statements to the contrary, he could never fully convince himself that God was not very much alive. That this is no mere speculation can be shown by Nietzsche's advice to his friend, Frau Overbeck, not to abandon the idea of God so that she could be spared the intense suffering that such abandonment had caused to himself. "I have abandoned it...but that does not bother me." These words, Frau Overbeck says, were pronounced by Nietzsche in 1882.[103] It is also about that time that Nietzsche confided to his friend and admirer, Lou-Salomé, whom at one time he had hoped to marry, that he was disenchanted with Schopenhauer and Wagner—both of whom had exerted a great influence on him—and concluded by saying: "Yes, thus the cycle began, and it goes on, but where will it end? After having run the full course, whither are we to turn?...Perhaps we will have to make a new start with faith? Perhaps a

---

[101] Cf. "The Idea of God," art. cit., p. 246.

[102] "Ecce Homo," in Basic Writings, p. 692.

[103] Cf. Carl A. Bernouilli, Franz Overbeck und Friedrich Nietzsche (Jena: E. Diederichs, 1908), I, 250. Quoted in Siegmund, art. cit., p. 286.

Catholic faith?"[104] Likewise, in a letter he wrote in 1885 to Frau Overbeck, Nietzsche expressed his dissatisfaction with his own philosophy and the wish that things be different from the way he understood them and that someone may one day prove him to be wrong.[105]

In the light of these statements, there seems to be sufficient evidence to suspect that Nietzsche had his doubts about the nonexistence of that God whom, in a moment of elation bordering on insanity, he had threatened to replace in the government of the world.[106] Whatever the nature and extent of his doubts, Nietzsche realized the truth of Pascal's statement that without God man becomes a monster. His claim to have fulfilled Pascal's prophecy stands as his own condemnation.[107]

V. SARTRE'S EXISTENTIAL ATHEISM

The existentialist movement that has characterized much of twentieth-century philosophy has given rise to a new attitude in man's approach to God. Man's concern for his own concrete, individual existence with all its problems and anxieties has led either to a deeper personal commitment to a transcendent Being as the ultimate solution to the mystery of life, or to the rejection of any such Being because of the anguish, dread, and apparent absurdities that beset human life. Because of such different views on the problem of God, existentialist philosophers are usually classified as either theists or atheists, although it is not easy in some individual cases to determine whether a philosopher belongs to one class or the other.

The typical representative of atheistic existentialism is Jean-Paul Sartre, who makes it quite clear that his philosophy "is nothing else but an attempt to draw the full conclusions from a consistently atheistic position."[108] Sartre acknowledges the two conflicting trends in existentialist philosophy and makes no secret about his own preference.

---

[104]Cf. Kurt F. Reinhardt, *The Existentialist Revolt* (Milwaukee: The Bruce Publishing Co., 1952), p. 94, for reference to Lou Andreas-Salomé's book, *Friedrich Nietzsche in seinen Werken* (Dresden: C. Reissner, 1924), p. 50. (Reference checked).

[105]Cf. Hans Pfeil, *Friedrich Nietzsche und die Religion* (Regensburg: J. Habbel, 1949), p. 140. Quoted in William A. Luijpen, O.S.A., *Phenomenology and Atheism* (Pittsburgh, Pa.: Duquesne University Press, 1964), p. 259, n. 115.

[106]Cf. "Ecce Homo," Appendix, in *Basic Writings*, p. 800.

[107]*The Will to Power*, no. 83, pp. 51–52: " 'Without the Christian faith,' Paschal thought, 'you, no less than nature and history, will become for yourselves *un monstre et un chaos.* ' This prophecy we have fulfilled." See also *Basic Writings*, p. 719, where Nietzsche speaks of himself as "a world-historical monster" and "the *Antichrist.* "

[108]Cf. his lecture, "Existentialism Is a Humanism," in *Existentialism from Dostoevsky to Sartre*, ed. Walter Kaufmann (Cleveland and New York: The World Publishing Company "Meridian Books," 1956), p. 310.

...there are two kinds of existentialists. There are, on the one hand, the Christians, amongst whom I shall name Jaspers and Gabriel Marcel, both professed Catholics; and on the other the existential atheists, amongst whom we must place Heidegger as well as the French existentialists and myself.[109]

Sartre's philosophy, especially as expounded in his major work, *L'être et le néant* (*Being and Nothingness*, 1943), is not easy to understand. Yet in spite of its obscurities, ambiguities, and apparent contradictions, the work has gone through several editions and has been translated into most modern languages. The existentialism of Sartre deserves special consideration because of its impact on contemporary man, even though Sartre's prestige is gradually declining even in his native France. In the words of Jean Wahl, Sartre's philosophy "is one of the incarnations of problematism and of the ambiguity of contemporary thought."[110] Gabriel Marcel, whose philosophical orientation is quite different from that of Sartre, does not seem to think otherwise. In fact he suggests that Sartre's philosophy ought "to be examined with the utmost seriousness and objectivity" because of its impressiveness, particularly among the young people.[111] This is what we propose to do in our study, which will be limited to Sartre's rejection of God within the context of his system.

Long before the publication of *Being and Nothingness*, or *An Essay on Phenomenological Ontology*, as the subtitle reads, Sartre had introduced its major themes in *La Nausée* (*Nausea*, 1938), a novel in the form of a diary where, under the disguise of a fictional character, Antoine Roquentin, he describes his own feelings and sensations about the world and people around him. Here we meet his concept of existence as a personal, unique experience that invades and conquers his entire being. "Existence—he writes—is not something which lets itself be thought from a distance: it must invade you suddenly, master you, weigh heavily on your heart like a great motionless beast—or else there is nothing more at all."[112] Borrowing a Heideggerian theme, Sartre describes existence as mere contingency, with no *raison d'être* and no relation to any outside cause or being.

---

[109]*Ibid.*, p. 289. Sartre's statement is not accurate, for neither was Jaspers a professed Catholic, nor was Heidegger an outright atheist.

[110]Cf. *A Short History of Existentialism*, trans. Forrest Williams and Stanley Maron (New York: The Philosophical Library, 1949), p. 30.

[111]Cf. *The Philosophy of Existentialism* (7th edition; New York: The Citadel Press, 1966), p. 48.

[112]Cf. *Nausea*, trans. Lloyd Alexander (Norfolk, Conn.: New Directions Books, 1959), p. 177.

...one cannot define existence as necessity. To exist is simply to be there: those who exist let themselves be encountered, but you can never deduce anything from them. I believe there are people who have understood this. Only they tried to overcome this contingency by inventing a necessary, causal being (a *causa sui*). But no necessary being can explain existence.[113]

The contingent, and therefore unexplainable nature of existence, is reasserted a little further in Roquentin's diary where we read: "Every existing thing is born without reason, prolongs itself out of weakness and dies by chance."[114]

If every individual thing exists without reason, what about the totality of things or the world as a whole? How did the world come into existence? Here is Sartre's answer:

There had been nothing *before* it [the world]. Nothing. There had never been a moment in which it could not have existed. That was what worried me: of course there was no *reason* for this flowing larva to exist. *But it was impossible* for it not to exist. It was unthinkable: to imagine nothingness you had to be there already, in the midst of the World, eyes wide open and alive; nothingness was only an idea in my head, an existing idea floating in this immensity: this nothingness had not come *before* existence, it was an existence like any other and appeared after many others."[115]

Sartre insists again and again that existence is an absurdity: "There is nothing, nothing, absolutely no reason for existing."[116] Yet he realizes that man cannot stop thinking about existence.

...this sort of painful rumination: *I exist*, I am the one who keeps it up. I. The body lives by itself once it has begun. But thought—*I* am the one who continues it, unrolls it, slowly....If I could keep myself from thinking! I try, and succeed: my head seems to fill with smoke... and then it starts again: 'Smoke...not to think...don't want to think ...I think I don't want to think. I mustn't think that I don't want to think. Because that's still a thought.' Will there never be an end to it?[117]

Finally, in his painful realization that he cannot stop thinking, Sartre, speaking as Roquentin, concludes:

[113]*Ibid.*, p. 176.
[114]*Ibid.*, p. 180.
[115]*Ibid.*, p. 181.
[116]*Ibid.*, p. 151.
[117]*Ibid.*, p. 135.

My thought is *me*: that's why I can't stop. I exist because I think...
and I can't stop myself from thinking. At this very moment—it's
frightful—if I exist, it is because I am horrified at existing. *I am the
one* who pulls myself from the nothingness to which I aspire: the
hatred, the disgust of existing, there are as many ways to *make* myself
exist, to thrust myself into existence.[118]

The self becomes then Sartre's principal concern, for man alone can
through his consciousness experience the meaning of existence. Accordingly, the phenomenological investigation of consciousness and its contents is the main theme of his work, *Being and Nothingness*. Here are
some of the ideas of this massive volume, which in many respects can be
compared to Heidegger's *Sein und Zeit (Being and Time)* and is largely
indebted to Husserl's phenomenology.

Consciousness is possible only in terms of an object, which, for the very
fact of being an object, is something distinct from consciousness itself.
Sartre calls the object the being-in-itself (*l'en-soi*) and consciousness the
being-for-itself (*le pour-soi*).[119] Since the being-in-itself, or the objective
world of things, is a massive, opaque, and uncreated entity that has no
reason for its existence, nothing can be said about it except that *it is*.[120]
Hence the principal concern of Sartre's analysis is the being-for-itself or
human consciousness.

The being-for-itself has no determinate structure and depends on the
being-in-itself for its origin. One of its features is the power of nihilation
(*néantisation*). This means that the being-for-itself negates the being-
in-itself, and since the latter includes everything that exists, the being-for-
itself emerges as a nothingness, or, to use Sartre's expression, as a hole at
the heart of being. "The For-itself, in fact, is nothing but the pure nihilation of the In-itself; it is like a hole of being at the heart of being."[121] This
does not mean that the for-itself is absolute nothingness; it is rather a
relative nothingness, in the sense that it represents the negation of *this*
particular being, not of being in general.[122]

The process whereby the for-itself nihilates the in-itself is not easy to
understand. Roughly stated, it amounts to saying that consciousness,
through its imagining power, can go beyond the actuality of the existing
things and think of their possibility of being other than what they are and
even of their nonexistence. In this way every act of consciousness includes

---

[118]*Ibid.*, pp. 135-36.

[119]Cf. *Being and Nothingness: An Essay on Phenomenological Ontology*, translated and
with an introduction by Hazel E. Barnes (New York: The Philosophical Library, 1956), pp.
li; 617.

[120]*Ibid.*, p. lxv.

[121]*Ibid.*, p. 617.

[122]*Ibid.*, p. 618.

the possibility of nothingness, an idea that Sartre expresses so characteristically by saying that "nothingness haunts being." On the other hand, since man is the being by whom nothingness comes into the world, man himself is Being and Nothingness.[123] It is at this point that Sartre introduces the notion of freedom, which plays such an important role in his philosophy.

Freedom, for Sartre, is not merely a property or power of man, but man himself. Since man, through his consciousness, is the being by whom nothingness comes into the world in the sense just explained, freedom is also the nihilation of the in-itself, it is nothingness. This does not mean that freedom does not exist, any more than consciousness can be said not to exist. Freedom is the ability of man to withdraw from the actual world and project himself into the future, to deny what he is so as to become what he is not. Freedom is an absolute that admits of no interference. In other words, man is free to determine his own essence, and the only limit to his freedom is freedom itself. Just as man is condemned to exist for no reason whatsoever, so he is condemned to be free, and only death can put an end to his freedom.

> I am condemned to exist forever beyond my essence, beyond the causes and motives of my act. I am condemned to be free. This means that no limits to my freedom can be found except freedom itself or, if you prefer, that we are not free to cease being free. To the extent that the for-itself wishes to hide its own nothingness from itself and to incorporate the in-itself as its true mode of being, it is trying also to hide its freedom from itself.[124]

Sartre says that consciousness of freedom produces anxiety, which no one can escape except through "bad faith" or self-deception. Likewise from freedom there arises responsibility, not in the sense that I am accountable to a superior being or to other men for my actions, but only inasmuch as I must carry the full weight of my decisions. These in turn are always determined by the particular set of facts that establish my facticity, i.e., my necessary connection with the world, my own past, and those environmental factors that constitute my situation. Sartre's emphasis on responsibility is evident from the following passage: "I am responsible for everything, in fact, except for my very responsibility, for I am not the foundation of my being. Therefore everything takes place as if I were compelled to be responsible."[125] Man, Sartre goes on to say, finds himself as if he were abandoned in the world; he feels like being left alone and without

---

[123]*Ibid.*, p. 11.
[124]*Ibid.*, pp. 439–40.
[125]*Ibid.*, p. 555.

help in a world for which he has to bear full responsibility without being able to tear himself away from it even for a moment. Yet such abandonment, he concludes, consists ultimately in the fact that man is condemned to be wholly responsible for himself.[126]

Despite the importance that he attaches to man by making him the supreme arbiter of his own destiny, Sartre maintains that man cannot avoid realizing his own radical insufficiency and ontological inferiority with regard to the in-itself in which the fullness of being is revealed. Hence man constantly strives to overcome his own limitation and attain to the plenitude of the in-itself in order to achieve a synthetic fusion of the in-itself with the for-itself. However, since this fusion is impossible without the consequent loss of self-identity on the part of the for-itself with its characteristics of consciousness and freedom, man's striving and aspiration are utterly frustrated. Thus in words that epitomize what Sartre calls his existential psychoanalysis, "man is a useless passion."[127]

So far our exposition of Sartre's reasoning in *Being and Nothingness* and in *Nausea* has included no reference to God, theism, or atheism. It has dealt only with man and his unrestrained freedom, along with the anguish and frustration that beset him in his striving for self-affirmation in a world that is deprived of meaning and without purpose. But Sartre could not ignore the fact that since the dawn of philosophy man has constantly tried to relate himself to a superior Being that gives him and the surrounding world reason and purpose for their existence. So Sartre must and does explicitly acknowledge that attempt, as well as the theistic orientation of great philosophical minds, both in the past and in the present, including some contemporary existentialist thinkers. Yet all this seems to leave him unimpressed. Having rejected God in his early youth, he develops a system entirely apart from Him, as though God would have no bearing on the solution of man's fundamental problems, especially the problem of his existence.

It is true that Sartre does not take upon himself the specific task of refuting the proofs for the existence of God with arguments of his own that would invalidate them. In this sense we can believe him when he affirms that his philosophy is not professedly atheistic.

Existentialism is not atheist in the sense that it would exhaust itself in demonstrations of the non-existence of God. It declares, rather, that even if God existed that would make no difference from its point of view. Not that we believe God does exist, but we think that the real problem is not that of His existence; what man needs is to find himself

---

[126]*Ibid.*, p. 556.
[127]*Ibid.*, p. 615.

again and to understand that nothing can save him from himself, not even a valid proof of the existence of God.[128]

We can go further and agree with Sartre that his *Being and Nothingness* is not a metaphysical work and should not be treated as such. It is merely "An Essay on Phenomenological Ontology," or, as he puts it, "the description of the phenomenon of being as it manifests itself."[129] Accordingly, the work attempts to answer the questions of the "how" and the "what" of being, man, and the world, not the question of the "why" of their existence. This at least is what Sartre claims. But is he really so unconcerned with the whole realm of metaphysical speculation that he leaves it completely out of his system? If we carefully analyze his work, this does not seem to be the case.

In fact, when he attempts to summarize the conclusions of *Being and Nothingness*, Sartre speaks of the "metaphysical implications" that can arise from his analysis of the two modes of being, the in-itself and the for-itself, and then he goes on to discredit metaphysics altogether. The metaphysician, he says, can only formulate "hypotheses" which can neither be validated nor invalidated. The only way to validate such hypotheses is to show the possibility of unifying the "givens" of ontology, namely, the for-itself and the in-itself. But since this unification cannot be made without suppressing the identity of either one of the two modes of being, then the metaphysician is bound to fail in his undertaking. Stated otherwise, the very concept of a being that would synthesize in a unique reality the for-itself and the in-itself is self-contradictory because of the radical incompatibility of the two modes of being. That, Sartre insists, is the concept of the *Ens causa sui*, or the God of Christian theology that contains within himself the reason for his own existence. Hence, not only does God not exist, but he cannot even be conceived as existing, for his very concept involves a contradiction. This is what in all appearance amounts to an "Ontological Argument" in reverse.[130]

Once the concept of God as the source of all reality is rejected, so also is the concept of creation from nothing which becomes an altogether meaningless issue.[131] Thus "everything happens as if the world, man, and man-in-the-world succeeded in realizing only a missing God."[132] Furthermore, the fundamental question of the "why" of man and the world,

---

[128]"Existentialism Is a Humanism," in Kaufmann, *op. cit.*, p. 311.

[129]*Being and Nothingness*, p. xlviii.

[130]Cf. the whole section "In-itself and for-itself: metaphysical implications," in *Being and Nothingness*, pp. 617-25. See also pp. 90 and 615 where Sartre attempts to show the contradictory nature of an *Ens causa sui*.

[131]*Ibid.*, pp. lviii, lxiv, and lxvi.

[132]*Ibid.*, p. 623.

which has puzzled philosophers of all times from Plato and Aristotle to Kierkegaard and Heidegger, becomes completely irrelevant. Man and the world, Sartre tells us, exist in their concrete reality—Sartre is not an idealist—but no reason can be given for their existence, since there is none.

So far we have seen how Sartre dismisses the concept of God on the ground that it involves a contradiction. But this is not the only reason for his refusal to accept the God of Christian theology, nor is it the most important one. Man, as previously explained, is for Sartre a being that is essentially free. He not only has the power of self-determination, but freedom is his very nature. Man is freedom itself, and because of his identification with freedom, he is also the source and supreme arbiter of all values in the moral order.

Given such a concept of human freedom, it is only logical for Sartre to eliminate from his system a God who is both creative and legislative. By his very nature, such a God would interfere, if we may so speak, with man's own creativity and ultimate responsibility. He writes: "Thus, the first effect of existentialism is that it puts every man in possession of himself as he is, and places the entire responsibility for his existence squarely upon his own shoulders."[133] Because of this radical freedom that is assigned to him, man becomes for Sartre something like an absolute being who automatically displaces God, even though the exercise of such freedom may be confined to the situation in which man finds himself.

> There is no difference between free being—being as self-committal, as existence, choosing its essence—and absolute being. And there is no difference whatever between being as an absolute, temporarily localized—that is, localized in history—and universally intelligible being.[134]

Once man has displaced God and become the arbiter of all values in the moral order, he alone will decide what is right and what is wrong, and his decisions will be morally justified as long as they represent a free act of self-commitment. Freedom, after all, Sartre insists, "can have no other end and aim but itself," because freedom is "the foundation of all values."[135]

To the objection that a self-centered, godless ethical theory may lead to moral permissiveness, as Dostoevsky had already seen, Sartre answers that that is correct, although he would perhaps qualify the meaning of "moral permissiveness." "Dostoevsky once wrote 'if God did not exist, everything would be permitted'; and that, for existentialism, is the star-

---

[133]"Existentialism Is a Humanism," in Kaufmann, *op. cit.*, p. 291.
[134]*Ibid.*, p. 304.
[135]*Ibid.*, p. 307.

ting point. Everything is indeed permitted if God does not exist."[136] Sartre is therefore fully aware of the consequences to which his atheistic morality will eventually lead, as evidenced by the life of the fictional characters of his novels and plays. Yet, far from retracting his own preconceived theory, he uses it as an argument for the nonexistence of God. He simply cannot bear the thought of a Being who would dictate to him a set of rules for his conduct and pose as his judge, or, in his words, "a being-who-looks-at and who can never be looked at."[137] This is perhaps the main reason for his persistent denial of God.

To evaluate fairly and adequately Sartre's system of philosophy and its built-in atheism, even within the restricted limits of the outline here presented, is no easy task. We would have first to analyze Sartre's concept of philosophy as a whole, as distinct from his phenomenological ontology and existential psychoanalysis, and see whether it is possible really to separate one from the others. If the answer is in the affirmative, then it remains to be seen whether Sartre's system of philosophy is also so independent as to be able to hold its ground apart from his ontology or the description of being taken as a totality, as Sartre understands it. Our impression is that philosophy, taken in its classic meaning as the ultimate explanation of reality, is not the direct concern of Sartre, who purposely avoids engaging himself in metaphysical issues. Rather, he is forced by the logic of his system to take some stand on the matter.

Having clarified, at least to our own satisfaction, this preliminary and more general issue, we may now turn to some specific points of doctrine and see whether Sartre's position can stand up to a sound critical analysis. Sartre conceives all reality in terms of being-in-itself and being-for-itself and claims that being-in-itself, which stands for all material reality, has no reason for existence; it just happens to be. Worse still, it does not even exist in the strict sense of the term, *it simply is*. This notion of being and its twofold modality may save Sartre from the pitfalls of both idealism and materialism, but it seems hardly realistic. How could those two aspects of being include everything that exists, especially if we consider that the being-in-itself is not self-explanatory? Sartre's understanding of reality is therefore too narrow and arbitrary; it rests on his preconceived view that being is not intelligible. Common sense will tell us that there must be a reason for a being to exist rather than not, or to be what it is rather than to be a different kind of being. Sartre refuses to accept this fundamental principle of reason and of reality which Leibniz, among others, has proved to be an absolute requirement for sound philosophical thinking.

While denying any intrinsic value to being-in-itself, Sartre depreciates

---

[136]*Ibid.*, pp. 294–95.
[137]*Being and Nothingness.* p. 423.

even further the being-for-itself whose unique feature seems to be its power to nihilate the being-in-itself. Sartre's description of the for-itself as "the being which is what it is not and which is not what it is"[138] is obviously not very helpful. In the words of a reputable contemporary critic, Sartre's explanation of the for-itself, both as negation and nothingness, is but an example of the tremendous confusion that exists in his entire system.[139]

A key point in Sartre's philosophy is his notion of freedom as the embodiment of human nature and the foundation of all morality. Freedom has for him the value of an absolute to the point that it determines man's own essence and confers upon the world its characteristic of rationality.[140] At the same time freedom, which for Sartre is essentially choice, is not a being but rather the non-being of man, a nothingness like consciousness itself. These seemingly contradictory statements about freedom are hard to explain and present the same problem we have just mentioned in connection with the being-for-itself. In the opinion of Gabriel Marcel, whose criticism of Sartre's philosophy is both sharp and devastating, Sartre's notion of freedom "is just as inexplicable and much more deeply unintelligible than the notion of creation which Sartre rejects and for which he has nothing but contempt.[141] What is clear is that Sartre uses the concept of freedom to justify almost anything in the realm of morality, if one can still speak of morality in a system where freedom becomes the measure of the good. In this context the commonly accepted distinction between freedom and license disappears altogether and it makes no difference, to use Sartre's example, "whether one gets drunk alone or becomes the leader of nations."[142] The unfortunate consequences of such an ideology are not difficult to foresee, and one can hardly disagree with Marcel's severe judgment that Sartre's philosophy may be one of the forces of self-destruction threatening to drive our unfortunate race into the abyss.[143]

There is one more question we would like to raise in connection with Sartre's concept of absolute freedom. How can Sartre be blind to the fact that man cannot possibly claim for himself a prerogative that so flatly contradicts his own limited and utterly imperfect nature? Surely it is obvious that man has not the right to determine his own moral law in a completely arbitrary fashion, as though he were a totally independent being and the supreme arbiter of his own destiny. It is true that Sartre does not seem to

---

[138]*Ibid.*, p. 621.
[139]Cf. Johannes Lotz, "Ateismo e esistenzialismo," in *L'ateismo contemporaneo*, II, 316.
[140]*Being and Nothingness*, p. 445.
[141]*The Philosophy of Existentialism*, p. 83.
[142]*Being and Nothingness*, p. 627.
[143]*Op. cit.*, p. 85.

be bothered by the evidence contradicting his view, but this is nevertheless another obvious weakness in his system.

One thing, however, must be said in Sartre's defense. If God does not exist, which is patently his basic assumption throughout his writings, then man can truly determine for himself what to do with his own life, as well as his own code of morality. On such an assumption, Sartre's concept of unrestricted freedom fits perfectly into his scheme of philosophy. But to build systems of philosophy on mere assumptions that are neither proved nor demonstrable could be a risky and even dangerous undertaking. In the case of Sartre it is both.

A final criticism concerns Sartre's concept of God as the identification of the in-itself and the for-itself which, in Sartre's terms, is a manifest contradiction. This is but another of Sartre's gratuitous assumptions. It rests on the concept that the in-itself and the for-itself are mutually incompatible and that their incompatibility becomes even more evident in a being that would integrate in himself an infinite self-consciousness (*le pour-soi*) and the plenitude of being (*l'en-soi*). Since, on the one hand, consciousness is always divided because of the distinction between the knower and the object known, even when the object is the self, and since, on the other hand, the plenitude of being is for Sartre a massive, undivided density of inert matter, it is obvious that the two cannot join together to form the ideal being that he calls God. Such a contradiction however would soon disappear, as a critic correctly observes, if the *en-soi* were conceived not as matter but as spirit, who would of necessity be an *en-soi-pour-soi*, or the perfect identification of the two seemingly contradictory modes of being.[144] But matter is apparently the only reality that Sartre is able to grasp,[145] so that any suggestion about God as pure Spirit leaves him completely indifferent.

Given such a materialistic view of reality, it is little wonder that Sartre also dismisses the concept of *creatio ex nihilo* as implying the existence of a Mind apart from the world, which is the exact opposite of what for him consciousness is. Indeed, consciousness or the *pour-soi* is always consciousness of the world or of the *en-soi* from which it derives. It is inconceivable, on Sartre's premises, that a Mind could exist that not only would not be the mere reflection of the world but would also be the creative power by which the world exists.

Sartre advances another reason for the impossibility of creation. A created world would either establish its own absolute autonomy and independence of the creator, or it would be coextensive with the act of creation itself from which it could not be distinguished. In either case *creatio ex*

---

[144]Cf. Reinhardt, *op. cit.*, p. 170.

[145]This is a verbal statement by Sartre quoted in Marcel, *op. cit.*, p. 89.

nihilo, taken in its traditional sense of the world's total dependence on the creator but with no loss of its identity and relative autonomy, is absolutely impossible. To exist, Sartre asserts, is to be contingent, i.e., to have no *raison d'être*. Thus, while rejecting creation as an absurdity, Sartre accepts the bare fact of the world's existence and calls it an absurdity. Accordingly, man too is an absurdity. Having been trapped into existence, he must solve for himself the tragedy of life which fills him with anguish and despair.

Obviously Sartre offers little hope to a twentieth-century man in search of meaning and purpose in his existence. His pessimistic outlook on life may further discourage those who have lost confidence in themselves and in the society in which they happen to live. Furthermore, such a view of life goes against man's deepest desires and aspirations. It is these aspirations that the great genius of St. Augustine, who himself went through much of the anguish and despair described by Sartre, expressed so vividly when he finally turned to God and said to him: "You have made us for yourself, and our heart is restless until it rests in you."[146] Having no God to turn to, since he makes it impossible for him to exist, Sartre turns to man only to discover how helpless and terrifying is a life enclosed within the narrow confines of an earthly existence. This is the inevitable but tragic conclusion to which his preconceived atheistic stance logically leads.

VI. EMOTIONAL ATHEISM AND MAN'S REBELLION AGAINST GOD IN CAMUS AND OTHER CONTEMPORARY THINKERS

A further denial of God that must be considered in this essay is what has been termed emotional atheism. It represents a rebellion of feeling rather than the outcome of a preconceived philosophical theory.[147] The existence of both physical and moral evil in the world is held to be incompatible with the notion of an omnipotent and infinitely good Being. "It is here in the grim fact that evil exists and the innocent suffer," asserts a contemporary author, "that atheism finds its permanent revitalizing bases."[148] The tragedy of this situation is reflected in the following statement by Roger Ikor, an avowed atheist:

---

[146]*The Confessions of St. Augustine,* trans. John K. Ryan (Garden City, N.Y.: Doubleday "Image Books," 1960), Book I, chap. 1, no. 1, p. 43.

[147]Cf. n. 10 above for reference to Hans Pfeil's article where emotional atheism is described.

[148]Robert W. Gleason, S.J., *The Search for God* (New York: Sheed and Ward, 1964), p. 9.

Evil exists: this is a fact. It strikes blindly the innocent and the wicked man. It strikes the infant; that's all; that's enough. The problem has been settled. Nothing and no one will ever be able to exonerate God from the suffering of an infant, of that innocent creature; nothing, except that he (God) does not exist.[149]

The murder of six million Jews in Nazi Germany has led Richard Rubenstein, who was Hillel Rabbi at the University of Pittsburgh, to reject the biblical notion of a creating and provident God in favor of the idea of a Holy Nothingness, a Sacred Void out of which man came and to which he will return for no apparent reason.[150]

The existence of evil in the world, which has been called "the biggest single stumbling block to belief in a God of love,"[151] is an age-old problem that has puzzled philosophers of all times and challenged such geniuses as St. Augustine, St. Thomas Aquinas, Leibniz, and Kant. It is reflected in Boethius' questioning of God's ways, which seemed unnatural to him, in accordance with which wicked men triumph and the innocent are persecuted. "If God is, whence come evil things? If he is not, whence come good?"[152]

While Boethius' questioning reminds us of Job's honest attempt to probe into the mystery of his own suffering, Hume, the skeptic, phrases the problem of evil in crude Epicurean terms and asks: "Is he [God] willing to prevent evil, but not able? Then he is impotent. Is he able, but not willing? Then he is malevolent. Is he both able and willing? Whence then is evil?"[153]

In a similar vein, John Stuart Mill, the utilitarian British philosopher, strongly objects to the idea of a just and omnipotent Creator on the ground that suffering and happiness in this world are not proportioned to a person's good or evil deeds, as the law of justice seems to demand. Hence his conclusion:

> Not even on the most distorted and contracted theory of good which ever was framed by religious or philosophical fanaticism can the government of nature be made to resemble the work of a being at once good and omnipotent.[154]

---

[149]Cf. *Dieu aujourd'hui,* p. 54.

[150]Cf. Richard L. Rubenstein, *After Auschwitz* (Indianapolis: Bobbs-Merrill, 1966), pp. 219-25.

[151]Ed. L. Miller, *God and Reason* (New York: Macmillan, 1972), p. 139.

[152]*The Consolation of Philosophy* (New York: The Modern Library, 1943), p. 12.

[153]Cf. "Dialogues Concerning Natural Religion," in *The Philosophy of David Hume* (New York: The Modern Library, 1963), p. 567. The questions to which Hume refers are contained in fragment 374 of *Epicurea,* ed. Hermannus Usener (Leipzig: In aedibus B. G. Teubner, 1887), p. 253.

[154]Cf. *Nature and Utility of Religion,* ed. George Nakhnikian (New York: The Liberal Arts Press, 1958), p. 27.

The opinions of many other philosophers could be mentioned who have passed pessimistic judgments on human life and the world and reached conclusions that in many ways resemble those we have mentioned and openly contradict traditional theistic belief. But instead of prolonging a list of more or less repetitious themes with little or no originality, we shall focus our attention on the view of a contemporary figure who has become the symbol of man's revolt against God because of the evil and injustice that beset man and our present-day society. We are referring to Albert Camus (1913–1960), Nobel Prize winning novelist, playwright, essayist, journalist, and political activist, whose career came suddenly to an end in a car accident in Paris when he was barely forty-seven years old. Like Jean-Paul Sartre, Camus is a representative of contemporary existential revolutionary thinking even though he disclaimed the label "existentialist." For better or for worse, he helped to shape the life and philosophy of a whole generation of young people, not only in France but in other countries as well. Unlike Sartre, he was not a professional philosopher or the author of a well-organized system of thought. However, in some of his essays he develops philosophical themes which pervade his entire literary production. These themes deserve careful study because of the far-reaching implications they have for man and society and also because of their antitheistic and antiauthoritarian overtones. It is to such philosophically oriented essays that we shall now direct our attention to discover the nature of Camus' antitheistic stance.

One such essay is *The Myth of Sisyphus*, whose original French text was written in 1940 "amid the French and European disaster" and published in 1942. Its fundamental theme is the meaning of life and the related issue of whether life should be accepted despite its absurdity or be terminated by an act of suicide.[155] The question of whether life is worth living, Camus asserts in terms reminiscent of Blondel's *L'action*, is truly the most fundamental problem of philosophy, because its solution is carried out in one's own actions. "I have never seen anyone die for the ontological argument," Camus argues rather convincingly; nor has Galileo's heliocentric theory ever had any practical application to man's concrete life. But many people die because they feel that their life is not worth living, or they are killed for those very ideas or illusions that give them reason for living.[156]

The relationship between the absurd and suicide and the degree to which suicide is a solution to the absurd become therefore the subject of Camus' essay.[157] One would expect him to produce some evidence of the

---

[155]Cf. Albert Camus, *The Myth of Sisyphus and Other Essays*, trans. Justin O'Brien (New York: Random House "Vintage Books," 1955), Preface, p. v.

[156]*Ibid.*, pp. 3–4.

[157]*Ibid.*, p. 5.

absurdity of human life before discussing its solution through suicide—a solution incidentally that he will reject—but no such discussion takes place. The absurd is assumed as a fact. Later, when in the course of his essay he points to the various aspects of the so-called absurdity of human life, Camus seems to identify absurdity with man's inherent limitations, his occasional uneasiness, suffering, and disappointments. In such a perspective, death becomes of course one of the absurdities, and the same thing must be said of man's attitude toward it.[158] The world as a whole is an absurdity, and the reason is that man cannot fully understand its meaning. "What I fail to understand is nonsense. . . . The world itself, whose single meaning I do not understand, is but a vast irrational."[159]

The notion of the absurd, Camus warns, is not merely the feeling of it; however, feeling lays the foundation for that notion and determines man's reaction to it. It is here that the problem of suicide arises and the conclusions of existential philosophy may be useful.[160] Anticipating such conclusions, Camus states that his purpose is to find a meaning even in the absurdity of the world and therefore a purpose for man's existence. "Our aim is to shed light upon the step taken by the mind when, starting from a philosophy of the world's lack of meaning, it ends up by finding a meaning and depth in it."[161] The meaning of life, Camus suggests, can be found only in man's revolt against the absurd that surrounds him. Revolt gives life its value and restores to it its majesty; suicide, on the contrary, is a repudiation of life which does not solve the problem of the absurd but engulfs the absurd in death itself. A man in revolt will die unreconciled and not of his own free will. The absurd will be "his extreme tension, which he maintains constantly by solitary effort," for he knows that it is in that day-to-day revolt that "he gives proof of his only truth, which is defiance."[162]

Here Camus introduces the notion of freedom, which is at the root of man's revolt against the absurd. He makes it clear, however, that he is not concerned with the problem of "metaphysical liberty," which has theistic connotations. He is convinced of his own freedom because he experiences it. To argue whether or not man is free is meaningless. There can be no question that man is free because there is no one above him who dictates his actions. The possibility that there is a God to whom man is responsible is irreconcilable with the presence of evil. "Either we are not free and God the all-powerful is responsible for evil. Or we are free and responsible but

---

[158]*Ibid.*, p. 12.
[159]*Ibid.*, p. 20.
[160]*Ibid.*, pp. 21–22.
[161]*Ibid.*, p. 31.
[162]*Ibid.*, pp. 40–41.

God is not all-powerful."[163] There is nothing new in this kind of reasoning, as should be clear from the introductory paragraph of this section, but Camus could not have missed the opportunity to exploit it for his own atheistic purposes. Yet, despite the emphasis on man's autonomy and independence, Camus realizes that man's freedom has many limitations, one being "the absurdity of a possible death." There can be no freedom in the fullest sense without assurance of eternity. Complete freedom is therefore a mere illusion, and freedom itself becomes an absurdity. Man should nevertheless accept his condition in a world full of absurdities and contradictions "and draw from it his strength, his refusal to hope, and the unyielding evidence of a life without consolation."[164]

Obviously Camus does not offer much of an alternative to suicide, and he himself feels the need to ask what meaning life may still have in such a perspective. His answer is that belief in the meaning of life implies the recognition of a scale of values, which is precluded by his own philosophy of the absurd. However, since man has been thrown, as it were, into the world, he must make the best out of it and live to the utmost of his potential by "substituting quantity of experiences for the quality." What counts, in other words, "is not the best living but the most living": to live with the greatest number and variety of experiences and, even more importantly, to be conscious of such experiences. It is the element of consciousness, more than the mere accumulation of experiences, that accounts for the highest form of living. "Being aware of one's life, one's revolt, one's freedom, and to the maximum, is living, and to the maximum."[165]

Having defined the goal of human existence in terms of a conscious revolt against the irrationality of the universe, Camus goes on to describe in detail what he means by an absurd man. This is "he who, without negating it, does nothing for the eternal."[166] He is courageous enough to get along with what he has and sufficiently reasonable to admit his own limitations. There can be no moral code for him, for he lives outside God and, in the words of Dostoevsky's hero, Ivan Karamazov, which Camus quotes approvingly, to such a man everything is permitted. This does not make the life of the absurd man any easier than the life of one who believes in God, "for the certainty of a God giving meaning to life far surpasses in attractiveness the ability to behave badly with impunity." Hence "everything is permitted" is not the same as "nothing is forbidden." The absurd does not commend crime or do away with a certain sense of duty; it

[163]*Ibid.*, p. 42.
[164]*Ibid.*, p. 44.
[165]*Ibid.*, p. 46.
[166]*Ibid.*, p. 49.

merely suppresses remorse and guilt. There may still be responsible persons but no guilty ones.[167]

A model of Camus' guiltless morality, if we can still speak of morality in a theory that admits of no binding moral code, is Don Juan, whose only purpose in life seems to have been the seeking of as much sensual pleasure as he could achieve through his ability to seduce women. "To anyone who seeks quantity in his joys," Camus writes, "the only thing that matters is efficacy."[168] Other models of what Camus calls "the absurd man" are the actor, the artist, the adventurer, or one who gets involved in a resistance movement against a tyrant, knowing full well that his is a lost cause. But the typical absurd hero is Sisyphus, the mythological figure that furnishes the title of the book. Sisyphus has been condemned by the gods ceaselessly to roll a rock to the top of a mountain, only to see it rush down to the plain again, with no end in sight to his hopeless effort. The tragic aspect of the myth is, according to Camus, the consciousness that Sisyphus has of the uselessness of his efforts. What makes him a hero and gives him the semblance of victory in the midst of his torture is his defiance of the gods and of the fate to which they have condemned him. Thus "the lucidity that was to constitute his torture at the same time crowns his victory," for "there is no fate that cannot be surmounted by scorn."[169]

Camus' second major essay, *The Rebel, An Essay on Man in Revolt,* is in many ways the continuation of the theme developed in *The Myth of Sisyphus,* but whereas this latter work attempts to solve the problem of suicide, the former aims at the solution of the problem of murder. *The Rebel* was written about ten years after *The Myth of Sisyphus* and reflects Camus' reaction to the new political climate determined by the Second World War. It is an attempt to understand those forms of crime, violence, and murder that seem to defy logic and yet pretend to have an ideological foundation. The idea of the absurd is again the starting point of this essay, as it was of his previous work, but here the absurd is open to a new field of investigation. It is discussed in relation to the notion of rebellion as an alternative to individual and universal murder, which Camus condemns just as he had condemned suicide in *The Myth of Sisyphus.*

It is not our intent to give even a brief summary of Camus' extensive work, which covers many aspects of rebellion that have no direct bearing on the subject of our discussion. We shall rather confine our presentation to that part of the essay that treats of metaphysical rebellion and shall implement it with some of the ideas expressed in a final section dealing with

---

[167]*Ibid.*, p. 50.
[168]*Ibid.*, p. 53.
[169]*Ibid.*, p. 90.

rebellion and murder. This will help us to understand better Camus' rationale for his denial of God.

"Metaphysical rebellion is the movement by which man protests against his condition and against the whole of creation."[170] The metaphysical rebel contests the purpose of human existence and of the whole of creation and declares that he is being frustrated by the universe. He fights for justice, order, and unity in a world that is saturated with injustice, suffering, and evil. While rejecting his own mortality, he refuses to recognize the power that has compelled him to live within the human condition. The rebel is not necessarily an atheist, but he is definitely a blasphemer. He blasphemes in the name of order and denounces God as the father of death and the cause of evil. Yet, by some strange inconsistency, he admits the existence of a supreme power at the very moment when he calls it into question. It is wrong nevertheless, says Camus, to confuse metaphysical rebellion with atheism. The rebel defies God more than he denies him. He argues with God on an equal basis with a view to conquering him. Once he has overthrown God from his throne, or believes he has done so, the rebel realizes that it is now up to him to create that kind of justice, order, and unity for which he is fighting. Here is where the positive aspect of metaphysical rebellion begins.[171]

Referring to the New Testament, Camus asserts that Christ came precisely to solve those two major problems that preoccupy the rebel, evil and death. Christ's solution consisted in experiencing both evil and death to the point of despair. "For God to be a man, he must despair."[172] Christ's voluntary sacrifice has contributed to make suffering acceptable to man. However, when Christianity was subjected to the critical analysis of reason, the freethinkers began to launch their attacks on Christ's morality and divinity and reduced Christ to the level of man. In so doing they paved the way for "the great offensive against a hostile heaven."[173]

It is to the description of this offensive that Camus devotes the remaining part of his section on metaphysical rebellion, where he discusses the works of men like the Marquis de Sade, Milton, Dostoevsky, Stirner, Nietzsche, Lautréamont, Rimbaud, and André Breton. He concludes his discussion by observing that all the leaders of the metaphysical rebellion and nihilism that shocked Europe for one hundred and fifty years had this in common: they decried the human condition and its creator and "affirmed the solitude of man and the nonexistence of any kind of

---

[170] Albert Camus, *The Rebel,* trans. Anthony Bower (New York: Alfred A. Knopf, 1961), p. 23.
[171] *Ibid.,* pp. 24–25.
[172] *Ibid.,* p. 32.
[173] *Ibid.,* p. 35.

morality."[174] Their protest was always directed at something in creation that was either irrational or obscure, such as unjustified suffering and death. Briefly, the very score of metaphysical revolt was a protest against evil in all its forms.[175]

The logic of the rebel, Camus argues in Part V of his essay where the relationship between rebellion and murder is considered, is to serve justice in order to lessen the injustice of the human condition. The rebel does not advocate murder, because rebellion is in principle a protest against death and murder would destroy the reason for one's revolt. However, the rebel may find himself in a situation where murder and violence become necessary for the achievement of the objective of his rebellion. As he faces this insuperable dilemma, the rebel cannot find peace within himself.[176] The solution to the dilemma, suggests Camus, lies in the realization that an authentic revolt has its own limitations, just as freedom has its limitations. Thus in no circumstance will the rebel claim the right to destroy the person and freedom of someone else without jeopardizing those very principles on which rebellion is based. "Either this value of limitation will be realized, or contemporary excesses will only find their principle and place in universal destruction."[177] Whatever the difficulties, the inspiring motive of man's rebellion against the evils and injustices of society is love of his fellowmen, especially of those who have been the victims of social and political abuses. Finding no rest in God, the rebel "rejects divinity in order to share in the struggles and destiny of all men."[178]

Such is the rationale of Camus' *Man in Revolt*, which, as previously indicated, is the subtitle of *The Rebel*. Like his other essay, *The Myth of Sisyphus*, the work is an attempt to solve the problem of evil within the context of a godless philosophy, or more precisely, of a philosophy of the absurd. We shall return to this theme later. Meanwhile we would like to refer the reader to a crucial episode from *The Plague*, a major novel in which Camus describes in vivid colors the horrors of a lethal epidemic that threatens everybody in the Algerian port of Oran. The episode is enlightening because it offers Camus the opportunity to present his own reflections on the mystery of evil in the face of a concrete tragic event. It concerns a plague-stricken boy, whose agonizing death becomes the subject of an animated dialogue between a Jesuit priest, Father Paneloux, and Dr. Rieux, the chief character in the book.

Horrified by the revolting scene witnessed a few minutes before, Dr.

---

[174]*Ibid.*, p. 100.
[175]*Ibid.*, p. 101.
[176]*Ibid.*, p. 285.
[177]*Ibid.*, p. 295.
[178]*Ibid.*, p. 306.

Rieux, with whom Camus identifies himself, recalls the explanation of
suffering that Paneloux had given in one of his sermons, namely, that suffering could be God's punishment for man's sin. Not quite convinced by
Father's reasoning, Dr. Rieux reacts with a deep sense of anger to the
tragic occurrence of the child's death and hurls in the Jesuit's face, "Ah!
That child, anyhow, was innocent, and you know it as well as I do!" As
Paneloux expresses his concern at such an outburst of anger and tries to
calm him down, Rieux turns to him and says: "I know. I'm sorry. But
weariness is a kind of madness. And there are times when the only feeling
I have is one of mad revolt." To this Paneloux replies: "I understand.
That sort of thing is revolting because it passes our human understanding.
But perhaps we should love what we cannot understand." Rieux gazes at
Paneloux, shakes his head and says: "No, Father. I've a very different
idea of love. And until my dying day I shall refuse to love a scheme of
things in which children are put to torture." "Ah, Doctor," the priest re-
joins sadly, "I've just realized what is meant by 'grace.' " "It's something
I haven't got, and I know that much," replies the Doctor more gently now.
Then he adds: "But I'd rather not discuss that with you. We're working
side by side for something that unites us—beyond blasphemy and prayers.
And it's the only thing that matters."[179]

Obviously disappointed at his failure to convince the Doctor that suffering is no argument against an all-loving God, Paneloux invites him to
another sermon that he would preach shortly at a Mass for men and prom-
ises that the subject will be of interest to him. Rieux accepts the invitation.
In the course of his sermon, the Jesuit priest points out that while no rational explanation can be found for human suffering, a true Christian
must look at his Master on the cross and renew his faith in him "who knew
all the pains of suffering in his body and his soul." Then he faces with
complete honesty the terrible problem of a child's suffering, and, looking
directly at his listeners, he challenges them in the following terms: "My
brothers, a time of testing has come for us all. We must believe everything
or deny everything. And who among you, I ask, would dare to deny everything?"[180]

Yes, in time of plague, Paneloux continues, there is no middle course,
no island of escape. We must accept the dilemma and choose either to
hate God or to love him. Since no true Christian would choose to hate
God, we must surrender ourselves to the love of God, even if this love is a
demanding one. Only this total self-surrender can reconcile us to suffering

---

[179] Albert Camus, *The Plague*, trans. Stuart Gilbert (New York: The Modern Library,
1948), pp. 196–97.
[180] *Ibid.*, p. 202.

and to the death of innocent children. Since these happenings are beyond our comprehension, we must make an act of faith. Cruel as they may be in men's eyes, faith alone will help us see things from a different and superior point of view. "On that lofty plane all will fall into place, all discords be resolved, and truth flash forth from the dark cloud of seeming injustice."[181]

The Jesuit priest's sermon—one must admit to Camus' credit—shows a profound understanding of the Christian teaching on the mystery of evil. This goes to show, among other things, how painful it must have been for the author of *The Plague* to make the choice he did in the presence of evil, since he was fully aware that his decision amounted to the acceptance of irrationality or absurdity as the only alternative to faith in God.

The reader who has followed our exposition of Camus' thought has no doubt been struck by his insistence upon the theme of absurdity. Camus' "obsession" with this theme is so well-known, that he has come to be regarded by many as "the philosopher of the absurd." It is true that an author, as Camus explains in one of his essays,[182] does not always write about himself in his books or represent necessarily his own personal thinking. But the fact remains that the absurd is not only at the center of many of Camus' writings, but also the starting point of his two major philosophical works discussed in this study. While comparing his absurdist position to Descartes' methodical doubt, Camus refuses to discuss the nature of the absurd. In itself, he says, the absurd has no content, and therefore no meaning; it is a contradiction. The absurd is incompatible with the act of living. This act presupposes a choice and a value judgment, but no such choice or judgment is possible in a world that is deprived of all meaning. The absurdist position cannot even be expressed in words, since such expression implies a minimum of coherence that is excluded by the very nature of the absurd. Thus the only logical attitude toward the absurd is to say nothing, since there is nothing that can be said about it. In Camus' words: "The only coherent attitude based on non-signification would be silence—if silence, in its turn, were not significant. The absurd, in its purest form, attempts to remain dumb."[183]

On the basis of these statements, one may seriously question Camus' right to assume the absurd as a starting point of his essays, especially *The Myth of Sisyphus*. By granting that the absurd is a contradiction, Camus reveals the fundamental inconsistency of this work, which, by his own ad-

---

[181]*Ibid.*, p. 206.
[182]Cf. "L'énigme," in *L'été* (Paris: Gallimard, 1954), pp. 131–32.
[183]*The Rebel.* p. 8.

mission, attempts to defend a position that clearly denies its premise.[184]
To hold, as he does, that his absurdist position is merely a point of departure helping him to reach certain practical conclusions, is no justification
for the fallacious character of his reasoning. And when he assures the
reader that no metaphysics and no belief are involved in his essay and
adds, "These are the limits and the only bias of this book,"[185] he no doubt
shows his honesty but he also discloses the book's basic weakness.

It is no easy task to evaluate a work that is admittedly based on a bias,
especially when such a bias involves the acceptance of the absurd as a
preconceived attitude toward human life, society, and the world. Perhaps
the best way to approach the subject is to question the author's right to
build up a whole philosophy of life—for that is what *The Myth of Sisyphus*
amounts to—on such a shaky foundation. Why and on what grounds, we
may ask, is human life such an absurdity that the only reasonable solution
of its problems is in terms of revolt and suicide? Life has of course many
negative aspects; it is subject to disillusionments and hardships that make
it difficult and may even drive a person to the point of despair. We are all
aware of this fact, just as we are aware of the hard reality that sooner or
later all life will come to an end, at least as far as earthly existence is concerned. But there are also many positive aspects of life that must be considered, and these far outweigh the negative ones. When Camus says that
life has no meaning except in terms of man's revolt against the absurd, he
completely ignores the brighter side of human experience.

The absurd, Camus would perhaps suggest in his own defense, is not
so much life itself as it is man's "sensitivity" to life and to the world.
Moreover, he would further explain, this kind of "absurd sensitivity" is
not something peculiar to himself; it is rather a widespread experience
among his contemporaries.[186] We do not contest the truth of these
statements. What we contest is Camus' right to capitalize on such an experience and make it the starting point of his whole approach to the problem of life.

The world, Camus tells us, is absurd. The reason is that he cannot
understand it, and what he cannot understand, he considers nonsense. It
is to bring some meaning into this "vast irrational" and to bring value to
life that he advocates revolt and discourages suicide. While Camus rightly
chooses the lesser of two evils, we must ask, is this the only possible

---

[184]This is also the conclusion reached by John Cruickshank, an admirer of Camus and
one of his best interpreters. He writes: "Camus...has the honesty...to admit a fundamental inconsistency in *Le Mythe de Sisyphe.* ... The book is even self-contradictory by the very
fact of having been written at all." *Albert Camus and the Literature of Revolt* (reprint; London: Oxford University Press, 1970), pp. 95-96.
[185]Cf. *The Myth of Sisyphus,* Dedication, p. 2.
[186]*Ibid.*

choice? A more realistic solution to the problem of life is to accept it as it is, with all its bright and dark moments, and try to find a meaning to it in terms of a transcendent and provident God. Such is the solution given by many outstanding philosophers and theologians in the course of history. Camus was aware of this, but his prejudice against God has made it impossible for him even to consider such a solution as an alternative to his own philosophy of defiance and revolt.

On the other hand, how can the notion of God be reconciled with man's absolute freedom? How can an omnipotent and provident God allow so much evil in the world? These are two crucial issues raised by Camus that have greatly concerned other philosophers before and after him, as well as his own contemporaries. We have already discussed Sartre's notion of freedom as an absolute and shown it to be incompatible with man's dependent and limited nature. Since Camus' view of freedom is basically the same as that of Sartre, we refer the reader to our discussion of it in the preceding section. The problem of evil is a far more complex issue, and we shall come to it shortly. Meanwhile we would like to continue with our analysis and bring forth certain other points of Camus' philosophy that deserve special consideration.

Camus holds that the absurd man has no moral code, since he lives apart from a God who alone could decree such a code. Similarly, man is not subject to remorse or guilt, although he does not cease because of that to be responsible for his own actions. What counts is the amount of pleasure that he can accumulate in his life, no matter what its source or quality. This is obviously an easy ethical theory that has a wide appeal, especially among the young and the disillusioned, and it partially explains the popularity of Camus' works. But what about the consequences of such guiltless morality? It would take little imagination to foresee them, if we were not already the involuntary witnesses of a society gradually moving toward a purely materialistic and pragmatic way of life that is not far from the ideal cherished by Camus. A guiltless morality, or a morality without God, can hardly be called morality. Even Nietzsche, who had no small influence on Camus, had seen this obvious truth.[187]

Thus far our observations have been directed mainly at *The Myth of Sisyphus*. Many of them can however be equally applied to Camus' second major essay, *The Rebel*, since it too rests on the basic assumption of the absurdity of both human life and the world. Yet in this latter work Camus makes more explicit the nature of man's rebellion in terms of an open de-

---

[187] Speaking of those philosophers who think that they can abolish religion and preserve morality, Nietzsche says: "Naiveté: as if morality could survive when the God who sanctions it is missing! The 'beyond' [is] absolutely necessary if faith in morality is to be maintained." *The Will to Power*, no. 253, p. 147.

fiance of God and creation, even though for the absurd man God seems to exist only at the moment of his revolt against him. This shows, among other things, how difficult it is for a man to be an outright atheist!

Camus' interpretation of Christ's reaction to suffering and death as nothing short of despair is evidently a distortion of the Gospel account. Nevertheless he is correct in saying that both the divinity of Christ and his moral teaching have long been the target of vigorous attacks by many agnostics or freethinkers. Such attacks, we agree with Camus, have paved the way for much of the ensuing anti-Christian and atheistic literature which took the form of a revolt against the evils of the world. Whether or not the revolt of Camus' absurd man is motivated by a genuine concern for his fellowmen who are the victims of social and political abuses is debatable. One thing however is beyond question, namely, that contrary to Camus' belief, love of God and love of our fellowmen are not necessarily irreconcilable; on the contrary, they are mutually complementary.

This leads us to the problem of evil, a problem that is very much at the center of Camus' essay and is so vividly portrayed in the episode from *The Plague*. Without repeating the comments made by Father Paneloux and Dr. Rieux on the tragic death of a plague-stricken child, we would like to observe that Camus' presentation of the two contrasting views is quite accurate. It reflects two different mentalities, one inspired by belief in a provident God and the other motivated by compassion for the innocent victim but lacking the support of faith and religion.

The existence of evil, especially physical and mental suffering with no apparent justification for it, has always been a stumbling block to belief in an all-loving and infinitely merciful God. In the beginning of this section we have mentioned the difficulties encountered by philosophers in this connection, and there is no need to repeat them. Camus has simply restated the problem, which he felt most acutely, in more emotional and passionate terms. Calling evil an absurdity, he sees it as the basic motive for denying God's existence.

Philosophy, it must be admitted, has no easy solution for this problem, which seems to transcend the limits of human understanding. But philosophy can point to certain principles that will prevent the mind from falling into open contradictions, such as making God responsible for any wrongdoing in the moral order, or what is commonly known as evil of sin. God permits sin because he respects human freedom, but man alone is responsible for his abuse of a power that was given to him for the attainment of the good, which is the proper object of the will. As for physical evil—suffering and death—God is certainly responsible for it in the sense that he is the creator of the universe and of the laws that direct it to its end. (Whether or not this was God's original plan is a question that can be answered only by a theologian.) It would be wrong, however, to infer from this that God wills physical evil as such or without any reference to a possible good to be achieved through it. Such a view would conflict with the notion of an infinitely good Being, whose purpose in creation can be only the good of his creatures. Hence if God willed a world in which man must suffer and die, often with no fault of his own, this can be only in view of a greater good that God wishes to achieve through his creatures' suffering. This good is thus the direct object of God's creative plan, and physical suffering, which as such involves no moral evil, is the unfortunate but inevitable means to its achievement. Looked at from this point of view, which is the only one consistent with the notion of a Creator, even the suffering and death of an innocent child become somewhat explainable. One may go further and say that the reality of physical and moral suffering, such as the tortures, brutal deaths, and injustices to which many innocent persons are subjected in this life, not only do not disprove the existence of a just and loving God, but they rather demand it, for only thus can order and justice be restored. If the restoration of order and justice is not achieved in the present life, which is clearly not the case, it must be achieved in a future life where proper sanction is provided by God for the good and evil deeds of man.

This, it seems to us, is as far as reason can go in its attempt to understand the mystery of evil. Yet, we must admit, this is an area where revelation may come to reason's help and partly lift the veil that surrounds the mystery. When God asked Job what right he had to complain about his own pain and misery, he reminded him that he should never dare to ask a reason for the divine actions. Since God's wisdom and power transcend the capacity of man's understanding, God meant to tell Job, it is wrong to judge divine actions by human standards. We may add that it is doubly wrong and blasphemous, as in the case of Camus' rebel, to challenge the ways of divine Providence and call them absurd simply because they are beyond human comprehension. A mystery is not the same as an absurdity. Life, as we all know, is full of mysteries; its very existence is mysterious, and so is the existence of the world. Should we then call life and the world an absurdity? It is easy to see how gratuitous and irresponsible is such an affirmation.

To move from purely philosophical speculation to the higher sphere of Christian theology is, as we have said, to see that pain, suffering, and death lose part of their mysterious nature. They become the necessary elements of a divine plan whereby man is called to share in the redemptive work of Christ, the Son of God. In a Christian context, to suffer is not a disgrace but a privilege. It offers man the opportunity to show his pure, unselfish love of his Creator and brings him closer to the Divinity. This is what Peter had in mind when he wrote to the Christian communities in Asia Minor: "Rejoice . . . in the measure that you share Christ's sufferings. When his glory is revealed, you will rejoice exultantly."[188] To be called to suffer is therefore to be called to a greater share in God's love, for just as it is out of love that God gave his only-begotten Son to the world,[189] so it is out of love that he created man and made him partaker of Christ's suffering and eternal glory.

To conclude these reflections on the mystery of evil prompted by Camus' works, we wish to quote a statement by the renowned French writer, François Mauriac, who saw life and suffering from a higher and much more optimistic viewpoint than did Camus.

I believe as I did as a child, that life has a meaning, a direction, a value; that no suffering is lost, that every tear counts, each drop of blood, and that the secret of the world is to be found in St. John's, *"Deus caritas est"*—God is Love.[190]

CONCLUSION

Certain conclusions may be drawn from this survey which will help us to appreciate better the results of our study.

If we look back and consider the various ways in which philosophers have denied God's existence, we see that in most cases atheism is a preconceived position rather than the conclusion of strictly philosophical reasoning. Certain men—for instance, Marx, Nietzsche, Sartre, and Camus—were atheists prior to their elaboration of a theory that was intended solely to confirm their atheistic belief. This is clearly the case with Sartre. In such other instances as Feuerbach and Freud, the denial of God is but the necessary consequence of premises that are either gratuitous or unjustified. This is a very important point that weighs heavily against certain forms of atheism and ought to make one very wary about taking them too seriously.

In line with this consideration, the question may be asked: Can an atheist be really convinced that there is no God? It is a very pertinent question, since none of the representative atheists whom we have considered has offered an actual proof for the nonexistence of God. To do so, one would have to demonstrate the contradiction latent in the very idea of God or, more specifically, the metaphysical impossibility that God exist. In fact, God is not like any other being that can be conceived either as existent or nonexistent without contradiction. A self-existent and therefore

---

[188]*I Peter* 4:13.
[189]*St. John* 3:16.
[190]Quoted in *Time* (Sept. 14, 1970), p. 34.

necessary Being who is the cause of all other beings—which is the philosophical concept of God—cannot be a merely possible Being, as Leibniz showed in his time and Duns Scotus had done long before him. Hence to prove the nonexistence of God is tantamount to proving the impossibility of his existence. To the best of our knowledge, no such proof has ever been produced, and we are quite sure that none will be forthcoming in the future.[191] The reason is obvious. In a realistic metaphysics it is inconceivable that mere possibility of existence be at the foundation of all reality, for possibility of existence is meaningless without a necessary Being to actualize it. To put it in other words, if all beings were merely possible, there would be nothing in existence today. This is so true that even Kant, in his precritical period, had come to realize that only an absolutely necessary Being can be the ground of all possibility.[192] Moreover, in his answer to the question, "Whether it is possible that there should be absolutely nothing," he said that this question is meaningless as long as there is someone to ask it, since thought is conceivable only in terms of a reality and this, in turn, demands an absolutely necessary Being as its foundation. Commenting on Kant's statement, Gilson observes:

> In a realistic epistemology, the question: *Could there be nothing?* does not arise, because in fact there is something, and if it were possible that nothing should be, there would be nothing. Not only would there be no thought, as Kant says, but Kant himself would not be there to ask the question. Because something is, then, there is necessary being, for actual reality is necessary by right. The only question still to be asked about it is: In all that necessary being, what has a right to be called God?[193]

The existence of a necessary Being as the ultimate ground of all reality is therefore an absolute requirement for any philosophical system that is not built on a metaphysical vacuum. It is our conviction that none of the atheists considered in this chapter has really been able to challenge this

---

[191]This is also the conviction of the author of the article on atheism in the *Encyclopédie*. He writes: "Even if we could not demonstrate the possibility of a supremely perfect Being, we would have the right to ask the atheist for his proof of the contrary. For, since we are convinced with reason that this idea does not include any contradiction, it is up to him to prove that the contrary is true. . . . This, we may add, is what he will never be able to do." Cf. "Athéisme," in *Encyclopédie ou Dictionnaire raisonné des sciences, des arts et des métiers* (Lausanne: Société Typographique, 1778), III, pt. II, 806–807. The article is signed X, which stands for M. l'abbé Yvon (Cf. vol. I, p. lxxxix) and not for Voltaire, as Jacques Duquesne claims in his work, *Dieu pour l'homme d'aujourd'hui*, p. 13.

[192]Cf. *Der einzig mögliche Beweisgrund zu einer Demonstration Daseins Gottes*, in Immanuel Kant: *Werke*, ed. Wilhelm Weischedel, I (Wiesbaden: Insel, 1960), 617–730. For a discussion of this point see our next chapter.

[193]Cf. "The Idea of God and the Difficulties of Atheism," in *The Great Ideas Today*, p. 273.

doctrine. Even the Marxist philosophers, in fact, who touch upon this problem indirectly, do not question the need of a necessary being as the ultimate explanation of reality; they simply identify the necessary being with matter. Thus what is at issue, as Gilson indicates, is not so much the existence of a necessary being, which reason seems to demand, but rather the nature of such a being. Conceived in these terms, the solution that atheists have given either explicitly or implicitly to this problem is both inadequate and philosophically untenable.

A necessary being, as the term indicates, is a being that must be able to preserve its own identity at all times and with no alteration whatsoever. Any change, whether essential or accidental, would make it a different kind of being. In fact, a change involves either the addition or the loss of a perfection, so that the being in question would be necessary and contingent at one and the same time. Nor can it be objected that a being could be partly necessary and partly contingent and thus involve no contradiction, since necessity and contingency would apply to it in different ways. This explanation would be valid if the being under discussion were a dependent, limited, and composite being—such as a man, or even an angel—, although it is hard to see how such a being could still be called necessary in the strict and unqualified sense of the term. But a self-existent, and therefore uncaused, Being depends on no other being for its existence. It is unlimited, just as existence itself with which it is identified, is unlimited. Most of all, it admits of no composition. Existence is in effect a simple perfection that excludes any metaphysical composition or limitation, unless it is received by or participated in by another being, which is obviously not the case with the Being whose nature is to exist. Furthermore, the reason for one's own existence cannot be the reason for one's own limitation in existence, as the case would be if a self-existent being were limited in its own nature.

In the light of these observations, it is not merely unlikely, but clearly impossible that a proof for the nonexistence of God will be forthcoming in the future, provided the term *God* is taken in the strict sense that we have indicated. Hence we agree with Gilson's statement concerning the difficulties encountered by atheistic philosophers:

> True atheists are not scarce; they do not exist, because true atheism—that is, a complete and final absence of the notion of God—is not only difficult, it is impossible. What indeed exists is an immense crowd of people who do not think of God, and perhaps a still larger crowd of worshipers of false gods, but that is something different from consciously accepting the world and man, without any further explanation, as self-sufficient cause and end. There is indeed ample justification for doubt, hesitations, and uncertainties in man's seeking for the

true God, but the very possibility of such a quest presupposes—no, it implies—that the problem of the existence of God remains for the human mind a philosophical inevitability.[194]

It is the "philosophical inevitability" of facing the problem of God's existence that has led philosophers of all persuasions to take stands on this issue. What remains to be seen is the degree of an atheist's conviction that there is no God. This is unquestionably a complex issue that admits of no easy answer. Each case must be studied in its unique context, which includes the family background, the cultural and philosophical training, the social and political environment, and the character and moral life of the individual atheist, as well as many other factors that contribute to the shaping of his personality and beliefs. It is not easy in many cases to point to any one particular cause of a former believer's loss of faith in God. On the other hand, a convert from atheism has made this revealing confession:

> Until I was twenty-seven years old, I was one of those people who had "always been atheist." Born into a family of freethinkers, I spent my childhood in an environment that was almost completely devoid of religious concern and practice.[195]

Sartre, like many other atheists, seems to have been deeply influenced by his family circle. School can be an even greater factor than the family in many instances of lost belief in God. Social and political conditions, especially in communistic countries, can also exert a decisive role in a person's rejection of God and religion.

In his study of the nature and causes of contemporary atheism, Gabriel Marcel comes to the conclusion that philosophical atheism consists not so much in a positive and constructive theory or system, but rather in the radical establishment of an absence, a privation, a negation. Then he adds: "The atheistic philosopher is brought to realize that his negation cannot be reduced to an observable fact or anything resembling it, but in the final analysis is based on passion."[196]

There are many people who are too proud to acknowledge the existence of a supreme Being whose rule over the world is sometimes inscrutable and mysterious. Others are too greatly involved in sensual pleasures to admit the existence of a supreme legislator and judge whose reproach they feel deeply in their conscience and whose threat of punishment for sins

---

[194] *Ibid.*

[195] Cf. Ignace Lepp, *Atheism in Our Time,* trans. Bernard Murchland, C.S.C., (New York: The Macmillan Company, 1963), p. 12.

[196] Cf. "Contemporary Atheism and the Religious Mind," *Philosophy Today,* 4 (1960), 256.

they strongly resent. As a result, there has gradually developed in our time a kind of morality that aims to do away with God and his eternal law and makes man the supreme arbiter of good and evil. This trend has led to the so-called secularization of morality or what has come to be known as morality without sin. While Sartre, Camus, and other atheistic European philosophers may have laid the foundation for this secularistic view of morality, many thinkers and writers in the United States must share some degree of responsibility for it. Lacroix writes in this connection:

> It is certainly true that in the United States certain forms of sociology and psycho-analysis combine to create a mentality which, if not atheist in principle, at least in practice rejects all true religious experience, and ends up as some brand of naturalism.[197]

Whatever the causes of the loss of religious belief, the question still remains of whether or not an atheist, especially a philosopher, can be absolutely convinced that there is no God. Our answer to this question is that, despite the apparent sincerity of many atheists who deny God for alleged rational motives, it seems unlikely that their conviction of the nonexistence of God is one of absolute certitude, or is such as to exclude any fear of error. The fact that most of the atheists analyzed in this study have either expressed occasional doubts about their disbelief in God or have not given the subject the consideration it deserves, supports our contention. Whether this opinion is correct or not, it remains true that no substitute for God has ever been found by a philosopher and that any attempt to construct a philosophical system without God has met with innumerable difficulties, contradictions and, more often than not, obvious absurdities.

BIBLIOGRAPHY

Afanasyev, V. *Marxist Philosophy*. 3d ed. rev. Moscow: Progress Publishers, 1968.
Andreas-Salomé, Frau Lou. *Friedrich Nietzsche in seinen Werken*. Dresden: C. Reissner, 1924.
Augustine, St. *The Confessions*. Translation, with an Introduction and Notes, by John K. Ryan. Garden City, N.Y.: Doubleday "Image Books," 1960.
Bernouilli, Carl A. *Franz Overbeck and Friedrich Nietzsche*. 2 vols. Jena: E. Diederichs, 1908.
Bochenski, J. M. *Soviet Russian Dialectical Materialism*. Dordrecht, Holland: D. Reidel Publishing Co., 1963.
Boethius. *The Consolation of Philosophy*. New York: The Modern Library, 1943.
Brinton, Crane. *Nietzsche*. Cambridge, Mass.: Harvard University Press, 1941.

---

[197]*Op. cit.*, p. 34. See also the discussion of Hesnard's work, *Morale sans péché* (Morality without Sin) for a better insight into the question. *Ibid.*, pp. 64-92.

Camus, Albert. *The Plague*. Trans. by Stuart Gilbert. New York: The Modern Library, 1948.

_____. *L'été*. Paris: Gallimard, 1954.

_____. *The Myth of Sisyphus and Other Essays*. Trans. by Justin O'Brien. New York: Random House "Vintage Books," 1955.

_____. *The Rebel*. Trans. by Anthony Bower. New York: Alfred A. Knopf, 1961.

Collins, James. *God in Modern Philosophy*. Chicago, Ill.: Regnery, 1959.

Cruickshank, John. *Albert Camus and the Literature of Revolt*; reprint. London: Oxford University Press, 1970.

De George, Richard T. *The New Marxism*. New York: Pegasus, 1968.

Delanglade, Jean, S.J. *Le problème de Dieu*. Paris: Aubier, 1960.

De Lubac, Henri. *The Drama of Atheist Humanism*. Trans. by Edith M. Riley. New York: Sheed and Ward, 1950.

Duquesne, Jacques. *Dieu pour l'homme d'aujourd'hui*. Paris: Grasset, 1970.

Engels, Friedrich. *Anti-Dühring: Herr Eugen Dühring's Revolution in Science*. Moscow: Progress Publishers, 1959.

Evans-Pritchard, E. E. *Theories of Primitive Religion*. Oxford: Clarendon Press, 1965.

Fabro, Cornelio. *God in Exile*. Trans. and ed. by Arthur Gibson. Westminster, Md.: The Newman Press, 1968. A thorough study of modern atheism and its original philosophical sources.

Feuerbach, Ludwig. *The Essence of Christianity*. Trans. by George Eliot. New York: "Harper Torchbooks," 1957.

Freud, Sigmund. *The Future of an Illusion*. Trans. by W. D. Robson-Scott. Garden City, N.Y.: Doubleday "Anchor Books," 1964.

Gemelli, Agostino, O.F.M. *Psychoanalysis Today*. New York: Kenedy and Sons, 1955.

Gilson, Etienne. "The Idea of God and the Difficulties of Atheism." In *The Great Ideas Today*, pp. 239–73. Ed. by R. M. Hutchins and M. J. Adler. Chicago: Encyclopaedia Britannica, 1969. Excellent study by a renowned historian of philosophy.

Gleason, Robert W., S.J. *The Search for God*. New York: Sheed and Ward, 1964.

Graneris, J. *La religion en la historia de las religiones*. Buenos Aires: Editorial Excelsa, 1946.

Heidegger, Martin. *An Introduction to Metaphysics*. Trans. by Ralph Manheim. Garden City, N.Y.: Doubleday "Anchor Books," 1961.

Holloway, Maurice R. *An Introduction to Natural Theology*. New York: Appleton-Century-Crofts, 1959.

Hume, David. "Dialogues Concerning Natural Religion." In *The Philosophy of David Hume*, pp. 501–596. Ed. by V. C. Chappell. New York: The Modern Library, 1963.

James, William. *The Varieties of Religious Experience*. New York: Collier Books, 1961.

_____. *Pragmatism*. 8th printing. Cleveland and New York: The World Publishing Company "Meridian Books," 1961.

Jones, Ernest. *The Life and Works of Sigmund Freud*. New York: Basic Books, 1957.

Jung, Carl Gustav. *Psychology and Religion*. New Haven, Conn.: Yale University Press, 1938.

Kant, Immanuel. *Der einzig mögliche Beweisgrund zu einer Demonstration Daseins Gottes.* In *Immanuel Kant: Werke*, vol. I, pp. 617–730. Ed. by Wilhelm Weischedel. Wiesbaden: Insel, 1960.

Kaufmann, Walter. *Nietzsche.* New York: The World Publishing Company "Meridian Books," 1959.

Konstantinov, F. V., ed. *Osnovy marksistskoj filosofii.* The Academy of Sciences of the Soviet Union, 1958.

Lacroix, Jean. *The Meaning of Modern Atheism.* Trans. by Garret Barden, S.J. New York: The Macmillan Company, 1966.

Lalande, André. *Vocabulaire technique et critique de la philosophie.* Paris: Presses Universitaires de France, 1960.

Lenin, Vladimir. *Collected Works.* Moscow: Foreign Languages Publishing House, 1960—.

Lepp, Ignace. *Atheism in Our Time.* Trans. by Bernard Murchland, C.S.C. New York: The Macmillan Company, 1963.

Lotz, Johannes. "Ateismo e esistenzialismo." In *L'ateismo contemporaneo*, vol. II, pp. 305–363. Ed. by the Facoltà della Pontificia Università Salesiana di Roma. Turin: Società Editrice Internazionale, 1968.

Luijpen, William A., O.S.A. *Phenomenology and Atheism.* Pittsburgh, Pa.: Duquesne University Press, 1964. A very accurate study of the principal atheistic trends in modern and contemporary times.

Macquarrie, John. *Twentieth-Century Religious Thought.* New York: Harper and Row, 1963.

Marcel, Gabriel. *The Philosophy of Existentialism.* 7th ed. New York: The Citadel Press, 1966.

————. "Contemporary Atheism and the Religious Mind," *Philosophy Today*, 4 (1960), 252–62.

Maritain, Jacques. *The Range of Reason.* New York: Scribner's Sons, 1952.

McPherson, Thomas. *The Philosophy of Religion.* Princeton, N.J.: Van Nostrand Company, 1965.

Miceli, Vincent P. *The Gods of Atheism.* New Rochelle, N.Y.: Arlington House, 1971. Good and informative study by a competent author.

Michelet, G. "Religion—Théorie sociologique," *Dictionnaire apologétique de la foi catholique*, IV, 857–74.

Mill, John Stuart. *Nature and Utility of Relgion.* Ed. by George Nakhnikian. New York: The Liberal Arts Press, 1958.

Miller, Ed. L. *God and Reason.* New York: Macmillan, 1972.

Murray, John Courtney, S.J. "On the Structure of the Problem of God," *Theological Studies*, 23 (1962), 1–26.

Nietzsche, Friedrich. "The Twilight of the Idols." In *The Complete Works of Friedrich Nietzsche*, vol. XVI, pp. 1–120. Ed. by Oscar Levy. New York: Macmillan, 1911.

————. *Thus Spoke Zarathustra.* Trans. by Marianne Cowan. Chicago: Regnery "A Gateway Edition," 1957.

————. *The Will to Power.* Trans. by Walter Kaufmann and R. J. Hollingdale. New York: Random House "Vintage Books," 1968.

————. *Joyful Wisdom.* Trans. by Thomas Common. New York: Frederick Ungar Publishing Co., 1960.

————. "Ecce Homo." In *Basic Writings of Nietzsche*, pp. 673–791. Trans. and ed. by Walter Kaufmann. New York: The Modern Library, 1968.

Norbeck, Edward. "Anthropological Views of Religion." In *Religion in Philosophical and Cultural Perspective*, pp. 414-35. Ed. by J. Clayton Feaver and William Horosz. Princeton, N.J.: Van Nostrand Company, 1967.

Ortegat, Paul, S.J. *Philosophie de la religion*. 2 vols. Paris: Vrin, 1948.

Pfeil, Hans. *Friedrich Nietzsche und die Religion*. Regensburg: J. Habbel, 1949.

_____. "The Modern Denial of God: Its Origin and Tragedy," *Philosophy Today*, 3 (1959), 19-26.

Reinhardt, Kurt F. *The Existentialist Revolt*. Milwaukee: The Bruce Publishing Co., 1952.

Rubenstein, Richard L. *After Auschwitz*. Indianapolis: Bobbs-Merrill, 1966.

Sartre, Jean-Paul. *Being and Nothingness: An Essay on Phenomenological Ontology*. Trans. by Hazel E. Barnes. New York: The Philosophical Library, 1956.

_____. "Existentialism Is a Humanism." In *Existentialism from Dostoevsky to Sartre*, pp. 287-311. Ed by Walter Kaufmann. Cleveland and New York: The World Publishing Company "Meridian Books," 1956.

_____. *Nausea*. Trans. by Lloyd Alexander. Norfolk, Conn.: New Directions Books, 1959.

Siegmund, Georg. "Friedrich Nietzsche." In *L'ateismo contemporaneo*, vol. II, pp. 259-86. Ed. by the Facoltà della Pontificia Università Salesiana di Roma. Turin: Società Editrice Internazionale, 1968.

Todoli, José, O.P. *Filosofía de la religion*. Madrid: Editorial Gredos, 1955.

Tylor, Edward Burnett. *The Origins of Culture*. New York: "Harper Torchbooks," 1958.

Usener, Hermannus, ed. *Epicuras*. Leipzig: In aedibus B. G. Teubner, 1887.

Van Steenberghen, Fernand. *Hidden God*. Trans. by Theodore Crowley, O.F.M. St. Louis, Mo.: Herder, 1966.

Various Authors. *Dieu aujourd'hui*. "Semaine des intellectuels catholiques." Paris: Desclée de Brouwer, 1965.

Various Authors. *L'ateismo contemporaneo*. 4 vols. Ed. by the Facoltà della Pontificia Università Salesiana di Roma. Turin: Società Editrice Internazionale, 1967-1969. The most comprehensive study of all cultural aspects of modern and contemporary atheism by competent authors of various nationalities.

Yvon, M. l'abbé. "Athéisme." In *Encyclopédie ou Dictionnaire raisonné des sciences, des arts et des métiers*, vol. III, pt. 2, pp. 805-828. Lausanne: Société Typographique, 1778.

Wahl, Jean. *A Short History of Existentialism*. Trans. by Forrest Williams and Stanley Maron. New York: The Philosophical Library, 1949.

PART TWO

ARGUMENTS FOR THE EXISTENCE OF GOD

CHAPTER II

THE IDEOLOGICAL ARGUMENT*

The ideological argument for the existence of God has been the object of so many studies that a further discussion of it might seem to be of little advantage to the philosopher. Yet the fact that ever since the argument was proposed by St. Augustine, thinkers of different trends and attitudes have felt the need of expressing their opinions on this highly controversial topic, and have reached conclusions that are often far apart from one another, is an indication that the issue is far from being closed to objective investigation. Perhaps one may go even a step further and affirm without fear of contradiction that the many conflicting comments on the argument have somewhat contributed to obscure the original issue. What for St. Augustine and his followers was a valid rational proof of God's existence became for others a purely logical device that provides no help to the philosopher in his ascent to God. Furthermore, even among those who stand for the validity of the argument, no agreement has been reached as to the actual basis of its demonstrative value. Whereas for some the ideological argument is a typically distinct Augustinian theistic proof, others prefer to view it within the general scheme of St. Thomas' five ways. Cases are likewise known in which commentators have shifted from one position to another and have repudiated at later times what they first considered to be a sound philosophical proof of God's existence.

In view of this state of things, the present writer has decided to reexamine the entire issue of the ideological argument. This will be done, first, by stating the real meaning of the argument; secondly, by studying the original Augustinian texts where the argument is presented; and thirdly, by submitting to careful consideration the pertinent views and opinions expressed by some leading philosophers over the centuries both in the scholastic and the non-scholastic fields. The inquiry will be followed by a discussion and personal evaluation of the argument on the basis of sound philosophical principles.

I.   STATEMENT OF THE ARGUMENT

The ideological argument has been proposed in different forms. Although the authors of scholastic manuals are not of one opinion as to its

---

*Reprinted, with revisions and additions, from *Studies in Philosophy and the History of Philosophy*, ed. John K. Ryan, I (Washington, D.C.: The Catholic University of America Press, 1961), 1–34.

exact meaning, they all seem to agree that the argument is an attempt to prove the existence of God from the nature of the intelligibles, i.e., those realities which are attained to solely by our mind and may or may not exist.[1] The argument takes its starting point either from possible essences of things, viz., the argument from the possibles; or from eternal truths, i.e., those statements which express necessary relations among the possibles or the first principles of reason, viz., the argument from eternal truths. Thus possible essences and eternal truths are what in scholastic terminology may be called the *terminus a quo* of the ideological argument.[2] An explanation of each is in order.

A thing is said to be possible insofar as it can exist, either because a power can bring it into existence, or because the elements by which it is constituted are such that they can be conceived as existing together without contradiction. In the first case, there is extrinsic possibility; in the second case, there is intrinsic possibility. It is with this latter type of possibles that the ideological argument is concerned.[3] An essence that is intrinsically possible has a potential but objective reality which of itself is intelligible. It can not only be the object of our knowledge, but it also determines our intellect to know. A circle, for example, must be known in its essential notes as a circle, and anything that does not belong to it must be excluded from the notion of a circle. The intrinsic reality of the possibles is therefore something that is necessary, unchangeable, and eternal. From this we may conclude that necessity, immutability, and eternity are the three characteristics of the possibles. They are also the notes on which the ideological argument is built.

Eternal truths, as previously stated, include both the necessary relations among the possibles and the first principles of reason. That mutual relations among the possibles exist is beyond doubt. The possibles in the quantitative order are ruled by geometrical and mathematical laws; the possibles of a rational nature are subject to logical and ethical laws; finally, all possibles, no matter what their nature may be, are governed by the same universal metaphysical principles, such as the principle of identity, the principle of contradiction, and the principle of sufficient reason, etc.[4] Hence there are truths which are absolutely necessary and universally valid in the logical, metaphysical, mathematical, geo-

---

[1] Pedro Descoqs, S.J., *Praelectiones theologiae naturalis,* I (Paris: Beauchesne, 1935), 77.

[2] Claudius Mindorff, O.F.M., "De argumento ideologico exsistentiae Dei," *Antonianum,* III (1928), 269-70.

[3] Iosephus Hontheim, S.J., *Institutiones theodicaeae sive theologiae naturalis* (Freiburg i. Br.: Herder, 1893), p. 737.

[4] Wenceslaus Pohl, *De vera religione quaestiones selectae* (Freiburg i. Br.: Herder, 1928), pp. 56-57.

metrical, and ethical orders. It is not merely a question, as has well been observed,[5] of a universal and necessary affirmation of such truths, but rather of the affirmation of truths which are absolutely universal and necessary. Furthermore, the ideological argument is concerned with objective, ontological truth, which is the conformity of reality with the mind, and not merely with logical and formal truth, or the conformity of the mind with reality.[6]

Just as the starting point of the argument is a being in the order of intelligibility and not an actually existing being, as in the traditional five ways, so the principle used for the demonstration is the principle of sufficient reason alone and not the principle of causality. This is another feature that distinguishes the ideological argument from St. Thomas' five ways and makes it a typically distinct proof of God's existence. Possibles and eternal truths, the upholders of the argument maintain, demand God as their ultimate foundation.

The question of the ultimate foundation of the beings in the ideal order (possibles and eternal truths) is also discussed in ontology. But here we approach the problem from a different point of view. We try to discover whether possibles and eternal truths are such that *by their very nature* they demand God as their ultimate reason. If a positive answer is given to this question, then we have in the ideological argument a real metaphysical proof of God's existence. In effect, we have a proof that is even more metaphysical in character than the five ways. The five ways take as their starting point a contingent reality, whereas the ideological argument argues to God from an ideal being that shares in the same characteristics of necessity and universality as God himself.

It must be made clear that the ideological argument, as proposed by its defenders, is completely different from St. Anselm's ontological argument. Whereas Anselm is said by some to have argued from the *content* of the idea of God to its objective correlate, the ideological argument is an attempt to reach God starting from an *objective reality* which, though it is itself in the ideal order, is a result of abstraction from, or reflection upon, the world of existing things. It is, in this sense, an argument *a posteriori* and involves no faulty passage from the ideal to the real order. This is one case in which the ideal is also real: it belongs to the realm of the intelligibles.[7]

---

[5]*Ibid.*, p. 59.

[6]Descoqs, *op. cit.*, II, 77. See also *ibid.*, n. 1, where the author takes exception to Father Mindorff's criticism of the ideological argument (cf. n. 2 above) on the ground that the argument does not proceed, as Father Mindorff claims, from a being in the purely logical order but rather from the metaphysical reality of possible essences. Yet it is questionable, remarks Descoqs, whether a possible essence could be called a metaphysical reality.

[7]We disagree, therefore, with Father Mindorff's position that the ideological argument

On these premises, we proceed now to state the argument in syllogistic form. It may be put as follows:

There are intrinsically possible beings whose essence and essential principles are necessary, immutable, and eternal.

But such beings demand as their ultimate foundation an actually existing being that is absolutely necessary, immutable, and eternal.

Therefore such a being exists, and it is what we call God.

The middle term of the syllogism includes all intrinsically possible essences, as well as their necessary relations and essential principles. These latter are better known as "eternal truths." If valid, the argument concludes directly and *per se* only to an eternal, necessary, and immutable intellect. But since such an intellect is possible only in an infinite being with which it is identified, the argument leads actually to the existence of God.

We shall return to the argument and make it the object of a thorough study; but first let us review briefly its historical background.

II. THE ARGUMENT IN ST. AUGUSTINE

The ideological argument has been so closely associated with St. Augustine, that sometimes it is called the Augustinian argument. To a certain extent this appellation is correct. For even though St. Augustine did not propose the argument explicitly and in as complete a form as it is presented today, he suggested all the elements with which the ideological argument may be constructed. There are many passages in St. Augustine's works which show him working his way out to God through the doctrine of eternal truths.[8] It is not that he considers this as the only rational approach to God,[9] or, for that matter, as an indispensable means

---

involves an illegitimate transition from the ideal to the real order, as some believe to be the case with the ontological argument. Cf. Mindorff, *art. cit.*, p. 273. For an evaluation of the ontological argument see the following chapter of this volume.

[8]See *De libero arbitrio*, Bk. II, chaps. 2-15; Migne, PL 32, cols. 1241-63; *Confessiones*, Bk. VII, chap. 17; Migne, PL 32, cols. 744-45; *Soliloquia*, Bk. II, chaps. 5-8; Migne, PL 32, cols. 888-92; chap. 11, no. 21; Migne, PL 32, col. 895; *De vera religione*, chaps. 29-31; Migne, PL 34, cols. 145-48; *De magistro*, chap. 11; Migne, PL 32, cols. 1215-16.

[9]St. Augustine makes use of other traditional proofs of God's existence. Thus in *Confessiones*, Bk. XI, chap. 4, no. 6 (Migne, PL 32, col. 811), he argues to God from the world order and design; in *De civitate Dei*, Bk. XI, chap. 6 (Migne, PL 41, cols. 321-22), he builds up a theistic argument on the basis of the change noticeable in the realm of perishable beings; in *De immortalitate animae*, chap. 8, no. 14 (Migne, PL 32, col. 1028), and in *Sermo* CCXLI, chaps. 1-2 (Migne, PL 38, cols. 1133-34), he makes explicit use of the principle of

to attain the knowledge of God's existence.[10] However, he places great emphasis on the mind's ascent to God through the consideration of the unchangeable and eternal character of truth. He does so particularly in his treatise *De libero arbitrio*, Bk. II, chaps. 2-15, where his approach to God through eternal truth is fully developed.

He establishes first as absolutely certain the fact of one's own existence. No one could possibly doubt his own existence if he did not exist. He next discusses the nature of man and distinguishes three orders of being in him: existence, life, and understanding. Just as life is above existence, since to live is better than merely to exist, so understanding is above life. To understand is a further perfection that presupposes both existence and life. This leads to the question of man's knowledge. Man knows first through his external senses, which he has in common with animals. Each external sense has its proper object to which it is necessarily confined. Over and above the external senses there is an inner sense, which distinguishes what is proper and what is common to the external senses. The inner sense, also shared by brutes and animals, is superior to the other senses in virtue of the principle that "whatever judges is better than that which is judged."[11] But since the inner sense is in turn subject to reason, this, St. Augustine concludes, is man's highest and most noble faculty.

Having thus proved the supremacy of reason, St. Augustine proposes to Evodius, with whom he is engaged in a dialogue, the problem of God's existence. "If we can find something which you are certain not only exists but also is nobler than our reason, will you hesitate to call this, whatever it is, God?"[12] To Evodius' observation that only that which is above everything else, not merely that which is above reason may be called God, Augustine replies: "That is plainly right. . . . But I ask you: if you find there

---

efficient causality as a rational means for his ascent to God. See also *Enarrationes in psalmum LXXIII*, no. 25 (Migne, PL 36, col. 944), where he argues against those who refuse to acknowledge the existence of a creator simply because they do not see him. For more information about St. Augustine's use of the traditional arguments for God's existence, cf. Martin Grabmann, *Die Grundgedanken des heiligen Augustinus über Seele und Gott* (2d ed.; Cologne: Bachem, 1929), pp. 89-98.

[10]For St. Augustine the idea of God is so natural to man that no one can ignore it: "Haec est enim vis verae divinitatis, ut creaturae rationali iam ratione utenti, non omnino ac penitus possit abscondi." *In Ioannis evangelium*, tract. 106, no. 4; Migne, PL 35, col. 1910. Furthermore, belief in God is a necessary condition for a proper understanding of God's existence: ". . . neque quisquam inveniendo Deo fit idoneus, nisi antea crediderit quod est postea cogniturus." *De libero arbitrio*, Bk. II, chap. 2, no. 6; Migne; PL 32, col. 1243.

[11]*De libero arbitrio*, Bk. II, chap. 5, no. 12; Migne, PL 32, col. 1247. For the English translation of *De libero arbitrio* cf. Dom Mark Pontifex, *The Problem of Free Choice* (Westminster, Md.: The Newman Press, 1955).

[12]*Ibid.*, chap. 6, no. 14; Migne, PL 32, col. 1248.

is nothing above our reason except the eternal and unchangeable, will you hesitate to call this God?" Evodius accepts the challenge and says: "I will confess clearly that to be God, which all agree to be higher than anything else." St. Augustine answers: "Very well. All I need do is to show that there is a being of such a kind, and you will admit this being to be God, or if there is anything higher, you will grant that the higher being is God. So, whether there is something higher or whether there is not, it will be clear that God exists, when, with his help, I shall show, as I promised, that there exists something higher than reason."[13]

In his search for something higher than reason, St. Augustine meets first the law and truth of number, i.e., mathematical truths. These truths, being independent of the senses and the sensible world, are eternal and immutable. In fact, whatever we perceive through our senses is contingent; as such, it may cease to exist at any time. But there has never been a time, nor will there ever be, when seven and three do not make ten.[14] Thus mathematical truths are not only above the senses, but also above intellect and reason. We discover them; we do not make them.

Turning to wisdom, St. Augustine describes it as "the truth in which we distinguish and grasp the supreme good."[15] Since the supreme good is the same for all, wisdom must also be shared in common by everyone. How is wisdom related to number? This, he says, is not an easy problem. However, one thing is plain, namely, that both wisdom and number are unchangeably true. Therefore unchangeable truth exists.

Something has thus been discovered that is higher than our minds and reason: truth. While our minds are subject to change, truth does not change. Moreover, we do not judge truth; we only judge in accordance with truth.

Having attained the end of his painstaking search, St. Augustine turns again to Evodius and says to him with evident satisfaction:

> If I showed there was something above our minds, you admitted you would confess it to be God, provided there was nothing else higher. I accepted your admission, and said it was enough that I should show this. For if there is anything more excellent, it is this which is God, but, if there is nothing more excellent, then truth itself is God. Whichever is the fact, you cannot deny that God exists, and this was the question we set ourselves to debate.[16]

---

[13]*Ibid.*, Migne, PL 32, cols. 1248–49.
[14]*Ibid.*, chap. 8, no. 21; Migne, PL 32, cols. 1251–52.
[15]*Ibid.*, chap. 9, no. 26; Migne, PL 32, col. 1254.
[16]*Ibid.*, chap. 15, no. 39; Migne, PL 32, col. 1262.

III. THE ARGUMENT IN MEDIEVAL SCHOLASTICS

St. Augustine's argument from eternal truths has been the source of endless discussion among philosophers. The nature of this study does not permit us to go into a detailed exposition of all the views and opinions expressed by scholars in this connection. We shall therefore confine ourselves to a brief presentation of the main attitudes towards the argument from the time of early scholasticism up to the present time.[17]

The first in the line of great thinkers to utilize the Augustinian argument for God's existence is St. Anselm, the initiator of the scholastic movement whose penetrating genius and Augustinian tendencies earned him the title of *alter Augustinus.*[18] St. Anselm had already outlined his theistic proof from the nature of eternal truth in the *Monologium,*[19] but he fully developed it in his dialogue *De veritate.*[20] Briefly stated, the argument runs like this: Truth is eternal, for one cannot think of a moment in which truth did not or will not exist. If at one time truth did not exist, then it was always true that truth did not exist. Likewise, if at some future time truth will not exist, it will always be true that truth will not exist. In either case truth must be eternal, and so is the supreme being with which eternal truth is to be identified.[21] Whether St. Anselm considered this argument as a strict metaphysical demonstration of God's existence, or wished simply to show that the supreme truth is eternal, is not agreed upon by his interpreters and commentators.[22]

---

[17]In this survey we shall make us of the following studies, even though we may occasionally depart from their point of view in the interpretation of the thought of some thinkers therein mentioned: Martin Grabmann, *op. cit.,* pp. 84-98; Claudius Mindorff, *art. cit.,* pp. 278-98; 407-419; Fernand Van Steenberghen, "La philosophie de St. Augustin d'après les travaux du centenaire," *Revue néoscolastique de philosophie,* XXXV (1933), 240-52; Michele F. Sciacca, *S. Agostino,* I (Brescia: Morcelliana, 1949); Fulbert Cayré, *Dieu présent dans la vie de l'esprit* (Bruges-Paris: Desclée de Brouwer, 1951).

[18]Commenting on the title, Alexandre Koyré says: "C'est le nom que lui donnait le moyen âge et c'est celui qui le désigne le mieux. Partout, dans l'oeuvre de Sant Anselme se montre l'influence profonde de Saint Augustin." *L'idée de Dieu dans la philosophie de St. Anselme* (Paris: Leroux, 1923), p. 3.

[19]Chap. 18, *al.* 17; Migne, PL 158, cols. 167 f.

[20]Chap. 1; Migne, PL 158, cols. 468 f.: "Quod veritas non habet principium vel finem."

[21]St. Anselm concludes his argument in the *Monologium,* chap. 18, *al.* 17, with the following statements: "si veritas habuit principium, vel habebit finem, antequam ipsa inciperet, verum erat tunc, quia non erat veritas; et postquam finita erit, quia non erit. Atqui verum non potest esse sine veritate: erat igitur veritas, antequam esset veritas; et erit veritas postquam finita erit veritas; quod inconvenientissimum est. Sive igitur dicatur veritas habere, sive intelligatur non habere principium vel finem, nullo claudi potest veritas principio vel fine: quare idem sequitur de summa natura, quia ipsa summa veritas est."

[22]Mindorff calls St. Anselm's demonstration from eternal truth neither an ideological argument nor a proof of God's existence. See *art. cit.,* pp. 278-80. Koyré, on the contrary, sees in it a new demonstration of God's existence and eternity. *Op. cit.,* p. 58. He adds:

In his *Summa theologica*, Alexander of Hales presents the argument from eternal truth in three different forms. The first two forms are taken from St. Anselm's *De veritate*, while the third form is from St. Augustine's *Soliloquia*.[23] It is not clear whether his statement of the argument amounts also to approval of it. At any rate, the argument, as stated in the Alexandrian *Summa theologica*, seems to rest on man's internal experience of truth rather than on the nature and existence of truth as such.[24]

Richard of St. Victor argues to God from the potentiality of existing things. His way of proving God's existence may be considered as an anticipation of the argument from the possibles. Yet the vehicle of his ascent to God is not so much the principle of sufficient reason as it is the principle of causality.[25]

For St. Bonaventure the existence of eternal truth in the human mind is an undeniable fact that he explains partially through the doctrine of divine illumination. However, his illumination theory does not so much propose a proof for God's existence as it calls upon God to aid us to attain certitude in knowledge. The eternal reason, of which our mind has some sort of intuition, is a norm that moves and directs the intellect in the

---

"L'origine augustinienne de cette preuve est indubitable. Elle est exposée longement par St. Augustin, qui lui-même la tient de Plotin. Nous ne pouvons exposer ici les théories de St. Anselme sur la vérité; il distingue la vérité d'énonciation, la vérité d'affirmation, la vérité d'action et la vérité de l'être. Toutes se réduisent en dernière analyse à la rectitude, à la conformité au but essentiel, au maximum de perfection possible. La vérité est réalisée quand tout est tel qu'il doit être, conforme à la perfection intrinsèque, à la volonté divine." *Ibid.*, n.2.

[23]Cf. Alexander of Hales, *Summa theologica* (Quaracchi: Typographia Collegii S. Bonaventurae, 1924-48), I, no. 25, pp. 41-42, where he refers to St. Anselm's *De veritate*, chap. 1, and St. Augustine's *Soliloquia*, Bk. II, chap. 15, no. 28, and chaps. 2 and 4. The authenticity of the *Summa theologica* of Alexander of Hales is discussed by Father Victorinus Doucet, O.F.M., in *Prolegomena in librum III necnon in libros I et II "Summae Fratris Alexandri"* (Quaracchi: Typographia Collegii S. Bonaventurae, 1948), where he reaches the following conclusion: "Quapropter, omnibus consideratis atque perpensis, nos ita concludendum esse censemus, ut nempe dicatur quod ipse Alexander quodammodo *Summam* fecit, sed collaborantibus aliis et maxime Ioanne de Rupella;...item, ex propriis maxime scriptis sed etiam ex alienis. Unde et authentica et halesiana *Summa* quodammodo dici potest, non autem simpliciter nisi forte quoad Librum II." *Ibid.*, p. 369.

[24]Cf. Efrem Bettoni, *Il problema della conoscibilità di Dio nella scuola francescana* (Padova: Cedam, 1950), p. 81.

[25]Cf. Richard of St. Victor, *De Trinitate*, Bk. I, chap. 12; Migne, PL 196, col. 896: "Illum autem certissimum est quod in tota rerum universitate nihil esse potest, nisi possibilitatem essendi vel de seipso habuerit, vel aliunde acceperit. Quod enim esse non potest, omnino non est; ut igitur aliquid exsistat, oportet ut ab essendi potentia posse esse accipiat. Ex essendi itaque potentia esse accipit omne, quod in rerum universitate subsistit. Sed si ex ipsa sunt omnia, nec ipsa quidem est nisi a semetipsa, nec aliquid habet nisi a semetipsa. Si ex ipsa sunt omnia, ergo omnis essentia, omnis potentia, omnis sapientia. Si omne esse ab illa est, ipsa summa essentia est. Si ab illa omne posse, summe potens. Si omne sapere, summe sapiens. Est enim maius aliquid dare quam habere."

understanding of truth; it does not give us truth as such, or at least not the complete truth.[26] When the theistic argument from truth is stated, then it is to the principle of causality that St. Bonaventure appeals to establish on metaphysical grounds the existence of God as the eternal and absolute truth.[27]

This does not prevent him from pursuing a form of reasoning that has close resemblances to the ideological argument. Actually, his reasoning ends in what may seem to be a paradoxical statement: "If God does not exist, [then] He exists."[28] For every proposition, whether it is affirmative or negative, contains some truth, and no truth is possible if God, the cause of all truth, does not exist.[29] Yet, as has been observed, it is not just by pure dialectical analysis of the abstract concept of truth that St. Bonaventure proceeds to infer the existence of God; nor is it simply a logical repugnance that makes it impossible for him to deny the existence of the supreme truth. "This repugnance is but a sign of a metaphysical impossibility with which we are in conflict.... This radical impossibility of denying God is...the effect left upon the face of our soul by the divine light."[30]

Thus far one thing is clear: the Scholastics whose opinion has been presented show in general a favorable attitude towards the ideological argument, even though their way of stating it may differ from its original formulation in St. Augustine. This may be due, at least partially, to the great influence that the Bishop of Hippo exerted upon the Catholic thinkers up to the thirteenth century. Be that as it may, none of the schoolmen we have examined dares to challenge the ideological argument, let alone to reject it. Can we say the same thing of St. Thomas Aquinas and John Duns Scotus, the leaders of the two largest schools of philosophy in the middle ages, who have played such an important role in the shaping of Catholic thought throughout succeeding centuries?

---

[26]Cf. St. Bonaventure, *Quaestiones disputatae de scientia Christi,* q. 4, in *Opera omnia* (Quaracchi: Typographia Collegii S. Bonaventurae, 1883-1902), V, 23: "...ad certitudinalem cognitionem necessario requiritur ratio aeterna ut *regulans et ratio motiva,* non quidem ut *sola* et *in sua* omnimoda claritate, sed cum ratione creata, et ut *ex parte* a nobis contuita secundum statum viae."

[27]Cf. *I Sent.,* in *Opera omnia,* I, 155: "Probat iterum ipsam [existentiam Dei] et concludit omnis *propositio affirmativa:* omnis enim talis aliquid ponit; et aliquo posito ponitur verum; et vero posito ponitur veritas quae est causa omnis veri." See also *De mysterio Trinitatis,* in *Opera omnia,* V, 50.

[28]Here is the full text: "Deum esse *primum,* manifestissimum est quia ex omni propositione, tam affirmativa quam negativa, sequitur, Deum ess; etiam si dicas: Deus non est, sequitur: si Deus non est, Deus est." *In Hexaëmeron Collatio X,* in *Opera omnia,* V, 378.

[29]*Ibid.* See also n. 27 above.

[30]Etienne Gilson, *The Philosophy of St. Bonaventure,* trans. by Dom Illtyd Trethowan (London: Sheed & Ward, 1940), pp. 131-132.

As far as the Angelic Doctor is concerned, we would look in vain in his works either for an explicit approval of the Augustinian argument or for an outright condemnation of it. Because he did not take any definite stand on the problem at issue, and because statements are to be found in his works both in favor of and against the argument, it is little wonder that his commentators are not of one opinion as to Aquinas' exact position in the present controversy. Some would have it that the Angelic Doctor constantly presupposes the Augustinian proof from eternal truths in his system.[31] Others believe that the ideological argument is implicitly included in St. Thomas' fourth way of which it would be but an application.[32] Members of a third group of interpreters flatly disagree with the preceding views and take a negative attitude in regard to Aquinas' use of the argument. In the words of one of its best exponents: "St. Thomas treats the problem of God's existence in several places of his works, and in none of them does he mention the argument from eternal truths. This is because the Angelic Master knew very well that we cannot demonstrate [that] God [exists] except as a cause, and consequently, by taking as a starting point some real, existing effects."[33] Sertillanges,[34] Cardinal Mercier,[35] Descoqs,[36] and Min-

[31]This is the opinion of P. B. Romeyer, S.J., who writes: "Bien que S. Thomas ne se soit nulle part attaché à développer, de dessein formé, la preuve augustinienne de la vérité subsistante à partir des vérités qui déterminent nos jugements certains, il la suppose toujours." Reference is also made by the writer to his article, "La doctrine de S. Thomas sur la vérité," *Archives de philosophie,* III, ca. 2 (1925), 46–50. See Descoqs, *op. cit.,* II, 93–95, for a critical appraisal of Romeyer's viewpoint.

[32]This is the teaching of R. Garrigou-Lagrange, *God: His Existence and His Nature,* trans. by Dom Bede Rose, I (St. Louis, Mo.: Herder, 1948), 324–31. He states: "Why did St. Thomas not develop this Augustinian argument [from eternal truths] in the article which he set aside for a special discussion of the proofs of God's existence? The reason is because this proof can be referred back to the *fourth,* which establishes the presence not only of a Primary Intelligence and of a Primary Being, but also of a Primary Truth (*maxime verum*)." *Ibid.,* pp. 329–30. The same view had been previously expressed by Father A. Lepidi in his *Elementa philosophiae christianae* (Paris: Lethielleux; Louvain: Peeters, 1875–79), vol. I: *Logica,* p. 382, and by P. De Munnynck in his *Praelectiones de Dei existentia* (Louvain: Uystpruyst—Dieudonné, 1904), p. 23. Cf. Descoqs, *op. cit.,* II, 91–92, for the criticism of this opinion and a discussion of the text from the *Contra gentiles,* II, chap. 84, which runs as follows: "Ex hoc quod veritates intellectae sint aeternae quantum ad id quod intelligitur, non potest concludi quod anima sit aeterna, sed quod veritates intellectae fundantur in aliquo aeterno. Fundantur enim in ipsa prima Veritate, sicut in causa universali contentiva omnis veritatis. Ad hoc autem aeternum comparatur anima non sicut subiectum ad formam, sed sicut res ad proprium finem; nam verum est bonum intellectus et finis ipsius." According to Descoqs this text, rather than being an argument for God's existence, presupposes that the existence of God has been previously demonstrated.

[33]Fr. M. Cuervo, O.P., "El argumento de 'Las Verdades Eternas' según Santo Tomás," *La ciencia tomista,* XXXVII (Jan.-June, 1928), 33.

[34]*La philosophie de S. Thomas d'Aquin* (new ed. rev.; Paris: Aubier, 1940), I, 45–48.

[35]*Cours de philosophie,* vol. II: *Métaphysique générale* (5th ed. rev.; Louvain: Institut supérieur de philosophie, 1910), pp. 40 ff.

[36]*Op. cit.,* II, 91–97.

dorff[37] share the same viewpoint. Their position can be summarized as follows: (1) St. Thomas does not admit the ideological argument in the purely analytical order; rather he denies that truth, considered in itself and independently of God otherwise known to us, is eternal and immutable; (2) the ideological argument can perhaps be reduced to the fourth way, but St. Thomas never attempts to do it.[38]

More recently, a Thomistic scholar claims that the Angelic Doctor acknowledges the value of the theistic argument from eternal truths, but he does not include it among his famous ways because of its complexity. Unlike the Thomistic ways, which proceed analytically by taking up one aspect of reality at a time, the Augustinian proof considers the various aspects of truth and of the mind that knows it *simultaneously*. However, if one analyzes carefully the complexity of the Augustinian proof, he will discover that it can be easily reduced to the scheme of several among the Thomistic ways.[39]

John Duns Scotus, like Aquinas, does not make explicit use of the ideological argument. Neither in the *Ordinatio*, Bk. I, dist. 2, Part I, qq. 1—3,[40] nor in the *De primo principio*,[41] where the proof of God's existence is worked out with a painstaking logic and a constructive reasoning that have no parallel in scholastic philosophy, is there found a trace of the argument from eternal truths. He approaches the problem from the three points of view of efficiency, finality, and eminence, and concludes to the existence of an infinite being which is most perfect, as well as the supreme efficient and final cause. In fact, for Duns Scotus infinity is the radical attribute of God which, more than any other attribute, characterizes the supreme being in his absolute unicity and perfection.[42] It is true that the starting point of Scotus' ascent to God is not, as with St. Thomas, the actual existence of things but rather their possibility; for the possibility that things exist is a necessary truth, whereas their actual existence is only a contingent fact. However, the possibility in question is not intrinsic possibility, as is the case with the ideological argument, but extrinsic possibility. Hence the principle on which his proof is based is the principle of causality and not merely the principle of sufficient reason, as the ideological argument demands. Moreover, when Duns Scotus describes

---

[37]*Art. cit.*, pp. 407–412.
[38]Emmanuel Gisquière, *Deus Dominus* (Paris: Beauchesne, 1950), I, 215.
[39]Cf. Marcolino Daffara, O.P., *Dio. Esposizione e valutazione delle prove* (2d ed. rev.; Turin: Società Editrice Internazionale, 1952), pp. 127-30.
[40]Duns Scotus, *Opera omnia*, II (Vatican edition, 1950), 125-243.
[41]*The "De Primo Principio" of Duns Scotus*. A revised text and translation by E. Roche, O.F.M. (St. Bonaventure, N.Y.: The Franciscan Institute, 1949).
[42]*Ordinatio*, I, d. 3, q. 2, no. 17; Vatican ed., III (1954), 40–42.

eternal truth with its characteristics of necessity and immutability, he affirms that strictly speaking such truth exists only in God.[43] Statements to the effect that Scotus admits the existence of eternal and necessary truths apart from God have been proved to be without foundation and contrary to his mind.[44] Thus the ideological argument based on eternal truths has no place in Scotus' philosophy, even though, in common with St. Thomas, he never takes upon himself the task of refuting it as an invalid theistic proof.

IV. MODERN FORMULATIONS OF THE ARGUMENT

In modern times we find that the ideological argument has been favorably received and defended by various outstanding philosophers, both scholastic and nonscholastic. Among nonscholastics, Leibniz and Kant deserve special consideration.

Leibniz takes up the argument in his *New Essays Concerning Human Understanding*, Bk. IV, chap. 11, where he discusses the value and foundation of purely essential propositions, that is, propositions about a subject that does not exist, and shows against John Locke that the truth of such propositions must have its ultimate foundation in a supreme and universal mind. He writes:

> The Scholastics have hotly disputed *de constantia subjecti*, as they called it, i.e., how the proposition made upon a subject can have a real truth, if this subject does not exist. The fact is that the truth is only conditional, and says, that in case the subject ever exists, it will be found such. But it will be further demanded, in what is this connection founded, since there is in it some reality which does not deceive. The reply will be, that it is in the connection of ideas. But it will be asked in reply, where would these ideas be if no mind existed, and what then would become of the real ground of this certainty of the eternal truths? This leads up finally to the ultimate ground of truths, viz., to that Supreme and Universal Mind, which cannot fail to exist, whose understanding, to speak truly, is the region of eternal truths, as St. Augustine has recognized and expresses in a sufficiently vivid way.[45]

---

[43]*Ibid.*, I, d. 8, q. 5, no. 22; Vatican ed., IV (1956), 321: "Dico...quod nihil aliud a Deo est immutabile...quia nihil aliud est formaliter necessarium." *Ibid.*, III, d. 32, no. 3; Vivès ed., XV (1894), 428b: "Nihil aliud a Deo in quocumque *esse* est ex se necessarium." *Ibid.*, I, d. 35, no. 12; Vatican ed., VI (1963), 261: "Quidquid autem est in Deo secundum quodcumque *esse*, sive rei sive rationis, per actum intellectus divini, est aeternum."

[44]Allusion is made here to certain erroneous statements by D. Bañez and A. Goudin, which Cuervo repeats but does not correct (cf. *art. cit.*, p. 22). For a full discussion of this subject cf. Mindorff, *art. cit.*, pp. 413–15.

[45]Cf. Gottfried Wilhelm Leibniz, *New Essays Concerning Human Understanding*, trans. by Alfred Gideon Langley (3d ed.; La Salle, Ill.: The Open Court Publishing Company, 1949), p. 516.

To emphasize his point, Leibniz states that eternal truths are the regulating principles of all existences, and as such they must preexist in a necessary substance from which all truth is derived.

And in order not to think that it is unnecessary to recur to this [the Supreme and Universal Mind], we must consider that these necessary truths contain the determining reason and the regulating principle of existences themselves, and, in a word, the laws of the universe. Thus these necessary truths being anterior to the existence of contingent beings, must be grounded in the existence of a necessary substance. Here it is that I find the original of the ideas and truths which are graven in our souls, not in the form of propositions, but as the sources out of which application and occasion will cause actual judgments to arise.[46]

From these statements it is clear that, although the starting point of Leibniz' ideological argument is found in the essential propositions that have no direct relation to existence, the eternal truths which such propositions contain are something real, since they are the determining reason and regulating principle of all existing things, as well as the source of our mind's judgments. Thus Leibniz is able to avoid the illicit transition from the ideal order to the order of reality, which for some is the main defect of the ontological argument, and his proof becomes an *a posteriori* argument for God's existence.

The ideological argument did not escape the attention of Immanuel Kant. In his early work, *The Only Possible Ground for a Demonstration of God's Existence,*[47] Kant reduces the arguments for the existence of God to four. Of these four arguments, two take as their starting point the idea of the possible, while the two others rest on the empirical idea of the existent. The idea of the possible may be considered as a ground from which God's existence is derived as consequence, in which case we have the so-called ontological argument proposed by St. Anselm and restated in their own ways by Descartes and Leibniz. Kant rejects such an argument because, he says, it is based on the false presupposition that existence is a predicate to be derived by analysis from essential possibility. Likewise, the third and fourth proofs, which Kant calls the cosmological and the teleological arguments, must be rejected as invalid demonstrations of God's existence. On the one hand, we cannot prove that a first cause must be what we call God, as the upholders of the cosmological argument maintain; on the other hand, order and design in the universe may lead to a be-

---

[46]*Ibid.,* pp. 516-17.
[47]The original title is *Der enzig mögliche Beweisgrund zu einer Demonstration Daseins Gottes* (Königsberg, 1763). The treatise can be found in *Immanuel Kants Werke* (ed. E. Cassirer; Berlin, 1912-1918), II, 67-172.

ing endowed with an extremely great intelligence but not to a creator in the strict sense of the term, as the defenders of the teleological argument proclaim. By excluding the first and the last two proofs, Kant is left with the second argument, which starts from the possible as consequence and argues to the existence of God *as its foundation*. This is exactly what we mean by ideological argument from the possibles. It is also what Kant reckons as the only possible basis for a demonstration of God's existence.

Kant has not just one way of stating the argument, but the essential features of his reasoning are as follows. There is no contradiction in saying that nothing whatsoever exists. But it is contradictory to say that nothing exists and affirm at the same time the real intrinsic possibility of things. For in real possibility the constitutive elements are always taken from an actually existing thing. We must admit such a possibility. To deny it is to think, and to think is to affirm implicitly the realm of possibility. Hence, given the intrinsic possibility of things, a being must exist which is its foundation and principle. This being is the absolutely necessary, existing God.

Kant arrives at the same conclusion by pursuing the following line of reasoning:

> All [intrinsic] possibility supposes something real in which and by means of which all thinkable is given. Hence a reality exists whose very destruction would entail the absolute destruction of all intrinsic possibility. But that whose destruction or denial destroys all possibility is absolutely necessary. Therefore something that is absolutely necessary exists.[48]

In other words, a being exists with real, absolute necessity, if its non-existence entails a real contradiction by removing the very ground on which the intrinsic possibility of things is founded. But such a being is God. Therefore God exists.

Kant does not consider his argument as an absolutely cogent proof of God's existence, or such a proof that would give us the certainty of a mathematical demonstration. However this kind of demonstration, he observes, is not really necessary. All we need to do is to convince ourselves that God exists. Nevertheless he believes that the line of thought suggested above is the only possible ground on which a demonstration of God's existence must rest.[49]

---

[48]*Ibid.*, pp. 87 f.

[49]For a more complete exposition and criticism of Kant's ideological argument cf. James Collins, *God in Modern Philosophy* (Chicago: Regnery, 1959), pp. 169-73. See also Frederick Copleston, S.J., *A History of Philosophy*, VI (London: Burns and Oates, 1950), 187-89; Mindorff, *art. cit.*, pp. 285-88. It is well known that the ideological argument, as

Another forceful presentation of the ideological argument is offered by a thinker of a cast of mind very different from that of Leibniz or Kant. This is Jaime Balmes, the greatest Spanish philosopher of the nineteenth century and one of the forerunners of the scholastic revival in Europe. Since Balmes' formulation of the ideological argument is so logical and complete that it served as a pattern for many later thinkers, we summarize it here in its essential points.[50]

Balmes considers the order of truth and the order of possibility as two separate ways of arriving at God. In the order of truth, he distinguishes between universal and particular truth. The former is the truth of a proposition in which the subject is universal, e.g., all the diameters of a circle are equal; the latter is the truth of a proposition in which the subject is particular, e.g., this circle has all its diameters equal. While agreement exists between these two kinds of truth, universal truth cannot depend on the truth of particular facts but only on a being that is superior to them. This can be proved in the following manner.

From a particular fact we cannot infer universal truth, but from universal truth we can infer the truth of all actual and possible facts. This is due to the necessary connection existing between subject and predicate in a proposition containing universal truth. Such necessity is not to be found in particular facts, since these facts are in themselves only of a contingent nature. Nor can it be found in our mind, for everyone perceives a necessary truth without giving even a thought to himself or others. Truth existed before us, and it will exist when we are no more without thereby losing anything of its nature. Hence, since there are necessary truths which are perceived by all independently of any previous agreement or understanding, there must be a universal reason (*ratio universalis*) from which all minds derive their knowledge as from their common source.[51]

This universal reason, Balmes goes on to say, cannot be a simple idea, as an abstraction from individual reason, for an idea has no existence apart from our mind. The universal reason must be an existing reality, a reality that is greater and more perfect than our mind. This reality cannot be but God.

A real fact must have a real principle; a universal phenomenon must have a universal cause; a phenomenon independent of all finite

---

well as all other theistic proofs, was later disposed of by Kant in his *Critique of Pure Reason*. However, that was due to his new approach to philosophy which made all strictly metaphysical speculation impossible.

[50]The argument runs through chaps. 24–26 of Balmes' *Fundamental Philosophy*, trans. by Henry F. Brownson (new ed. rev.; New York: Kenedy, 1903), II, 96–104.

[51]*Ibid.*, pp. 96–99.

intelligence must spring from some cause independent of all finite intelligence. There is, then, a universal reason, the origin of all finite reason, the source of all truth, the light of all intelligences, the bond of all beings. There is, then, above all phenomena, above all finite individuals, a being, in which is found the reason of all beings, a great unity, in which is found the bond of all order, and of all the community of other beings.

The unity, therefore, of all human reason affords a complete demonstration of the existence of God. The universal reason is; but universal reason is an unmeaning word, unless it denotes an intelligent, active being, a being by essence, the producer of all beings, of all intelligences, the cause of all, and the light of all.[52]

Having established the existence of God from eternal truths, Balmes proposes to do the same thing from the standpoint of the possibles. Our mind, he says, does not understand existing things alone; its range of knowledge extends also to the realm of the possibles and their necessary relations. But if no reality existed in which such possibility were grounded, possibility itself would be an absurdity. If nothing existed, nothing would be possible. Moreover, a foundation must be something real; a foundation that is nothing is no foundation at all, nor can it serve as a ground for the possibles. The same holds true of the necessary relations existing among the possibles. They demand real models and exemplars. Hence necessary truths exist prior to human reason and must be related to a being that is the source of all reality and the foundation of all possibility, as well as the principle from which we receive the power to perceive such truths. This being is God.[53]

---

[52]*Ibid.*, p. 100.

[53]*Ibid.*, pp. 100-101. This same line of thought is more fully developed by Balmes in chap. 26 of his *Fundamental Philosophy*, where he illustrates his viewpoint by analyzing the truth of the proposition "Two circles of equal diameters are equal." The proposition, Balmes says, is evidently true. It refers to the possible order, and abstracts absolutely from the existence of the circles and of the diameters. The truth of the proposition does not refer to our mode of understanding; on the contrary, we conceive it as independent of our thought. Nor does it depend on the corporeal world, for even if no body existed, the proposition would still be true, necessary, and universal.

"What would happen, if, withdrawing all bodies, all sensible representations, and even all intelligences, we should imagine absolute and universal nothing? We see the truth of the proposition even on this supposition; for it is impossible for us to hold it to be false. On every supposition, our understanding sees a connection which it cannot destroy: the condition once established, the result will infallibly follow.

"An absolutely necessary connection, founded neither on us, nor on the external world, which exists before any thing we can imagine, and subsists after we have annihilated all by an effort of our understanding, must be based upon something, it cannot have nothing for its origin: to say this, would be to assert a necessary fact without a sufficient reason. . . . In pure nothing, nothing is possible; there are no relations, no connections of any kind; in nothing there are no combinations, it is a ground upon which nothing can be pictured.

Thus Balmes defends the ideological proof in its twofold aspect of argument from eternal truths and argument from the possibles.

V. VIEWS OF CONTEMPORARY PHILOSOPHERS

In recent times the ideological argument has again been the object of study by many thinkers, especially among Scholastics. As it would be outside the scope of this essay to make a survey of all the opinions expressed in this connection in scholastic manuals or in special studies, we shall limit our exposition to some among the most original and authoritative views, beginning with those favoring the argument.

A. Defenders of the Argument

In his lengthy and valuable article on St. Augustine, E. Portalié takes a stand against Jules Martin,[54] and says that it is wrong to see in the Augustinian proof from eternal truths a prelude to St. Anselm's ontological argument. St. Augustine does not argue from the idea of God to his existence. Rather he analyzes the characteristics of truth and finds that their only explanation lies in the admission of an actually existing being which is above truth and the source of all truth.[55] This, Portalié says, is confirmed by St. Augustine's profound observation[56] that all our theistic proofs show that God exists, not that he must exist. In other words, they are not *a priori* proofs from the idea of God but proofs *a posteriori*.

Grabmann calls the Augustinian argument for God's existence a psychological-metaphysical proof, in which facts of consciousness constitute the premises of a metaphysical train of thought.[57] While recognizing the proof as the work of a powerful mind,[58] he says that it is not without its dark spots and difficulties.[59] Grabmann rejects the opinion of Malebranche and other ontologists who interpret St. Augustine's doctrine of illumination in such wise as to imply man's direct knowledge of God.[60] He

---

"The objectivity of our ideas and the perception of necessary relations in a possible order, reveal a communication of our understanding with a being on which is founded all possibility. This possibility can be explained on no supposition except that which makes the communication consist in the action of God giving to our mind faculties perceptive of the necessary relation of certain ideas, based upon necessary being, and representative of his infinite essence." *Ibid.,* pp. 102–104.

[54]*Saint Augustin* (Paris: Alcan, 1901), pp. 101–188.

[55]E. Portalié, "Augustin (saint)," *Dictionnaire de théologie catholique,* I, 2, col. 2345.

[56]Quoted *ibid.,* col. 2344.

[57]Grabmann, *op. cit.,* p. 76.

[58]*Ibid.,* p. 77.

[59]*Ibid.,* p. 83.

[60]*Ibid.*

also points out the important role that the principle of causality—exemplary causality more than efficient causality—plays in St. Augustine's argument for God's existence.[61]

According to Etienne Gilson, the proof of God's existence is not so great a problem for St. Augustine as it is for modern philosophy. For Augustine the idea of God is something like a universal knowledge that cannot be separated from the human soul.[62] Hence, rather than attempt to prove to an unbeliever that God exists, he tries to show the rational character of our faith. The formula *credo ut intelligam* is at the basis of the Augustinian proof of God's existence, just as it is at the basis of the entire Augustinian philosophy.[63]

In Gilson's view, the Augustinian argument from eternal truths must be interpreted in the light of the doctrine of illumination. No matter how this doctrine is understood, the fact remains that for St. Augustine the problem of God's existence is strictly bound up with the problem of knowledge. "To know how we conceive truth and to know the existence of truth is one and the same question."[64] The Augustinian proof is completed entirely within our thought, and no consideration of the sensible order has a necessary part in it.[65] While St. Thomas' five ways take their lead from the data of sense experience, St. Augustine's proof from eternal truths, along with his other theistic arguments, has as its starting point certain modes of being for which an ultimate reason is sought in a being of a different order, which alone can be the reason for those modes and limited perfections. Briefly, while the Thomistic five ways move in the order of existence, St. Augustine's proofs are developed basically, although not exclusively, in the order of essence.[66]

In a profound study of the Augustinian argument, J. Hessen stresses the point that in it there is no transition from the ideal to the real order, since for St. Augustine the intelligibles are true realities, the necessary ontological foundation of truth. Basically, the proof consists in showing that the multitude of intelligibles demands as their ultimate foundation a unity that transcends them, namely, eternal truth. In this respect, the Augustinian proof is equally distant from both the Anselmian argument and the Aristotelian argument. Just as it does not imply a passage from the ideal to the real order, so the proof does not have recourse, in the real

---

[61]*Ibid.*, pp. 88–89.
[62]Etienne Gilson, *Introduction à l'étude de saint Augustin* (2d ed. rev.; Paris: Vrin, 1943), p. 11.
[63]*Ibid.*, p. 13.
[64]*Ibid.*, p. 22.
[65]*Ibid.*
[66]*Ibid.*, pp. 26–27.

order, to the principle of causality. It merely affirms a norm of truth without which the characteristics of our knowledge would remain unexplained.[67] Yet, Hessen remarks, the dialectic process whereby St. Augustine argues from what is incommutably true (*incommutabiliter verum*) to incommutable truth (*veritas incommutabilis*) as something self-existing and personal, cannot satisfy our modern critical mind. The process must be completed and integrated with the consideration that the ideal order is not something isolated from, but related to, the real. Thus interpreted and implemented, the Augustinian argument for God's existence may be considered, if not a proof in the strict sense of the term, at least a rational justification of our faith in God. This, affirms Hessen with Gilson, is precisely what St. Augustine wanted his argument to be.[68]

Charles Boyer does not quite agree with Hessen's viewpoint that the principle of causality has no part in the Augustinian proof; nor does he accept the distinction that Gilson introduces between an essential and an existential approach to the problem of God's existence, as though, in contrast with the existential character of the Thomistic ways, St. Augustine would have developed his proof on a purely essential plane. After a careful study of all the pertinent texts, which he lines up and interprets in what he believes to be a logical sequence, Boyer concludes that St. Augustine's theistic arguments constitute various stages of a unique demonstration, in which the sensible world is the starting point and the nature of our ideas a further step in our mind's ascent to God. Hence no clear-cut distinction can be made in St. Augustine's system between the cosmological and the ideological argument. The two arguments are but two different stages of a unique demonstrative process that rests ultimately on the principle of causality.[69]

One of the strongest supporters of the apodictic value of the Augustinian argument is Prof. Ioachim Sestili. In an extensive and well-documented study,[70] he contends that this proof of God's existence is truly metaphysical, inasmuch as our mind has a direct intuition of the ideal properties and principles of truth which are like norms or regulating principles of our knowledge and judgments.[71] For Sestili the special characteristic of the proof consists in this: the *incommutabilis ratio* of the intelligible, such

---

[67]J. Hessen, *Augustins Metaphysik der Erkenntnis* (Berlin: Dümmler, 1931), pp. 138–46.

[68]*Ibid.*, pp. 189–91.

[69]Charles Boyer, "La preuve de Dieu augustinienne," *Archives de philosophie,* VII, 2 (1930), 105–141.

[70]Cf. Prof. Ioachim Sestili, "Argumentum augustinianum de existentia Dei," *Acta hebdomadae augustinianae-thomisticae* (Turin-Rome: Marietti, 1931), pp. 241–65. The study is followed by a very interesting and enlightening discussion, pp. 265–270.

[71]*Ibid.*, p. 242.

as the concept of a square body, expresses an absolute truth of the ideal order which serves as a basis for our ascent to self-existing truth.[72] The Augustinian proof is an argument *a posteriori*, for it is grounded in the essences of things that exist outside our mind.[73] Moreover, we arrive at the knowledge of God as the source of all truth by means of the principle of both efficient and exemplary causality.[74] To this extent the proof is similar to the Thomistic ways, especially the fourth way, which argues to God from the various degrees of being.[75] However, unlike the Thomistic fourth way, the Augustinian proof rests exclusively on knowledge of the pure intelligible through the eternal forms or ideas that are impressed, as it were, in the very core of reality and assist our mind as illuminating principles in its attainment of truth.[76]

If we wish, observes Prof. Sestili, we may speak of abstraction and separation in the attainment of the intelligible; but in St. Augustine's system the intellect does not rest ultimately on a logical and subjective universal whose characteristics of necessity and eternity are purely negative. The universal in question is a universal of an ideal order, but an *objective* and *positive* universal. It is not a pure abstraction, since it manifests in its objective notion an absolute, simple, and definite mode of eternal possibility of an essence with regard to existence. This mode, it is worth noting, will be easily identified with those Augustinian ideas or forms which lead necessarily to the exemplary idea of participability of the divine essence and conclude to the divine essence itself as to their ultimate foundation.[77] Thus understood, he concludes, the Augustinian proof is the best and most effective argument for God's existence, for, rather than rest on the judgments derived from the principles of truth, it rests on the direct contemplation of truth itself in the ideal order.[78] Besides, all other theistic arguments, including St. Thomas' five ways, are somehow grounded in the Augustinian proof.[79]

An enthusiastic defense of the argument from eternal truths can be

---

[72]*Ibid.*, pp. 242; 251.

[73]*Ibid.*, p. 243. See also Prof. Sestili's answer to P. Blasius Romeyer, p. 266.

[74]*Ibid.*, pp. 251; 252.

[75]*Ibid.*, p. 243. See also Prof. Sestili's answer to P. Bernardus Jansen, p. 269.

[76]*Ibid.*, p. 243.

[77]*Ibid.*, 243–44.

[78]*Ibid.*, p. 246: "Hinc concludimus, augustinianum argumentum omnium rei demonstrandae argumentum praestantissimum extare et illo neque maius neque praestabilius inveniri. Illud namque dicimus quasi mathesim puram ceteris applicandam. De bonitate enim argumentorum ceterorum iudicare debemus ex principiis incommutabilis veritatis; iamvero, Augustinus ad argumentum conficiendum, contemplatur directe hanc ipsam incommutabilem veritatem in ordine ideali. Et excellentia ipsius thomistici argumenti, quo ex rebus mobilibus ad ens immobile devenitur, ad illud Augustini reduci debet."

[79]Cf. Prof. Sestili's answer to Father Jérôme of Paris: "Teneo cetera argumenta in illo fundari, non autem ad illud reduci." *Ibid.*, p. 266.

found in another contemporary thinker, an informed and devoted advocate of St. Augustine, Prof. Michele Federico Sciacca.[80] In his opinion, the problem of God's existence is essentially the problem of the truth or existence of every finite being; it is the problem of the metaphysical intelligibility of the real. To inquire whether God exists is to search for the truth of the truth of my own being and that of every other existing being, as well as for the truth that is within myself.[81] Hence all demonstration of God's existence must begin with truth.[82] Even the theistic argument from the existence of the external world rests ultimately on the objective validity of the principle of causality. This, too, is a truth.[83] To affirm that the human mind can attain to absolute truth, but to deny the existence of a transcending truth, is to contradict oneself. One denies truth in the very moment that he makes truth the product of his finite and changeable mind.[84]

In an attempt to give the argument from truth its concrete and precise formulation, Prof. Sciacca reduces it to the following syllogism.

An intelligent being has the intuition of truths that are necessary, immutable, absolute.

[But] a contingent and finite intelligible being can neither create nor receive from things, through the senses, the absolute truths that it knows intuitively.

Therefore, there exists a necessary, immutable, absolute truth, which is God.[85]

In a fairly recent reappraisal of St. Augustine's ideological argument, Father Marcolino Daffara affirms its unquestionable value, provided, he says, the argument is properly understood.[86] He holds that the innatistic trend of St. Augustine's gnoseology, according to which truth is possessed by our mind even prior to the mind's activity, in no way prejudices the value of the argument. The ideological argument is only accidentally related to the primary origin of our ideas. Whatever this origin may be, it is absolutely necessary that the truths which we know and the activity itself of our mind that knows them, find their ultimate explanation in a first mind and first truth that makes them intelligible.[87]

---

[80] We refer especially to his work, *Filosofia e metafisica* (Brescia: Morcelliana, 1950), pp. 146–68.

[81] *Ibid.*, p. 147.

[82] *Ibid.*, p. 148.

[83] *Ibid.*

[84] *Ibid.*, p. 149.

[85] *Ibid.*, p. 163.

[86] Cf. Marcolino Daffara, *op. cit.*, p. 110. The entire discussion of the argument runs from p. 110 to p. 136.

[87] *Ibid.*, p. 125.

As to the argument from the possibles, which Daffara presents in the light of St. Thomas' *De veritate*, q. 1, arts. 2-6, we find this penetrating observation:

> [Just as] things exist because they are possible, and they are not possible because they exist, [so] they are known to us because they are knowable, and not vice versa, [i.e.] knowable because they are known. Possibility and the truth that concerns it are something above things and our mind; they transcend both. But the possibility and intelligibility of things are inferred from their relation to an efficient power which is capable of bringing them to existence and from their relation to an intellect that is capable of understanding them. According to this relationship, the truth of things is eternal. [Therefore] the foundation [of the truth of things] is to be found in an intellect that eternally comprehends them, and in a power that can eternally draw them from nothing.[88]

Obviously, this intellect and power is God. Therefore God exists.

Since the publication of this essay in 1961, the ideological argument has been the subject of several studies, among which the following are worth mentioning.

Jean-Dominique Robert, O.P., in a work entitled *Approche contemporaine d'une affirmation de Dieu*,[89] purports to show that science leads to God as the ultimate foundation of the scientific act. In fact, he argues, a scientific act, like any other act of thinking and reasoning, is necessarily subject to the general laws of thought. These laws, in turn, presuppose certain "intelligible necessities" that guarantee the internal coherence and value of scientific truth and depend neither on the thinking subject nor on the concrete objects of our experience. Hence scientific truth, with its characteristics of unity and necessity, demands a foundation that transcends the contingent nature of both the thinking subject and the object of his thought. This can only be Truth itself, or a Thought that is at once existence, truth, and necessity, i.e., God; for our acts of thinking are real and so are the objects of our mind.

Having shown in the course of his study how philosophical reflection upon the scientific act leads to God as the source and foundation of all truth, Robert takes up the question of whether his "proof of God's existence" is in line with St. Thomas' philosophy. His answer is that it is. To

---

[88]*Ibid.*, p. 132, continuation and conclusion of n. 3 from p. 130.

[89]Brussels: Desclée de Brouwer, 1962. This book is a development of a previous study, "Essai d'une preuve de Dieu comme fondement ultime de la vérité scientifique," which appeared in *L'existence de Dieu* by Henri Birault, *et al.* (Tournai: Casterman, 1961), pp. 267-94.

support his claim, he refers to several texts from Aquinas' works and singles out two for special consideration. The first is a passage from the *Summa contra gentiles*, Book II, chap. 84, where Aquinas states that the truths understood by our intellect must be grounded "in the first truth, as in the universal cause embracing all truth."[90] The second text is from St. Thomas' Commentary on the Gospel of St. John which, the author says, was brought to his attention by Etienne Gilson. Here is the text's English translation:

> Certain people have arrived at the knowledge of God from the incomprehensibility of truth. In fact, all the truth that our intellect can comprehend is limited, for, as Augustine says, "whatever is known, is limited by the understanding of the knower," and, if limited, it is determined and particularized. Hence it is necessary that the first and supreme truth, which transcends every intellect, be incomprehensible and infinite; and this is God.[91]

Whether or not this text, like the preceding passage from the *Summa contra gentiles*, can be construed as an argument for the existence of God, acknowledged as such by Aquinas, is questionable. What is certain is that the two texts do support Robert's contention that "within the perspective of a research for the foundation of truth, it is possible to build an argument that comes close to St. Thomas' fourth way, of which it is the concrete realization."[92]

In a more recent study,[93] Stanislas Kowalczky first analyzes the ideological argument in its original form in St. Augustine's *De libero arbitrio* and sets it in relation to other Augustinian texts. Next he makes a brief survey of the argument's interpretations by modern and contemporary philosophers, which he classifies in five categories: ontological, phenomenological, Thomistic, Neo-Platonic, and moderately realistic. He does mention specifically the interpretations of Cayré, Sciacca, and, last in the order of time, the one by Robert which we have just discussed. In the final section of his study, the author offers his own interpretation of the argument, which is consistent with Augustine's thought, namely, that from the analysis of truth and its characteristics, the human mind can, in virtue of the principle of sufficient reason, argue to the existence of God as personal Truth.

In response to the question whether the Augustinian proof might

---

[90]Cf. n. 32 above for the complete Latin text.

[91]St. Thomas Aquinas, *Expositio in evangelium Ioannis,* ed. by R. Cai, O.P. (5th ed.; Turin-Rome: Marietti, 1952), Prologus, p. 2, no. 6.

[92]*Approche contemporaine,* p. 221, n. 3.

[93]"L'argument idéologique de la vérité de Saint Augustin," *Giornale di metafisica,* 23 (1968), 586–99.

perhaps involve an illicit transition from the order of ideas to the order of reality, Kowalczky denies any ground for claiming there is such a transition, for, although "the eternal truths (logical, ethical, esthetic, etc.) have only an intentional existence, the human intellect is an actual reality. Our intellect is made in such a way that it has the perception of being subordinated to truth." Moreover, "the metaphysical structure of the human mind is real and enduring." That is why, the author concludes, "the Augustinian proof is essentially different from the proof of St. Anselm."[94]

Lope Cilleruelo, an Augustinian scholar, has once more submitted the argument from eternal truths to a thorough investigation.[95] In the first part of his study, which serves as an introduction to the discussion of the proof itself, the author reviews some of the previous studies on the subject. While he disagrees with Cayré's Aristotelian interpretation of the Augustinian proof [96] and praises Sciacca for what he calls the best possible interpretation of it,[97] he takes issue with certain authors who venture to interpret Augustine without taking into account the historical and critical exegesis of his thought. He also criticizes those writers who like to indulge in interpretations that are either supernatural and mystic, existentialist and affective, or pietistic and experimental. Cilleruelo believes that the Augustinian proof moves within the framework of Platonic philosophy and is entirely rational in character, even though it presupposes faith as one of its necessary conditions.

In the second part of his article, Cilleruelo discusses the actual proof of Augustine through three distinct stages, i.e., the world, the *cogito*, and transcendence. In an effort to present the proof in all its details and complexities, he brings into his discussion elements drawn from Augustine's works other than *De libero arbitrio*, namely, *De musica, De vera religione, Confessiones*, and *De Trinitate*. Cilleruelo's study amounts to an endorsement of the Augustinian argument from eternal truths, which he approaches from the perspective of Augustine's entire system of thought and with a good knowledge of the literature on the subject.[98]

---

[94]*Ibid.*, p. 598.

[95]See his article, "La prueba de la existencia de Dios *(Intellectus quaerens fidem),"* whose first part appeared in *Archivo teológico Agustiniano,* 2 (1967), 515-34, and second part in the same but newly renamed periodical *Estudio Agustiniano,* 4 (1969), 239-73.

[96]See Fulbert Cayré, *Dieu présent dans la vie de l'esprit,* already cited.

[97]See Michele F. Sciacca, *L'existence de Dieu,* trans. by Régis Jolivet (Paris: Aubier, 1951). The original Italian title is *Filosofia e metafisica,* above mentioned.

[98]Other defenders of the ideological argument in modern and contemporary times are:
a) *Among scholastics:* R. Arnou, S.J. *Theologia naturalis* (Rome: The Gregorian University, 1942), pp. 92-94; P. De Munnynck, O.P., "L'idée de l'être," *Revue néoscolastique de philosophie,* XXXI (1929), 182-203; 415-37; L. De Raeymaeker, *Metaphysica generalis* (Louvain: Institut supérieur de philosophie, 1931), pp. 58 ff.; T. de Diego Diez, S.J., *Theologia naturalis* (Santander: "Sal Terrae," 1955), p. 114; I. Di Napoli, *Manuale philoso-*

B.   Opponents of the Argument

Despite the seemingly strong line of reasoning offered by the supporters of the ideological argument, the argument does not go unchallenged. Its validity has been seriously questioned by several influential Neoscholastics who, following the lead of Cardinal Mercier and the Louvain School, subject the argument to a severe criticism.[99] Their position can be summarized in the following statements.

1. The possibles may be considered in the purely ideal or analytical order, inasmuch as the formal elements by which they are constituted imply no contradiction (negative intrinsic possibility). In this case, they can be explained by the operation of our mind without having recourse to God. They may also be considered as essences or realities abstracted from actually existing things, and then they may constitute the basis for a theistic proof. However, this will not be the ideological argument in ques-

---

phiae, III (Turin-Rome: Marietti, 1951), 36-37; J. Donat, S.J., *Theodicea* (6th ed. rev.; Innsbruck: F. Rauch, 1929), pp. 60-63; R. Garrigou-Lagrange, O.P., *God: His Existence and His Nature*, trans. by Dom Bede Rose from the 5th French ed., I (St. Louis, Mo.: Herder, 1948), 324-31; I. Gredt, O.S.B., *Elementa philosophiae aristotelico-thomisticae*, II (9th ed. rev.; Barcelona: Herder, 1951), 201-202; Ch. V. Héris, O.P., "La preuve de l'existence de Dieu par les vérités eternelles," *Revue thomiste*, XXXI (1926), 330-41; J. H. Hickey, O. Cist., *Summula philosophiae scholasticae*, III (4th ed.; Dublin: M. H. Gill and Son, 1920), 33; I. Hontheim, S.J., *Institutiones theodicaeae* (Freiburg i. Br.: Herder, 1893), pp. 128-39; J. Kleutgen, S.J. *Die Philosophie der Vorzeit*, I (Innsbruck: F. Rauch, 1878), 767 ff.; F. X. Maquart, *Elementa philosophiae*, III-2 (Paris: Blot, 1938), 316-20; W. Pohl, *De vera religione quaestiones selectae* (Freiburg i. Br.: Herder, 1928), pp. 53-69; Bl. Romeyer, S.J., "S. Augustin," *La philosophie chrétienne*, II (1936), 146-77; *Idem*, "La doctrine de S. Thomas sur la vérité," *Archives de philosophie*, III, ca. 2 (1925), 46-50; *Idem*, "Dieu," *Dictionnaire pratique des connaissances religieuses*, II, cols. 845-46; A. D. Sertillanges, O.P., *Les sources de la croyance en Dieu* (Paris: Perrin et Cie., 1908), pp. 202-238. Later the author rejected the argument.

Other scholastics who favor the argument: Bossuet, Boedder, Chossat, De Broglie, Del Campo, Farges, Fénelon, Janssens, Jolivet, Kwant, Lacordaire, Lehmen, Lepidi, Liberatore, Maréchal, Monaco, Pesch, Piat, Reinstadler, Schaaf, Schiffini, Van der Aa, Willems, Zacchi.

b) *Among nonscholastics:* Blondel, Cousin, Malebranche, Parodi, Rosmini, Ruyssen. This latter wrote: "J'ai toujours pensé que, s'il est possible de sauver des assauts de la critique quelqu'une des preuves traditionnelles de l'existence de Dieu, c'est sourtout celle dite des 'vérités eternelles'." Th. Ruyssen, "Le Dieu lointain et le Dieu proche," *Revue de métaphysique et de morale*, XXXVII (1930), 349.

[99]Cardinal Désiré Mercier discusses the ideological argument in connection with the problem of the ultimate foundation of the possibles in his *Métaphysique générale*, pp. 29-48. A summary of the discussion can be found in N. Balthasar's article, "Le métaphysicien," *Revue néoscolastique de philosophie*, XXVIII (1926), 163-66. Descoqs reproduces substantially Card. Mercier's argumentation with some additional reflections of his own in his *Praelectiones theologiae naturalis*, II, 80-87. The works of both Mercier and Descoqs served as a basis for Gisquière's treatment of the question in his work, *Deus Dominus*, I, 215-20. The author, however, does not fail to express some personal views on the matter. For a presentation in English of Card. Mercier's standpoint, cf. Peter Coffey, *Ontology* (New York: Smith, 1938), pp. 91-95.

tion, but either the third or fourth way of St. Thomas, depending on whether we look upon them from the viewpoint of their contingency or of their limited perfection.[100]

2. The reason why the possibles considered in the purely ideal order— the only order in which an ideological argument can be built—do not constitute a basis for an ascent to God is that they can be sufficiently explained without God both as to their formal elements and as to their characteristics.[101] The elements that make up possible essences are those abstracted from concretely existing things, even though their association may be the construct of our mind, e.g., a golden mountain. The possibility of those essences, considered formally as the truth of essences in the order of intelligibility, involves necessarily a relation to an intellect, either human or divine, provided that such an intellect exist. But since in our hypothesis the existence of God has not yet been demonstrated, the formal reason of that possibility can and must be found in the thing itself, from which the essence is abstracted, and in the human mind, which is responsible for the process of abstraction. Hence the so-called independence of the possibles from any contingent reality is but an apparent independence.

Furthermore, the characteristics of necessity, eternity, and immutability of the possibles are only hypothetic and relative. These characteristics find their explanation in the nature of our intellect and its abstractive process, whereby the essences of finite things, which exist in reality as contingent, mutable, and temporary, become in the ideal order necessary, immutable, and eternal.[102]

In conclusion, the object and the human mind, both of which are con-

---

[100]Cf. Descoqs, *op. cit.*, II, 80. Gisquière, *op. cit.*, I, 219-20, believes that the ideological argument cannot be reduced to St. Thomas' fourth way, because no degrees of perfection are to be found in beings or essences of a purely ideal order, with which the ideological argument is concerned.

[101]This is substantially the first part of the thesis that Cardinal Mercier defends in his discussion of the possibles. He writes: "Les objects abstraits de l'expérience et analysés par la pensée sont, dans l'ordre analytique, la raison suffisante dernière des possibles et de leurs propriétés." *Métaphysique générale*, p. 37. The second part of the thesis is an attempt to prove that the theory that makes God the necessary foundation of the possibles leads directly to ontologism. *Ibid.*, pp. 45-46. This conclusion has been disavowed by many neoscholastics, including some who deny the validity of the ideological argument. See, for example, Gisquière, *op. cit.*, I, 219, where he states: "Illam tamen Ontologismi accusationem *non putamus esse legitimam*, saltem ut a Mercier proponitur."

[102]Cardinal Mercier sums up his discussion of the possibles and their characteristics by saying: "Les possibles et leurs charactères trouvent une explication *suffisante* dans les choses d'expérience. L'intelligence a le pouvoir de concevoir les choses abstraitement, et de réfléchir ensuite sur ces types abstraits; cette analyse réflexive fait surgir devant la pensée des rapports universels, nécessaires, supérieurs aux conditions particulières de l'espace et du temps, qui deviennent alors, pour nous, les normes des choses et des jugements." *Ibid.*, pp. 44-45.

tingent realities, furnish us with the explanation of all possibles in the purely ideal order.

3. The observations that have been made about the nature and foundation of the possibles can also be applied to the question of eternal truths and first principles. These truths and principles are all based on the nature of being as such, with which they are coextensive. They may help us attain to the supreme being, but unless we want to fall into a perfect *petitio principii,* they have a value of their own even prior to the demonstration of God's existence.[103] Their characteristics of necessity, eternity, and immutability, which they share in common with the possibles, are likewise hypothetical and relative. They become absolute only when the existence of an intellect endowed with those properties has been demonstrated. But this is precisely the point at issue.[104]

To speak of truth as something absolute and eternal is to forget that truth is essentially a relation. In themselves, things are neither true nor false; they become true only when they are related to an intellect. If there were no intellect, there would be no truth; if there were no being, there would be no truth either.[105]

Evidently, a being does not have to exist in act to be true; it can be potentially true as regards its future existence even as it exists in its cause. Hence if an eternal cause exists, the truth of things may be called eternal, inasmuch as it is grounded in an eternal creative power and will. However, the existence of such a cause must first be demonstrated. To argue to the existence of that cause from the existence of eternal truth is to invert the order of ideas and realities.[106]

The foregoing considerations, the opponents of the ideological argument take care to observe, have the sole purpose of showing that no valid proof of God's existence can be drawn from the nature of possibles and eternal truths considered in the *ideal* or *analytical* order. But once the existence of God has been demonstrated, the doctrine of possibles and eternal truths retains its full value in the *ontological* or *synthetic* order. The whole controversy therefore is not about the foundation of possibles and

---

[103] See Descoqs, *op. cit.,* II, 86.

[104] *Ibid.*

[105] "La vérité n'est pas chose absolue, c'est une proportion: la proportion de l'être à l'intelligence. Si donc il n'y a point d'intelligence, il n'y a point de vérité; s'il n'y a point d'être, il n'y a point de vérité davantage, et la fiction que la vérité se précède elle-même en tant que future, ou se survit à elle-même en tant que passée n'est qu'une imagination creuse, si l'on ne présuppose, d'une part, un *sujet* qui puisse concevoir la vérité et, de l'autre, un *objet* qui la fonde." Sertillanges, *La philosophie de S. Thomas d'Aquin,* I, 46. See also Card. Désiré Mercier, *Critériologie générale* (8th ed.; Louvain: Institut supérieur de philosophie, 1923), pp. 20 ff., and commentary on Mercier's statements by Mindorff, *art. cit.,* pp. 440 ff.

[106] Sertillanges, *La philosophie de S. Thomas d'Aquin,* I, 46-47.

eternal truths as such, which all admit to be God, but about the question whether possibles and eternal truths may be considered as a valid *terminus a quo* for a demonstration of God's existence.[107]

VI. CRITICAL EVALUATION OF THE ARGUMENT

It is our contention that the ideological argument is a valid theistic proof, provided it is correctly understood. In this section we will present some of the reasons on which we base our conviction, and answer the objections that have been raised against the argument. But first some clarifications are needed.

We do not take the ideological argument in the sense that its opponents have sometimes given to it, namely, that it is an argument based on ideas considered only in their logical or analytical order. Rather, as already stated at the beginning of this chapter, we consider ideas as mental concepts with a foundation in reality; not inasmuch as they represent an actually existing thing or the truth of an actually existing object, but in the sense that their content reflects a being or truth in the essential and metaphysical order.[108] Thus understood, the argument keeps its distinctive feature as an argument from the ideal order, and at the same time it is kept free of an illicit passage from the ideal to the real order. In our case, the ideal is also real, and the transition is simply from one order of reality to another order of reality.

It must also be made clear that although the ideological argument

---

[107]Cf. Mercier, *Métaphysique générale*, pp. 46–47; Descoqs, *op. cit.*, II, 81; Gisquière, *op. cit.*, I, 215. Other opponents of the ideological argument, besides Mercier, Descoqs, Gisquière, Mindorff, Coffey and Sertillanges (this last at least in his work, *La philosophie de S. Thomas d'Aquin*), are: N. Balthasar, "Deux théodicées," *Annales de l'Institut supérieur de philosophie de Louvain* (1912), 436–47; L. Billot, *De Deo uno et trino* (6th ed. rev.; Rome: The Gregorian University, 1920), pp. 36–38; M. Cuervo, O.P., "El argumento de 'Las Verdades eternas' según Santo Tomás," *La ciencia tomista*, XXXVII (Jan.-June, 1928), 18–34 (the author maintains that St. Thomas denies the validity of the argument); I. Hellin, S.J., *Cursus philosophicus*, vol. V: *Theologia naturalis* (Madrid: B. A. C., 1950), pp. 229–35; G. Manser, *Das Wesen des Thomismus* (Fribourg: St. Paulus Druckerei, 1932), pp. 267–98; 407–450; J. Van der Meersch, *De Deo uno et trino* (Bruges: Beyaert, 1917), pp. 74–75; Z. Van de Woestyne, O.F.M., *Cursus philosophicus*, II (Malines: Typographia S. Francisci, 1925), 680, n. 1; J. Webert, *Essai de métaphysique thomiste* (Paris: Éditions de la revue des jeunes, Desclée et Cie., 1927), p. 151.
    To these we must add all the nominalists.
[108]As has been observed, the possibles are neither actual beings nor nothing. They are not actual beings, because as such, i.e., inasmuch as they are possibles, they do not exist; they are not nothing, because *nothing* cannot exist, nor can it be the object of our understanding, whereas the possibles can exist and are intelligible. The possibles have therefore a reality of their own which is properly called *a potential reality*. This reality is not physical but metaphysical; it is not false but true, for the possibles can truly exist. Hontheim, *Institutiones theodicaeae*, pp. 35–36.

originated with St. Augustine, we shall not attempt to evaluate it in the light of St. Augustine's works. Nor is it our concern to investigate the exact attitude of St. Thomas or any other Scholastic towards it. The reason is simple. Ours is not an exegetical study of the thought of any particular philosopher but only an effort to evaluate the argument on its own merit, that is, on a purely objective basis. While this will render our task less difficult, it will also save us the trouble of setting the argument in relation to any particular system of philosophy. This is in itself a very complex problem, especially in the case of St. Augustine, where the argument is closely connected with his illumination theory and the doctrine of eternal reasons.

Keeping this in mind, we shall proceed to a critical evaluation of the proof, beginning with the argument from the possibles.

A. Argument from the Possibles

There is no doubt that our mind can conceive intrinsically possible beings whose reality and essential principles are altogether independent of any contingent factor. In fact, the intrinsic reality of the possibles does not and cannot depend on their existence, since of their very nature they are indifferent to exist or not to exist. On the contrary, the existence of things depends on their intrinsic possibility. Nor does the intrinsic reality of the possibles depend on our intellect. The intellect discovers but does not make the possibility of things.

It is true that the proximate reason of the possibles as such is to be found in the compatibility of their notes. But, we may ask, where does this compatibility come from? What is the ultimate foundation of these notes? Since, on the one hand, the possibles are not the reason for their own reality,[109] and, on the other hand, the human intellect cannot be held responsible for their intrinsic possibility, the answer must be that a being exists which is their ultimate ontological reason and possesses in itself the characteristics of necessity, immutability, and eternity proper to the possibles.

This being cannot be a contingent reality whose internal possibility depends on another, for in this case we would only have displaced the problem, not solved it. It must be a necessary being, a being that has within

---

[109]Cf. J. Donat, *Theodicea,* p. 63: "Si possibilia a se realitatem possibilitatis haberent, etiam exsistentiam haberent. Nam possibilitas nihil est nisi ordo ad exsistendum; ideo inter utramque concordantia est. Si igitur a se extra purum nihil per possibilitatem ponuntur, ad suam exsistentiam vero se actuare non possunt, disharmonia est inter eorum gressum primum in ordine realitatis et ultimum; quae concipi nequit." This doctrine, the author remarks, is better grasped *by intuition* than by a lengthy demonstration. *Ibid.*

itself the reason for its own existence; a being, in other words, whose essence is to exist. That being is God.

Thus, in our search for the ultimate foundation of the possibles, we arrive, by the aid of the principle of sufficient reason alone, at the existence of an absolutely necessary being, which is also immutable, eternal, and infinite: God. Since the demonstration fulfills all the requirements set down for a genuine theistic proof, we conclude that the ideological argument is a valid demonstration of God's existence.

To the objection that the possibles and their characteristics of necessity, immutability, and eternity can be sufficiently explained through an abstractive intellect and the object, the answer will be that the human mind and the object are the *proximate* causes and foundation of the possibles, but not their *ultimate* reason. Indeed, by their very nature, the possibles transcend all created mind and reality; they are such even if no contingent being or human intellect ever existed. Far from being the ultimate foundation of the possibles, the human mind and all created beings would not exist at all, were they not themselves intrinsically possible.

Another objection that is often raised against the argument from the possibles is this. The possibles are eternal and immutable negatively, not positively; they prescind from time but are not above time. Hence they do not demand as their foundation a being that is positively eternal and immutable.

In answer to this objection it must be said that even if the possibles were only negatively eternal and immutable, their ultimate foundation would still have to be something positive. To hold the contrary is to fall into nominalism, which maintains that the nature and essence of things, considered as such, is only a fiction of the mind and needs no other foundation than the mind itself.

A further objection, which has already been answered implicitly in the course of our discussion but which we wish to mention here again for the sake of completeness, takes the form of a dilemma. It reads: the possibles are considered either as mere ideas, and then we have essentially the same procedure as in St. Anselm's ontological argument where from the idea of God it is argued to God's existence; or they are considered as contingent and limited entities, in which case the argument is but another version of the third or fourth way of St. Thomas.

Our answer to the dilemma is that neither alternative is true. The possibles are not considered as mere ideas, but as ideas of a possible or potential essence for which an ultimate reason is sought in a necessary and eternal being. Thus, whereas in the ontological argument one argues to God from the very concept of God, in the ideological argument we argue to God as the ultimate reason of a possible entity. Consequently, ours is not an argument *a priori* or *a simultaneo*, as the Anselmian proof is supposed to be, but an argument *a posteriori*.

On the other hand, the ideological argument should not be identified with any of St. Thomas' five ways. It is worth repeating: in the ideological argument the vehicle of our ascent to God is not the principle of causality but the principle of sufficient reason. On this account the argument from the possibles stands as an altogether independent and distinct theistic proof.

B. Argument from Eternal Truths

The argument from eternal truths has many points in common with the argument from the possibles. In both cases the *terminus a quo* is a being in the ideal order, the means of demonstration is the principle of sufficient reason, and the *terminus ad quem* is God. But whereas in the argument from the possibles the ideal being is an intrinsically possible reality, in the argument from eternal truths the ideal being is those eternal and immutable principles and relations which lie at the basis of all thought and reality. Here is how the argument runs.

The mutual relations existing among the possibles are governed by certain principles, such as the principle of identity, contradiction, and sufficient reason, that are absolutely necessary and universal not only in the order of knowledge but also in the order of reality. These relations and principles find their ultimate explanation neither in the existing things of this world nor in our mind. Not in the things of this world, for even if all things ceased to exist, these relations and principles would still be intelligible and therefore true. Thus, even if no man ever came into existence, it would still be true that in order to exist a man would have to possess rationality and animality as his essential principles. Likewise, even if no circle ever existed, the geometrical laws about the circle would still be true and valid. Obviously, these truths are grasped by our mind in the study of reality. But in grasping them our mind also understands that such truths are neither its own product nor the product of any existing being. Briefly, they are independent of all contingent reality; they are necessary and universal, and as such they demand a necessary being as their ultimate ground and foundation. That being is God.

Thus, by examining the nature and characteristics of eternal truths and following the same line of reasoning we used in the argument from the possibles, we argue by the aid of the principle of sufficient reason to God, who alone can furnish us with the ultimate explanation of truth. While these truths are *fundamentally* in the divine essence, they are *formally* in the divine mind, the source of all truth and intelligibility. It becomes clear, then, that our search for the ultimate foundation of eternal truths is a quest for the ultimate source of intelligibility of the laws and principles that govern all reality.

The objections that have been raised against the argument from the possibles have also been put forward against the argument from eternal truths. To avoid repetition, we shall mention here only those objections which are directed primarily against the argument from eternal truths.

Truth, it is said, is essentially a relation; it is a conformity of mind with reality. Therefore, it is wrong to speak of truth as something absolute, independent of all contingent being, and from such a notion of truth argue to God as its ultimate foundation. God is of course the cause of all truth, but this cannot be known from the mere notion of truth as such. To arrive at God as the source of all truth from the truth of our judgment—for it is in judgment that truth consists properly—is to use the term "truth" equivocally.

This objection would have a certain value if by truth we meant purely logical truth, or truth as it is in our mind apart from reality. This is not our contention. The starting point of our argument is ontological or metaphysical truth, that is, the conformity of reality with the mind. If defenders of the argument sometimes speak of truth in the logical order along with truth in the mathematical and metaphysical orders, they do not intend to oppose one kind of truth to another. They want only to emphasize the different order of reality from which truth is taken. Hence truth in the logical order is truth in the order of thought, not inasmuch as thought is divorced from reality, but in the sense that it expresses those necessary and eternal principles that are at the basis of all knowledge. Such is the truth of the first principles. These, let us always remember, are not merely logical principles but also metaphysical principles, i.e., principles of reality. It is with the ultimate objective foundation of these principles that the ideological argument is concerned.[110]

The opponents of the ideological argument insist further that if there were no contingent being, then prior to the demonstration of God's existence we could hardly speak of truth, since there would be no truth. Hence truth and its properties of eternity and necessity are purely hypothetical, and cannot serve as a springboard for our ascent to God.

Here again we must disagree with critics of the argument. Before

---

[110]It is true that some authors try to justify the ideological argument from the nature and characteristics of logical truth rather than from ontological truth. However, they would never consider truth a pure product of our mind, but rather as the relationship of conformity between mind and reality in the order of possibility and intelligibility. Thus the intelligibles and their metaphysical principles and relations are in fact the real basis of the ideological argument.

knowing that God exists, I perceive truth, such as the truth of the first principles, as something that is absolutely independent of any contingent reality, and from it I argue to God as its ultimate foundation. The existence of contingent things, or of any intelligible reality for that matter, is the immediate cause of my knowledge of truth, but it is not the ultimate foundation of truth, which prescinds from both contingent reality and my mind. Certainly, if nothing ever existed there would be no truth; but there is truth, and so there must be that eternal and necessary foundation without which truth is impossible.

* * *

Before concluding this discussion, we wish to make the following observation: the ideological argument is and remains a debatable philosophical issue. It has been the purpose of this chapter to present the argument in its historical background from its first appearance in St. Augustine up to the present time, and to evaluate it on the basis of a sound criticism. The positions of both defenders and opponents have been stated with fairness and objectivity. Some obscure points have been clarified, so as to pave the way for an impartial discussion of the two opposing views. This led us to accept the argument as a valid proof of God's existence and to reject as groundless the objections raised against it. Owing to the inherent difficulty of the problem and the reigning confusion of the issue in some philosophical manuals and treatises, the writer is more than willing to admit that the task has not been an easy one. It was only after a great deal of thinking and a serious balancing of the arguments pro and con that he has decided for the positive side in the controversy. Was he justified in doing so? The answer is left to the reader. Meanwhile, if the foregoing discussion has succeeded in arousing some interest in a fascinating, although often neglected and discarded, theistic proof that has challenged the abilities of many great philosophical minds, the writer feels that his efforts have been sufficiently rewarded.

BIBLIOGRAPHY

Alexander of Hales. *Summa theologica*. 4 vols. Quaracchi: Typographia Collegii S. Bonaventurae, 1924-1948.

Anselm, St. *De divinitatis essentia Monologium*. Migne, PL 158; cols. 141-224.

Arnou, R., S.J. *Theologia naturalis*. Rome: The Gregorian University, 1942.

Augustine, St. *De libero arbitrio*. Migne, PL 32. English translation by Dom Mark Pontifex under the title: *The Problem of Free Choice*. Westminster, Md.: The Newman Press, 1955. Also in Migne, PL 32: *Confessiones, Soliloquia, De immortalitate animae* and *De magistro;* Migne, PL 34: *De vera religione;*

Migne, PL 35: *In Ioannis evangelium*; Migne, PL 36: *Enarrationes in Psalmum LXXIII*; Migne, PL 38: *Sermo CCXLI*; Migne, PL 41: *De civitate Dei*.

Balmes, Jaime. *Fundamental Philosophy*. 2 vols. Trans. by Henry F. Brownson. New ed. rev. New York: Kenedy, 1903.

Balthasar, N. "Deux théodicées," *Annales de l'"Institut supérieur de philosophie de Louvain* (1912), 436–47.

_____. "Le métaphysicien," *Revue néoscolastique de philosophie*, XXVIII (1926), 153–85.

Bettoni, Efrem. *Il problema della conoscibilità di Dio nella scuola francescana*. Padova: Cedam, 1950.

Billot, L. *De Deo uno et trino*. 6th ed. rev. Rome: The Gregorian University, 1920.

Bonansea, Bernardine M., O.F.M. "The Ideological Argument for God's Existence." In *Studies in Philosophy and the History of Philosophy*, vol. I, pp. 1–34, Ed. by John K. Ryan. Washington, D.C.: The Catholic University of America Press, 1961.

Bonaventure, St. *Opera omnia*. 10 vols. Quaracchi: Typographia Collegii S. Bonaventurae, 1882–1902.

Boyer, Charles. "La preuve de Dieu augustinienne," *Archives de philosophie*, VII, 2 (1930), 105–141.

Cayré, Fulbert. *Dieu présent dans la vie de l'esprit*. Bruges-Paris: Desclée de Brouwer, 1951.

Cilleruelo, Lope, O.S.A. "La prueba de la existencia de Dios (*Intellectus quaerens fidem*)," *Archivo teológico Agustiniano*, 2 (1967), 515–34, and *Estudio Agustiniano*, 4 (1969), 239–73.

Coffey, Peter. *Ontology*. New York: Smith, 1938.

Collins, James. *God in Modern Philosophy*. Chicago: Regnery, 1959. An excellent and authoritative study.

Copleston, Frederick, S.J. *A History of Philosophy*. 9 vols. Westminster, Md.: The Newman Press, 1950–1975.

Cuervo, M., O.P. "El argumento de 'Las Verdades Eternas' según Santo Tomás," *La ciencia tomista*, XXXVII (Jan.-June, 1928), 18–34.

Daffara, Marcolino, O.P. *Dio: Esposizione e valutazione delle prove*. 2d ed. rev. Turin: Società Editrice Internazionale, 1952.

De Diego Diez, T., S.J. *Theologia naturalis*. Santander: "Sal Terrae," 1955.

De Munnynck, Marc, O.P. *Praelectiones de Dei existentia*. Louvain: Uystpruyst-Dieudonné, 1904.

_____. "L'idée de l'être," *Revue néoscolastique de philosophie*, XXXI (1929), 182–203; 415–37.

De Raeymaeker, L. *Metaphysica generalis*. Louvain: Institut supérieur de philosophie, 1931.

Descoqs, Pedro, S.J. *Praelectiones theologiae naturalis*. 2 vols. Paris: Beauchesne, 1932–1935. Fundamental work.

Di Napoli, Ioannes. *Manuale philosophiae*. 4 vols. Turin-Rome: Marietti, 1950–1951. Excellent manual of Thomistic philosophy.

Donat, J., S.J. *Theodicea*. 6th ed. rev. Innsbruck: F. Rauch, 1929.

Doucet, Victorinus, O.F.M. *Prolegomena in librum III necnon in libros I et II "Summae Fratris Alexandri"*. Quaracchi: Typographia Collegii S. Bonaventurae, 1948.

Duns Scotus, John. *Opera omnia*. Editio nova iuxta editionem Waddingi. 26 vols. Paris: Vivès, 1891–1895.

_____. *Opera omnia*. Studio et cura Commissionis Scotisticae ad fidem codicum edita. Vols. I to VII of the *Ordinatio* published. Civitas Vaticana: Typis polyglottis Vaticanis, 1950-1973. Also published by the same Vatican Press is Scotus' *Lectura in I Sententiarum*, vols. XVI-XVII, 1960-1966.

_____. *De Primo Principio*. A revised text and a translation by Evan Roche, O.F.M. St. Bonaventure, N.Y.: The Franciscan Institute, 1949.

Garrigou-Lagrange, Reginald, O.P. *God: His Existence and His Nature*. 2 vols. Trans. by Dom Bede from the 5th French ed. St. Louis, Mo.: Herder, 1948-1949.

Gilson, Etienne. *The Philosophy of St. Bonaventure*. Trans. by Dom Illtyd Trethowan. London: Sheed and Ward, 1940.

_____. *Introduction à l'étude de saint Augustin*. 2d ed. rev. Paris: Vrin, 1943.

Gisquière, Emmanuel. *Deus Dominus*. 2 vols. Paris: Beauchesne, 1950. Most fundamental study of all the issues concerning God: his existence, his nature, and his operations.

Grabmann, Martin. *Die Grundgedanken des heiligen Augustinus über Gott*. 2d ed. Cologne: Bachem, 1929. Very informative study of St. Augustine's use of classic theistic arguments.

Gredt, Iosephus, O.S.B. *Elementa philosophiae aristotelico-thomisticae*. 2 vols.; 9th ed. rev. Barcelona: Herder, 1951. Classic text of Thomistic philosophy.

Hellin, I., S.J. *Cursus philosophicus*. Vol. V: *Theologia naturalis*. Madrid: B.A.C., 1950.

Héris, Ch. V., O.P. "La preuve de l'existence de Dieu par les vérités éternelles," *Revue thomiste*, XXXI (1926), 330-41.

Hessen, J. *Augustins Metaphysik der Erkenntnis*. Berlin: Dümmler, 1931.

Hickey, J. S., O.Cist. *Summula philosophiae scholasticae*. 3 vols. 4th ed. Dublin: M. H. Gill and Son, 1919-1920.

Hontheim, Iosephus, S.J. *Institutiones theodicaeae naturalis*. Freiburg i. Br.: Herder, 1893.

Kant, Immanuel. *Der einzig mögliche Beweisgrund zu einer Demonstration Daseins Gottes*. In *Immanuel Kants Werke*, vol. II, pp. 67-172. Ed. by E. Cassirer. Berlin, 1912-1918.

Kleutgen, J., S.J. *Die Philosophie der Vorzeit*. 2 vols. Innsbruck: F. Rauch, 1878.

Kowalczky, Stanislas. "L'argument idéologique de la vérité de Saint Augustin," *Giornale di metafisica*, 23 (1968), 586-99.

Koyré, Alexandre. *L'idée de Dieu dans la philosophie de St. Anselme*. Paris: Leroux, 1923.

Leibniz, Gottfried Wilhelm. *New Essays Concerning Human Understanding*. Trans. by Alfred Gideon Langley. 3d ed. La Salle, Ill.: The Open Court Publishing Company, 1949.

Lepidi, Alberto, O.P. *Elementa philosophiae christianae*. 3 vols. Paris: Lethielleux; Louvain: Peeters, 1875-1879.

Manser, G. *Das Wesen des Thomismus*. Friburg: St. Paulus-Druckerei, 1932.

Maquart, F. X. *Elementa philosophiae*. 3 vols. Paris: Blot, 1937-1938.

Martin, Jules. *Saint Augustin*. Paris: Alcan, 1901.

Mercier, D. J. *Cours de philosophie*. Vol. II: *Métaphysique générale*. 5th ed. rev. Louvain: Institut supérieur de philosophie, 1910.

_____. *Critériologie générale*. 8th ed. Louvain: Institut supérieur de philosophie, 1923.

Mindorff, Claudius, O.F.M. "De argumento ideologico exsistentiae Dei," *Antonianum*, III (1928), 267-98; 407-450.

Pohl, Wenceslaus. *De vera religione quaestiones selectae*. Freiburg i. Br.: Herder, 1928.

Portalié, E. "Augustin (saint)," *Dictionnaire de théologie catholique,* I, 2, col. 2345.

Richard of St. Victor. *De Trinitate*. Migne, PL 196.

Robert, Jean-Dominique, O.P. *Approche contemporaine d'une affirmation de Dieu*. Brussels: Desclée de Brouwer, 1962.

Romeyer, Blasius, S.J. "S. Augustin," *La philosophie chrétienne*, II (1936), 146-77.

————. "La doctrine de Saint Thomas sur la vérité," *Archives de philosophie*, III, ca. 2 (1925), 1-54.

————. "Dieu," *Dictionnaire pratique des connaissances religieuses*, II, cols. 845-46.

Ruyssen, Th. "Le Dieu lointain et le Dieu proche," *Revue de métaphysique et de morale*, XXXVII (1930), 337-66.

Sciacca, Michele, F. *S. Agostino*. Vol. I: *La vita e l'opera. L'itinerario della mente*. Brescia: Morcelliana, 1949.

————. *Filosofia e metafisica*. Brescia: Morcelliana, 1950.

————. *L'existence de Dieu*. Trans. by Régis Jolivet. Paris: Aubier, 1951. This is a translation of the preceding work, *Filosofia e metafisica*.

Sertillanges, A. D., O.P. *Les sources de la croyance en Dieu*. Paris: Perrin et Cie., 1908.

————. *La philosophie de St. Thomas d'Aquin*. 2 vols.; new ed. rev. Paris: Aubier, 1940.

Sestili, Ioachim. "Argumentum augustinianum de existentia Dei." In *Acta hebdomadae augustinianae-thomisticae*, pp. 241-65; discussion, pp. 265-70. Turin-Rome: Marietti, 1931.

Thomas Aquinas, St. *Expositio in evangelium Ioannis*. Ed. by R. Cai, O.P. Turin-Rome: Marietti, 1952.

Van der Meersch, Joseph. *Tractatus de Deo uno et trino*. Bruges: Beyaert, 1917.

Van de Woestyne, Zacharias, O.F.M. *Cursus philosophicus*. 2 vols. Malines: Typographia S. Francisci, 1921-1925. Excellent and well documented text of Franciscan philosophy, with special emphasis on Scotus' thought.

Van Steenberghen, Fernand. "La philosophie de St. Augustin d'après les travaux du centenaire," *Revue néoscolastique de philosophie*, XXXV (1933), 230-81.

Various Authors. *L'existence de Dieu*. 2d ed. Tournai: Casterman, 1963.

Webert, J. *Essai de métaphysique thomiste*. Paris: Éditions de la Revue des jeunes, Desclée et Cie., 1927.

CHAPTER III
THE ONTOLOGICAL ARGUMENT*

St. Anselm's ontological argument is one of the most provocative and fascinating topics in the field of philosophy. Although the subject of endless discussion, the argument continues to draw the attention of philosophers of different persuasions. New interpretations have superseded those of the past and new insights into the controversy have been revealed which point out, among other things, the difficulty and complexity of the issue.

It has been customary to dismiss the Anselmian argument for the existence of God on the ground that it involves a transition from the ideal to the real order, from a concept in our mind to the existence of the being so conceived. This transition, it is asserted, is never permissible, not even in the case of the greatest conceivable being, as the argument seems to imply. The fact that many great thinkers, such as Aquinas and Kant, have felt a need to refute the argument is a further proof, so it is claimed, that the *ratio Anselmi* has little more than a historical value. St. Anselm would have fallen victim to an illusion, and no dialectical effort could ever rescue his argument from the attacks of its critics, even though no serious scholar would subscribe today to Schopenhauer's view that the *ratio Anselmi* is merely a charming joke.

Yet, despite the many attacks and "refutations," the argument has a peculiar power of survival. There is a growing realization, even among those whose philosophical background is very different from St. Anselm's way of thinking, that the argument is not as simple as it first appears to be and that much of the criticism directed against it is due to a superficial knowledge of its context and the general framework of Anselm's thought. As a contemporary author points out, "If Anselm is to be refuted, it should be for what he said, taken in something like the context which he provided, and not for something someone else said he said, or a fragment

---

*This chapter is a combination, with some minor changes, of two essays which appeared in *Studies in Philosophy and the History of Philosophy*, ed. John K. Ryan (Washington, D.C.: The Catholic University of America Press), i.e., "Duns Scotus and St. Anselm's Ontological Argument," vol. IV (1969), pp. 128–41, and "The Ontological Argument: Proponents and Opponents," vol. VI (1973), pp. 135–92. The first essay is the development of a paper read at the International Scotistic Congress held at Oxford and Edinburgh in 1966, and published in *Studia Scholastico-Scotistica. Acta Secundi Congressus Scholastici Internationalis Oxonii et Edimburgi diebus 11–17 Sept. 1966 celebrati septimo expleto saeculo ab ortu Ioannis Duns Scoti*, vol. II (Romae: Cura Commissionis Scotisticae, 1968), pp. 461–75.

of what he said, torn wholly out of context."[1] The Anselmian argument, which has been called "one of the boldest creations of man's reason and a credit not only to its inventor, but to human reason itself,"[2] is not to be treated lightly, nor are some of its later formulations.

An objective study of the Anselmian argument in its actual context and historical development may reveal that, while undue credit has been given to certain modern and contemporary thinkers for their role in the controversy about it, the actual contribution of philosophers who long preceded them in the academic arena has often been neglected or even completely ignored. Yet it is perhaps in the writings of these forgotten masters, who both historically and intellectually are closer to the "father of scholasticism" than their later contenders, that one may find a clue to a better appreciation of the celebrated argument.

To avoid misunderstanding, a distinction must be made at the very outset between two different issues: first, the nature and scope of the argument in the mind of its author, and second, the validity of the argument as an attempt to prove the existence of God. The first issue must be solved in terms of the argument's original text as contained in the *Proslogion* and set in relation to Anselm's other writings where his philosophical, and especially his epistemological, doctrines are more clearly stated. The solution of the second issue rests to a great extent on the critic's conviction as regards the possibility, ways, and means of attaining to any knowledge of a Supreme Being by unaided reason. The failure to make such a distinction has contributed to much of the confusion in appraisals of the Anselmian proof.

The purpose of this chapter is to present the essential features of the ontological argument as stated in the *Proslogion* and follow the history of the controversy it has generated from Anselm's first debate with his fellow-monk Gaunilo down to the present day. The presentation will be followed by a critical evaluation of the argument itself and of the argument's interpretations by succeeding philosophers and commentators.

I. ANSELM'S ARGUMENT

The chief objective that St. Anselm proposed to himself in his *Proslogion* was to present an argument that would in itself alone suffice to prove

---

[1]Charles Hartshorne, Introduction to the Second Edition of *Saint Anselm: Basic Writings,* trans. by S. W. Deane (La Salle, Ill.: The Open Court Publishing Company, 1962), p. 2.

[2]Richard Taylor, Introduction to *The Ontological Argument from St. Anselm to Contemporary Philosophers,* ed. by Alvin Plantinga (Garden City, N.Y.: Doubleday "Anchor Books, 1965), p. xviii.

the existence of God. "I began to ask myself whether there might be found a single argument which would require no other for its proof than itself alone, and alone would suffice to demonstrate that God truly exists."[3] This thought had caused him so much trouble that, in the words of Eadmer, his first biographer and disciple, he had for a while lost all desire for food, drink, and sleep. Worst of all, the thought had been interfering even with his prayers and devotions.[4] But suddenly one night during matins, his biographer continues, the light was shown to him and his heart was filled with an overwhelming joy. He had finally discovered the argument he was looking for. He wrote it down immediately on tablets, and later, after some mysterious happenings which resulted in the loss of the first draft and the partial destruction of the second, Anselm was able to restore the argument to its original form and put it down on parchment for the benefit of future generations.[5] The origin and early history of the argument may well foreshadow its later destiny.

The argument, as the subtitle of the treatise indicates, takes the form of a discourse on the existence of God. It was written primarily for the "brethren" of his monastery, and therefore for believers who, like Anselm himself, try to understand the meaning and import of their belief. "I have written the following treatise, in the person of one who strives to lift his mind to the contemplation of God, and seeks to understand what he believes."[6] Anselm does not conceal the limited scope of his argument; on the contrary, he states explicitly that faith is required for its understanding. "I do not seek to understand that I may believe, but I believe in order to understand. For this also I believe, that unless I believed, I should not understand."[7]

This last statement is enlightening. It shows that Anselm clearly distinguishes between the intrinsic value of the argument and conviction of such value. Since this latter depends on many factors extraneous to the argument itself, it is quite possible that the same logical reasoning may appeal to one person and not to another. More precisely, the argument is not meant to convince an atheist or an agnostic—no theistic argument will ever do so—but only those who have been enlightened by faith and are favorably disposed towards it. It is true that in his reply to Gaunilo's ob-

---

[3]Preface to the *Proslogion;* Migne, PL 158, col. 223. For the English translation of the *Proslogion* and other Anselmian works cf. *Saint Anselm: Basic Writings,* above mentioned, to which reference will henceforth also be made for the reader's convenience.
[4]Cf. *The Life of St. Anselm, Archbishop of Canterbury, by Eadmer,* ed. by R. W. Southern (London-New York: Thomas Nelson and Sons, 1962), pp. 29-30.
[5]*Ibid.,* pp. 30-31.
[6]Preface to the *Proslogion;* PL 158, col. 224; *Basic Writings,* p. 2.
[7]*Proslogion,* chap. I; PL 158, col. 227; *Basic Writings,* p. 7.

jections Anselm writes: "It was a fool against whom the argument of my *Proslogion* was directed."[8] However, this does not mean that the argument was written *for* a fool but rather *against* a fool, i.e., one whom we would today call an unbeliever. Anselm's aim was to show to his fellow monks the truth of the biblical statement that only a fool will say there is no God.[9] To have set the exact limits of the argument according to the mind of its author is already a big step towards the understanding of the argument itself.

Addressing himself to God, Anselm says: "We believe that you are a being than which nothing greater can be conceived." This, he goes on to say, even a fool is able to understand, and yet he cannot convince himself that this being exists in reality. Anselm now tries to prove the inconsistency of such a position by arguing that a being than which no greater is conceivable cannot possibly exist in the understanding alone but must also exist in reality. "For, suppose it exists in the understanding alone, then it can be conceived to exist in reality also, which is greater." Hence, if the notion of the greatest conceivable being has any meaning at all, it must include the actual existence of the being so conceived, since existence is a perfection and the greatest conceivable being must possess all perfections.[10]

Further, existence is so essential to the greatest conceivable being that without it the being in question cannot even be conceived. Indeed, how can one conceive of a being whose nature is to exist—since existence is one of its essential perfections—and deny its existence without denying the very content of his concept? One can form the concept of man and still know nothing about his actual existence, because the nature of man is not such as to demand existence. Man, Anselm would say, can exist in our mind as a mere concept without contradiction. But in the case of the greatest conceivable being this is not possible, since existence enters to form the concept itself of that being. It is not the question of mere possible existence, for that is excluded by the very nature of the greatest conceiv-

---

[8]Introduction to *Liber apologeticus contra Gaunilonem respondentem pro insipiente;* PL 158, col. 247; *Basic Writings,* p. 153.

[9]*Proslogion,* chap. II; PL 158, col. 227; *Basic Writings,* p. 7. M. J. Charlesworth does not seem to have given sufficient consideration to Anselm's statement, "This I also believe, that unless I believed, I should not understand" (*Proslogion,* chap. I), when he wrote that Anselm could not mean that "the whole *Proslogion* argument...would only be persuasive for those who already believe in God." *St. Anselm's Proslogion* (Oxford: Clarendon Press, 1965), p. 57. As Thomas McPherson states, "Anselm does not suppose that his Ontological Argument will convert the sceptic: it is the person who believes in God already who can profit from it." *The Philosophy of Religion* (Princeton, N.J.: Van Nostrand Company, 1965), p. 28.

[10]*Proslogion,* chap. II; PL 158, cols. 227-28; *Basic Writings,* pp. 7-8.

able being;[11] it is the question of actual, real existence. In other words, a being than which nothing greater can be conceived either exists in reality or is not that kind of being; it is a contradiction, and therefore a non-being.[12] Hence Anselm's conclusion: "There is, then, so truly a being than which nothing greater can be conceived, that it cannot even be conceived not to exist; and this being you are, O Lord, our God."[13]

This is the general structure of the Anselmian proof. To understand it better, we shall find some observations in order. The argument rests on the idea that existence is a perfection, a teaching that is not peculiar to Anselm but has been widely accepted by philosophers before and after him. Existence is also called a pure perfection, since its concept, whether simple or complex, direct or indirect, implies no imperfection whatsoever. When Kant challenged the argument on the ground that existence is not a predicate, since it does not add anything to the concept of a thing, he failed to see—perhaps one should say that his antimetaphysical approach to philosophy prevented him from seeing—the difference between the beings of our experience, whose nature is indifferent to existence and non-existence, and the greatest conceivable being, whose nature is to exist. In this latter case, and in this case alone, existence is so much of a perfection that without it the being in question cannot even be conceived. This does not mean that we can form a simple and direct concept of such a being, for we have no immediate knowledge of it; nor does it mean that we can attain to the knowledge of the existence of such a being merely through a concept. Nowhere in Anselm's writings can we find support for this view. It is only by reasoning and inferential judgment that we can attain to such a knowledge, and reason will tell us that not only in the case of the greatest conceivable being but in the case of any being whatsoever existence is a perfection.[14] As such, it *can* be predicated of any being that is not in a

---

[11]This point has been strongly emphasized by Charles Hartshorne: "A common method of seeking to trivialize Anselm's claim is to hold that 'necessarily existing' (to use a non-Anselmian phrase) means only 'existing necessarily if it exists at all'. 'Divinity exists' is perhaps necessary if true; however, it may be false." *Anselm's Discovery. A Re-Examination of the Ontological Argument for God's Existence* (La Salle, Ill.: The Open Court Publishing Company, 1965), p. 6.

[12]Alexandre Koyré pertinently observes: "... *l'ens quo maius cogitari nequit* ne peut pas être envisagé comme n'existant pas, et cela non seulement parce que c'est une impossibilité *quoad rem,* mais aussi et sourtout parce que c'est une pensée impossible à penser, une pensée qui contredit les lois immanentes de la pensée elle-même." *L'idée de Dieu dans la philosophie de St. Anselme* (Paris: Éditions Ernest Leroux, 1923), p. 202.

[13]*Proslogion,* chap. III; PL 158, col. 228; *Basic Writings,* pp. 8–9.

[14]In his short but penetrating analysis of the Anselmian argument, P. Franciscus Spedalieri, S.J., makes the following remark: "Igitur, potius ad artem studiumque attendas, quibus sanctus Doctor ad opusculum istud conscribendum processit, atque animadvertas illum plane dicere omnique vi asserere se non ex mero conceptu, verum ex iudicio argumentum deducere: et hoc quidem non...quia mens nostra Deum quodammodo intueatur, sed quia omne, quod intelligitur vel iudicatur, cum sit in intellectu quia et sicut intelligitur, in-

purely potential state, and *must* be predicated of a being that cannot be conceived otherwise than as existing.

Another presupposition of the Anselmian argument is that we already have a notion of God as a supremely perfect being. This is evident from the very nature of the *Proslogion* as an attempt to understand the God known by faith, and from Anselm's explicit statement that anyone can arrive at such a notion from the degrees of goodness of the beings of our experience. "It is therefore evident to any rational mind, that by ascending from the lesser good to the greater, we can form a considerable notion of a being than which a greater is inconceivable."[15] Anselm does not imply in any way that the proposition "God exists" is self-evident, as Aquinas seems to suggest. On the contrary, the knowledge of God's existence is the result of a complex process of reasoning which extends to at least two chapters of the *Proslogion* and the whole *Liber apologeticus*, and which even a trained philosopher has difficulty in following. The argument is definitely not for the ordinary man but for the intellectual elite, such as Anselm's fellow monks for whom it was originally written.

Again—and this is the most crucial point of the entire issue—the Anselmian proof does not involve an illegitimate transition from the ideal to the real order, as though Anselm would attempt to prove the existence of God from a purely abstract concept or the notion of a supreme conceivable being in the logical order.[16] Rather, Anselm wants to show that the notion of the supreme conceivable being, which according to the Augustinian ideological realism has an objective intelligibility of its own and is not therefore a pure abstraction, implies of its very nature the existence of the being in question. It is the ontological value of the idea that forces the mind to accept the existence of that being as its necessary implication.[17]

---

dependenter a mentis cogitatione, quadantenus saltem, ordinem ad esse dicit." *Selectae et breviores philosophiae ac theologiae controversiae* (Rome: Officium Libri Catholici, 1950), pp. 22-23.

[15]*Liber apologeticus*, chap. VIII; PL 158, col. 258; *Basic Writings*, p. 167.

[16]Charlesworth writes in this connection: "The objection that St. Anselm argues directly from the conceptual logical order to the real order, that is, from the idea of God to the actual existence of God, is simply a vulgar travesty of his argument." *St. Anselm's Proslogion*, p. 63. The same observation had already been made by Spedalieri, *op. cit.*, p. 38: "Et longe a recta eius mentis interpretatione aberrant quotquot Anselmum de transitu ab ordine logico ad ordinem ontologicum, nostris etiam diebus, arguere volunt."

[17]The objective nature of the concept that serves as a starting point for the Anselmian argument is clearly stated by Cardinal José Aguirre, an eminent scholar and recognized authority on Anselmian studies. He writes: "Itaque Anselmus ex mente omnium *supponit* conceptum obiectivum, significatum hoc nomine *Deus*, esse id quo nihil melius aut excellentius cogitari potest. Eiusmodi autem conceptus, si recte intelligatur aut penetretur, habet immediatam connexionem cum existentia. Qui enim recte concipit optimum cogitabilium omnium, eo ipso concipit ipsum ut simpliciter existens, et existens necessario." Quoted in Josephus M. Piccirelli, S.J., "De mente S. Anselmi in Proslogio," *De Deo: disputationes metaphysicae* (Paris: Lecoffre, 1885), pp. 521-22. It is wrong, therefore, to interpret the

Briefly, the *ratio Anselmi* is an attempt to show that it is impossible for the human mind fully to understand the meaning and ideological content of the notion of a being than which nothing greater is conceivable and simultaneously deny the existence of that being. This goes to prove, Anselm would insist, the truth of the biblical statement that only a fool can say, there is no God. "For God is that than which a greater cannot be conceived. And he who thoroughly understands this, assuredly understands that this being so truly exists, that not even in concept can it be non-existent. Therefore, he who understands that God so exists, cannot conceive that he does not exist."[18] Anselm is so convinced of the value of his discovery, that he concludes the argument by thanking God for his enlightenment and does not hesitate to say that, as a result of it, it would now be impossible for him to deny his existence. "What I formerly believed by your bounty I now so understand by your illumination, that if I were unwilling to believe that you exist, I should not be able not to understand this to be true."[19]

What was Anselm's precise intention in setting forth his famous and much debated argument? To judge from the trouble he went to in reaching its final formulation and the enormous importance he attached to his discovery, it would seem that he was quite certain that he had arrived at a solution of the problem that had beset him for so long a time, namely, to find a single argument which would of itself suffice to demonstrate that God truly exists.[20] This is undoubtedly the impression one gets from reading the preface to the *Proslogion* written by Anselm himself and the historical account of the argument's composition transmitted to us by his disciple Eadmer.

If such was Anselm's conviction, we must carefully analyze his claim and see what it really amounts to in terms of his own thinking and the general context of the argument. The reader of the *Proslogion* is immediately struck by the close relationship between faith and reason that runs through the entire work. Hence it is only natural to ask what role, if any, faith plays in Anselm's approach to God, and especially in the argument under consideration.

To state the problem more clearly, is the argument strictly philosophical, and hence completely independent of the data of revelation, or is it merely a "discourse on the existence of God"—this is the subtitle of the treatise—as known to us by faith? If it is held that the argument is purely

Anselmian argument in the light of Aristotelian-Thomistic philosophy according to which the objective value of our ideas can be derived only from sensible experience through the process of abstraction.

[18] *Proslogion,* chap. IV; PL 158,col. 229; *Basic Writings,* p. 10.
[19] *Proslogion, loc. cit.; Basic Writings, loc. cit.*
[20] See Preface to the *Proslogion;* PL 158, col. 223; *Basic Writings,* p. 1.

philosophical, we may ask further, is Anselm's really an a priori demonstration arguing from the concept of God to his existence, or is there any way to justify his reasoning and avoid at the same time what has been termed an illicit transition from the logical to the real order? If, on the other hand, the *ratio Anselmi* is only a reflection on a doctrine known by revelation, can we still speak of it as a rational argument for the existence of God? These are vital questions that have been raised by critics in their attempt to penetrate the mind of Anselm and discover his real intention in the writing of the *Proslogion* .

There can be no doubt that Anselm approached the problem of God's existence from the point of view of a believer who tries to understand the meaning of his own belief. This he tells us explicitly in the preface to his work.[21] The fact that the original title of the *Proslogion* was *Fides quaerens intellectum* (Faith Seeking Understanding) is a confirmation of this point. Likewise, there seems to be no doubt that Anselm was convinced that faith is a necessary requirement for understanding the full import of his argument.[22]

That much granted, it still remains to be seen whether in Anselmian terms a rational demonstration of God's existence is possible. Despite all arguments to the contrary, it is our contention that faith does not affect or weaken the value of a demonstration as long as this is kept within the limits of man's reasoning ability. And this, we believe, is precisely the case with the Anselmian proof. Indeed, Anselm does not take as starting point of his demonstration the existence of God as known by faith, in which case he would simply beg the question. What he assumes as a major premise of his reasoning is the idea of God as "that than which nothing greater can be conceived." This, he says, is what we believe about God. Then he goes on to work on this idea, which the human mind can understand even apart from revelation, and tries to show by the principle of contradiction that it is impossible to grasp its full ideological content and deny at the same time the existence of the being for which the idea stands. The reasoning may fail to convince an unbeliever, or even a believer for that matter, but there is nothing in it that would seem to demand faith as its necessary element. To state it another way, faith may be required as a necessary condition for the conviction of the validity of Anselm's reasoning, but not for the validity of the reasoning itself.

Further to clarify our point, we cannot see any inconsistency in seeking

---

[21]Preface to the *Proslogion;* PL 158, col. 224; *Basic Writings,* p. 2: "I have written the following treatise, in the person of one who strives to lift his mind to the contemplation of God, and seeks to understand what he believes."

[22]*Proslogion,* chap. I; PL 158, col. 227; *Basic Writings,* p. 7: "For this also I believe, that unless I believed, I should not understand." See also *Proslogion,* chap. IV; PL 158, col. 229; *Basic Writings,* p. 10.

to prove by reason a doctrine that is already held to be true by a superior source of knowledge such as revelation, just as we cannot see how one can disprove Anselm's claim that faith may help towards, or even be required for, convincing a person of the validity of his reasoning about God. The value of an argument and conviction of its value, especially when the argument in question concerns the existence of a being that transcends all empirical evidence, are two different things.[23]

If our understanding of the problem is correct, then the alternate interpretation of the *ratio Anselmi* as a mere reflection on the doctrine of God's existence known by revelation is *ipso facto* ruled out as incompatible with a strict rational demonstration. The question then arises: What kind of demonstration is it? If the starting point of Anselm's reasoning is merely a concept of the being whose existence it purports to prove, no matter what the source of that concept, how is Anselm able to move from a concept to the existence of the being so conceived? This is unquestionably the major difficulty Anselm had to face in defending the value of his argument.

II. ANSELM AND GAUNILO

As is well known, Gaunilo, a monk of the abbey of Marmoutiers near Tours, was the first to attack Anselm's argument "on behalf of the fool." Gaunilo's observations deserve special consideration because they anticipate most of the objections subsequently raised against the argument and also because they offered Anselm an opportunity to clarify certain points of the *Proslogion* that either had been left obscure or had not been fully developed.

Gaunilo's objections may be summarized as follows. The notion of a being than which no greater can be conceived is not different from the notion of a fictional being or a being whose existence has not been ascertained. To hold the contrary, one must show that the being in question is of such a nature that it cannot be understood without grasping at the same time its actual existence. But if this were the case, then there would be no difference between having an object in the mind prior to its actual existence, such as the idea of a painting in its potential state, and understanding the object in its concrete reality, such as the idea of a painting once it has been completed. Besides, if the existence of that being is so evident that its nonexistence cannot even be entertained in thought, why should one bother himself with proving it? Would it not be enough to think of that being to know that it really exists? But obviously this is not

---

[23]For a development of this point see chapter VII of this volume.

the case, for despite their idea of God there are still those who persist in denying his existence.

To support his point, Gaunilo brings forth his example of the "lost island," i.e., an island "more excellent than any other lands" and such that no better can be conceived. Yet, he says, despite the fact that we can form a clear concept of it, it does not follow that the island in question is actually existent. As a matter of fact, the island has never existed except in the imagination of men. Similarly, Gaunilo argues, I can very well form the concept of a being greater than any other being, and still doubt whether this being is anything but a fiction of my mind. Briefly, Gaunilo wants to say that existence is not something that can be inferred from a mere concept in the mind, whether it is the concept of God or of any other being. To think otherwise is to make an illicit transition from the ideal order to the order of reality.[24]

To judge from the nature and length of Anselm's refutation of Gaunilo's objections, it is clear that he made a serious effort to correct certain ideas about his argument that had led his critic to a wrong interpretation of it. As a result, his *Reply* to Gaunilo, made up of ten chapters, is extremely enlightening and is indispensable for an objective evaluation of the whole issue. His answer is as follows.

In the first place, Anselm sharply criticizes Gaunilo's comparison of the notion of God with the notion of a purely fictional being or "a being that is altogether inconceivable in terms of reality." If the two notions were alike, then either God would not be a being than which a greater is inconceivable, or he would not be able to be conceived at all. Now both of these suppositions are false, and to this effect he appeals to Gaunilo's faith and conscience. Granting therefore that the being in question is conceivable, it follows that such a being must also exist in reality. If not—and here Anselm gives a new turn to his argument—it would be possible for it to have a beginning and this would make it a different kind of being. It is indeed greater to exist without a beginning than to come into existence at a particular moment of time. (As far as Anselm's reasoning is concerned, an eternally contingent being seems to be out of question). Likewise, a being than which a greater is inconceivable cannot exist only at any particular place or time; it must exist as a whole everywhere and always. The reason is that whatever exists only temporarily or at a particular place can be conceived as not existing at all, which again is in direct contradiction to a being whose nonexistence is inconceivable.

A further observation of the greatest importance for a proper grasp of the Anselmian proof is that if the being under discussion is in the

---

[24]Cf. *Liber pro insipiente adversus S. Anselmi in Proslogio ratiocinationem.* PL 158, cols. 241–48; *Basic Writings,* pp. 145–53.

understanding, as it certainly is whenever I grasp its meaning, it is possible to think of it as existing also in reality. But as soon as this possibility is realized, it will be seen that the inference from possibility to actuality is demanded by the logic of reasoning. In fact, how could a being than which a greater is not conceivable exist only in the understanding if I can think of it as existing also in reality—which is undoubtedly greater than to exist in the understanding alone—and at the same time remove such a reality from it? Would not that be a contradictory notion, since on the one hand I form the concept of a greatest conceivable, and therefore possible, being, and on the other hand I remove from it one of the essential features of its greatness, i.e., existence?

It must be noted that it is not a question here of mere conceptual existence, in which case the argument would be self-defeating; it is a question of actual, real existence, which, in Anselm's thinking, is a perfection that has to be included in the notion of the greatest conceivable being. It is possible to disagree with Anselm's viewpoint, but it cannot be denied that that is his position, as the following text clearly indicates: "What more consistent inference, then, can be made than this: that if a being than which a greater cannot be conceived is in the understanding alone, it is not that than which a greater cannot be conceived?"[25]

On the basis of the foregoing observations, it was easy for Anselm to dismiss Gaunilo's analogy of the "lost island." The analogy simply did not apply to his own reasoning. First, there cannot be such a thing as an island than which no greater can be conceived, since no matter how excellent the island may be, it is always possible to think of a better one. Secondly, an island, by its very nature, is a limited reality and hence only relatively perfect, whereas Anselm's being must possess all perfections to the ultimate possible degree. Thirdly, an island, like any other creature, is a contingent being or such that it is indifferent for it to exist or not to exist. In other words, one can think of it as nonexisting without any contradiction, which is precisely the opposite of the kind of being Anselm had in mind in the formulation of his argument. It is because of these contrasts between the two kinds of being, which were no doubt in the back of Anselm's mind, even though he did not spell them out in exactly the way we have done, that he could challenge Gaunilo in the following terms: "I promise confidently that if any man shall devise anything either in reality or in concept alone to which he can adapt the sequence of my reasoning, I will discover that thing, and will give him his lost island, not to be lost again."[26]

Having clarified the problem of the fictional island, Anselm turns to

[25]*Liber apologeticus*, chap. II; PL 158, col. 252; *Basic Writings*, p. 158.
[26]*Liber apologeticus*, chap. III; PL 158, col. 252; *Basic Writings*, p. 158.

Gaunilo's final remark, which at first sight may appear to be a purely semantic subtlety but in truth is something much more significant. Referring to Anselm's oft-repeated statement that the nonexistence of the being in question is inconceivable, Gaunilo had suggested that a better term for it would be "unintelligible." For, he added, just as unreal things are unintelligible yet their existence is conceivable, so it is with God, whose nonexistence or even the possibility of his nonexistence is unintelligible and yet can be conceived, as is the case with the fool. Anselm takes issue with Gaunilo's observation on the ground that no comparison is possible between the nonexistence of God and the nonexistence of unreal things, even as far as our thinking is concerned. While there is no contradiction in thinking of the nonexistence of unreal things—indeed, that is the only way we think of them—it is impossible to think of the nonexistence, or even the possibility of the nonexistence, of God. Furthermore, if the nonexistence of God is said to be only unintelligible, there would be no difference between God and creatures, since all existing beings are intelligible to the extent that they exist.

To understand the logic of Anselm's reasoning, one must keep in mind the distinction between conceiving (*cogitare*) and understanding (*intelligere*), a distinction that was accepted by him as well as by Gaunilo. Whereas conceiving may refer to both existing and nonexisting beings, although not at the same time and in the same respect, understanding can only be in terms of actually existing beings, both material and spiritual. It is precisely because God is a unique being to which existence is necessarily due that, in Anselm's view, our mind is unable even to think of him as nonexisting. That explains his statements that while "nothing, so long as it is known to exist, can [at the same time] be conceived not to exist," and "whatever exists, except that being than which a greater cannot be conceived, can be conceived not to exist, even when it is known to exist,...of God alone it can be said that it is impossible to conceive of his nonexistence."[27]

With this last remark one might think that Anselm had refuted all the objections that Gaunilo had marshaled against his argument; but that is not the case. Going once more through the script of his objector, he discovers more weak spots, inconsistencies, and even misrepresentations which he feels must be brought into the open and thus further reveal some of the peculiarities of the argument. One first point he finds necessary to clarify is the notion of the being whose existence he is attempting to prove. To this effect he accuses Gaunilo—and rightly so—of having misquoted him by having him say that he wanted to demonstrate the existence of God

---

[27]*Liber apologeticus*, chap. IV; PL 158, col. 254; *Basic Writings*, p. 161.

merely from the notion of a being greater than all other beings. "Nowhere in all my writings," he asserts emphatically, "is such a demonstration found. For the real existence of a being which is said to be *greater than all other beings* cannot be demonstrated in the same way as the real existence of one that is said to be *a being than which a greater cannot be conceived*."[28] In fact, it is not altogether clear, and certainly not so on the strength of Anselm's reasoning, that a supreme being must exist merely because it is greater than all other beings, since it is always possible, at least in theory, to think of its nonexistence without contradiction. This very possibility would seem to make it inferior to a being whose nonexistence is absolutely inconceivable.

But the main point at issue is not so much the difference between the two kinds of being under discussion, but rather the question as to whether or not an argument for their existence can be made from their concept. It is Anselm's contention that while a cogent argument for the existence of God can be built on the idea of a being than which no greater is conceivable, no such argument is possible in the case of a being that is simply greater than all other beings. In point of fact, he adds, it is not difficult to see that the former will also be the latter; the reverse position, however, need not necessarily be true.[29]

In his analysis of the argument in the *Proslogion*, Gaunilo not only finds fault with Anselm's reasoning; he also questions the value of its premise, namely, the idea of the greatest conceivable being, since, in his view, there is no way of forming such an idea either from the being itself or from any other being. This is obviously a very serious objection which Anselm cannot let go unheeded, for, if it were proved valid, his whole argument would crumble. His answer is swift and to the point, if we take care to place it within the perspective of Platonic-Augustinian thought common at his time.

Granting the Platonic principle that a limited good is conceivable only in terms of a supreme good in which it participates, Anselm argues that by understanding the limited goods of our experience and by ascending from the lesser to the greater good, one can form a sufficiently valid notion of a being than which a greater is inconceivable. "So easily, then, can the fool who does not accept sacred authority be refuted, if he denies that a notion may be formed from other objects of a being than which a greater is inconceivable."[30] As for a Christian, Anselm simply reminds his objector of St. Paul's statement in Romans, I, 20, that the invisible things of God can

---

[28]*Liber apologeticus*, chap. V; PL 158, col. 254; *Basic Writings*, pp. 161–62.
[29]See the whole chapter V of *Liber apologeticus*, PL. 158, cols. 254–56; *Basic Writings*, pp. 161–64.
[30]*Liber apologeticus*, chap. VIII; PL 158, col. 258; *Basic Writings*, p. 168.

be understood from the things he has made, including his eternal power and divinity.[31]

But even if it were true, Anselm goes on to say, that we cannot conceive or understand a being than which a greater is inconceivable, it will nevertheless be possible for anyone to understand at least the meaning of such an expression. Just as we understand the meaning of the term *ineffable*, even though we may not grasp what is said to be ineffable, so we understand what is meant by the term *inconceivable*, although that to which the word applies is not conceivable. In other words, Anselm wants to say that the value of his argument does not depend on the actual understanding of the being under discussion, but simply on the understanding of what is meant by a being than which a greater cannot be conceived. This, he suggests, can be understood by everyone, including him who denies the existence of that being, for "whoever...makes this denial, understands and conceives of that than which a greater is inconceivable."[32]

Having made this concession, Anselm is still convinced that it is possible for everyone both to conceive and to understand a being than which a greater is inconceivable, and not merely the logical content, as it were, of such an expression. It is likewise possible for everyone to understand that the being so conceived must exist, "for anything whose nonexistence is possible, is not that which he conceives."[33]

Anselm is obviously satisfied with his refutation of Gaunilo's objections, none of which, he insists, carries such weight as to invalidate his argument. Hence he feels justified in making a final statement which reaffirms his conviction and summarizes the entire argument: "So great force does the signification of this reasoning contain in itself, that this being which is the subject of discussion, is of necessity, from the very fact that it is understood or conceived, proved also to exist in reality, and to be whatever we should believe of the divine substance."[34] This statement makes it clear, in case there is still doubt about Anselm's contention, that the existence of God, along with all other attributes ascribed to him on the basis of revelation, can be proved from the very fact that we understand not only the meaning or logical content, but the full dimension, that is, the ideological as well as the ontological content of the notion of "that than which no greater can be conceived."

The argument, it is worth repeating, is not so much an attempt to prove God's existence from the idea that we have of a supremely conceivable being in the abstract or logical order, as though it were enough to

---

[31]*Liber apologeticus, loc. cit.; Basic Writings, loc. cit.*
[32]*Liber apologeticus,* chap. IX; PL 158, col. 259; *Basic Writings,* p. 169.
[33]*Liber apologeticus, loc. cit.; Basic Writings, loc. cit.*
[34]*Liber apologeticus,* chap. X; PL 158, col. 260; *Basic Writings,* p. 170.

have such an idea to know for sure that God exists. Rather, Anselm's purpose is to show that one cannot possibly think of a being than which a greater cannot be conceived without admitting at the same time that such a concept, or better, such a notion—for it is not merely a concept—includes necessarily, if it is to have any value, the existence of the being in question. In other words, according to Anselm's reasoning, we do not arrive at God from the idea of him as a purely mental construct, but we cannot have an idea of him that does not include his existence, or to be precise, his real existence. This may appear to be a subtle distinction, but it is not. It is a distinction that must be made for a proper understanding of the argument in light of the ideological realism that, as we have already indicated,[35] Anselm shared with the entire Augustinian tradition.

It will perhaps be objected that if this observation is correct, one can no longer speak of the *ratio Anselmi* as a demonstration a priori in the strict sense of the term. We are inclined to agree with such a view and suggest that demonstration *a simultaneo* is a better term for it. We would further suggest that "argumentation" is also a better translation of the Anselmian term *ratio* and more in keeping with the general character of the *Proslogion* as "a discourse on the existence of God."

III. BONAVENTURE AND AQUINAS

It would be a long and perhaps fruitless task to analyze all the aspects of the problem that the controversy between Anselm and Gaunilo has aroused in the history of philosophy. However, it is important to consider the reactions of various philosophers both to Anselm's argument and to his debate with Gaunilo and to evaluate them on the basis of our understanding of the problem at issue.

The first major figures in the history of the argument are St. Bonaventure and St. Thomas Aquinas, the representatives of the two largest schools of thought in the thirteenth century. Their attitude toward the *ratio Anselmi* is of primary importance because of the enormous influence it exerted on later philosophers, especially within scholastic circles.

Bonaventure discusses the Anselmian argument in his *Commentary on the Sentences* of Peter Lombard and the opuscule *De mysterio Trinitatis*.[36] The two treatments move along the same line, but whereas in the first work the *ratio Anselmi* is introduced at the beginning of the question, "Whether the existence of God is so true that his nonexistence cannot

---

[35] See the preceding section of this chapter.

[36] Cf. St. Bonaventure, *Opera omnia* (Quaracchi: Typographia Collegii S. Bonaventurae, 1882-1902), vol. I: *In I Sent.*, d. 8, pt. 1, a. 1, q. 2, pp. 153-55; vol. V: *De mysterio Trinitatis*, q. 1, a. 1, pp. 45-51.

be conceived," in the second Anselm's proof is incorporated into a more extensive article dealing with the general question, "Whether truth is a property of the divine being." In fact, the proof is but an application of the answer to the question at issue. Once it has been established that truth is an absolute property of God, it is only logical to ask whether God's existence shares in the same degree of truth as the divine nature with which it is to be identified. Clearly, then, Bonaventure's approach to Anselm's argument is from the point of view of the divine nature itself rather than from the viewpoint of our knowledge of it.

In his answer to the question whether the existence of God is indubitably true, Bonaventure appeals both to the author of the *Proslogion*, whose reasoning he completely endorses,[37] and to St. Augustine's notion of divine truth as the source and foundation of all other truths, including the truth of the statement that God exists.[38] Likewise, in accordance with Aristotle's principle that the more basic and universal a truth is the better it is known,[39] Bonaventure argues that the truth of God's existence is most certain and evident because it is the first of all truths, both in itself and in our understanding. Its evidence is such that it excludes even the possibility of its denial.[40] In concluding his series of arguments in favor of the absolute necessity of God's existence from the idea we have of him, Bonaventure writes: "If God is God, God exists. The antecedent is so true that its contradictory is unthinkable. Therefore, the existence of God is indubitably true."[41] In a parallel conclusion in the *Commentary* he writes: "God, or the supreme truth, is being itself, [and such] than which no better can be conceived. Hence, since the predicate is included in the subject, [God] cannot not exist, nor can he be conceived as nonexistent."[42]

Evidently Bonaventure's reasoning, even more than Anselm's, rests on the assumption that we already have a notion of God either from revelation[43] or from some other source, such as reason or experience. Just as we can argue from creatures to their creator on the basis of the principle of causality,[44] so we can know the privations and limitations of the beings of our experience only through the knowledge of the opposite perfections. This means that "our mind experiences necessarily within itself some sort of light through which it knows the first being.[45] Furthermore, Bonaven-

---

[37]*De myst. Trin.*, nos. 21-24, p. 47.
[38]*Ibid.*, nos. 25-26, p. 47.
[39]Cf. Aristotle, *Posterior Analytics*, Bk. I, chap. 2.
[40]*De myst. Trin.*, q. 1, a. 1, no. 27, p. 48.
[41]*Ibid.*, no. 29, p. 48.
[42]*In I Sent.*, d. 8, pt. 1, a. 1, q. 2, *Conclusio*, p. 155.
[43]*De myst. Trin.*, q. 1, a. 1, no. 21, p. 47.
[44]*Opera omnia*, vol. V: *In Hexaëmeron*, V, no. 29, p. 359.
[45]*Ibid.*, no. 30, p. 359.

ture shares Augustine's view that the human soul, by being present to itself, knows itself directly, and since God is present to the soul even more than the soul is to itself, then the knowledge of God is inserted, as it were, into our soul.[46]

To the objection that many people, including the fool described by the Psalmist, are not aware of the knowledge in question, Bonaventure answers with Anselm that such ignorance is not due to the fact that God is not knowable or that our mind has no ability to know him, but rather to the knower's lack of reflection on what the term *God* really means.[47] As for the kind of knowledge of God man can attain in this life, Bonaventure agrees with most of the schoolmen that it is neither perfect or comprehensive, since such knowledge belongs to God alone, nor clear and distinct, such as that of the blessed in heaven. It is only partial and confused knowledge inasmuch as God is known to be the first being from whom all other beings derive their existence.[48]

With Bonaventure, as with Anselm, there is no question of an illicit transition from the idea of God to God's existence, the objection commonly raised against the ontological argument. As Gilson puts it, "the idea is for him [Bonaventure] simply the mode whereby the being is present in his thought: there is therefore no real gap to be bridged between the idea of God whose existence is necessary, and this same God necessarily existing."[49] On the other hand, Bonaventure does not simply accept Anselm's reasoning without bringing into it new insights that are no doubt in keeping with the general context of the *Proslogion*, but nevertheless have not been made explicit by its author. To quote once more from Gilson:

> With St. Bonaventure the truths presupposed in St. Anselm's argument come into the foreground and, shown in their full evidence, in some sense absorb the proof. If, in fact, the line of argument of the *Proslogion* draws its value from the profound contacts that our idea of God maintains with its object, it is rather the realization of this action of God in our thought that constitutes the proof of His existence, and not the analytical working out of the consequences involved in the notion we have of Him.[50]

To turn from Bonaventure to Aquinas is to see a totally new picture, that is, a completely different interpretation of the *ratio Anselmi*. This dif-

[46]*De myst. Trin.*, q. 1, a. 1, no. 10, p. 46. See also no. 1, p. 45.
[47]*Ibid.*, *Conclusio*, nos. 1, 2, 3, p. 50.
[48]*Ibid.*, *Conclusio*, no. 13, p. 51.
[49]Etienne Gilson, *The Philosophy of St. Bonaventure*, p. 129.
[50]*Ibid.*, pp. 129-30. For St. Bonaventure's teaching on man's knowledge of God and the arguments for God's existence see P. Léon Veuthey, O.F.M. Conv., "Le problème de l'existence de Dieu chez S. Bonaventure," *Antonianum*, XXVIII (1953), 19-38.

ference of approach should not surprise anyone who is acquainted with the relative degree of freedom with which the thirteenth-century school-men moved within the area of philosophy and the conflict into which they were gradually drawn by the introduction of Aristotle's thought into what was predominantly a Platonic-Augustinian tradition. Thus, although Bonaventure made extensive use of Aristotle's works, he adhered basically to the Augustinian tradition which he saw as being more in keeping with Christian thought and his own theological speculation. On the other hand, Aquinas had no strong tradition behind him in his own Order, was more directly exposed to Aristotle's profound and ingenious metaphysical thinking, and went all the way in an attempt to absorb Aristotelian philosophy into his own synthesis. His attitude toward the Anselmian argument is a case in point.

Aquinas discusses the *ratio Anselmi* in several of his works but with no appreciable difference of approach.[51] In both the *Summa theologiae* and the *Summa contra gentiles* he fails to name Anselm as the author of the argument, while in the second work he speaks of not just one but several authors as defenders of the argument under discussion.[52] This has led historians to suspect that in his polemic Thomas had in mind not so much Anselm himself as certain contemporary philosophers and theologians, especially Bonaventure.[53] Whoever may have been the objects of his criticism, neither Anselm nor Bonaventure or any other upholder of the argument had presented the problem in quite the same terms as Thomas does, namely, "Whether the existence of God is self-evident."[54] As a matter of fact, none of those authors would have subscribed to the view that the existence of God is self-evident. They all thought of this as a demonstrable truth and as such the opposite of what a self-evident pro-position is.[55] Anselm and Bonaventure, as we have seen, devote a con-siderable amount of space to the demonstration of the existence of a being than which no greater can be conceived. In addition, both of them have

---

[51] The principal texts where Aquinas discusses the *ratio Anselmi* are: *In I Sent.*, d. 3, q. 1, a. 2, ed. Mandonnet (Paris: Lethielleux, 1929), I, 93–95; *Summa contra gentiles*, Bk. I, chaps. 10–11; *Summa theologiae*, I, q. 2, a. 1; *De veritate*, q. 10, a. 12; *In Boethii De Trinitate*, q. 1, a. 3, obj. 6 and ad 6, ed. Decker (Leiden: Brill, 1955), pp. 70, 73–74.

[52] Anselm's name is mentioned by Aquinas in *In I Sent.*, d. 3, q. 1, a. 2, obj. 4 and ad 4, pp. 93 and 95; *De veritate, loc. cit.*; and *In Boethii De Trinitate, loc. cit.*

[53] Cf. Anton C. Pegis, "St. Anselm and the Argument of the 'Proslogion'," *Mediaeval Studies*, XXVIII (1966), 262 ff.; Etienne Gilson, *The Christian Philosophy of St. Thomas Aquinas*, trans. L. K. Shook, C.S.B. (New York: Random House, 1956), p. 48.

[54] See, for example, *Sum. theol.*, I, q. 2, a. 1: "Utrum Deum esse sit per se notum"; *Con. gent.*, I, 1: "De opinione dicentium quod Deum esse demonstrari non potest cum sit per se notum."

[55] Cf. Pegis, *art. cit.*, pp. 262 ff. for a discussion of this point.

recourse to the traditional theistic arguments which have been so well synthesized by Thomas in his well-known five ways.

Having stated the problem in these terms, Aquinas goes on to describe a self-evident proposition as that which is known immediately upon the knowledge of its terms, such as the proposition that a whole is greater than a part. Now the proposition "God exists," Aquinas writes, is held by some philosophers to be such a proposition, for once we understand the meaning of the two terms we see immediately that existence is of the very nature of God. Hence they hold that it is self-evident that God exists.[56]

In refutation of the argument Thomas states, first, that a distinction must be made between a proposition that is self-evident in itself and one that is self-evident to us. The proposition "God exists" is self-evident in the former sense, since the subject and the predicate are identical, but not in the latter sense, for it is not evident to us that God is his own existence. This truth must be demonstrated and that can be done only by starting from the objects of our experience, which are more evident to us.[57] Moreover, referring specifically to Anselm's notion of a being than which no greater can be conceived, Aquinas argues that such is not the meaning conveyed to everyone as soon as he hears the word *God*. Indeed, some people have an entirely different notion of God, a statement with which Anselm would perfectly agree. But even if the word *God* were generally recognized to mean a being than which no greater can be conceived, Aquinas stresses that it would still be uncertain whether such a being exists in reality or whether it is but a concept of our mind. It remains to be proved therefore, especially to an unbeliever, that such a being does actually exist. Finally, Anselm's reasoning that if God can be thought not to be then it is possible to think of something greater than God, is not valid. For the possibility of thinking of God as nonexistent is not due to the imperfection or uncertainty of the divine being but rather to the weakness of our mind which cannot behold God himself and can argue to him only from the effects of his creation.[58]

Such is Aquinas' position on the *ratio Anselmi*. In all fairness it must be said that, apart from his initial misrepresentation of the problem as seen above, his objections to the argument are strong and quite consistent with his Aristotelian background. If ideas have no value-content except insofar as they reflect a concrete material object or are derived from it through the process of abstraction, it is useless to try to construct an argument for the existence of a being merely from the idea we have of it in our mind, be it the idea of the greatest conceivable being. From the Aristotel-

---

[56]Cf. *Sum. theol.*, I, q. 2, a. 1, obj. 2 and *Respondeo; Con. gent.*, I, 10, no. 1.

[57]*Sum. theol.*, I, q. 2, a. 1, *Respondeo; Con. gent.*, I, 11.

[58]*Sum. theol.*, I, q. 2, a. 1, ad 2; *Con. gent.*, I, 11.

ian viewpoint the idea in question has no ontological value and any attempt to build a theistic argument on it is doomed to fail. It falls short of bridging the gap between mind and reality, and it incurs the charge, so often leveled against the Anselmian proof, of being an illicit transition from the ideal to the real order.

Aquinas was therefore right in refuting the Anselmian argument on Aristotelian premises, and so are his followers who for centuries have been repeating the same objections with no appreciable effort to place the argument within its proper historical and ideological context. But the question is: Is the Aristotelian epistemology the only valid one? Is it true that the formal and proper object of our intellect, even in this life, is only a material quiddity and that sense experience and abstraction are the only valid process of acquiring knowledge? These are fundamental issues that have received different solutions in the course of history, and none of them seems to be completely satisfactory. Hence the value of Aquinas' criticism of the *ratio Anselmi* is conditioned upon the acceptance of the Aristotelian theory as the only valid cognitive theory. Once this is questioned—and there is an entire school of thought from Plato to Augustine, from Anselm to Bonaventure, and from Duns Scotus to many present-day thinkers who question it—then the criticism itself becomes questionable.

Whatever side one may take in the controversy, it seems clear that Aquinas did not give Anselm the credit he deserves for his discovery. Stated more bluntly, he did not show himself to be completely objective in his presentation of Anselm's view. However, the truth of the matter is that this lack of objectivity in the presentation of opposite views is not something peculiar to Aquinas or to his treatment of the ontological argument. It is rather a common attitude among medieval schoolmen whenever in their writings they want to make a particular point of doctrine. A notable exception in the case under consideration is John Duns Scotus, who was neither an all-out Aristotelian nor a complete Augustinian, although he had great esteem for both Aristotle and Augustine. It is to him that we shall now turn our attention in the study of the argument throughout the Middle Ages.

IV. DUNS SCOTUS

Duns Scotus, whose attempts to work out a most complete and thorough proof for the existence of God have perhaps never been matched in the history of human thought, could not remain indifferent to Anselm's argument. In addition to its highly stimulating nature, the argument had a special appeal to him because of the spiritual kinship of Anselm and the

Franciscan school in which he had been raised. The fact that St. Bonaventure and other Franciscan masters had adopted a different view from Aquinas' and sponsored the Anselmian argument made it all the more necessary for him to examine the issue and, setting aside all school prejudices, see whether the argument could be put to use for his own approach to God.

Scotus discusses the argument in several works. His most complete treatment of it is found in the *Ordinatio*, otherwise known as the *Opus Oxoniense*, and in *De primo principio*, a short tract whose striking similarities to the Anselmian work have led some historians to call it the thirteenth-century *Proslogion*.[59] Since the treatment of *De primo principio* follows along the general lines of that of the *Ordinatio*, from which the greater part of the tract has been taken,[60] the text of the *Ordinatio* will be used in this study. However, references to *De primo principio* will be given whenever they are relevant.

Scotus' first approach to the Anselmian argument takes the form of an objection to the question whether the existence of an infinite being—the aim of his theistic proof—is a self-evident truth. It is logical for him to discuss such a question at the very outset of his demonstration, for if a positive answer is given to it, all demonstrations will be superfluous. One does not have to prove what is obvious. As an alleged indication of the self-evidence of God's existence, he quotes Anselm's statement that a being than which nothing greater can be conceived must exist, or else it would not be such a being.[61] Before answering the question, Scotus makes a detailed analysis of what he considers to be a self-evident proposition. Disregarding the distinction between a proposition that is evident in itself (*per se nota*) and one that is evident to us (*nota quoad nos*), which serves as a basis for Aquinas' rejection of the Anselmian proof,[62] he states that a proposition is self-evident if its terms and their relationship are im-

---

[59]Cf. Etienne Gilson, *Jean Duns Scot. Introduction à ses positions fondamentales* (Paris: Vrin, 1952), p. 178: "Cet écrit *[De primo principio]* peut être comparé sans trop d'inexactitude à un *Proslogion* de type anselmien dont l'auteur aurait maîtrisé, outre les resources de la dialectique, celles de la métaphysique de son temps." See also the study of Robert Prentice, O.F.M., "The 'De primo principio' of John Duns Scotus as a Thirteenth-Century Proslogion," *Antonianum*, 39 (1964), 77–109, where the author shows the similarities of Anselm's and Scotus' works as regards their spirit, their purpose, their outline, and their argumentation.

[60]Cf. Charles Balić, "The Life and Works of John Duns Scotus," in *John Duns Scotus, 1265-1965*, ed. by John K. Ryan and Bernardine M. Bonansea (Washington, D.C.: The Catholic University of America Press, 1965), p. 23. While affirming the unquestionable authenticity of the *De primo principio*, Father Balić maintains that conceivably Scotus is not the only author of the treatise. *Ibid.*

[61]*Ord.* I, pt. 1, q. 2; Vatican ed., II, 129.

[62]*Sum. theol.*, I, q. 2, a. 3 c. For a recent study of the subject cf. Anton C. Pegis, "St. Anselm and the Argument of the 'Proslogion'," 228–67.

mediately known.[63] Hence if the terms of a proposition are not known as soon as their meaning is understood but a third concept must be introduced to define them, the proposition is not self-evident. Likewise, if the relationship between the subject and the predicate of a proposition is not evident but becomes so only through demonstration, the proposition is not self-evident either. Furthermore, just as there is no distinction between a proposition that is evident in itself and one that is evident to us,[64] so for Scotus there is no distinction between a proposition that is known by itself (*per se nota*) and one that is knowable by itself (*per se noscibilis*), for the evidence of a proposition does not depend on its actual cognition but on the aptitude of its terms to cause self-evident knowledge.[65] More specifically, a proposition is and remains self-evident despite the fact that its terms are not immediately known to us, if the evidence of the proposition can be known by a superior mind, such as the divine intellect and the angelic minds, or even by the blessed in heaven, whose intellect is in direct contact with the divinity.

Having clarified the meaning of a self-evident proposition, Scotus goes on to apply his principles to the question at issue, namely, whether the proposition "God exists" is self-evident. Surprisingly enough, he says "Yes," but he immediately qualifies his answer. Since the terms of the proposition are apt to produce evident truth in the intellect that perceives them, such as the divine intellect and the minds of the blessed in heaven, the proposition must be called self-evident or *per se nota*.[66] Moreover, since there is no distinction between a proposition that is evident in itself and one that is evident to us, it follows that the proposition in question is also known to us as self-evident—or else how could we say it is so in regard to God? However, since in the present state our knowledge of God is possible only through common concepts derived from creatures, we do not have a direct grasp of the terms of the proposition under discussion or any evidence that existence belongs to the divine nature. Hence the proposi-

---

[63]*Ord.* I, d. 2, pt. 1, q. 2; Vatican ed., II, 131: "Dicitur igitur propositio per se nota, quae per nihilum aliud extra terminos proprios, qui sunt aliquid eius, habet veritatem evidentem"; *ibid.*, p. 135: "Est ergo omnis et sola propositio illa per se nota, quae ex terminis sic conceptis ut sunt eius termini, habet vel nata est habere evidentem veritatem complexionis."

[64]*Ibid.*, p. 136: "Nulla est distinctio de per se nota in se et naturae et nobis, quia quaecumque est in se et per se nota, cuicumque intellectui, licet non actu cognita, tamen quantum est ex terminis est evidenter vera et nota si termini concipiantur."

[65]*Ibid.:* "Non est distinguere inter propositionem per se notam et per se noscibilem, quia idem sunt."

[66]*Ibid.*, pp. 137–38. "Est igitur ista 'Deus est' sive 'haec essentia est' per se nota, quia extrema illa sunt nata facere evidentiam de ista complexione cuilibet apprehendenti perfecte extrema istius complexionis, quia esse nulli perfectius convenit quam huic essentiae." *Ibid.*, p. 138.

tion "God exists" is not precisely understood by us as self-evident and its truth can and must be demonstrated.[67]

What has been said of the proposition "God exists" is equally true, Scotus argues, of any other statement in which existence is predicated of God in a concept by which he is known to us, such as "A necessary being exists" or "An infinite being exists." These propositions are not self-evident for three reasons: first, because they can be demonstrated, whereas a self-evident proposition admits of no demonstration; second, because their terms, far from being self-evident, are known to us either by faith or by demonstration; and third, because none of the proper concepts we have of God, such as "infinite being," "necessary being," and the like, are absolutely simple (*simpliciter simplex*) but all are composite. Since they are composite, no proposition about them is self-evident unless it is also evidently known that the components of such concepts go together. If this is true in the quidditative order, it is much more so in the existential order when the being in question is not immediately known. Hence, Scotus concludes, the proposition "An infinite being exists" is not self-evident and must be demonstrated.[68]

Turning then to the problem under discussion, Scotus rightly says that Anselm does not assert that "a being than which nothing greater can be conceived exists" is a self-evident proposition. In fact, Anselm's reasoning implies at least two syllogisms. The first is: "A being is greater than a nonbeing; but nothing is greater than the supreme; therefore, the supreme is not a nonbeing." The second syllogism is: "What is not a nonbeing is a being; but the supreme is not a nonbeing; therefore, the supreme is a being." That Anselm's proposition is not self-evident is proved by the fact that it is not immediately known to us that the nonexistence of a supreme conceivable being involves a contradiction, or that the components of the concept of a supreme conceivable being do actually go together. The two requirements are necessary for a self-evident proposition.[69]

To say that Anselm's proposition is not self-evident and to say that it is not true are two entirely different things. As a matter of fact, Scotus holds to the truth of the proposition but says that this must be proved. Anselm,

---

[67]*Ibid.*: "Sic igitur intelligendo per nomen Dei aliquid quod nos non perfecte cognoscimus nec concipimùs ut hanc essentiam divinam, sic est per se nota 'Deus est'." The apparent ambiguity of Scotus' position is explained by Gilson, *Jean Duns Scot,* p. 123, n. 2, in the following terms: "L'ambiguité apparente de la position de Duns Scot tient à ce que l'on ne distingue pas comme lui les moments du problème. Le fait que la proposition *Deus est* ne nous soit pas, en fait, *per se nota* n'empêche pas qu'elle doive rester pour nous, en droit, la proposition *per se nota* qu'elle est en soi. Autrement dit, une proposition est *per se nota* lorsqu'elle est évidente à l'intellect qui en appréhende les termes. C'est le cas de la proposition *Deus est*. Que nous n'en appréhendions pas les termes, ne change rien à sa nature."
[68]*Ord.* I, d. 2, pt. 1, q. 2; Vatican ed., II, 138–42.
[69]*Ibid.,* pp. 145–46.

it is worth mentioning, never attempts to prove the possibility of a supreme conceivable being in his *Proslogion*. He takes it for granted, or perhaps he holds that if a proof were needed, he has already offered it in his previous work, the *Monologium*, where not only the possibility but the actual existence of a supreme being is demonstrated by a posteriori arguments. If we look then at the *Proslogion* as a mere continuation of the *Monologium*, we have in it an added reason for believing in God based on the analysis of the notion of a supreme conceivable being whose existence is already known to us. However, in such a case the *ratio Anselmi* will lose its specific characteristic and can no longer be called an argument for God's existence, as its author holds it to be. Scotus realizes the weakness of the Anselmian argument and attempts to provide it with a rational foundation that will give it strength and solidity and make it more acceptable.

The *ratio Anselmi*, Scotus says, can be "colored" or reformulated this way. "God is such a being that, if it is possible for it to be conceived without contradiction, no greater being can be conceived without contradiction."[70] The introduction of the principle of contradiction to justify the notion of God on which the argument is based is most important. Indeed, if the *summum cogitabile*—this is Scotus' contracted form of "a being than which nothing greater can be conceived"—were found to be self-contradictory, no argument whatsoever could be built on it; the argument would have failed its preliminary test. But far from being self-contradictory, the *summum cogitable* seems to satisfy completely my intellect, which finds in it a certain delight, as though it were confronted with the supreme object of its knowing ability. Moreover, if there were any contradiction in the notion of a *summum cogitabile*—which for Scotus is the same as the infinite being whose existence he purports to prove—my intellect, whose primary and proper object is being, could not fail to notice it, just as my sense of hearing immediately notices discordant sounds.[71] Thus the notion of a *summum cogitabile* is not contradictory, and since whatever implies no contradiction is possible, "a being than which nothing greater can be conceived" is possible.

To have proved the possibility of a supreme conceivable being is already a major and perhaps decisive step in the reformulation of the Anselmian argument. Scotus is able to take such a step because of his theory of being as the proper object of the human intellect and his doctrine of the

---

[70]*Ibid.*, p. 209. See also *De primo principio*, in John Duns Scotus, *A Treatise on God as First Principle*, trans. and ed. by Allan B. Wolter, O.F.M. (Chicago, Ill.: Franciscan Herald Press, 1966), p. 123. Henceforth the *De primo principio* will be quoted from the Latin text in the above work.

[71]*Ord.* I, d. 2, pt. 1, q. 2; Vatican ed., II, 208; *De primo principio*, pp. 121-23.

univocity of the concept of being. No recourse is necessary in his case to the ideological realism in the light of which, as we have shown, the *ratio Anselmi* must be understood.

Once the possibility of a supreme conceivable being has been established, it remains to prove its actual existence. The transition from the essential to the existential order, or, to use Scotus' terminology, from the *esse quiditativum* to the *esse existentiae*, is done by the Subtle Doctor in a way that anticipates Leibniz' reasoning and helps to substantiate the *ratio Anselmi*. Scotus' reasoning is as follows.

The supreme conceivable being cannot be merely in our mind, for then it would be possible, since it can be conceived as existing without contradiction, and at the same time it would not be possible, i.e., it could not exist, since of its very nature it cannot depend on any cause for its existence.[72] In other words, we can think of the supreme conceivable being only as self-existing, for, on the one hand, it admits of no extrinsic cause for its existence and, on the other hand, it is against its nature not to exist. It is greater, in fact, to exist in reality than to exist merely in the mind.[73] Hence, if our thoughts have any objective value, the very nature of the supreme conceivable being demands its actual existence.

To add further strength to the Anselmian argument, Scotus submits another reason. Whatever exists, he argues, has a greater degree of intelligibility, and therefore a greater degree of perfection, than that which does not exist, since the former can be known intuitively, whereas the latter, not being present or visible, can be known only abstractively. Hence the supreme conceivable being must exist, or else it would lack one of the perfections that go along with supreme intelligibility, namely, the perfection of being apt to be known intuitively.[74] This is in line with Scotus' teaching that intuitive cognition, whereby an object is directly known in its actual existence, is superior to abstractive cognition, which is knowledge either of a nonexisting object or of an object that exists but is not known precisely as existing.[75]

With this, Scotus concludes his "coloration" of the Anselmian argument. Much discussion has taken place among Scotus' interpreters as to whether such a coloration amounts to a conditional approval of the argu-

---

[72]*Ord.* I, d. 2, pt. 1, q. 2; Vatican ed., II, 209-210; *De primo principio,* p. 123.

[73]*Ord.* I, d. 2, pt. 1, q. 2; Vatican ed., II, 210: "Maius ergo cogitabile est quod est in re quam quod est tantum in intellectu. Non est autem hoc sic intelligendum quod idem si cogitetur, per hoc sit maius cogitabile si exsistat, sed, omni quod est in intellectu tantum, est maius aliquod quod exsistit." See also *De primo principio,* p. 123.

[74]*Ord.* I, d. 2, pt. 1, q. 2; Vatican ed., II, 210-211; *De primo principio,* pp. 123-25.

[75]*Ord.* I, d. 1, pt. 1, q. 2; Vatican ed., II, 23-24. See also *ibid.,* d. 2, pt. 2, q. 4; Vatican ed., II, 352.

ment—an outright endorsement of it is out of the question—or whether it is simply a touching up or reformulation of the argument without ascribing to it any real value as a theistic proof. The two interpretations can perhaps be brought together by saying that the *ratio Anselmi* is integrated, as it were, into Scotus' proof for the existence of an infinite being, not as an essential and indispensable element of it—Scotus' proof is self-sufficient and equally valid without it—but as a confirmatory argument to the effect that a supreme conceivable being, or what amounts to the same thing, an infinite being, is not contradictory and hence is at least intrinsically possible. This seems to be the mind of Scotus himself, who states that, while no a priori demonstration of the existence of an infinite being is possible,[76] some persuasive reasons can be used to support Anselm's reasoning.[77]

Thus Scotus' position shows a balanced judgment that avoids two extremes: the view of those who reject the Anselmian argument altogether because they make little or no effort to understand it in its true perspective, and the view of those who accept it as a theistic proof without any reservation as to its demonstrative value. Scotus' main contribution to the argument consists in providing it with a truly rational basis by showing the noncontradiction, and hence the possibility, of the supreme conceivable being and by pointing out, more effectively than St. Anselm did and long before Descartes and Leibniz were to do in their own way, the real contradiction that would result from accepting such a concept and denying the existence of the being so conceived.

In the period immediately following the Middle Ages no important contribution to the understanding of the argument was made. We therefore pass to the consideration of the Anselmian proof in modern times.

---

[76]*Ord.* I, d. 2, pt. 1, q. 2; Vatican ed., II, 206–207: "[Quod] enti non repugnat infinitas. . .non videtur posse a priori ostendi." See also *De primo principio,* p. 121.

[77]*Ord.* I, d. 2, pt. 1, q. 2; Vatican ed., II, 207–208; *De primo principio,* p. 121. Bettoni holds that although in Scotus' view the *ratio Anselmi* has no cogency of its own as an argument for the existence of God, the Subtle Doctor developed it for the purpose of his own theistic proof and gave it a full demonstrative value. See Efrem Bettoni, *Duns Scotus: The Basic Principles of His Philosophy,* trans. and ed. by Bernardine Bonansea (Washington, D.C.: The Catholic University of America Press, 1961), p. 144. Gilson maintains that Scotus' coloration of the Anselmian argument is for the purpose of proving God's infinity rather than his existence. *Jean Duns Scot,* pp. 166–67. This view had already been advanced by Séraphin Belmond, *Dieu: existence et cognoscibilité* (Paris: Beauchesne, 1913), p. 21, n. 1, and Van de Woestyne, *Cursus philosophicus,* II, 712–13, n. 2, who base their position on Scotus' statement: "Quomodo autem ratio eius [Anselmi] valeat dicetur in sequenti quaestione, argumento sexto, de infinitate probanda." *Ord.* I, d. 2, pt. 1, q. 2; Vatican ed., II, 146.

V. DESCARTES, LEIBNIZ, AND KANT

The name of René Descartes is so closely associated with the ontological argument that in some cases his version of it has been given preference over its original formulation by St. Anselm. A conspicuous example of this is Kant, who, as we shall see, ignores completely the *Proslogion* and attributes the argument to Descartes, even though he presents it in a form more similar to that of Leibniz. It is to these three representatives of modern philosophy that we direct our attention for their view of the argument.

Descartes discusses the ontological argument in his *Discourse on Method*, the *Meditations on First Philosophy*, and *The Principles of Philosophy*, as well as in his *Replies* to the objections to his works raised by some contemporary philosophers and theologians. Suprisingly enough, throughout the discussion Descartes never mentions the name of Anselm and there is some evidence to the effect that he was not even acquainted with the *Proslogion* at the time he wrote. In his answer to Père Mersenne, who had pointed out the affinity of his argument with the one presented by Anselm, Descartes says simply that he will read Anselm at the first opportunity.[78] Since this letter was written in December 1640, that is, long after he had finished writing his *Discourse* and his *Meditations*, the question has been asked by historians of philosophy as to the immediate source of his argument. In Gilson's view, Descartes knew the argument only through the criticism of Thomas Aquinas whom he had studied at the Jesuit college of La Flèche. The fact that he shares Aquinas' criticism against his supposed objector concerning the non-self-evidence of the proposition *God exists* and the impossibility of arguing to God merely from his verbal definition—two propositions Anselm himself would have readily accepted—seems to support the view that Descartes had not read Anselm's *Proslogion*, or if he had, he completely ignored it.[79]

---

[78]Cf. *Oeuvres philosophiques de Descartes,* ed. Ferdinand Alquié, II (Paris: Garnier, 1967), 290: "Je verrai saint Anselme à la première occasion."

[79]For the relationship between Descartes and Anselm see Etienne Gilson, *Études sur le rôle de la pensée médiévale dans la formation du système cartésien* (Paris: Vrin, 1930), chap. IV, "Descartes et Saint Anselme," pp. 215-23. Gilson admits that some authors, among whom he mentions Alexandre Koyré, defend the thesis that Descartes had read Anselm's *Proslogion* before writing his own *Meditations*. If this view is correct, Gilson remarks, then it becomes more difficult to explain Descartes' misunderstandings about Anselm's thought. *Ibid.*, p. 222, n. 1. Descartes' apparent disregard for the contributions of the past has been pointed out by Leibniz, who mentions the ontological argument specifically: "Argumentum pro existentia Dei ab ipsa eius notione sumtum, primus quantum constat, invenit proposuitque Anselmus Cantuariensis Archiepiscopus in libro contra insipientem qui extat. Et passim examinatur a Scholasticae Theologiae scriptoribus, ipsoque Aquinate, unde videtur hausisse Cartesius, eius studii non expers, *postquam apud Jesuitas Flexiae literas hausit.*" (This last sentence is an additional note by Leibniz himself). Cf. *Die philosophischen Schriften von*

Be that as it may, there seems to be little doubt that in his formulation of the argument Descartes depends on Anselm, whether directly or indirectly. The substance of his reasoning as it appears in his *Fifth Meditation* where the argument is most fully developed, will now be summarized.

Everything of which I have a clear and distinct idea is true, and whatever is true is real, for I cannot have the idea of a pure negation. This is most certain in the realm of mathematics which deals with shapes and numbers. For instance, I have the idea of a triangle, and by analyzing its nature I see clearly that its three angles are equal to two right angles. This is true even if no triangle had ever been anywhere in the world except as a figure in my imagination or a thought in my mind. The idea of triangle and whatever belongs to it is therefore the idea of something and not of nothing. Nor can it be said that it is merely a product of my mind, for a triangle is and remains what it is whether I think of it or not.

Now, just as I have the idea of a triangle, so I have also in my mind a clear and distinct idea of God as a supremely perfect being in which [actual] existence is seen to belong to its nature not otherwise than it belongs to the nature of a triangle to be equal to two right angles. Hence the existence of God is no less certain to me than any truth in the mathematical order.[80] "It is at least as certain that God, who is a being so perfect, is, or exists, as any demonstration of geometry can possibly be."[81]

Descartes acknowledges that this truth is not immediately evident, so that it is possible for us to think of God as non-existent. However, he insists that on closer study it becomes manifest that it is no more possible to separate existence from essence in God than it is to deny the equality of three angles to two right angles in a triangle. Therefore, since existence is a perfection and the idea of God is the idea of a most perfect being, to think of God as nonexistent is just as impossible as to think of a mountain without a valley.[82]

In anticipation of the objection that although I cannot think of God as nonexistent, any more than I can think of a mountain without a valley, still it does not follow that either God or a mountain exists in actual reality, Descartes—in the same fashion as Anselm before him in regard to the analogy of the perfect island—answers that the objection rests on a fallacy. Because I cannot think of a mountain without valley it does not indeed follow that either mountain or valley exists, since existence is not

---

Gottfried Wilhelm Leibniz, ed. C. J. Gerhardt (7 vols.; Hildesheim: Olms, 1960-1961), IV, 358.

[80]Cf. *Meditations on the First Philosophy,* in *The Philosophical Works of Descartes,* ed. E. S. Haldane and G. R. T. Ross, I (New York: Dover Publications, 1955), 180-81.

[81]*Discourse on Method, ibid.,* p. 104. See also Proposition I in *Arguments Demonstrating the Existence of God, ibid.,* II, 57.

[82]*Meditations, ibid.,* I, 181.

part of their concepts. On the contrary, in the case of God existence is included in the very concept of him in such a way that it becomes impossible for me to think of him as nonexistent. It is not a necessity brought about by my thought, but rather a necessity imposed on me by the object of my thought, that is, the necessity of God's existence.[83]

As for the other objection, which was to be raised later by Kant, that his reasoning rests on the presupposition that God possesses all perfections and that existence is itself one of these perfections, Descartes insists that there is no presupposition involved in his argument. Indeed, one does not have to think of God at all, but as soon as he conceives the idea of a supremely perfect being, he cannot but include in it all perfections, one of which is of course the perfection of existence.[84]

It would be interesting at this point to analyze, in addition to Descartes' own anticipation of these objections, all the other objections marshaled by philosophers and theologians against the argument and forwarded to him after the manuscript of the *Meditations* had been circulated among them by Père Mersenne: objections that were later published by Descartes along with his own reply. However, such an analysis, useful as it might be, would carry us beyond the limits of this survey. We shall instead confine ourselves to certain points that emerged from the discussion and may serve to throw further light on Descartes' understanding of the argument.

Thus, in his answer to Caterus, Descartes stresses the distinction between possible and necessary existence and affirms that possible existence is contained in the idea of everything that is clearly and distinctly conceived, but not so necessary existence, which is peculiar to the idea of God.[85]

Likewise, in reply to an unidentified group of philosophers and theologians who took exception to his conclusion that God's existence can be inferred from the clear and distinct idea we have of his nature and suggested that the only conclusion to be derived from that idea is that existence belongs to the divine nature but not that such a nature exists unless we otherwise know that to be a fact, Descartes says that they have completely misunderstood his argument. If their suggestion were followed, the major premise should then be worded like this: "That which we clearly understand to belong to the nature of anything, can truthfully be asserted to belong to its nature," which is a pure tautology. Instead of this, Descartes insists that the major premise of his argument is: "That which we clearly understand to belong to the nature of anything can truly

---

[83]*Ibid.*, pp. 181–82.
[84]*Ibid.*, p. 182.
[85]Cf. *A Reply by the Author to the First Set of Objections, ibid.*, II, 20.

be affirmed of that thing," and not merely of that nature. Hence he feels justified in clinging to the original conclusion of his argument that the existence of God can be truly affirmed from the clear and distinct idea we have of him. Even if our idea of God is not adequate, as the same group of objectors hold, it is nevertheless sufficiently clear, Descartes retorts, to give us assurance that God's nature is possible, or not contradictory, and that necessary existence belongs to him.[86]

In the same vein, Descartes rebuts Gassendi's objection that existence is neither a property nor a perfection of an essence, not even in the case of God. Descartes argues that if by property is meant an attribute or perfection that can be predicated of a thing, then necessary existence in God is a true property in the strict sense of the term and that as such it belongs to him exclusively, just as omnipotence and other divine attributes do.[87] Then, somewhat annoyed by Gassendi's remark that his argument does not prove anything, since it assumes what has to be proved, namely, that existence is a perfection included in the idea of a supreme being, Descartes concludes: "I pass over the rest, because, though saying that I explain nothing, you yourself explain nothing and prove nothing, save only that you are able to prove nothing."[88]

If we compare the Cartesian formulation of the ontological argument with that of Anselm, the striking similarity between the two is evident. Although the starting point is somewhat different, in the sense that for Anselm it is the idea of a supremely conceivable being, whereas for Descartes it is the idea of a supremely perfect being, nevertheless in each case it is an idea that is forced upon our mind by the very nature of the being under consideration, and not merely a product of our mind. It is a unique kind of idea, for it represents a unique kind of being, i.e., a being that admits of no comparison with any other being, whether existent, possible, or fictitious. The conclusion of both arguments is likewise the same, namely, the existence of God. Again, in both instances the means of reaching this conclusion is the analysis of the value-content of the idea.

Yet, despite the similarity in the general structure of the arguments, there are important differences at the basis of the two formulations which make them quite distinct from one another. Anselm, the theologian, presupposes that we already believe in God, and his argument is but an attempt rationally to justify such a belief. Descartes, the mathematician, by accepting the principle of clear and distinct ideas as a criterion of truth, tries to prove the existence of God from the analysis of the idea of a supremely perfect being which, in accord with his innatism, is clearly and

---

[86]Cf. *Reply to the Second Set of Objections, ibid.,* pp. 45–47.
[87]Cf. *The Author's Reply to the Fifth Set of Objections, ibid.,* p. 228.
[88]*Ibid.,* p. 229.

distinctly present to our mind even prior to any contact with outside reality. It is precisely because of his innatism and his proposed criterion of truth based upon it that, despite certain strong points, Descartes' version of the ontological argument becomes more vulnerable to the attacks of the critics than Anselm's original statement of it.

Another chief proponent of the ontological argument in modern times is Gottfried Wilhelm Leibniz, whose system is in many respects compatible with the way of thinking developed by both Anselm and Descartes, especially the latter. A respected mathematician like Descartes, Leibniz attempts to construct a system of philosophy on a purely rational basis and by the use of a rigorous mathematical method. He admits the theory of innate ideas and innate truths, among which he includes the idea of God and the truth of his existence;[89] he teaches that existence is a perfection and a predicate;[90] and he shares the view that ideas have an ontological value of their own. Despite these similarities and his favorable attitude toward the Cartesian form of the ontological argument—he never directly mentions the *ratio Anselmi*—Leibniz takes issue with Descartes' reasoning and terms it an imperfect demonstration of God's existence. The reason is that the argument assumes as true something that is not mathematically evident, namely, that the idea of a supremely perfect being implies no contradiction and is therefore the idea of a possible being. Until this assumption is justified, the argument—which is not a paralogism, as some scholastics, including Thomas Aquinas, maintained—is not convincing.[91] The most that can be drawn out of the argument is that if God is possible, it follows that he exists.[92]

Elaborating further on this point, Leibniz remarks that it is not uncommon to fall into error by drawing conclusions from ideas whose truth has not been previously established. There are indeed true and false ideas, depending on whether or not the thing in question is possible. Thus we are

[89]Cf. *New Essays on the Human Understanding*, in *Leibniz: Selections*, ed. P. Wiener (New York: Charles Scribner's Sons, 1951), p. 471.

[90]For Leibniz' teaching on existence as a perfection cf. Gerhardt, *Die philosophischen Schriften von G. W. Leibniz*, IV, 401–402, or *On the Cartesian Demonstration of the Existence of God*, in *The Philosophical Works of Leibniz*, trans. George M. Duncan (New York: Tuttle, Morehouse and Taylor, 1890), p. 135. Leibniz speaks of existence as a predicate in *New Essays*, Bk. IV, chap. I, par. 7. See *Selections*, p. 461.

[91]*New Essays*, in *Selections*, p. 472. As pointed out in connection with his reply to the second set of *Objections*, Descartes had actually tried to show that God is possible because the idea that we have of him implies no contradiction (cf. text referred to in n. 86 above). However, this reflection is somewhat incidental and is not found in Descartes' original presentation of the argument to which Leibniz refers.

[92]See *Meditations on Knowledge, Truth and Ideas*, in *Gottfried Wilhelm Leibniz: Philosophical Papers and Letters*, trans. Leroy M. Loemker, I (Chicago, Ill.: University of Chicago Press, 1956), 451.

likely to speak in terms of the fastest possible motion or the highest possible number, and at first glance we seem to have a fairly good idea of what we are talking about. But on closer study we realize that there can be no such thing as a fastest motion or a highest number, simply because their notions involve an absurdity. In fact, one can always think without contradiction of a faster motion or a higher number than the preceding ones, since motion and number are of their very nature limited quantities.

Applying this line of reasoning to the argument for the existence of God based on the idea of a most perfect being, Leibniz says that, to make it a valid and cogent proof, one must first show that the idea in question is a true idea or such that it involves no contradiction.[93] Leibniz proposes a way to show this.

A most perfect being is that which possesses all perfections, i.e., those simple qualities which are positive and absolute inasmuch as they express what they do without any limitation whatsoever. Now, there is nothing in the nature of such qualities that would make them incompatible with one another, since they are simple realities that cannot be resolved into, or defined by, any other reality short of losing their characteristic of absolute simplicity. On the other hand, there is no evidence that such perfections are not compatible with one another. Hence a being that embodies all such perfections is possible because it is conceivable, and if it is possible, it must exist, since existence is supposedly one of its perfections.[94]

The same argument is presented in a slightly different way in the *Monadology*. Whatever reality there is in essences, whether they are actual or only possible, must be grounded in an actually existing being. This being must be necessary, that is, one in which essence includes existence, or else it could not be the source of all other essences and possibilities. Hence this being, which we call God, has the unique prerogative that it must exist if it is possible. And since nothing can hinder the possibility of that which is the source of all possibilities and is therefore infinitely perfect, the existence of God is thus established a priori.[95]

Leibniz' arguments can perhaps be reduced to the following syllogism. It is possible for a necessary being to exist, for its notion implies no contradiction. But if a necessary being is possible, it must exist, for existence is part of its nature. Therefore a necessary being, i.e., God, exists.

This, then, is Leibniz' version of the ontological argument, and he pre-

---

[93]*Ibid.* See also *Discourse on Metaphysics,* in *Selections,* p. 324.

[94]The substance of this argument is contained in a paper entitled "Quod Ens perfectissimum existit," which Leibniz showed to Spinoza at the Hague in November, 1676. See Gerhardt, *op. cit.,* VII, 261-62. See also *New Essays Concerning Human Understanding by Gottfried Wilhelm Leibniz,* trans. Alfred G. Langley (3d ed.; Chicago, Ill.: The Open Court Publishing Company, 1949), Appendix X, pp. 714-15.

[95]Cf. *Monadology,* nos. 44-45, in *Selections,* pp. 541-42.

sents it both as an improvement upon the Cartesian proof and as an original contribution to the solution of the problem at hand. Was he justified in his claims? As for his first contention, Koyré seems to disagree on the grounds that by reducing the argument to the analytic proposition "The necessary being exists," Leibniz deprives the Cartesian proof of its ontological foundation and makes it an easy target for Kant's criticism. "In truth," says Koyré, "it is in its analytic character that lies its weakness. He [Leibniz] failed to see that the idea of perfection constituted a necessary foundation of the argument and that by eliminating it he deprived the demonstration of all its strength."[96] On the other hand, Hartshorne praises Leibniz for his attempt "to establish the logical possibility of the theistic concept," but observes at the same time that his failure to distinguish between existence and necessary existence as a perfection of an essence "betrays the persistent influence of Anselm's initial blunder."[97] The opponents of the ontological argument in any of its forms would of course blame Leibniz for confusing the logical or ideal order with the order of reality and for equating negative possibility, i.e., mere absence of evident contradiction, with positive possibility, which in the case of God can be known only through a clear and distinct idea of the divine essence or as a result of arguments a posteriori. Clearly, then, the value of Leibniz' version of the ontological argument, not otherwise than that of Descartes' version, rests on whatever strength and validity their rationalistic tendencies may have, as we have previously indicated.

With regard to Leibniz' second contention, namely, that his version of the argument represents an original contribution to the understanding of the issue at hand, it is clear that historical evidence is against it, although Leibniz may not have known this. Duns Scotus, as shown in our preceding section, had long before preceded Leibniz in pointing out the need to strengthen the Anselmian proof by showing, first, the noncontradiction, and hence the possibility, of a being than which no greater can be conceived, and secondly, the necessity for such a being to exist. Moreover, because Scotus had a more realistic approach to philosophy, he was able to prove these two points much more effectively than Leibniz did. The difference between the Leibnizian and the Scotistic versions of the argument is due mainly to the different philosophical background of their authors, but with an added qualification. Whereas Leibniz thought of his allegedly newly revised argument as a strict demonstration of God's existence, Scotus was much more cautious and said that his "coloration" of the argument made it more acceptable but refrained from labeling it a strict philosophical demonstration. It is regrettable that while historians of

[96] *L'idée de Dieu dans la philosophie de St. Anselme,* p. 232.
[97] *Anselm's Discovery,* p. 178.

philosophy, today even more than in the past, devote considerable study to Leibniz' rendition of the argument, they give only a passing reference to Scotus' interpretation of the *ratio Anselmi*, which is not only original but also more objective and better balanced.

Any treatment of the *ratio Anselmi* must include the name and doctrine of Immanuel Kant, who is responsible for the coining and popularization of the term ontological argument[98] and who, more than anybody else, has influenced the course of the entire philosophical movement after him. Kant has set a pattern for most of the criticism of the argument in modern and contemporary times, even though few of the argument's opponents would be willing to subscribe to the fundamental positions of the *Critique of Pure Reason* which have determined its author's rejection of the argument. It is necessary, therefore, to place Kant's criticism within its literary and historical context in order to get a full understanding of his position on what appeared to be then, perhaps even more than now, a very controversial issue.

Kant discusses the ontological argument in Chapter III, Section IV of his Transcendental Dialectic. The chapter carries the title: "Of the Impossibility of an Ontological Proof of the Existence of God." In the course of his discussion he never mentions Anselm's name or his *Proslogion,* and only toward the end of it does he speak of "the famous ontological argument of Descartes" after a somewhat casual reference to "the celebrated Leibniz." The study of the text of the *Critique* and its immediate sources seems to indicate that Kant did not know that Anselm was the true author of the argument, which he attributes to Descartes but presents in the form given to it by Leibniz. Actually, Kant does not even present Leibniz' own version of the argument but only its reformulation by Christian Wolff as found in Baumgarten's *Metaphysica* and Eberhard's *Vorbereitung zur natürlichen Theologie*, a teacher's manual.[99] Needless to say, Gaunilo seems to have been completely unknown to Kant, despite the fact that Gaunilo had anticipated by many centuries most of the objections made by Kant and others against the Anselmian proof. One ought not to be surprised, however, at this obvious disregard for basic rules of scholarship in a man who, even more than Descartes, attempted to revolutionize the whole course of philosophy by setting it on a new foundation and giving it an entirely new direction. His ambitious work, *Prolegomena to Any Future Metaphysics*, is an anticipation of the revolutionary plan

[98]Cf. Dieter Henrich, *Der Ontologische Gottesbeweis* (Tübingen: Mohr, 1960), p. 1, n. 1.

[99]Cf. Koyré, *op. cit.,* p. 231; James Collins, *The Emergence of Philosophy of Religion* (New Haven: Yale University Press, 1967), p. 102. n. 10.

that culminated in his three *Critiques*. It is within this plan that his criticism of the ontological argument must be studied and evaluated.

Kant states categorically that there are and there can be only three ways by which speculative reason can prove the existence of God. Two of these ways take their start from sensible experience and are called the physico-theological and cosmological arguments, while the third way proceeds from mere mental concepts and is therefore entirely a priori. This he calls the ontological argument, that is, an attempt to prove the existence of God from the concept we have of a most perfect or most real being (*ens perfectissimum* or *ens realissimum*), or simply from the idea of a necessary being.

Kant recognizes that men at all times have tried to prove the existence of an absolutely necessary being, but he claims that they have seldom made an effort to understand whether or not that idea makes any sense at all. He does not question the possibility of a verbal definition of the concept but rather raises doubts as to the content or reality underlying that concept. He maintains that the stereotyped examples taken from geometry, such as the absolute necessity that a triangle have three angles, are deceitful, for such necessity refers to judgments alone. It is a purely logical necessity which has no bearing on the reality of things, let alone on their existence.

In propositions of this kind, which Kant calls identical propositions, it is of course contradictory to reject the predicate while retaining the subject, because the predicate necessarily belongs to the subject. Thus it is contradictory to accept a triangle and reject its three angles; but there is no contradiction in rejecting both the triangle and its three angles. The same principle holds true, Kant argues, for the concept of an absolutely necessary being. One can simply dismiss its notion altogether by removing the existence of that being along with all its predicates, and if this is done no question of contradiction will ever arise.

At this point Kant realizes that his opponents, such as Descartes and Leibniz—and to them we must add Anselm—would not be impressed by this line of reasoning and that at best it would appear naive to them. Indeed, the concept of a necessary being, or of a most real being for that matter, is precisely such that one cannot remove the existence of its object without contradicting himself. The analogy of the triangle, they would suggest, is besides the point, for existence is not of the nature of a triangle. In the case of a necessary being, however, existence is so much part of its nature that one cannot, not even mentally, separate the one from the other.

Kant's answer to this objection is in accord with his preconceived theory that every proposition involving existence is synthetic, i.e., it must be based on experience, and this in the case at hand is completely lacking. To attempt to derive existence from a mere concept, be it the concept of a necessary being, is to state a mere tautology. This holds true, Kant remarks, even in the case of a possible being, which becomes an empty concept unless it rests on principles of possible experience. Briefly, it is wrong to argue directly from the logical possibility of concepts to the real existence of things.

This last observation leads Kant to discuss the distinction between logical predicate and real predicate. A logical predicate is one that abstracts from the content of the concept, for logic has no bearing on the reality of things. A real predicate, on the other hand, is one that determines a thing by adding something to its concept. Now being or existence, Kant continues, is not a real predicate, for it adds nothing that is not already contained in the concept of the subject. It is merely the positing of a thing, or of certain determinations, as existing in themselves.[100] Thus, when I say "God is," or "There is a God," I only posit the subject (God) with all its predicates, such as omnipotence and omniscience, as an object in relation to my concept. On this score, any distinction between the real and the possible disappears, since both are on the same conceptual level. "A hundred real dollars"—Kant uses the term *thalers* —"do not contain a penny more than a hundred possible dollars."

Needless to say, Kant observes, my financial position is affected quite differently by a hundred real dollars than it is by the same amount of merely possible dollars, but this is due to the fact that in the former case the object has been added to my concept synthetically. This, Kant suggests, is possible when the object in question can be known experimentally; but in the case of the supreme being no such knowledge is possible. Our only way of thinking of its existence is through a purely a priori form or category of the understanding which does not allow us to distinguish between actual and possible existence.

Hence, Kant concludes, even though the concept of a supreme being is in many respects a very useful concept, it in no way helps us to attain to the knowledge of God's existence, or even the possibility of his existence. "The attempt to establish the existence of a supreme being by means of the famous ontological argument of Descartes is therefore merely so much labor and effort lost.[101]

---

[100]For a detailed analysis of Kant's notion of logical and real prediates and their application to the problem under discussion see S. Morris Engel, "Kant's Refutation of the Ontological Argument," in *Kant: A Collection of Critical Essays*, ed. Robert P. Wolff (Garden City, N.Y.: Doubleday "Anchor Books," 1967), pp. 189–208.

[101]Cf. *Immanuel Kant's Critique of Pure Reason*, trans. Norman K. Smith (reprint; London: Macmillan, 1933), p. 507. For Kant's discussion of the ontological argument as presented in this study see *ibid.*, pp. 499–507.

At first glance this appears to be a devastating analysis of the ontological argument: an analysis that has far-reaching consequences, inasmuch as it is to this form of argument that Kant will ultimately reduce what he believes to be the only two other possible proofs of God's existence, namely, the cosmological and the physico-theological arguments.[102] As we go through Kant's systematic and unrelenting demolition of all the structures on which the argument has been so carefully built by its authors, we may get the impression that the argument would never be able to survive the severe blow administered to it by the author of the *Critique*. But history has proved that this is not true. In the words of a recent author, "the [ontological] argument is like an eel: now you think that you have it in a conclusive form, and it slips away: now you think that you have killed it, and lo it lives again. The eel has wriggled for centuries, and will go on wriggling, for all the handling of Descartes and Leibniz, Kant, and you and me."[103]

Despite Kant's vigorous attacks, the argument is as alive today as it was at his time. The growing literature on the subject is sufficient evidence of this. However, this fact does not dispense us from taking a closer look at Kant's criticism in order to see whether he really accomplished what he hoped to do.

Simply stated, Kant's position is that it is impossible to infer God's existence merely from the concept we have of him as of a most perfect or necessary being, because existence is not a perfection or predicate contained in that concept. Taken at its face value, Kant's reasoning is not much different from that of Gaunilo or Aquinas, and even his analogy of the hundred dollars is very similar to, although less pertinent than, Gaunilo's celebrated example of the most beautiful island. But if we analyze Kant's criticism carefully, we will see that it is much more destructive than it may first appear to be. At the root of the whole problem is Kant's epistemological theory that makes it impossible for speculative reason to attain to any knowledge that is not confined to sensible appearances of the objects of our experience. On this assumption it is pointless to speak of a proof for the existence of God, who by his very nature transcends all sense experience, whether such a proof be based on the concept we have of him or be grounded in the reality of the material world, for even this reality cannot be reached by our reason. There is no way, in

---

[102] *Ibid.*, p. 524: "Thus the physico-theological proof of the existence of an original or supreme being rests upon the cosmological proof, and the cosmological upon the ontological."

[103] Joseph Rickaby, S.J., *Studies on God and His Creatures* (London and New York: Longmans, Green and Co., 1924), pp. 63–64.

Kant's system, to attain to the knowledge of things in themselves or noumena; all we know is their appearances or phenomena.

Kant, it must be admitted, does not completely eliminate existence from his critical philosophy, but he reduces it to one of those a priori forms of the understanding—the power of thinking or judging as distinct from both pure and practical reason—by means of which the data of our sensible experience are synthesized. Consequently, for him existence is no longer a mode of an essence, as it is for rationalists such as Leibniz and Wolff, but a modality of judgment expressing the relationship of the object of sense intuition, the phenomenon, to our cognitive faculty. "The categories of modality," Kant writes in this connection, "have the peculiarity that, in determining an object, they do not in the least enlarge the concept to which they are attached as predicates. They only express the relation of the concept to the faculty of knowledge."[104]

As can be seen, Kant's attack on the ontological argument is part of a major systematic attack on the whole of natural theology and metaphysics, precisely as he had planned in his *Prolegomena to Any Future Metaphysics*. In its introduction he writes: "My purpose is to persuade all those who think metaphysics worth studying that it is absolutely necessary to pause for a moment and, regarding all that has been done as though undone, to propose first the preliminary question, 'Whether such a thing as metaphysics be even possible at all.' "[105] His answer, as we know, is a categorical "No." It is true that the metaphysics he had in mind is primarily the metaphysics of Leibniz and Wolff, which is concerned with essences and the possibles rather than with actually existing things; but there is no doubt that in his mind even traditional metaphysics had lost all right to existence. It is in this broader context that Kant's attack on the ontological argument must be seen. Yet, despite Kant's negative attitude toward the ontological argument and metaphysics, it remains to his credit that he admitted in his precritical period the value of the theistic proof based on the possibles[106] and acknowledged in his *Critique of Pure Reason* the value of the idea of God, whose existence, together with freedom of the

[104]Cf. *Critique of Pure Reason*, p. 239.

[105]Immanuel Kant, *Prolegomena to Any Future Metaphysics*, ed. Lewis White Beck (Indianapolis and New York: Bobbs-Merrill, 1950), p. 3.

[106]Cf. *Der einzig mögliche Beweisgrund zu einer Demonstration des Daseins Gottes*, in *Immanuel Kant: Werke in sechs Bänden*, ed. Wilhelm Weischedel, I (Wiesbaden: Insel, 1960), 617–738. Hartshorne writes in this connection: "In spite of his negative attitude toward theoretical theism, Kant, in the essay *Der einzig mögliche Beweisgrund des Daseins Gottes*, makes a contribution to theism which should never again be lost and which is not invalidated by anything he himself later said." *Anselm's Discovery*, p. 211. It must be said, however, that Leibniz had already anticipated Kant's reasoning in his *Monadology* (see text referred to in n. 95 above). For a discussion of the theistic argument from the possibles see the preceding chapter of this book.

will and immortality of the soul, became for him postulates of practical reason.

VI. KOYRÉ, BARTH, AND GILSON

While Kant has set a pattern of criticism of the ontological argument that has been adopted in various degrees by many subsequent thinkers both within and outside the Kantian tradition, there have been philosophers who accepted the argument and adapted it to their own particular system, such as G. W. F. Hegel[107] and Maurice Blondel.[108] A study of these variations of the argument would carry us too far, and besides it would contribute little, if anything, to the understanding of the issues connected with the original Anselmian proof. We therefore pass them by and take up certain more recent interpretations of the argument with a view to broadening our perspective of it.

A penetrating analysis of Anselm's proof within the general context and historical background of his entire philosophical and theological thought has been made by Alexandre Koyré, whose work, *L'idée de Dieu dans la philosophie de St. Anselme*, has been widely acclaimed by the experts. Convinced that the argument of the *Proslogion* "which alone would have assured the immortality of its author" is but the conclusion and crowning of Anselm's entire theodicy,[109] Koyré discusses it only in the last two chapters of his volume, while in Appendix I he examines the psychological interpretation of the argument given by Dom Beda Adloch[110] and in Appendix II he makes a comparative study of Kant's criticism and Gaunilo's objections to the argument.[111]

In Koyré's view the *Proslogion* is an apologetic work concerned chiefly with the existence of God, which Anselm attempts to prove indirectly by showing against the fool of the Psalmist the logical impossibility of denying it. The basis of the demonstration is the neo-Platonic principle of per-

---

[107]For Hegel's formulation of the ontological argument see *Beweise für das Dasein Gottes,* Appendix to his *Vorlesungen über die Philosophie der Religion,* ed. Philipp Marheineke, II (Berlin: Duncker und Humblot, 1832), 466–83, trans. by E. B. Spiers and J. B. Sanderson as *Lectures on the Philosophy of Religion by Georg Wilhelm Friedrich Hegel,* III (reprint; New York: The Humanities Press, 1968), 347–67. See also Hegel's *Vorlesungen über die Geschichte der Philosophie,* ed. Karl L. Michelet, III (Berlin: Duncker und Humblot, 1836), 164–69, trans. by E. S. Haldane and F. H. Simson as *Hegel's Lectures on the History of Philosophy* (reprint; New York: The Humanities Press, 1968), 61–67.

[108]Cf. *L'action* (reprint of 1893 edition; Paris: Presses Universitaires de France, 1950), p. 348. See also James M. Somerville, *Total Commitment: Blondel's L'action* (Washington, D.C.: Corpus Books, 1968), pp. 221–23. For a study of Blondel's original way of arguing to God see chapter VI of this volume.

[109]Koyré, *L'idée de Dieu.* p. vii.

[110]*Ibid.,* pp. 228–30.

[111]*Ibid.,* pp. 231–40.

fection, which makes it possible to assert a priori a real existence and to argue from perfection to being. Although it is a demonstration a priori, it is not an ontological proof in the strict sense of the term. Moreover, contrary to what is held by many commentators, there is no textual evidence to the effect that Anselm identified being and perfection. What he says is that a being endowed with perfection and existence is more perfect than a being with the same nature but without existence. This does not imply in any way that existence itself is a perfection.[112]

By combining the principles of perfection and contradiction, Anselm endeavors to prove not only the metaphysical impossibility of the nonexistence of God but also, and even more so, the logical impossibility of conceiving his nonexistence. It is precisely by showing the impossibility of denying the existence of God that he argues to its affirmation. This, contends Koyré, is the characteristic of Anselm's proof that distinguishes it from the Cartesian proof based on clear and distinct ideas of the divine nature.[113] Furthermore, Anselm's proof is autonomous, in the sense that it presupposes neither the existence of creatures nor any concept derived from them. Its only basis is the concept of God.[114]

If the proof does not convince the fool, and if it is unable to convert an unbeliever, to do so is not the purpose of its author. His purpose is to show to a believer that no argument can ever undermine his belief in God simply because no argument affects or even touches upon the content of his faith.[115]

Koyré believes, as do many other commentators, that Anselm's debate with Gaunilo is not only extremely enlightening, but that it contains the answer to most of the objections raised against the argument since Gaunilo's time. Anselm's demonstration, as evidenced by his *Reply* to Gaunilo, can be synthesized in the formula: if God is possible, he exists necessarily. The inference from possibility (*posse*) to existence (*esse*) is made through the impossibility of conceiving the nonexistence of the being in question (*non posse concipi non esse*), from which follows the necessity of conceiving it as existing (*necesse concipi esse*), or, if one prefers, the necessity of existence can be inferred directly from the impossibility of not existing *(non posse non esse ergo necesse esse).*[116] We can therefore distinguish two different parts or moments in the Anselmian argument: the hypothetical part, which is the a priori element of the proof, and

---

[112]*Ibid.*, pp. 195–99.

[113]*Ibid.*, pp. 200–201 and n. 1.

[114]*Ibid.*, p. 202.

[115]*Ibid.*, pp. 204–205.

[116]Koyré bases his formula on Anselm's *Liber apologeticus*, chap. I; PL 158, col. 249; "Certe ego dico: si vel cogitari potest esse, necesse est illud esse. . . . Si ergo potest cogitari esse, ex necessitate est. Amplius. Si utique vel cogitari potest, necesse est illud esse."

the synthetic part—Koyré calls it *thétique*—which is a factual truth. The first part of the argument contains an absolutely necessary truth, namely, that if God is possible, he must exist. But this truth does not involve in any way the actual existence in God. It merely affirms the necessary relationship between possibility and necessity of existence in God: a unique and extremely interesting relationship whose discovery and formulation are a perennial credit to Anselm. Yet the actual transition from possibility to existence in God can be made only in terms of another premise that turns conceptual possibility into real, factual possibility. In other words, it is necessary to prove first that God is possible, unless of course one is willing to accept such possibility without the benefit of a proof.

As far as a believer is concerned, Anselm would say that the assurance of the possibility of God is given to him by faith. Hence for him the synthetic part of the argument needs no proof: all he needs is the hypothetical part. It is only for the fool or the unbeliever that the two parts of the argument are needed. The fool will no doubt be able to understand the absurdity of denying God, but there is no way to prove to him the possibility of God. All one can do is to reduce him to silence, and that is precisely what Anselm intended to do. However, Koyré suggests, if we consider the *Monologium,* where the possibility of God is solidly established, as a preparation for or an introduction to the *Proslogion,* then we have in the two works a complete demonstration a priori of the existence of God.[117]

On the strength of this analysis, it is only to be expected that Koyré will consider the *ratio Anselmi* a much better argument than the one transmitted to us by Descartes and Leibniz, especially the latter. It will also be easy for him to refute both Gaunilo's objections to the argument, to which he devotes the entire Chapter X of his work,[118] and the criticism of Kant, whom he blames "for demanding something that is absolutely impossible and has no sense whatsoever."[119] This is a severe judgment to pass on so towering a figure as Kant, but no more severe than the judgment Kant passed on the ontological argument when he termed it a waste of labor and effort. Such remarks are obviously due to radically opposed ideologies and call for no further comment at this time. Instead we shall proceed in our survey and consider another prominent and much better known figure, whose interpretation of the Anselmian proof has stirred a great deal of discussion and controversy.

Like Koyré, whom he frequently quotes, Karl Barth has made Anselm's argument the object of extensive study. Approaching the subject

---

[117]Koyre, *ibid.,* pp. 209–211.
[118]*Ibid.,* pp. 212–25.
[119]*Ibid.,* p. 234.

from the viewpoint of a theologian and within the context of Anselm's theological scheme, he prefaces his book, *Anselm: Fides quaerens intellectum*, with the observation that Anselm's proof of the existence of God is "a model piece of good, penetrating and neat theology...that has quite a bit to say to present-day theology, both Protestant and Roman Catholic."[120] Barth does not consider the Anselmian *argumentum* as being limited to the proof of Chapters 2-4 of the *Proslogion*, but rather as a kind of *argumentatio* that extends throughout the entire work, even though the largest part of it is devoted to the study of the nature of God. However, for the purpose of his inquiry he confines himself to an analysis of the proof as set forth in *Proslogion* 2-4.

Beginning with the concept of proof, Barth claims that in Anselm the term has not precisely the meaning of *probare* but rather the more general connotation of *intelligere*: it is an *intelligere* that issues in a *probare*. Hence *to prove* means that "the validity of certain propositions advocated by Anselm is established over against those who doubt or deny them; that is to say, it means the polemical-apologetic result of *intelligere*."[121] Besides, the only *intelligere* that concerns Anselm is that which is aroused by faith. This, he says, is the meaning of the Anselmian *Credo ut intelligam*, I believe in order to understand.[122]

Barth's initial position on the notion of the Anselmian proof affects his treatment of the *Proslogion* by limiting its scope and depriving it of that particular probative feature that, rightly or wrongly, has fascinated philosophers of different persuasions. In Barth's view only theologians will profit from Anselm's proof which, having been reduced chiefly to *intelligere*, "can consist only of positive meditation on the object of faith" but "cannot establish this object of faith as such."[123] Barth feels however that although Anselm's proof—if we can still speak of proof—is directed primarily to a believer, it remains the same even from the viewpoint of an unbeliever, for "the unbeliever's quest [for knowledge of God] is not simply taken up in a casual fashion and incorporated into the theological task but all the way through it is in fact treated as identical with the quest of the believer himself.[124]

Once the nature of the *Proslogion* has been defined in terms of *Faith in Search of Understanding*, which was indeed the original subtitle of the work, Barth goes on to analyze the relationship between *ratio* and *necessi-*

---

[120]Karl Barth, *Anselm: Fides quaerens intellectum* (Cleveland and New York: The World Publishing Co. "Meridian Books," 1962), p. 9.

[121]*Ibid.*, p. 14.

[122]*Ibid.*, pp. 16–18.

[123]*Ibid.*, pp. 39–40.

[124]*Ibid.*, p. 67.

tas in Anselm's approach to faith, with special reference to the problem of our knowledge of God. Here are some of his conclusions: (1) The *necessitas* that is characteristic of the object of faith is the impossibility of this object not to exist or to be otherwise than it is, as well as the impossibility for thought to conceive it as not existing or as existing differently. (2) The *ratio* peculiar to the object of faith is the fact that its existence conforms to law (the hidden law of the object of faith) and that it exists in this particular way, along with the other fact that the knowledge of it is the conception of that conformity and of that particular kind of existence. From these considerations it follows that, with regard to the object of faith, ontic necessity precedes noetic necessity. This means that the rational knowledge of the object of faith is derived from the object of faith and not vice versa. Ultimately, both the object of faith and its knowledge are derived from Truth, i.e., from God and his will.[125]

On these premises Barth approaches the actual "proof" of *Proslogion* 2–4, which he claims to be based on the assumption of a name of God whose meaning implies that the statement "God exists" is necessary. Anselm translates this name in terms of a being than which no greater can be conceived, but this is not a concept of his own; it is a revealed concept, just as the existence of God is a revealed doctrine. What Anselm tries to do is show that the existence of God, which he accepts on faith, must be recognized and proved on the presupposition of the name of God likewise accepted on faith and must be understood "as necessary for thought."[126] Furthermore, he wants to show that the necessity of the existence of God that is forced, as it were, upon our mind, cannot be merely a conceptual necessity, but is such that it belongs to God himself and makes it impossible for us even to think of his nonexistence. This is of course a development of the data of our faith and the particular contribution that Anselm has made to Christian theology.[127]

In his work Barth follows the various steps of the Anselmian proof, which he presents on the strength of the first chapters of the *Proslogion* and integrates with many valuable insights from Anselm's dialogue with Gaunilo. He concludes his analysis by saying that "the whole effort of *Proslogion* 2–3 has been to prove conclusively that God cannot be conceived as not existing. The demonstration that this is impossible is Anselm's proof of the existence of God."[128] Then, summing up his understanding of the proof, he insists once more that "it is a question of theology;...a question of the proof of faith by faith which was already

---

[125]*Ibid.*, pp. 49–52.
[126]*Ibid.*, p. 78.
[127]*Ibid.*, pp. 94–95.
[128]*Ibid.*, p. 165.

established in itself without proof."[129] Hence any interpretation of the Anselmian argument along the lines of Descartes and Leibniz is altogether inaccurate, while Kant's criticism of the proof "is so much nonsense on which no more words ought to be wasted."[130]

As was to be expected, Barth's theological interpretation of the Anselmian proof led a number of scholars to take a new look at the *Proslogion* and see whether his conclusions were warranted by the text. One of these scholars is Etienne Gilson, whose exceptional competence in the field of scholastic philosophy is universally recognized. Gilson had already touched upon the *Proslogion* argument in other writings, but the appearance of Barth's volume induced him to take up the issue anew and give it a fuller consideration. In his article, *Sens et nature de l'argument de Saint Anselme*, [131] which contains the last four lectures of a course on the doctrine of Saint Anselm offered at the Collège de France in 1934, he first presents his own interpretation of the Anselmian proof, then he compares it with the theological and mystical interpretations of Karl Barth and Anselm Stolz respectively, and finally he concludes with a section on the nature of the *Proslogion*. Our concern here is chiefly his reaction to Barth's view of the proof.

Gilson agrees with Barth that the argument of the *Proslogion* presupposes a concept of God from revelation that represents an object or *res* by which the concept is determined. Hence, for Anselm the question of whether it is possible to draw existence from thought is irrelevant, since the starting point of the argument is a real concept and not merely a logical one.[132] Gilson also agrees with Barth's theory that for Anselm a truth of faith is independent of rational speculation, so that a doctrine of faith does not need to be understood to be believed but may nevertheless be an aid to our intelligence to understand it: *credo ut intelligam.* He goes further and grants Barth the fundamental point that for Anselm reason will never be able to create its own truth, as if it were possible to have a double set of truths, one from faith and one from reason. To hold the contrary is directly to contradict Anselm, who admits that thought must submit to, or be determined by, the object. Having made these concessions, Gilson asks himself whether the *Proslogion* argument is merely a piece of theology, as Barth thinks it to be, and his answer is an unequivocal "No." Here are his reasons.

---

[129]*Ibid.*, p. 170.

[130]*Ibid.*, p. 171.

[131]The article appeared in *Archives d'histoire doctrinale et littéraire du Moyen Age*, IX (Paris: Vrin, 1934), 5–51.

[132]*Ibid.*, pp. 6–8.

To begin with, Gilson remarks that Barth seems to have very little use for philosophy, which he considers to be a worldly subject foreign to God and whatever pertains to him. Because this Calvinistic attitude toward philosophy permeates his whole approach to Anselm, Barth is unable to see how it is possible to have a rational argument for the existence of God, such as that of the *Proslogion,* without falling into ontologism. Hence, if it is not an ontological argument, Barth sees no other alternative: it must be purely theological or, in other words, no argument at all, for one does not prove the existence of God which he accepts on faith as an assumption of his proof. All he can do is to show how God's existence is possible, and that is precisely what in Barth's view Anselm would have done.[133]

Yet, Gilson continues, this is not what we read in the *Proslogion,* where Anselm states explicitly his intention of producing an argument which alone could establish that God truly exists (*ad astruendum quia Deus vere est*). Likewise, in his *Reply* to Gaunilo he speaks of the force of his proof: *Tantam enim vim huius probationis in se continet significatio,* an expression that Barth, to Gilson's surprise, has wrongly translated to fit into his own preconceived theory. It is not true, therefore, that Anselm builds his argument on the *name* of God known to us by revelation, for nowhere in Scripture is God called "a being than which no greater can be conceived," which is Anselm's point of departure. If the argument were built on the name of God known by revelation, then it would be the name of a person and the existence of God would be assumed at the very outset of the proof. This is of course what Barth wants us to accept, but textual evidence seems to contradict him. The truth is that Anselm's argument takes as its starting point the *concept* of God as the supreme conceivable being, which is quite different from what Barth says.[134]

This raises the issue as to whether or not, despite the concept of God that Anselm assumes from revelation, it is still possible to speak in terms of a demonstration of God's existence. This is an important issue that has to be solved in order to establish the legitimacy of his claim, especially because there are historians who refuse to see in Anselm's argument any attempt at a real demonstration of the existence of God. To solve this problem, Gilson suggests, one must go once more to Anselm himself and see what was his intention in structuring the argument.

Anselm tells us that as a result of his discourse on God he has shown that the being than which no greater can be conceived exists not only in our mind (*in intellectu*) but also in reality (*in re*). Besides, unless he wanted to deceive us about his intention, he has also made it clear that by proving the rational necessity of affirming the existence of God, or the

[133]*Ibid.,* pp. 22–24.
[134]*Ibid.,* pp. 25–28.

rational impossibility of denying it, he has truly proved God's existence. He must have been convinced therefore, if we are willing to grant him that minimum of logical coherence one can expect from a philosopher, that the necessity for reason to affirm an existence—the existence of God in this case—fully guarantees the fact of that existence. Short of this his whole demonstration becomes useless. This in turn leads us to admit that the necessity of the above affirmation supposes the necessity of its object. Hence, Gilson argues, "unless the argument of the *Proslogion* be devoid of meaning, it must necessarily be inserted within a doctrine of truth to be conceived in such a way that the very existence of truths always presupposes the existence of their objects." And that is precisely the case with the *Proslogion*, a work that presupposes Anselm's previous treatise *De veritate*, where he laid down the epistemological foundation of his entire doctrine, including his doctrine on God.[135]

In this sense Gilson endorses without reservation Barth's view that in Anselm's teaching there can be no question about the creative and normative role of human reason in regard to truth, because it has none. "There will never be a God," he rightly observes, "because our reason has devised proofs for his existence, but there are proofs for the existence of God because there is a God."[136] Where ontic necessity precedes noetic necessity, as Barth well states, truth is caused by its object, which in the case of Anselm's argument is God himself. Summing up Anselm's reasoning, Gilson writes that Anselm starts from the word "God," next proceeds to analyze the meaning of that word, and then, from the analysis of that meaning in terms of "a being than which no greater can be conceived," concludes that God, the being in question, cannot exist merely in our understanding but must also exist in actual reality. And since there is nothing to stand between our thought and God except the meaning of that term, the cause of the truth of the argument's conclusion can only be sought in God himself, the source of all truth.[137]

On the basis of this analysis of the Anselmian proof, which he offers as a corrective to Barth's understanding of it, Gilson concludes that between the two interpretations there stands the whole distance that separates Catholicism from Calvinism. "There is a Catholic way of maintaining that the *Proslogion* is the work of a theologian," and this aims to safeguard the rights of God without jeopardizing the rights of a reason created by God. "There is a Calvinistic way of maintaining the same thing," and it consists in safeguarding the rights of God at the expense of human reason, whose only right, or rather duty, is to repeat the word of God. Gilson feels

---

[135]*Ibid.*, pp. 8–9.
[136]*Ibid.*, pp. 10–11.
[137]*Ibid.*, p. 12.

that Barth has committed the mistake of trying to draw Anselm over to his own side.[138]

If we now look back at these last three interpretations of the Anselmian argument, we can see that, despite their obvious differences, they have many points in common. For one thing, each of them attempts to visualize the argument from the perspective of its author's Platonic-Augustinian thought and present it as a reflection on a concept of God known by revelation, whose truth-value is ultimately determined by God himself. The three authors do not quite agree whether or to what extent the argument is a proof for the existence of God, but all of them are apparently convinced that the value of the argument cannot be determined merely on logical or empirical grounds. Moreover, it seems to be their common understanding, which Gilson for one states explicitly,[139] that for the complete argument both Chapters 2 and 3 of the *Proslogion* must be considered, the third chapter being the necessary complement of the second.

Recently some of these ideas have been challenged, especially since the advent of logical positivism and analytic philosophy, whose followers have submitted the argument to their own criterion of truth.[140] It would be a long and tedious task to make even a brief survey of the massive amount of contemporary literature on the subject.[141] We shall rather focus our atten-

---

[138]*Ibid.*, pp. 28-29.

[139]"Le chapitre III du *Proslogion* ne doit, sous aucun prétexte, être considéré comme séparable du chapitre II, ni inversement." *Ibid.*, p. 13.

[140]Surprisingly enough, even Bertrand Russell thought at one time that the ontological argument was valid. He writes: "I remember the precise moment, one day in 1894, as I was walking along Trinity Lane, when I saw in a flash (or thought I saw) that the ontological argument is valid. I had gone out to buy a tin of tobacco; on my way back, I suddenly threw it up in the air, and exclaimed as I caught it: 'Great Scott, the ontological argument is sound'." Cf. Bertrand Russell, "My Mental Development," in *The Philosophy of Bertrand Russell*, ed. Paul A. Schilpp (Evanston and Chicago, Ill.: Northwestern University, 1944), p.10.

[141]Besides the useful collection of studies by Plantinga in *The Ontological Argument from St. Anselm to Contemporary Philosophers* (cf. n. 2 above), see *The Many-Faced Argument*, ed. by John Hick and Arthur C. McGill (New York: Macmillan, 1967). The work has an excellent bibliography (pp. 357-70) covering the history of the argument from Anselm to the present time and including the principal studies of it by both European and American philosophers. A special section of *Religious Studies*, IV (The Cambridge University Press, 1968-1969), is devoted to the ontological argument. It includes the following articles: Leroy T. Howe, "Existence as a Perfection: A Reconsideration of the Ontological Argument," pp. 78-101; David A. Pailin, "Some Comments on Hartshorne's Presentation of the Ontological Argument," pp. 103-122; Charles Crittenden, "The Argument from Perfection to Existence," pp. 123-32; M. J. A. O'Connor, "New Aspects of Omnipotence and Necessity in Anselm," pp. 133-46; Donald F. Henze, "Language-Games and the Ontological Argument," pp. 147-52. The ontological argument is also the subject of several scholarly studies in the *Analecta Anselmiana* (5 vols.; Frankfurt-am-Main: Minerva GMBH, 1969-1976). Of particular importance for the history of the argument is "Das Ontologische

tion on two recent interpretations of the argument whose originality and challenging nature make them particularly interesting and worthy of our consideration. These are the interpretations of Norman Malcolm and Charles Hartshorne.

VII. MALCOLM AND HARTSHORNE

Malcolm contends that the *Proslogion* argument contains two distinct pieces of reasoning, and therefore two distinct arguments for the existence of God. Anselm's failure to make a proper distinction between them has caused great confusion among his interpreters.[142] The first argument is stated in Chapter 2 and is essentially the argument that later was taken up by Descartes and developed by him in his own way. It consists in saying that a being than which no greater can be conceived cannot exist in our understanding alone but must also exist in reality, since otherwise we could think of a greater being that would exist both in the understanding and in reality. Such reasoning presupposes the notion that existence is a perfection, a doctrine that Descartes shared with Anselm. This doctrine, says Malcolm, is not only strange but fallacious as well, and to this effect he quotes Kant's criticism, discussed earlier in this chapter. In doing so, Malcolm makes the interesting observation: "It would be desirable to have a rigorous refutation of the doctrine [that existence is a perfection] but I have not been able to provide one. I am compelled to leave the matter at the more or less intuitive level of Kant's observation."[143] We admire Malcolm's honesty in making such a concession, but we cannot but wonder how seriously his charge that the doctrine holding existence as a perfection is fallacious must be taken. To leave the matter at the intuitive level of Kant's observation is little comfort to those who lack such an intuition and even less to those who may disagree with Kant altogether.

Regardless of what one may think of this issue, which separates two distinct schools of thought and hence two distinct interpretations of the argument, Malcolm does not attach much importance to it, since he does not accept the "first" argument as a valid proof. He notes, however, that Gassendi had already anticipated Kant's criticism when he asserted against Descartes that "existence is a perfection neither in God nor in anything else"—a statement, incidentally, that amounts to a rejection of much of what Malcolm himself will try to defend.

Argument in der Geschichte der Philosophie," *op. cit.*, IV (1975), 59–364, a joint study by several authors, each one competent in his own field.

[142]Cf. Norman Malcolm, "Anselm's Ontological Arguments," in Plantinga, *op. cit.*, p. 136. (The article is a reprint from *The Philosophical Review*, LXIX [1960], 41–62.)

[143]*Ibid.*, p. 140.

The second ontological proof, Malcolm says, is to be found in Chapter 3 of the *Proslogion*. In it Anselm affirms two things: first, that a being whose nonexistence is logically impossible is "greater" than a being whose nonexistence is logically possible (and therefore that a being a greater than which cannot be conceived must be one whose nonexistence is logically impossible); second, that *God* is a being than which a greater cannot be conceived.[144] It is worth noting that Anselm never speaks of "logical" possibility or "logical" impossibility: the qualification is Malcolm's own addition. This may appear to be a minor point, but in the light of his subsequent observation it is not. In fact, commenting on the second assertion, he remarks that the statements to be drawn from it, namely, that "God is the greatest of all beings," "God is the most perfect being," and the like are *logically* (italics are his) necessary truths in the same way that the statement "A square has four sides" is a logically necessary truth.[145] We do not question the truth of Malcolm's remark. What we do question is the correctness of approaching the Anselmian proof exclusively from the viewpoint of a logician, as he seems to do.

Discussing Anselm's alleged first assertion, namely, that a being whose nonexistence is logically impossible is greater than a being whose nonexistence is logically possible, Malcolm finds it difficult to accept in this connection the term "greater," which means of course superior or more perfect. This should not come to us as a surprise, since he has already rejected the idea that existence is a perfection. But what puzzles us is his inference from the above assertion that Anselm does not say that existence is a perfection, but rather that *the logical impossibility of nonexistence is a perfection* (Malcolm's italics). In other words, *necessary existence* is a perfection, not existence as such. From this Malcolm concludes that, whereas the first ontological proof rests on the principle that a thing is greater if it exists than if it does not exist, the second proof rests on a quite different principle, namely, that a thing is greater if it exists necessarily than if it exists contingently.[146]

This line of reasoning seems to imply that Anselm has used the term "greater" in two entirely different ways, since in Malcolm's view only the latter use of the term is justified, while the former rests on a faulty principle. However, a reading of Anselm's text does not seem to bear out Malcolm's view, nor does the general context of the *Proslogion* where "greatness" stands for perfection and refers, although in different degrees, to both contingent and necessary existence. Is it not perhaps Malcolm's concern to safeguard, on the one hand, the value of the argument and, on the other hand, the soundness of his own principle, in-

---

[144]*Ibid.*, p. 141.
[145]*Ibid.*
[146]*Ibid.*, p. 142.

herited from Kant, that existence is not a perfection that led him to interpret Anselm the way he did? This, at least, it seems to us, is a good question to ask of him.

To illustrate his point, Malcolm has recourse to the concept we have of
God as an absolutely independent and unlimited being and shows that
such a being cannot be thought of as dependent on any other being for his
existence, any more than it can be conceived as nonexistent at any particular moment of time. Accordingly, he quotes Anselm's *Reply* to Gaunilo to
the effect that the notion of contingent existence or contingent nonexistence has no application to God, and concludes:

> His [God's] existence must either be logically necessary or logically im-
> possible. The only intelligible way of rejecting Anselm's claim that
> God's existence is necessary is to maintain that the concept of God, as
> a being a greater than which cannot be conceived, is self-contradictory
> or nonsensical. Supposing that this is false, Anselm is right to deduce
> God's necessary existence from his characterization of him as a being,
> a greater than which cannot be conceived.[147]

The argument, Malcolm insists, is an a priori proof, for "the proposition
'God necessarily exists' entails the proposition 'God exists,' if and only if
the latter also is understood as an a priori proposition: in which case the
two propositions are equivalent. In this sense Anselm's proof is a proof of
God's existence."[148]

Malcolm must be commended for his ingenuity in defending what he
considers to be the second Anselmian argument against the objection—
the strongest proposed since Kant's time—that existence is not a perfection or a real predicate of an essence. By making a distinction between
contingent and necessary existence and claiming for the latter the same
role of predication as for the other perfections of God, such as necessary
omnipotence and necessary omniscience, he seems to avoid the extremes
both of those who identify existence with other perfections in God as well
as in creatures, and of those who deny any possibility for existence to serve
as a real predicate, even in the case of God. This compromise solution has
been hailed by some authors as an important discovery that enhances the
value of the Anselmian argument and one that escaped the attention even
of its author. But is it really so? Is Malcolm's discovery really so important
as to determine for the first time the precise nature and value of the argument and rescue it from the centuries-old attacks of its opponents? This
question must be asked because, as will be seen in connection with the
next and last man to be dealt with in this survey, some rather strong

---

[147]*Ibid.*, pp. 145–46.
[148]*Ibid.*, p. 147.

language has been used to characterize those who refuse to endorse Malcolm's line of reasoning. Our answer will be brief and to the point. Any attempt to prove the existence of God solely from the analysis of an a priori proposition such as "God necessarily exists" is bound to fail. The gap between mind and reality outside it cannot be bridged by a logical concept, not even in the case of a necessary being. To bridge such a gap something is needed to transform a logical concept into a real, metaphysical concept, or, as in the case in point, a proposition about a real being, either material or spiritual. An a priori proposition can only be an analysis of the meaning of its terms, and this will never give us a clue as to the actual existence of the being the terms are held to stand for.[149] Logic, after all, deals only with what scholastic philosophers, following Aristotle, have called beings of second intention, i.e., concepts of concepts. We must go beyond logic and even beyond physics to attain to the realm of existence; we must enter into the realm of metaphysics. True, the term *metaphysics* is not popular today, especially among logical positivists and analysts, but popularity is not always a criterion of truth. We submit that it is not in this case.

The way to rescue the Anselmian proof from apparent shipwreck, if we may use this expression, is either the way indicated by men like Koyré and Gilson, or the more sophisticated way of Duns Scotus. But since to Malcolm and those who agree with him both of these ways are systematically closed to investigation, it makes little sense to proceed any further in our criticism. A final remark is in order. Malcolm's presupposition that [contingent] existence is not a perfection and his frank admission of not being able to refute the opposite "fallacious" doctrine, is a weak spot in his analysis. So also is the fact that he discusses at some length the notion of perfection but gives no definition or clear indication of what perfection is, let alone of what Anselm meant it to be. This is a weakness that is common to many other present-day analysts.[150]

---

[149]That is why, incidentally, Findlay, arguing on purely logical grounds, has arrived at a conclusion exactly opposite to Malcolm's, namely, that the existence of God is impossible! Cf. J. N. Findlay, "Can God's Existence Be Disproved?", in Plantinga, *op. cit.*, pp. 111-22. (The article is a reprint from *Language, Mind, and Value* [New York: The Humanities Press, 1963], but was originally published in *Mind*. LVII [1948], 176-83). Although Findlay later admitted that the conclusion of his argument could be reversed (*ibid.*, p. 121), the fact of having accepted it as a possibility shows the obvious limitations of logic and linguistic analysis in dealing with such metaphysical issues as the existence of God. As he correctly observes, when "necessity in propositions merely reflects our use of words, the arbitrary conventions of our language," one can hardly expect to see a proof of God's existence derived from the proposition "God necessarily exists," unless "we have made up our minds to speak theistically *whatever the empirical circumstances might turn out to be*" (italics in the text). *Ibid.*, p. 119.

[150]Recently an attempt has been made to show that in the case of God there is no real distinction between factual (or ontological) necessity and logical necessity, so that the form of

No contemporary philosopher has written so much and so earnestly on the ontological argument as Charles Hartshorne, whose thought will be discussed here as a fitting conclusion to our survey. Hartshorne approaches the argument systematically in two works, *Man's Vision of God* and *The Logic of Perfection,* and historically in a more recent volume, *Anselm's Discovery.* In addition to these extensive treatments, he has made the Anselmian proof the subject of many articles and papers.[151] In keeping with the nature of this study, we shall present only the basic features of his interpretation, which in many respects is similar to that of Malcolm. As a matter of fact, Hartshorne had already pointed out long before Malcolm the need of distinguishing between two different forms of the Anselmian proof and said that the standard criticisms are relevant only to the first of them, namely, that of *Proslogion* 2.

Despite their similarities, there are substantial differences between the two philosophers in their understanding of the argument, which differences are determined by their diverse conception of philosophy in general and of metaphysics in particular. Also, the conclusion that Hartshorne draws from *Proslogion* 3 is not in line with Malcolm's theism but with what he himself terms neoclassical theism, a view of God inspired mainly by the process philosophy of Alfred North Whitehead. Hartshorne does not conceal the fact that his interpretation is intended to be original and that it will shed new light on a subject that "has been scandalously mishandled" by "nearly all schools of philosophy which have attempted to deal with it."[152] He feels that Anselm himself, whom he credits with "a discovery greater than he knew," did not realize all the implications of his argument because he was "blinded" by "prejudices derived chiefly from Greek and Roman sources."[153] Whether such statements are fully justified or not will be seen later.

Hartshorne correctly observes that Anselm's ontological argument presents a metaphysical issue that must be solved on metaphysical

---

the ontological argument based on the logical necessity of God's existence is valid. Cf. Alan G. Nasser, "Factual and Logical Necessity and the Ontological Argument," *International Philosophical Quarterly,* XI (1971), 385–402.

[151] The following sources will be used in this study: *Man's Vision of God and the Logic of Theism* (New York: Harper and Row, 1941), chap. IX, pp. 299–341; *The Logic of Perfection and Other Essays in Neoclassical Metaphysics* (La Salle, Ill.: The Open Court Publishing Company, 1962), chap. II, pp. 218–117; *Anselm's Discovery, op. cit.;* "Introduction" to *St. Anselm: Basic Writings, op. cit.,* pp. 1–19; "The Necessarily Existent," in Plantinga, *op. cit.,* pp. 123–35 (a partial reprint from *Man's Vision of God* mentioned above); "What Did Anselm Discover?", in Hick and McGill, *The Many-Faced Argument, op. cit.,* pp. 321–33 (an expanded version of a previous paper which appeared under the same title in *Union Seminary Quarterly Review,* XVII [1962], 213–22).

[152] *The Logic of Perfection,* p. viii.

[153] Introduction to *St. Anselm: Basic Writings,* p. 4.

grounds.[154] This explains why those philosophers, especially in recent times, who dismiss the argument as a mere sophistry, also dismiss the possibility of metaphysical inquiry.[155] The argument centers on the unique relationship between possibility and actuality, essence and existence in God. With ideas of finite things there can be three distinct cases as to the nature and value of their contents: (1) the thing conceived is impossible and hence nonexistent; (2) the thing is possible but not actualized; (3) the thing is possible and actual. The ontological argument holds that with the idea of God only the first and third cases need be considered, since the second case is meaningless. Moreover, if there is no God, there is no possibility for him to come into existence, and thus the very concept of God is nonsensical. Finally, if it can be shown that the idea of God is not nonsensical but must represent at least a possible object, it follows that the idea must refer to an actual object, since a merely possible God is inconceivable. Hence "where impossibility and mere unactualized possibility are both excluded, there nothing remains but actuality, if the idea has any meaning at all."[156]

The argument, Hartshorne remarks, is not in itself sufficient to exclude the impossibility or meaninglessness of God; rather it shows the contradiction of a notion of God as a merely possible being. Once this is granted, the transition from possibility to actuality in God becomes necessary. Indeed—and here Hartshorne uses the same line of reasoning as Malcolm—the idea of God is the idea of a being everlasting in duration and independent of any other being. For such a being to be produced would imply both dependence on the producer and limitation in its duration—Hartshorne excludes the possibility of an eternally dependent being admitted by Aquinas among others—two conditions that contradict the very nature of the being under discussion. Hence it is only logical to con-

---

[154]"What Did Anselm Discover?", in Hick and McGill, *op. cit.*, p. 321.

[155]*The Logic of Perfection*, p. 30. Obviously, Hartshorne's statement refers to a trend among modern and contemporary thinkers who reduce philosophy either to scientific knowledge or to linguistic analysis.

[156]"The Necessarily Existent," in Plantinga, *op. cit.*, p. 124. Hartshorne's line of reasoning is basically that of Scotus, Leibniz, and the more recent authors, Lepidi and De Munnynck. These latter present the ontological argument in the following terms: God is either a being of reason *(ens rationis)*, whose nature is to exist only in our mind, or a real being, actual or possible. But God, the plenitude of being represented in our mind through a created likeness, cannot be merely a being of reason, for, if he were, the objectivity of all our concepts would be endangered. Nor can he be a merely possible being, for his existence would then depend on the causality of another being, which is obviously wrong. Hence he must be an actual being. Cf. Lepidi, *Elementa philosophiae christianae*, II, 14–17; III, 348–54; *Idem*, "La preuve ontologique de l'existence de Dieu et Saint Anselme," *Revue de philosophie*, XV (July-Dec., 1909), 655–64; De Munnynck, *Praelectiones de Dei existentia*, pp. 18–23; *Idem*, "L'idée de l'être," *Revue néoscolastique de philosophie*, XXXI (1929), 182–203.

clude that to think of God as a merely possible being is to think an impossible idea. God must be thought as existent or cannot be thought at all.[157]

At this point Hartshorne becomes aware that the argument's opponents will take issue with the inference of reality from mere logical possibility. All that can be inferred from it is self-consistency on a purely conceptual level. To this Hartshorne answers that self-consistency cannot be the referent of the meaning whose consistency is granted; it is rather the presupposition of there being any meanings, consistent or otherwise. "If a consistent meaning means something, but something not even possible, then it means something very odd indeed. If it means only its own consistency, then it is really meaningless."[158] To explain his position more fully, Hartshorne insists on the unique nature of God as existence itself. To think of God is not to think of a being that might exist; it is to think of what "existence" itself must be, unless the idea is devoid of any meaning. That God must be conceived this way can be proved also by the fact that all other beings can exist only through him, while he in turn cannot exist through another being but must be self-existent, as the cosmological argument puts it. Besides, mere possibility of existence is inconceivable without a being in which such possibility is ultimately grounded, and since the possibility is real, the source of it must also be real; it must be reality itself. This is the argument from the possibles, that is, the ideological argument.[159]

Nor can it be objected that existence is not a predicate and hence cannot be signified by the predicate "perfection." For even if existence is not a predicate, the "mode" of a thing's existence is included in every predicate. Thus contingency of existence is implied in every predication concerning creatures, whereas necessary existence or self-existence is a predicate that belongs exclusively to God. Hence "that God's essence should imply his existential status (as contingent or necessary) is not an exception to the rule, but an example of it, since the rule is that contingency or noncontingency of existence follows from the kind of thing in question."[160]

Further developing his notion of modality of existence as a property deducible from the definition of a thing, Hartshorne goes on to apply it to three specific kinds of existence proper to a definition. With the modality of *contingency,* existence and non-existence are equally conceivable; with the modality of *impossibility,* existence is not conceivable; but with the modality of *necessity,* only the existence, but not the nonexistence, is con-

---

[157]"The Necessarily Existent," in Plantinga, *op. cit.*, pp. 124–26.

[158]*Ibid.*, p. 128.

[159]*Ibid.*, p. 129.

[160]*Ibid.*, pp. 129–30.

ceivable. In this latter case, and in this case alone, existence must be affirmed, since its denial is contradictory. This is the gist of the Anselmian argument and that is why it makes no sense to argue, as some of its critics do, that God's existence is necessary only upon condition that he exists. "God's existence can only be unconditioned. We assert it, or we ignore it; we cannot logically deny it."[161]

Yet, despite the apparent logic of this reasoning, Hartshorne concedes that the ontological argument is only hypothetical. "If 'God' stands for something conceivable," the argument holds, "it stands for something actual," an expression that reminds us of St. Bonaventure's statement, "If God is God, God exists." But this hypothetical character of the argument should not be construed in a way that would deprive the Anselmian proof of all demonstrative value, as it would be if one were saying, as previously stated, that if God exists, he exists necessarily. It must rather be understood in the sense that "if the phrase 'necessary being' has a meaning, then what it means exists necessarily, and if it exists necessarily, then, a fortiori, it exists." To deny this is to deny all value to our idea of God, which, for all practical purposes, would be less than an idea; worse than that, no idea at all.[162]

It has been our concern to present Hartshorne's interpretation of the ontological argument as faithfully as possible and to quote verbatim some of his most significant statements. If we follow carefully the dialectic of his reasoning, we cannot fail to see that, regardless of his introductory remark that the argument is a metaphysical problem, all we have seen thus far is an attempt to solve the problem on purely logical grounds. If this is the case, then his presentation of the Anselmian proof is not much different from that of Malcolm and hence open to the same kind of criticism. But Hartshorne is too keen a philosopher not to have seen this obvious inconsistency with his claim about the metaphysical nature of the argument. As a matter of fact, this is precisely the reproach he makes—whether rightly or wrongly is not our immediate concern here—that Anselm attempts to derive the concrete actuality of God from a mere abstract definition.[163] Actuality, he says, is much more than bare existence, and while Anselm is right in deducing existence from the definition of God, he overlooks the enormous gulf between bare existence and actuality. Actuality can never be deduced from a definition, not even in the case of a supreme conceivable being.

---

[161]"What Did Anselm Discover?", in Hick and McGill, *op. cit.*, pp. 325-27. See also "A Theory of Existential Modality," in *The Logic of Perfection*, pp. 84-89.

[162]"The Necessarily Existent," in Plantinga, *op. cit.*, pp. 134-35.

[163]"What Did Anselm Discover?", in Hick and McGill, *op. cit.*, p. 329: "Here, I think, is the innermost reason for the opposition to Anselm's Proof. From an abstract definition it *seems* to derive a concrete actuality; for God is not supposed to be a mere abstraction."

If this sounds a little puzzling to a "classic theist" who is used to think-ing of God as a most simple being in whom essence and existence are iden-tified, Hartshorne explains that a distinction must be made between ex-istence and actuality in God, existence being God's abstract nature and actuality his concrete reality. Thus "God merely qua 'necessarily-existing individual' is not God in his concrete actuality, but is merely the abstract necessity that there be some such actuality."[164] On this assumption, the ontological proof for the existence of God will have to include two steps, one going from essence to existence and the other from existence to actual-ity. Anselm's mistake, as well as the mistake of his opponents, Hartshorne asserts, is to have reduced these two steps to one. While Anselm was right in showing that in God the step from essence to existence is a necessary one, his argument fell short of showing how God's existence is actualized in concrete reality.

If we ask Hartshorne whether actuality can ever be proved to follow necessarily from existence in God, he will tell us that that can never be the case, for the divine actuality is not necessary at all, neither in itself nor for our knowledge. "I hold that the divine actuality must be contingent, not only for us, but in itself."[165] Quite consistently, he then claims that if God is contingent in his concrete actuality, he is also limited and able to sur-pass himself, as for instance by coming to know a greater and better world. Thus Hartshorne's God is a being that is at one and the same time, although not in the same respect—it would be openly absurd to hold this latter—both necessary and contingent, infinite and finite, immutable and mutable...and the list could go on![166] In short, it is a God that, while ab-solute and transcendent in his perfections, is at the same time "a living, sensitive, free personality, preserving all actual events with impartial care and forever adding new events to his experience."[167] Hartshorne holds that

---

[164]*The Logic of Perfection*, p. 94.

[165]"What Did Anselm Discover?", in Hick and McGill, *op. cit.*, p. 331. See also *The Logic of Perfection*, p. 100: "God as necessary is not God in his concrete actuality."

[166]"What Did Anselm Discover?", in Hick and McGill, *op. cit.*, p. 331.

[167]Cf. Charles Hartshorne and William L. Reese, *Philosophers Speak of God* (Chicago, Ill.: The University of Chicago Press, 1953), p. 514. For Hartshorne's concept of God and his relation to the world see the whole essay, "The Logic of Panentheism," *ibid.*, pp. 499–514. For a more comprehensive study of the subject see his major works: *The Divine Relativity: A Social Conception of God* (Third printing; New Haven and London: Yale University Press, 1967); *Reality as Social Process: Studies in Metaphysics and Religion* (Glencoe, Ill.: The Free Press, 1953); *A Natural Theology for Our Time* (La Salle, Ill.: The Open Court Pub-lishing Company, 1967); *Creative Synthesis and Philosophic Method* (London: S. C. M. Press, 1970). The following articles are also worth consulting: "The Formal Validity and Real Significance of the Ontological Argument," *The Philosophical Review*, LIII (1944), 225–45; "God as Absolute, Yet Related to All," *The Review of Metaphysics*, I (1947), 24–51; "The Dipolar Conception of Deity," *The Review of Metaphysics*, XXI (1967), 273–89.

once this new concept of God is accepted and the proper distinction between divine existence and actuality is made, then the ambiguity of the
Anselmian proof is removed and the proof becomes very strong. However,
he insists, it will be a proof of God's necessary *existence,* not of his
necessary actuality.[168]

Such, then, is Hartshorne's understanding of the Anselmian proof.
Needless to say, his approach to the argument raises so many issues that it
is almost impossible to pass a fair judgment on it without getting involved
in a much wider discussion than the present study allows. Thus in our criticism we will have to be selective and choose those points which in our
estimation are particularly important for a proper evaluation of both
Anselm's argument and Hartshorne's interpretation of it.

We feel that Hartshorne's interest in the argument—an interest that
he describes as going back to his student days when he made the Anselmian proof the subject of a thesis written in 1923 at Harvard University—
coupled with a sharp and original mind, makes him particularly qualified
for the discussion of a topic whose complexity has baffled some of the
greatest philosophers. It is refreshing therefore to see how a man like
Hartshorne, whose cast of mind sets him quite apart from the eleventh-
century's "father of scholasticism," has the courage to stand up and sus-
tain the value of Anselm's discovery in an unfriendly philosophical climate
and against logicians who, in his own words, "would rather be seen in beg-
gars' rags than in the company of the ontological argument."[169] While we
admire his courage and the depth and subtlety of his reasoning, we cannot
ignore the challenge offered to us by certain of his new and daring ideas on
the subject.

First of all, Hartshorne believes that the argument of *Proslogion* 3, implemented with elements from Anselm's *Reply* to Gaunilo, is a valid proof
of God's existence, as distinct from the divine actuality, on the strength of
pure logical reasoning. We have discussed this problem in connection with
Malcolm's view, and need only repeat what we said in his regard. As long
as the starting point of the argument is found in ideas as pure mental entities or propositions looked upon merely from the viewpoint of their
logical contents, there seems to be no way of reaching God as an extramental reality, even when he is conceived as a necessary being. Hartshorne's subtle distinction between existence and concrete actuality in God
is no solution to the problem, as long as existence is considered as a mode
of the divine nature with its characteristics of necessity, independence, immutability, and the like. If, on the other hand, divine existence is a pure
abstraction or concept of our mind with no foundation in the reality of

---

[168]"What Did Anselm Discover?", in Hick and McGill, *op. cit.,* p. 333.
[169]*The Logic of Perfection,* p. 57.

God—which does not seem to be Hartshorne's understanding of it—then the argument has even less of a chance of reaching God, for the reason previously mentioned. On either alternative, then, the argument fails to meet the requirements for a proof of the existence of God, as Hartshorne intends it to be.

But what appears to us an even weaker point in Hartshorne's theory is his conception of God as the embodiment of all those contradictory attributes listed above. To conceive God as a self-existent and necessary being, the absolute and independent cause of all other beings which owe him *totally* whatever they have in the way of essence and existence, and then to make this self-same being dependent on the effects of his creative act, and hence contingent, relative, and subject to the limitations and imperfections of his creatures,[170] is to suggest a notion of God that defies the most fundamental principles of metaphysics. There is always room for suggestions and ideas that may help us better to understand the mysterious nature of God and his relation to the world, but not at the expense of those principles that are the foundation of traditional natural theology, unless these principles are shown to be inadequate. In our opinion, Hartshorne has failed to show that they are. On the other hand, the panentheistic doctrine he proposes as a conciliatory theory between the "extremes" of classical theism and pantheism, raises more problems than it can solve. Hence his distinction between existence and actuality in God, which he presents as the key to the solution of the problems involved in the Anselmian proof, is either too subtle or too unrealistic. We submit that it is the latter.[171]

[170]*Philosophers Speak of God,* pp. 501–502. See also *The Divine Relativity,* p. 74, where Hartshorne speaks of God as being bound to create, although not necessarily this world or any given creature.

[171]For a more sympathetic but equally critical appraisal of Hartshorne's view see David A. Pailin, *art. cit.* in n. 141 above. See also Eugene H. Peters, *Hartshorne and Neoclassical Metaphysics: An Interpretation* (Lincoln: University of Nebraska Press, 1970). The author concludes his evaluation of Hartshorne's philosophy with the following statement: "He is to many of us the foremost of contemporary philosophers." *Ibid.,* p. 127.

One of the latest works on the ontological argument is *Le Dieu d'Anselme et les apparences de la raison* by Jules Vuillemin (Paris: Aubier Montaigne, 1971). In the first two parts of his volume (pp. 11–52) the author restates the usual objection that the ontological argument of the *Proslogion* is a rational proof based on rational data that involves an illicit transition from the concept of God in our mind to God's actual existence. In the third and fourth parts of the book (pp.a 53–131) Vuillemin attempts to show the epistemological and mathematical antinomies that result from the "negative" concept of a being than which no greater can be conceived. Thus he rules out the argument as a valid proof for the existence of God. Vuillemin, like many other writers before him, does not seem to do justice to the inventive genius of Anselm.

The same observation must be made with regard to an even more recent work by Jonathan Barnes, *The Ontological Argument* (New York: St. Martin's Press, 1972), where the Anselmian proof and some of its later formulations are analyzed almost exclusively from the point of view of their logic and semantics rather than their philosophical content. It

CONCLUSION

In an attempt to summarize the result of our inquiry, we can say that Anselm's ontological argument has found supporters in Bonaventure, Duns Scotus, Descartes, Leibniz, and Barth, while its strongest opponents have been Gaunilo, Aquinas, and Kant. Between these two opposite positions, there is the view of Malcolm and Hartshorne, who see in the *ratio Anselmi* two distinct pieces of reasoning and claim that only that of *Proslogion* 3 is valid. Koyré and Gilson do not really take a stand for or against the argument. Rather, they try to show how the argument should be understood by placing it within the context of the entire *Proslogion* and other Anselmian works, especially the *Monologium* and *De veritate*. In this sense Koyré and Gilson can be considered as being somewhat favorable to the Anselmian proof. Actually they assign to it greater philosophical value than Barth does, since Barth sees the proof merely within a theological framework. In some respects they even come closer to Anselm than Malcolm and Hartshorne, who refuse to grant dialectic value to the reasoning of *Proslogion* 2. Whatever their stand, all the authors discussed in this chapter have contributed, either directly or indirectly, to a better understanding of the issue at hand.

Our appraisal of the position of each individual author, as well as our remarks on Anselm's own presentation of the argument, seems to dispense us from any further comment. However, there are a few observations that we wish to make by way of conclusion in an effort to bring forth, even more effectively than we have already done, the positive aspects of the Anselmian proof.

The strong point of Anselm's reasoning consists in his attempt to show that it is impossible to form a proper concept of a supremely conceivable being and at the same time deny the existence of the being so conceived. Existence is indeed a necessary element of that concept. One may question the ontological value of the concept but not the logic of Anselm's reasoning, provided this is placed within the context of the ideological realism which he shares with Augustine and the entire Augustinian school.

In such a context ideas have a value of their own and cannot be considered as mere logical constructs. The idea of perfection as something that is better to have than not to have, which is the traditional understanding of the term, has a positive content, and so too has the being understood as possessing that perfection. When the concept of perfection is raised to the highest possible degree and personified, as it were, in a being, as in the case of God, then the concept does not lose its ontological

should be clear from our presentation that, although logic may be useful for determining the correctness of a particular piece of reasoning, the ontological argument is a metaphysical issue and its value must be determined primarily on metaphysical grounds.

value. On the contrary, it acquires a new dimension, an infinite dimension, if we are allowed to speak in such terms in regard to the human intellect.

The idea of God, it is worth repeating, does not prove God's existence, but without existence the idea has no meaning. Worse still, it is no idea at all; it is a contradiction. Indeed, if the notion of a supremely conceivable being does not stand for an actual reality, it becomes the notion of the least conceivable being, for such a being, in addition to having no reality of its own, would never be able to receive one without losing its identity. The greatest conceivable being cannot possibly depend on another being for its existence and remain what it is supposed to be. Thus the human mind would be placed in the embarassing situation, already pointed out by Scotus, that it would be deceived in the attainment of that very object which seems best to satisfy its inner tendency as a knowing faculty. It becomes evident, therefore, that the validity of Anselm's reasoning is closely connected with the question of the objective value of our concepts and the related issue of the proper object of our intellect.

A final remark. The idea of the greatest conceivable being, and hence of a self-existent being, would be proved to be groundless, and consequently false, if to exist meant exclusively to exist by and because of another. Until this is shown, which is not only most unlikely but patently impossible because of the contradictions involved in all attempts to do so, the Anselmian argument will continue to fascinate philosophers as a unique piece of profound and original thinking whose logic it is easier to reject than it is to refute.

BIBLIOGRAPHY

Anselm, St. *Proslogion seu Alloquium de Dei existentia.* Migne, PL 158, cols. 223–42.

_____. *Liber apologeticus contra Gaunilonem respondentem pro insipiente.* Migne, PL 158; cols. 247–60.

_____. *Basic Writings.* 2d ed. Trans. by S. W. Deane. La Salle, Ill.: The Open Court Publishing Company, 1962.

Aristotle. "Posterior Analytics." In *The Basic Works of Aristotle.* 10th printing. Edited and with an Introduction by Richard McKeon. New York: Random House, 1941.

Balić, Charles. "The Life and Works of John Duns Scotus." In *John Duns Scotus, 1265–1965,* pp. 1–27. Ed. by John K. Ryan and Bernardine M. Bonansea. Washington, D.C.: The Catholic University of America Press, 1965.

Barnes, Jonathan. *The Ontological Argument.* New York: St. Martin's Press, 1972.

Barth, Karl. *Anselm: Fides quaerens intellectum.* Cleveland and New York: The World Publishing Company "Meridian Books," 1962.

Belmond, Séraphin. *Dieu: Existence et cognoscibilité.* Paris: Beauchesne, 1913.

Bettoni, Efrem. *Duns Scotus: The Basic Principles of His Philosophy.* Trans. and ed. by Bernardine Bonansea, O.F.M. Washington, D.C.: The Catholic University of America Press, 1961.

Blondel, Maurice. *L'action (1893);* reprint. Paris: Presses Universitaires de France, 1950.

Bonansea, Bernardino M. "Duns Scotus and St. Anselm's Ontological Argument." In *Studies in Philosophy and the History of Philosophy,* vol. IV, pp. 128–41. Ed. by John K. Ryan. Washington, D.C.: The Catholic University of America Press, 1969.

_____. "The Ontological Argument: Proponents and Opponents." In *Studies in Philosophy and the History of Philosophy,* vol. VI, pp. 135–92. Ed. by John K. Ryan. Washington, D.C.: The Catholic University of America Press, 1973.

Bonaventure, St. *Opera omnia.* 10 vols. Quaracchi: Typographia Collegii S. Bonaventurae, 1882–1902.

Charlesworth, M. J. *St. Anselm's Proslogion.* Oxford: Clarendon Press, 1965.

Collins, James. *The Emergence of Philosophy of Religion.* New Haven: Yale University Press, 1967. A penetrating analysis of the beginnings of philosophy of religion as a modern discipline.

Crittenden, Charles. "The Argument from Perfection to Existence," *Religious Studies,* IV, 123–32. The Cambridge University Press, 1968–1969.

De Munnynck, Marc, O.P. *Praelectiones de Dei existentia.* Louvain: Uystpruyst-Dieudonné, 1904.

_____. "L'idée de l'être," *Revue néoscolastique de philosophie,* XXXI (1929), 182–203; 415–37.

Descartes, René. *Oeuvres philosophiques.* Ed. by Ferdinand Alquié. Vol. II. Paris: Garnier, 1967.

_____. *The Philosophical Works.* 2 vols. Ed. by E. S. Haldane and G. R. T. Ross. New York: Dover Publications, 1955.

Duns Scotus, John. *Ordinatio.* Vol. II. Civitas Vaticana: Typis polyglottis Vaticanis, 1950.

_____. *A Treatise on God as First Principle.* Trans. and ed. by Allan B. Wolter, O.F.M. Chicago, Ill.: Franciscan Herald Press, 1966.

Findlay, J. N. "Can God's Existence Be Disproved?". In *The Ontological Argument,* pp. 136–59. Ed. by Alvin Plantinga. Garden City, N.Y.: Doubleday "Anchor Books," 1965.

Gaunilo. *Liber pro insipiente adversus S. Anselmi in Proslogio ratiocinantem.* Migne, PL 158; cols. 241–48.

Gilson, Etienne. *The Philosophy of St. Bonaventure.* Trans. by Dom Illtyd Trethowan. London: Sheed and Ward, 1940.

_____. *The Christian Philosophy of St. Thomas Aquinas.* Trans. by L. K. Shook, C.S.B. New York: Random House, 1956. A masterpiece of scholarship by a leading historian of medieval philosophy.

_____. *Jean Duns Scot. Introduction à ses positions fondamentales.* Paris: Vrin, 1952.

_____. *Études sur le rôle de la pensée médiévale dans la formation du système cartésien.* Paris: Vrin, 1930.

_____. "Sens et nature de l'argument de Saint Anselme," *Archives d'histoire doctrinale et littéraire du Moyen Age,* IX, 5–51.

Hartshorne, Charles. *Anselm's Discovery: A Re-Examination of the Ontological Argument for God's Existence.* La Salle, Ill.: The Open Court Publishing Company, 1965.

_____. *Man's Vision of God and the Logic of Theism.* New York: Harper and Row, 1941.

_____. *The Logic of Perfection and Other Essays in Neoclassical Metaphysics.* La Salle, Ill.: The Open Court Publishing Company, 1962.

_____. "The Necessarily Existent." In *The Ontological Argument from St. Anselm to Contemporary Philosophers,* pp. 123–35. Ed. by Alvin Plantinga. Garden City, N.Y.: Doubleday "Anchor Books," 1965.

_____. "What Did Anselm Discover?". In *The Many-Faced Argument,* pp. 321–33. Ed. by John Hick and Arthur C. McGill. New York: Macmillan, 1967.

_____. *The Divine Relativity: A Social Conception of God.* 3d printing. New Haven and London: Yale University Press, 1967.

_____. *Reality as Social Process: Studies in Metaphysics and Religion.* Glencoe, Ill.: The Free Press, 1953.

_____. *A Natural Theology for Our Time.* La Salle, Ill.: The Open Court Publishing Company, 1967.

_____. *Creative Synthesis and Philosophic Method.* London: S.C.M. Press, 1970.

_____. "The Formal Validity and Real Significance of the Ontological Argument," *The Philosophical Review,* LIII (1944), 225–45.

_____. "God as Absolute, Yet Related to All," *The Review of Metaphysics,* I (1947), 24–51.

_____. "The Dipolar Conception of Deity," *The Review of Metaphysics,* XXI (1967), 273–89.

Hartshorne, Charles, and Reese, William L. *Philosophers Speak of God.* Chicago: The University of Chicago Press, 1953.

Hegel, Georg W. F. *Lectures on the Philosophy of Religion.* 3 vols. Trans. by E. B. Spiers and J. B. Sanderson; reprint. New York: The Humanities Press, 1962.

_____. *Lectures on the History of Philosophy.* Trans. by E. S. Haldane and F. H. Simson; reprint. New York: The Humanities Press, 1968.

Henrich, Dieter. *Der Ontologische Gottesbeweis.* Tübingen: Mohr, 1960.

Henze, Donald F. "Language-Games and the Ontological Argument," *Religious Studies,* IV, 147–52. The Cambridge University Press, 1968–1969.

Hick, John, and McGill, Arthur C., eds. *The Many-Faced Argument.* New York: Macmillan, 1967.

Howe, Leroy T. "Existence as a Perfection: A Reconsideration of the Ontological Argument," *Religious Studies,* IV, 78–101. The Cambridge University Press, 1968–1969.

Kant, Immanuel. *Prolegomena to Any Future Metaphysics.* Ed. by Lewis White Beck. Indianapolis and New York: Bobbs-Merrill, 1950.

_____. *Der einzig mögliche Beweisgrund zu einer Demonstration des Daseins Gottes.* In *Immanuel Kant: Werke,* vol. I, pp. 617–730. Ed. by Wilhelm Weischedel. Wiesbaden: Insel, 1960.

_____. *A Collection of Critical Essays.* Ed. by Robert P. Wolff. Garden City, N.Y.: Doubleday "Anchor Books," 1967.

_____. *Critique of Pure Reason.* Trans. by Norman K. Smith; reprint. London: Macmillan, 1933.

Koyré, Alexandre. *L'idée de Dieu dans la philosophie de St. Anselme.* Paris: Éditions Ernest Leroux, 1923.

Leibniz, Gottfried Wilhelm. *Die philosophischen Schriften von Gottfried Wilhelm Leibniz.* 7 vols. Ed. by C. J. Gerhardt. Hildensheim: Olms, 1960-1961.

_____. *Leibniz: Selections.* Ed. by P. Wiener. New York: Charles Scribner's Sons, 1951.

_____. *The Philosophical Works of Leibniz.* Trans. by George M. Duncan. New Haven: Tuttle, Morehouse and Taylor, 1890.

_____. *Philosophical Papers and Letters.* 2 vols. Trans. by Leroy M. Loemker. Chicago: University of Chicago Press, 1956.

_____. *New Essays Concerning Human Understanding.* Trans. by Alfred G. Langley. 3d ed. Chicago, Ill.: The Open Court Publishing Company, 1949.

Lepidi, Alberto, O.P. *Elementa philosophiae christianae.* 3 vols. Paris: Lethielleux; Louvain: Peeters, 1875-1879.

_____. "La preuve ontologique de l'existence de Dieu et Saint Anselme," *Revue de philosophie,* XV (July-Dec., 1909), 655-64.

Malcolm, Norman. "Anselm's Ontological Argument." In *The Ontological Argument from St. Anselm to Contemporary Philosophers,* pp. 136-59. Ed. by Alvin Plantinga. Garden City, N.Y.: Doubleday "Anchor Books," 1965.

McPherson, Thomas. *The Philosophy of Religion.* Princeton, N.J.: Van Nostrand Company, 1965.

Nasser, Alan G. "Factual and Logical Necessity and the Ontological Argument," *International Philosophical Quarterly,* XI (1971), 385-402.

O'Connor, M. J. A. "New Aspects of Omnipotence and Necessity in Anselm," *Religious Studies,* IV, 133-46. The Cambridge University Press, 1968-1969.

Pailin, David A. "Some Comments on Hartshorne's Presentation of the Ontological Argument," *Religious Studies,* IV, 103-122. The Cambridge University Press, 1968-1969.

Pegis, Anton C. "St. Anselm and the Argument of the 'Proslogion'," *Medieval Studies,* XXVIII (1966), 228-67.

Peters, Eugene H. *Hartshorne and Neoclassical Metaphysics: An Interpretation.* Lincoln: University of Nebraska Press, 1970.

Piccirelli, Josephus, S.J. "De mente S. Anselmi in Proslogio." In *De Deo: disputationes metaphysicae.* Paris: Lecoffre, 1885.

Plantinga, Alvin, ed. *The Ontological Argument from St. Anselm to Contemporary Philosophers.* Garden City, N.Y.: Doubleday "Anchor Books," 1965.

Prentice, Robert, O.F.M. "The 'De primo principio' of John Duns Scotus as a Thirteenth-Century Proslogion," *Antonianum,* 39 (1964), 77-109.

Rickaby, Joseph, S.J. *Studies on God and His Creatures.* London and New York: Longmans, Green and Co., 1924.

Russell, Bertrand. "My Mental Development." In *The Philosophy of Bertrand Russell.* Ed. by Paul A. Schilpp. Evanston and Chicago, Ill.: Northwestern University, 1944.

Somerville, James M. *Total Commitment: Blondel's L'action.* Washington, D.C.: Corpus Books, 1968.

Southern, R. W., ed. *The Life of St. Anselm, Archbishop of Canterbury, by Eadmer.* London and New York: Thomas Nelson and Sons, 1962.

Spedalieri, Franciscus, S.J. *Selectae et breviores philosophiae ac theologiae controversiae.* Rome: Officium Libri Catholici, 1950.

Thomas Aquinas, St. *In I et II Sententiarum.* 2 vols. Ed. by Pierre Mandonnet. Paris: Lethielleux, 1929.

_____. *Summa theologiae.* Vol. I. Ed. by P. Caramello. Turin-Rome: Marietti, 1948.

_____. *Summa contra gentiles.* Editio Leonina Manualis. Turin-Rome: Marietti, 1946.

_____. *De veritate.* Vol. I of *Quaestiones disputatae.* Ed. by R. M. Spiazzi, O.P. Turin-Rome: Marietti, 1949.

_____. *In Boethii De Trinitate.* Ed. by B. Decker. Leiden: Brill, 1955.

Van de Woestyne, Zacharias, O.F.M. *Cursus philosophicus.* 2 vols. Malines: Typographia S. Francisci, 1921–1925.

Various Authors. "Das Ontologische Argument in der Geschichte der Philosophie." In *Analecta Anselmiana,* IV, 59–364. Frankfurt-am-Main: Minerva GMBH, 1975.

Veuthey, Léon, O.F.M. Conv. "Le problème de l'existence de Dieu chez S. Bonaventure," *Antonianum,* XXVIII (1953), 19–38.

Vuillemin, Jules. *Le Dieu d'Anselme et les apparences de la raison.* Paris: Aubier Montaigne, 1971.

CHAPTER IV

THE FIVE WAYS OF ST. THOMAS

*THEIR METAPHYSICAL STRUCTURE**

A complete study of St. Thomas' "five ways" would call for a whole book. It is impossible, therefore, to encompass within the narrow limits of a chapter the exposition of the Thomistic proofs for the existence of God with all their developments and implications. Hence we shall confine ourselves to presenting Aquinas' authentic thought on the subject and showing that the five ways have a true and genuine metaphysical structure.

The question of the validity of the theistic proofs set forth by the Angelic Doctor depends in no small degree on the related issue of their correct interpretation. The proofs are sometimes presented in a way that may jeopardize not only their probative value but also their authenticity. Thus we must go to the root of the problem and try to rediscover the original thought of the Master.

It must be said at the very outset that the interpretation of the five ways is no easy task. This is so, first, because Aquinas, as he avows in the prologue to the *Summa theologiae,* has condensed his thought in a few concise propositions, whose development must be found in other parts of the *Summa* or in his other works; secondly, because the five ways involve a series of notions that are more clearly stated and worked out elsewhere; and thirdly, because the five ways must be placed in their proper context, if we want to see them in their true perspective. In short, the correct interpretation of the five ways requires great familiarity with Aquinas' texts and some sort of congeniality with his way of thinking.

In the following pages we shall discuss three main issues, the first two of which are preliminary to the third. First, we shall show that the five ways are presented within a theological context. Once this has been established, we shall ask ourselves whether the five ways still retain their value as rational proofs. Secondly, we shall discuss the human mind's itinerary to God in its present state and see how Aquinas' theory of knowledge underlies the philosophical procedure of each of the five ways. Finally, we

---

*This chapter is the author's translation from the French and adaptation of a study by Louis Charlier, which appeared in *L'existence de Dieu,* vol. 16 of "Cahiers de l'actualité religieuse" (Tournai, Belgium: Casterman, 1963), pp. 181-227. All quotations and references have been carefully checked against the original sources and, whenever necessary, corrected.

shall examine the metaphysical structure of the five ways and show that in treating each one of them Aquinas kept himself on a metaphysical level.

I. THE THEOLOGICAL CONTEXT OF THE FIVE WAYS

St. Thomas is first and foremost a theologian. This fact does not prevent him from exercising the metaphysical vigor of his genius. Nevertheless, he is a theologian and it is from a theological perspective that he has visualized the five ways. Are we, therefore, caught within some sort of theological authoritarianism? Is he going to dictate to us in such a way that we can already know beforehand the outcome of his teaching? The five ways are, in fact, contained in the *Summa theologiae;* they are part of so-called sacred doctrine. It is true that they fall within the realm of the *praeambula fidei,* i.e., doctrines that precede faith; but according to medieval mentality, and especially St. Thomas, the *praeambula fidei* are not merely preambles to theology. They are also an integral part of sacred doctrine (*sacra doctrina*).

There are indeed certain natural truths that are a prerequisite for the knowledge of faith[1] and yet are so much a part of theology that man's salvation also depends on their acceptance. That is why their revelation in man's present state is held to be morally necessary for salvation.[2] These natural truths belong to the domain of theology from a twofold point of view: as preambles to faith (*aliquid praecedens articulos fidei*) and as revealed truths (*veritatem quam fides profitetur et ratio investigat*). At least, this is the case as regards those natural truths which are also an object of revelation and upon which revelation confers a new meaning. Thomas writes:

> That God exists is not an article of faith but a preamble to an article of faith, unless we understand something else along with God's existence, for example, that he has a unity of essence with a trinity of persons, and other similar things.[3]

Although inserted within theology, the *praeambula fidei* are truths that the human mind, by virtue of its own light, can prove with

---

[1]*In III Sent.,* d. 24, q. 1, a. 3: "Sicut autem est in gratia perficiente affectum quod praesupponit naturam, quia eam perficit; ita et fidei substernitur naturalis cognitio quam fides praesupponit et ratio probare potest: sicut Deum esse et Deum esse unum, incorporeum, intelligentem et alia huiusmodi."
[2]For St. Thomas' view on the natural truths required for salvation and whose revelation is morally necessary see *S.T.,* I, q. 1, a. 1 and II–II, q. 2, a. 4. See also *Con. gent.,* I, c. 4; *De ver.,* q. 14, a. 10; *In Boeth. de Trinit.,* q. 3, a. 1.
[3]*De ver.,* q. 10, a. 12, and 5 *in contrarium.* See also *ibid.,* q. 14, a. 9, ad 8; *S.T.,* II–II, q. 1, a. 8, ad 1.

demonstrative reasons (*rationes demonstrativae*) and not merely with probable reasons (*rationes probabiles*).[4] Still it is within a theological framework and in the service of the data of revelation that the demonstrative reasons concerning the preambles to faith are developed. Consequently, they also move within an atmosphere of serenity rather than of anguish.

There is no question that Aquinas wants to prove the existence of God and intends to do so by truly demonstrative arguments. Yet it is a God whom he has already found and who has already spoken to him. Hence he emphasizes not the discovery of God but the establishment of a solid foundation for his whole theology. His axiom is: "Faith presupposes natural knowledge, even as grace presupposes nature."[5] He also writes in this connection:

> Among the inquiries that we must undertake concerning God in himself, we must set down in the beginning that whereby his existence is demonstrated, as the necessary foundation of the whole work. For, if we do not demonstrate that God exists, all consideration of divine things is necessarily suppressed.[6]

We are concerned even more fundamentally, in Aquinas' mind, with the question of making possible the dialogue between man and the living God of revelation. If reason is radically incapable of attaining God (*an sit Deus*), the dialogue becomes impossible and God's call to the beatific vision is nothing but a snare or an illusion.

We must look at man in his concrete, existential condition. When so considered—and this is the way Thomas the theologian views him—he is not merely the man known in philosophy or one who lives in a purely natural state (*in puris naturalibus*); he is man as God wants him to be in accord with the plan he deigned to reveal to us. He is a man placed within an economy of elevation to the supernatural life, an economy that leads ultimately to eternal happiness. Moreover, he is a man who, historically, has fallen from his original state and is now beclouded by sin. Finally, he is a man who finds himself within an economy of salvation achieved by Christ and who, under Christ's salvific influence, is involved in a process of perfect restoration. This influence is being exerted in the first place on

---

[4]The *rationes demonstrativae* produce scientific knowledge and belong to the demonstrative syllogism, whereas the *rationes probabiles* produce only opinion and belong to the dialectic syllogism. For the technical meaning of these expressions see St. Thomas' Commentary on Aristotle, especially *In Post. anal.*, L. 1.

[5]*S.T.*, I, q. 2, a. 2, ad 1. This axiom occurs frequently in Thomas' writings, although not always in the same form. See, for example, *S.T.*, I, q. 60, a. 5; I, q. 62, a. 7, *sed contra;* I-II, q. 4, a. 5; III, q. 69, a. 8; *De ver.*, q. 14, a. 10.

[6]*Con. gent.*, I, c. 9 *in fine.*

man's intellect and by him who, as the light of the mind, enlightens every man who comes into the world. It is first of all from the point of view of God's wisdom manifested through his revealing and creative Word, that we must approach the problem of God in all its dimensions.

Since he has been called to see God as he is in himself, man has the potentiality for the vision of the divine essence as his ultimate perfection. Hence there is no doubt that the adequate object of our intellect is the divine essence itself seen face to face.

> The divine substance is not beyond the capacity of the created intellect in such a way that it is altogether foreign to it...; in fact, the divine substance is the first intelligible object and the principle of all intellectual cognition.[7]

Here we have the whole explanation of our knowledge in this life. Whether it be natural, i.e., from reason, or supernatural, i.e., from faith, our knowledge is related to the supreme act of our intellect.

Faith and reason are, therefore, two beams of light that meet in their common root, the human intellect, which they partially actualize in reference to its adequate object. They are two kinds of illumination that come from the same source, and both of them derive ultimately from the light of God.

> The intellectual power of the creature is called an intelligible light, as it were, derived from the first light, whether this be understood of the natural power, or of some superadded perfection of grace or of glory.... We understand and judge of all things in the light of the first truth, inasmuch as the light itself of our intellect, whether natural or gratuitous, is nothing but the impression of the first truth upon it.[8]

Thus both the natural light of the intellect and the light of faith can be called "the impression of the first truth." This is an impression of the divine light by which God teaches us interiorly. The two lights are not opposed to or separated from each other; rather they are mutually complementary. The natural light of our intellect is perfected and driven to its maximum degree of intensity by the supernatural light. What occurs is like a reflection of the divine light upon the soul, in virtue of which the light of faith and of the wisdom of the Holy Spirit shines on human reason and its principles, which are thus enlightened by a supernatural luminosity.[9] Nevertheless, it remains true that the light of reason and the light of

---

[7]*Con. gent.*, III, c. 54.
[8]*S.T.*, I, q. 12, a. 2; I, q. 88, a. 3, ad 1.
[9]*In Boeth. de Trinit.*, q. 1, a. 1, c and ad 2.

faith are distinct and so different from one another that it is impossible to believe and to demonstrate the same thing at one and the same time.[10]

The intellect is able, in virtue of its own power and without the aid of faith or revelation, to offer demonstrative reasons for the *praeambula fidei* and, more specifically, the existence of God. Yet in the present state of man these proofs are inaccessible to many people. That is why in the economy of salvation God comes to man's support through revelation and the gift of faith. In Thomas' words,

> Even as regards those truths about God which human reason can investigate, it was necessary that man be taught by a divine revelation. For the truth about God, such as reason can know it, would be known only by a few, and that after a long time, and with the admixture of many errors; whereas man's whole salvation, which is in God, depends upon the knowledge of this truth.[11]

It is worth noting that, in addition to the general reasons given for the knowledge of the natural truths necessary for salvation, Thomas offers some specific reasons why it is difficult to attain to the knowledge of God by way of demonstration (*per viam demonstrationis*):

1) The depth and subtlety of the matter. 2) The weakness of the human intellect from the beginning. 3) The many preambles required for a knowledge of God according to reason. For this there is needed knowledge of almost all the sciences, since cognition of divine things is the end of them all. But few indeed would comprehend these preambulatory truths or investigate them completely. 4) Many men, on account of their natural constitution, are unfitted for perfect intellectual investigation according to reason. 5) The numerous occupations with which men are busied.[12]

One thing especially must be kept in mind, namely, that no one can argue to the existence of God except at the end of all philosophical speculation, that is, at the end of metaphysics, which for Thomas is "the last science to be learned and the end of all sciences" (*ultima in addiscendo et finis omnium scientiarum*).[13] And very few people, according to Aquinas, arrive at

---

[10]*S.T.*, II–II, q. 1, a. 5.

[11]*S.T.*, I, q. 1, a. 1.

[12]*In Boeth. de Trinit.*, q. 3, a. 1; *Con. gent.*, I, c. 4; *De ver.*, q. 14, a. 10.

[13]*In Metaph.*, L. I, lect. 2: "Illa enim quae sunt a materia penitus separata secundum esse, sicut substantiae immateriales, sunt magis difficilia nobis ad cognoscendum, quam etiam universalia: et ideo ista scientia quae sapientia dicitur, quamvis sit prima in dignitate, est tamen ultima in addiscendo." *Ibid.*, lect. 3: "[Ista philosophia, sive sapientia] est circa altissimas causas; quia inter causas altissimas etiam est finalis causa, ut supra dictum est. Unde oportet quod haec scientia consideret ultimum et universalem finem omnium. Et sic omnes aliae scientiae in eam ordinantur sicut in finem; unde sola ista maxime propter se est." It is worth noting that metaphysics leads us to God as the final cause.

this knowledge. Hence, through the gift of faith, God in his mercy compensates for those who cannot attain this philosophical knowledge of himself with all its implications. Will there be, then, a special kind of faith, or what might be called natural faith, for those who are unable to demonstrate by reason the existence of God? No; Thomas knows only one kind of faith, and that is the supernatural faith by which man accepts God, the Truth itself, "inasmuch as it is not seen" (*in quantum non visa*). For him there are not and there cannot be two kinds of faith, just as there are not two kinds of revelation. Faith is a gift offered by God to man with a view to his eternal happiness. That is why by believing in God (*Deum esse*), a person believes in everything that is eternally contained in him who is our happiness.[14]

It is clear, however, that revelation presents us with an existing God in the act itself of revelation, and that by the gift of faith a person knows also the existence of a creative God, the very same being that reason can attain by itself. It is in this sense that faith supplements reason in its own domain. For those who can attain to the knowledge of God by reason, this knowledge becomes an introduction or preamble to faith. The *praeambula fidei* are the normal ways, wisely graded and proportioned to our mind, by which we are raised to the consideration of the mysteries of faith. They are admittedly imperfect ways, but such that they can be perfected by revelation.

There are, then, three degrees in the knowledge of things divine: the first is furnished by the light of reason that, starting from creatures, raises itself up to God; the second rests on the fact that divine truth, which transcends our human mind, comes down to us by revelation and makes itself known to us, not by demonstration, but by the word of faith; the third degree is attained when the human spirit is raised to the contemplation of the divine realities in the perfect revelation of celestial vision.[15]

It is from this perspective that the role of the Thomistic five ways must be viewed: they are five ways for man to reach up to God by natural reason. They represent a vigorous effort of the human mind to raise itself to the divinity in order better to understand the content of revelation. It is within an atmosphere of serenity and of trust in the resources of human

---

[14]*S.T.*, II-II, q. 1, a. 7: "In esse enim divino includuntur omnia quae credimus in Deo aeternaliter existere, in quibus nostra beatitudo consistit."

[15]*Con. gent.*, IV, c. 1: "Quia perfectum hominis bonum est ut quoquo modo Deum cognoscat, ne tam nobilis creatura omnino in vanum esse videretur, velut finem proprium attingere non valens, datur homini quaedam via per quam in Dei cognitionem ascendere possit, ut scilicet, quia omnes rerum perfectiones quodam ordine a summo rerum vertice Deo descendunt, ipse ab inferioribus incipiens et gradatim ascendens in Dei cognitionem proficiat...per has igitur vias intellectus noster in Dei cognitionem ascendere potest."

reason that the five ways unfold and develop. If faith comes to support the data of reason, still it does not simply and purely replace it. There are no traces of fideism in Thomas, who is convinced that a philosophical and natural knowledge of God is possible and that God's existence can be demonstrated from creatures. If only a few achieve such a demonstration, that shows only that in its present condition the human intellect is affected by a congenital weakness that makes it hard for it to understand reality as such, or to raise itself to the level of metaphysics. Since it is beclouded by sin, the human intellect is not quite capable of a connatural knowledge of God.[16]

II. THE HUMAN MIND'S ITINERARY TO GOD IN ITS PRESENT STATE

St. Thomas has constantly refused to admit an innate knowledge of God. He acknowledges no doubt that a certain general and confused knowledge of God is embedded in our nature, that is, inasmuch as God is man's ultimate happiness. Man has a natural desire for happiness and what he naturally desires he must also naturally know. But this is not, properly speaking, the knowledge that God exists, any more than to know that someone is approaching is to know Peter, even though the one who approaches happens to be Peter. In fact, many people believe that happiness, man's perfect good, does not consist in God but in wealth, riches, pleasure, or some other type of good.[17]

Since for Thomas there is no innate knowledge of God, nor for that matter any a priori knowledge of him, the only way to attain God is by knowledge a posteriori or from his effects (ex effectibus). This is due to the very structure of our intellect in the present life. Since the intellect is incarnated, as it were, in the body, all natural knowledge must take its rise from the senses. Consequently, our natural knowledge can go only as far

---

[16]In Ioan., c. I, lect. 5: "Una [ratio] est perversitas humanae naturae, quae ex sui malitia iam obtenebrata erat vitiorum et ignorantiae obscuritate."

[17]S.T., I, q. 2, a. 1, ad 1. See also Con. gent., I, c. 11: "Sic enim homo naturaliter Deum cognoscit sicut naturaliter ipsum desiderat. Desiderat autem ipsum homo naturaliter in quantum desiderat naturaliter beatitudinem, quae est quaedam similitudo divinae bonitatis. Sic igitur non oportet quod Deus ipse, in se consideratus, sit naturaliter notus homini, sed similitudo ipsius. Unde oportet quod per eius similitudines in effectibus repertas, in cognitionem ipsius homo ratiocinando perveniat." See also Con. gent., III, c. 38: "Est enim quaedam communis et confusa Dei cognitio quae quasi omnibus hominibus adest." However, this common and confused knowledge does not lead us as yet to the true knowledge of a personal God: "Quis autem vel qualis vel si unus tantum est ordinator naturae, nondum statim ex hac communi consideratione habetur" (ibid.).

as it can be driven by means of sensible things.[18] The proper object of the human intellect in its present state is then the essence of a material reality.[19] The intellect, however, does not know anything directly except the universal, and so the nature of a thing is conceived universally even though it is actualized in a concrete individual being. Hence the proper and immediate object of the human intellect united to the body is neither God, nor the human soul, but the nature of a sensible thing.

Aquinas says indeed in many places that the object of the intellect is being, and goes as far as to affirm that being is that which is first conceived by the mind.[20] But by these statements he does not mean to say that the intellect immediately attains the knowledge of being precisely as being. The knowledge of being as such or *in universali* is the result of a metaphysical reflection that is already quite mature. The *ratio entis* is first perceived by the intellect in a being that is the object of our senses. Furthermore, in perceiving being or truth as a universal, Thomas says, the intellect perceives also its own cognitive act. But this is not what the intellect knows in the first place, for the primary object of the intellect in our present life, it is worth repeating, is not any kind of being or truth, but being and truth as grounded in a material reality. This is the intellect's starting point for its knowledge of all reality.[21]

Granted that every intellect is capable of knowing being in all its dimensions,[22] the proper and proportionate object of the human intellect in our present state remains the essence of a sensible being. It is from this object that the human mind is able to ascend, by metaphysical reflection, to the cause or principle of the being that is the object of its immediate knowledge. Thus, although God as such is not the subject of metaphysics

---

[18]*S.T.*, I, q. 12, a. 12: "Unde tantum se nostra naturalis cognitio extendere potest, in quantum manuduci potest per sensibilia." See also *Con. gent.*, I, c. 12: "Etsi Deus sensibilia omnia et sensum excedat, eius tamen effectus, ex quibus demonstratio sumitur ad probandum Deum esse, sensibiles sunt. Et sic nostrae cognitionis origo in sensu est etiam de his quae sensum excedunt."

[19]*S.T.*, I, q. 88, a. 3: "Primum autem quod intelligitur a nobis secundum statum praesentis vitae, est quidditas materialis, quae est nostri intellectus obiectum, ut multoties dictum est." See also *S.T.*, I, q. 84, a. 7; q. 85, a. 1 and a. 8; q. 87, a. 2, ad 2.

[20]*De ver.*, q. 1, a. 1: "Illud autem quod primo intellectus concipit quasi notissimum, et in quo omnes conceptiones resolvit, est ens."

[21]*S.T.*, I, q. 87, a. 3, ad 1.

[22]*Con. gent.*, II, c. 98: "Est enim proprium obiectum intellectus ens intelligibile, quod quidem comprehendit omnes differentias et species entis possibilis; quidquid enim esse potest, intelligi potest...Ex hoc autem quod substantia aliqua est intellectualis, comprehensiva est totius entis." In *S.T.*, I, q. 79, a. 2, Thomas asserts that every intellect, by the very fact that it is an intellect, has as its object being in all its dimensions: "Intellectus...habet operationem circa ens in universali." But whereas the divine intellect is all being in act *(se habet sicut actus totius entis)*, the created intellect can only be its object in potentiality, for if it were in act, it would be infinite *(quia sic oporteret quod esset ens infinitum)*.

or, in Aquinas' terminology, its *genus subiectum*, he pertains to metaphysics as the principle of its subject, the *principium subiecti*.[23] In other words, I attain to God as the principle of being when I reach the terminus of my knowledge of the being abstracted from sensible reality. I discover God as an existing reality that gives the reason for existence to all things that participate in his own being. Indeed, everything outside him is but a participation in being, the *Ipsum Esse*; it is its reflection or a distant approximation to it.

It is this beam of light that leads me, in a somewhat obscure yet most certain way, to the discovery of being. Through it I am assured, Thomas says, that the object of my intellect is being,[24] and that I have the capacity to attain it, for I come to know and discover being, not as it is in itself, but as it manifests itself in its reflection and in its participation. In other words, I discover that being exists and that the object of my immediate knowledge is nothing else than a participation in it. For it is he, the *Ipsum Esse*, that in the last analysis gives intelligibility to all that I know.

There is then an ascent from the being of material things to being itself, the *Ipsum Esse*. Such is the normal process followed by our intellect in its search for knowledge, and such is also the process we shall find in each of the five ways. The starting point is a concrete, existential datum of our sense experience. "It is certain, and evident to our senses, that in the world some things are in motion...." "In the world of sensible things we find there is an order of efficient causes...," etc. Having established the fact of our experience from the sensible world, Thomas raises the issue immediately to the level of being: "Motion is nothing else than the reduction of something from potentiality to actuality...." "Nothing can be the efficient cause of itself, for in such case a thing would be prior to itself, which is impossible...," etc. In each case, the metaphysical reflection on the ex-

---

[23]*In Boeth, de Trinit.*, q. 5, a. 4: "Res divinae non tractantur a philosophis, nisi prout sunt rerum omnium principia; et ideo pertractantur in illa doctrina, in qua ponuntur illa quae sunt communia omnibus entibus; quae habet subiectum ens in quantum est ens...in qua considerantur res divinae, non tamquam subiectum scientiae, sed tamquam principium subiecti."

[24]*S.T.*, I, q. 12, a. 4, ad 3. The created intellect is in passive potentiality to all being, including the divine essence, but it cannot attain it by its own power alone. Hence, in order to be raised to the beatific vision, the created intellect needs the light of glory and union with the divine essence. The proof of the possibility of this elevation is that the created intellect can apprehend form itself and being itself in a concrete sensible reality. *Ibid.*: "Et huius signum est quod...intellectus noster potest in abstractione considerare quod in concretione cognoscit. Etsi enim cognoscat res habentes formam in materia, tamen resolvit compositum in utrumque, et considerat ipsam formam per se....Et ideo, cum intellectus creatus per suam naturam natus sit apprehendere formam concretam et esse concretum in abstractione, per modum resolutionis cuiusdam, potest per gratiam elevari ut cognoscat substantiam separatam subsistentem, et esse separatum subsistens."

periential data leads us to the same necessary conclusion: God exists. Whether it be under the aspect of a first immovable mover (first way), a first efficient cause (second way), a self-existent and necessary being (third way), a supremely perfect being (fourth way), or the first intelligent being (fifth way) that God appears to us at the end of the proof, we arrive in each case at a transcendent being, or a being that is outside every series of causes and above the entire order of creation. While it itself is not ordered to any other being, all other beings are totally and necessarily ordered to it as to their efficient, exemplary, and final cause.

Since, therefore, God is outside the whole order of creation, and all creatures are ordered to him, and not conversely, it is manifest that creatures are really related to God himself; whereas in God there is no real relation to creatures, but only a relation of reason, inasmuch as creatures are referred to him.[25]

III.   THE METAPHYSICAL STRUCTURE
OF THE FIVE WAYS

A.   A General View

Before we give an account of the five ways, an observation is in order. In the *Summa theologiae* Aquinas introduces his answer to the question of "Whether God exists" by saying: "The existence of God can be proved in five ways." He wants, therefore, to set forth five proofs and takes care to number them one by one in the course of the article. This reveals a two-fold intent on his part.

In the first place, if there are five ways, each of them must be distinct from the others and sufficient by itself to prove that God exists. Stated otherwise, one way cannot be reduced to any of the others, nor can the five ways together be reduced to one single proof that would contain all of them. The five ways are undoubtedly complementary to one another in the sense that, while each of them takes as its starting point a particular aspect of created being in order to argue to God from that point of view, all together they give us a complete view of both the radical exigency of creatures for God and the richness of the divine perfections that the ways manifest to us. It remains true, however, that each way unfolds along its own particular line of thought and truly leads to God: "And this," we read at the end of each way, "we call God," or "everyone calls God."

Here a second question arises. Did Thomas really intend to reduce all his theistic proofs to five, to the exclusion of any other? It seems that a

---

[25]*S.T.*, I, q. 13, a. 7.

positive answer must be given to this question. Aquinas' general line of reasoning is this: by analyzing the beings of our sense experience, we discover that they cannot be adequately explained through themselves. Indeed, they manifest a quintuple insufficiency, which is revealed, upon reflection, by the fact that they are composite beings. 1) They are composed of act and potency, for they go from potentiality to actuality (first way). 2) They are composed of essence and existence, for their *esse* is caused and is not part of their essence (second way). 3) They are also composed of matter and form, because, as corruptible, their being can be dissolved (third way). 4) Likewise, they are composed of the *quod* and the *ex quo (ex esse et quod est),* since every being that is the object of our experience is a subject (*quod*) that is qualified as good and true and a being of such and such a kind (*ex quo*). These beings are multiple and diverse; they possess being but are not being itself (fourth way). 5) Finally, they are composed of substance and accidents. They possess in effect a triple perfection: first, that by which they are constituted in their own particular entity or reality (substantial perfection); second, that by which they are endowed with certain specific powers (accidental perfections); and third, that by which they achieve an end outside themselves. To act for an end implies an intention: this is the thrust of the fifth way.

In the third question of the first part of the *Summa theologiae,* where he deals with divine simplicity, Thomas excludes from God the quintuple composition that he finds in concrete material beings. God is composed of neither matter and form (art. 2), nor supposit and nature (art. 3), nor supposit and *esse* (art. 3), nor *esse* and *essentia* (art. 4), nor finally of substance and accidents (art. 6). Fundamentally—and this is a notion that pervades the entire question—there is in God no composition whatsoever of act and potency.

St. Thomas does not distribute the five ways at random or in a merely casual order; rather he sets them down according to a rational plan, beginning with the first fact of our experience.

The First Way. This represents the point of departure for our metaphysical reflection. The first, and therefore most manifest fact of our experience, is change or becoming. It is from here, from this most evident fact, that we initiate our ascent to God: something passes from potentiality to actuality, something is "moved." How are we going to explain this transition from potentiality to act? Will it not be necessary to ascend to a first immovable mover, a pure act, to explain it?

The Second Way. There is something more fundamental than change or becoming, and this too must be accounted for. We must explain not only the actual production of something by way of change, but also the underlying reality, the being itself of the things that change. This is what is known as the way of causality applied to the production of the very being of the objects of our experience. It will not be difficult to show that the being in question depends on its causes for its coming into existence. The acknowledgment of a series of causes that contribute, each in its own way, to the production of the effect is of course the starting point of our investigation. But are these causes, no matter what their number, sufficient to explain the being itself of the effect, or must we not attain to a first cause, a self-existing being?

The Third Way. The beings of our experience are of a fragile and corruptible nature. Not only do they have no reason in themselves for their existence, but their existence itself is ephemeral. They do not last, for they are generated and corrupted, they are born and die. Since they exist only for a limited span of time, they are only contingent, that is, "they are possible to be and not to be." If all existing beings were of this nature, how could we ever explain their emergence into existence, their *inceptio*? Shall we not be forced to admit that beyond that which is possible to be and not to be there is a being that is necessary? That beyond time, which is the measure of corruptible beings, there is a being that is eternal and immutable?

The Fourth Way. Here we are faced with a new line of reasoning, which is formally grounded in the multiplicity and diversity of the beings of our experience. Everything that exists in the universe (*in rebus*) has a certain amount of being, truth, and goodness, but not in the same degree: one has more being, is truer and better (ontologically) than another. Now degrees are so called because of their relation to a maximum of the same kind (*maxime tale*). How can we, then, explain the existence of beings with a limited amount of perfection without a being that is unrelated to any other, and is therefore unique, unlimited, and self-existent? This is but another way of saying that the beings of our experience participate in being itself, which in turn is the cause of their participated being.

The Fifth Way. A final observation shows us that the beings of our experience act and operate. They come out, as it were, of their inner selves in order to enrich themselves at the expense of other beings. They tend to an end, and in so doing, they achieve their greatest perfection. What is this end? Who directs them toward it? If we consider the universe at large, which, far from being in a chaotic state, manifests a magnificent order, shall we not be compelled to admit that there is a final end that transcends the entire realm of creation and a government that brings about the order devised by a first intelligence directing everything toward that end?

In the foregoing pages it has been our intention to show only the nature and scope of Aquinas' procedure in setting forth his five ways and the logical sequence of his reasoning that takes its start from what he calls the most obvious datum of our experience. Hopefully, this brief exposition will suffice to convince everyone of the faultless logic and comprehensive character of the Thomistic proofs, which omit no fundamental aspects of concrete reality as it presents itself to our experience and reflection. We must now show the basic features of Aquinas' reasoning in each of the five ways and point out their fundamental metaphysical structure.

B. A Detailed Analysis of the Five Ways

1. THE FIRST WAY

"The first and more manifest way is the argument from motion."

a. The starting point is the fact of motion (*motus*) in the world. "It is certain, and evident to our senses, that in the world some things are in motion." One cannot deny motion, Thomas says. But what does he really mean by motion or *motus*? Before answering this question, it is worth noting that Aquinas uses the terms *movere* and *immutare*, motion and change, indiscriminately.[26] As for the meaning of the two terms, here is what Aquinas says: "To move is nothing else than to reduce something from potentiality to actuality." Or more explicitly: "That which is in potentiality needs to be reduced to act by something that is in act; and that is to move."[27] The general meaning of motion is therefore to pass from one state to another: "It is of the nature of change that something should be different now from what it was before."[28]

Yet change is conceivable only in terms of an end or act to be achieved. This is what specifies change as such: "Changes receive species and dignity, not from the terminus *a quo*, but from the terminus *ad quem*."[29] Now the idea of act involves the idea of perfection: "Every act is some sort of perfection."[30] And, as we have already seen, for Thomas there are three kinds of perfection in beings: an essential perfection, an accidental perfection or the principle of operation, and finally, the operation itself as tending toward an object or end. The transition from potentiality to actuality can refer either to a substantial or accidental form or to operation. Hence the starting point of the first way is not merely a change in the physical order such as local motion, but includes all the changes that take place in

---

[26]Here are some references: *Movere, S.T.*, I, q. 2, a. 3; I, q. 5, a. 4; *Immutare, S.T.*, I, q. 106, a. 2; *Motio, S.T.*, I–II, q. 9, *per totum;* I–II, q. 109, a. 1; I–II, q. 111, a. 2; I–II, q. 113, a. 3; *Mutatio, S.T.*, I, q. 45, a. 3; I, q. 105, *per totum.*

[27]*S.T.*, I–II, q. 9, a. 1. Henceforth all the texts without explicit reference will be taken from *S.T.*, I, q. 2, a. 3.

[28]*S.T.*, I, q. 45, a. 2, ad 2.

[29]*S.T.*, I, q. 45, a. 1, ad 2.

[30]*S.T.*, I, q. 5, a. 3.

nature, such as the birth or emergence of a being and the movement involved in the activity of the human soul, as when we perform an intellective or voluntary act.[31]

b. Thomas defines *motus* and *movere* in terms of potentiality and actuality: "Motion is the act (or actualization) of a being in potentiality." "To move is to reduce something from potentiality to actuality." This notion calls for an analysis. Potentiality and actuality are said primarily and frequently of beings that are subject to movement. However, potentiality and actuality are more fundamentally said of all finite beings.[32] This, says Aquinas, is the first division of being as such: "Potentiality and actuality divide being and every kind of being."[33] The notion of potentiality and actuality is, in Thomas' philosophy, a primary notion of metaphysics. By referring to it in his first way, he clearly shows that, from the very beginning, he raises himself to the metaphysical level.

One cannot, properly speaking, define actuality and potentiality, for the first simple notions admit of no definition.[34] It is possible, however, to form a concept of them by analyzing their mutual relationship. Actuality and potentiality are, in effect, correlative notions.[35] Actuality is perfection, achievement.[36] Since existence is the ultimate achievement inasmuch as it is through it that a thing truly becomes a reality, *esse* is the actuality of every form or nature.[37]

---

[31] This is how Thomas understands the transition from potentiality to actuality. See, for example, with regard to intellect: *S.T.*, I, q. 105, a. 3; I-II, q. 109, a. 1; and with regard to will: *S.T.*, I-II, q. 9, a. 6; I-II, q. 10, a. 4; I-II, q. 109, a. 2. By applying the principles laid down in the first way, Thomas can very well use the spiritual movement of either intellect or will as a starting point for his proof.

[32] *In Metaph.*, L. 9, lect. 1: "Potentia enim et actus, ut plurimum, dicuntur in his quae sunt in motu, quia motus est actus entis in potentia. Sed principalis intentio huius doctrinae non est de potentia et actu secundum quod sunt in rebus mobilibus solum, sed secundum quod sequuntur ens commune. Unde et in rebus immobilibus invenitur potentia et actus, sicut in rebus intellectualibus." *In Metaph.*, L. 11, lect. 9: "Ens dividitur per actum et potentiam. Et hoc est quod dicit, quod entium quoddam est actu, sicut primum movens, quod Deus est; quoddam potentia tantum ut materia prima, quoddam potentia et actu, sicut omnia intermedia."

[33] *S.T.*, I, q. 77, a. 1. See also *De spir. creat.*, a. 1: "Cum potentia et actus dividant ens et cum quodlibet genus per actum et potentiam dividatur"; *Con. gent.*, II, c. 54: "Compositio actus et potentiae est in plus quam compositio formae et materiae. Unde materia et forma dividunt substantiam materialem, potentia autem et actus dividunt ens commune."

[34] *In Metaph.*, L. 9, lect. 5: "Prima simplicia definiri non possunt, cum non sit in definitionibus abire in infinitum. Actus autem est de primis simplicibus; unde definiri non potest."

[35] *Con. gent.*, I, c. 22: "Omne autem cui convenit aliquis actus, aliquid diversum ab eo existens, se habet ad ipsum ut potentia ad actum: actus enim et potentia ad se invicem dicuntur."

[36] *S.T.*, I, q. 5, a. 3: "Omne enim ens in quantum est ens, est in actu et quodammodo perfectum: quia omnis actus perfectio quaedam est."

[37] *S.T.*, I, q. 3, a. 4: "Esse est actualitas omnis formae vel naturae: non enim bonitas vel humanitas significatur in actu nisi prout significamus eam esse. Oportet igitur quod ipsum

Just as actuality implies a relationship to potentiality, so potentiality is correlative to actuality.[38] Moreover, potentiality is not known except through its relation to act.[39] Whether considered from its active or passive viewpoint, potentiality is a principle of motion or change (*motus*). There is then a twofold potentiality, active and passive. Active potentiality is a principle of activity (*principium agendi*), or a principle of change in something else precisely as it is something else (*principium transmutationis in alio in quantum est aliud*); it is a capacity for action. Passive potentiality, on the other hand, is a principle of change whereby the recipient is moved or transformed by something else inasmuch as it is something else (*est principium quod aliquid moveatur ab alio in quantum est aliud*); it is a capacity for receiving. Passive potentiality is related to active potentiality: "This [passive] potentiality is related to the first active potentiality, for passion is caused by an agent. And for this reason passive potentiality is related to active [potentiality]."[40]

We thought it appropriate to furnish the preceding explanations for a proper understanding of Thomas' text. As a primary metaphysical reality, the composition of actuality and potentiality is found everywhere. However, it is clear that the starting point of the first way is not this composition as such but rather the transition from potentiality to actuality that is represented by *motus*. It is the reality of *motus* that is at issue here, a reality that is distinct from the agent (*movens*), the subject (*patiens*), the movable (*mobile*) that passes from potentiality to actuality, and the terminus of the change or the perfected act (*actus perfectus*).[41] To deny the

---

esse comparetur ad essentiam quae est aliud ab ipso, sicut actus ad potentiam." *S.T.*, I, q. 4, a. 1, ad 3: "Ipsum esse est perfectissimum omnium: comparatur enim ad omnia ut actus. Nihil enim habet actualitatem, nisi in quantum est: unde ipsum esse est actualitas omnium rerum et etiam ipsarum formarum."

[38]*S.T.*, I, q. 5, a. 1, ad 1: "Cum ens dicat aliquid proprie esse in actu, actus autem proprie ordinem habeat ad potentiam."

[39]*S.T.*, I, q. 84, a. 2: "Unde nec ipsa potentia cognoscitur nisi per actum."

[40]The texts on active and passive potentiality are taken from St. Thomas' Commentary on Aristotle's *Metaphysics*, L. 9, lect. 1.

[41]St. Thomas has devoted no fewer than five lectures to the study of *motus* in his Commentary on Aristotle's *Physics*, i.e., L. 1, lects. 1 to 5. These lectures are an indispensable source for a thorough understanding of the Thomistic concept of *motus*, which underlies the whole first way. Let us recall the definition of *motus* as "actus existentis in potentia." *Motus* is thus the act of the movable "in quantum est mobile," and this act is received in the movable and caused by the *movens*: "actus motus est in mobili, cum sit actus mobilis, causatus tamen in eo a movente" (lect. 4).

Action and passion do not constitute two different realities, but are one and the same reality: "Actio et passio non sunt duo motus, sed unus et idem motus: secundum enim quod est ab agente, dicitur actio; secundum autem quod est in patiente, dicitur passio." As far as action is concerned, this is in the patient or receiver: "actio est actus ab agente in aliud. Idem actus est huius, id est agentis, ut a quo, et tamen est in patiente ut receptus in eo" (lect. 5).

There are in *motus* a real element and a conceptual element: "Ratio motus completur

reality of *motus* is to affirm either that there is an actualization of being without any becoming, in which case being would have come from nothing, or that at the very starting point being was already in act, i.e., was already what was supposed to have come to be at the end of the process of becoming.

But how is the transition from potentiality to actuality accomplished in *motus*? Needless to say, we speak of the reality of *motus*, but what, in fact, is such a reality? *Motus*, let us remember, refers to both the agent and the patient or recipient. From the point of view of the agent it is called action, whereas from the point of view of the patient it is called passion. The truth of the matter is that it is one and the same reality that is properly said to take place in the patient, for action is in the subject that is being acted upon (*actio est in passo*).

c. From the preceding discussion it is evident that *motus* implies an action received as a perfection in the thing that is moved. Now an agent acts inasmuch as it is in act: "Every action is caused by an existing being in act, for nothing acts except in so far as it is in act." Hence the principle enunciated in the first way, "Whatever is moved is moved by another," and the subsequent explanation of the term *moveri*: "For nothing can be moved unless it is in potentiality to that toward which it is moved." Accordingly, for a thing to be moved, it must be in passive potentiality with regard to the terminus of the movement which is its perfection or act. *Movere*, on the other hand, means to cause something to go from passive potentiality to actuality: "For to move is nothing else than to reduce something from potentiality to actuality." To move, a being must therefore be in active potentiality, i.e., in act: "A thing moves inasmuch as it is in act."

If the movable thing moved itself or caused itself to go from potentiality to actuality, it would itself already have to be in act when it is only in potentiality. But to be in potentiality and actuality at one and the same time and in the same respect is a contradiction: "It is not possible that the same thing should be at once in actuality and potentiality in the same respect, but only in different respects." Hence the conlusion: "It is therefore impossible that in the same respect and in the same way a thing should be both mover and moved, i.e., that it should move itself." From which it follows that the statement, "Whatever is moved must be moved by another," is true and correct.

d. This is how Aquinas proceeds from the moved mover (*movens*

non solum per id quod est de motu in rerum natura, sed etiam per id quod ratio apprehendit. De motu in rerum natura, nihil aliud est quam actus imperfectus qui est inchoatio quaedam actus perfecti in eo quod movetur...sed quantum ad id quod ratio apprehendit circa motum, scilicet esse medium quoddam inter duos terminos, sic iam implicatur ratio causae et effectus: nam reduci aliquid de potentia ad actum non est nisi ab aliqua causa agente. Et secundum hoc motus pertinet ad praedicamentum actionis et passionis" (lect. 5).

motum) to the first immovable mover (*primum movens immobile*). If the
agent that moves is itself moved, it must be moved by another, and that by
another again. But this cannot go on to infinity, because then there would
be no first mover, and consequently, no other mover, for subsequent
movers move only inasmuch as they are moved by the first mover.

Here we are confronted with the problem of the movers that are themselves moved (*moventia mota*), that is, agents which, while being the principle of action, are in turn moved: "They move and are moved." The
mover that is moved (*movens motum*) does not undergo any change in so
far as it moves (or as *movens*); it is rather the cause of the change in the
thing moved. But inasmuch as it itself is moved, the change is in that
which moves (*in movente moto*), i.e., in itself, because it itself passes from
potentiality to actuality. The agent cannot be identified with its operation.

The mover that is moved (*movens motum*) is said to be moved as
regards the last act to which the movable is reduced, that is, a movable
that is moved but itself does not move (*motum non movens*). In fact, what
is only moved is in potentiality to the act to be achieved (*ad actum perfectum*). Not having in itself this perfection in act, it must receive it from
another. Now the moving agent moves only inasmuch as it is in act as
regards the perfection to whose acquisition it leads the movable. Were it
in act by itself, it would be moving without being moved (*movens non
motum*), it would be purely and simply in act, it would not pass from
potentiality to actuality; in other words, it would be identical with its own
acting. But if it is not identical with its own acting, it must first be in potentiality toward the performance of its operation. And to pass from
potentiality to the actuality of its operation, it must be moved by another
which, itself, is an act that moves but is not moved (*movens non motum*).

"This cannot go on to infinity..." (*Non est procedere in infinitum*).
The subordination of secondary agents is a *per se* subordination, in the
sense that all secondary movers are said to move with regard to the last effect. It is always a question, let us not forget, of explaining the reduction
of the movable (*motum non movens*) to its act. Since the movable is only
potentially moved (*motum*), it cannot possibly give this perfection to itself;
it must receive it through motion or *motus*. More specifically, the movable
is moved by the mover, which in turn is moved by another mover but
always with regard to the last act. Thus each of the movers contributes its
share to the perfection or act of the movable, and does so inasmuch as it is
actually moving (*actu movens*). But since each secondary mover does not
actually move except in so far as it itself is moved in its own turn, in order
to explain change or motion one must arrive at a first immovable mover.[42]

In every moved mover (*movens motum*) there is only a single motion by

---

[42]Here are some texts illustrating the conclusion of the first way. *De pot.*, q. 3, a. 7:

which the mover passes from the potentiality of acting to act, the act by which it itself operates on the movable. Thus one and the same motion activates all the secondary movers so as to achieve the last effect which is exterior to themselves and is found within the movable. This motion comes to them from the immovable mover (*movens immobile*).

The immovable mover is not part of the series of secondary movers but transcends them all. Since it is above them, it guarantees all motion and change, all passage from potentiality to actuality. The immovable mover does not act in the sense that it accomplishes something by which it acquires a new perfection. Its acting is its very self. It does not pass, as it were, into action, and yet everything is moved by it: it is pure act and the source of all activity.

2.   THE SECOND WAY

"The second way is from the nature of efficient cause."

a. The second way is based on the reality of efficient causality. It is not a duplication of the first way. Whereas in the first way we were concerned with motion (*motus*), the becoming of an effect and its actual production by way of change, here we shall analyze the end or terminus of the becoming (*fieri*). The very being of the effect (*esse effectus*) must be explained and not merely its becoming. It is for this reason that recourse must be had to the notion of cause.

Cause is commonly understood in terms of *fieri* or becoming, because motion (*motus*) is the first object of our experience.[43] However, when taken more formally, cause refers to the very being of the effect, so that to cause is to produce the being of the effect: "Cause indicates some sort of

---

"Sed quia nulla res per seipsam movet vel agit nisi sit movens non motum; tertio modo dicitur una res esse causa actionis alterius in quantum movet eam ad agendum; in quo non intelligitur collatio aut conservatio virtutis activae, sed applicatio virtutis ad actionem... Et quia natura inferior agens non agit nisi mota, eo quod huiusmodi corpora inferiora sunt alterantia alterata; caelum autem est alterans non alteratum, et tamen non est movens nisi motum, et hoc non cessat quousque perveniatur ad Deum: sequitur de necessitate quod Deus sit causa actionis cuiuslibet rei naturalis ut movens et applicans virtutem ad agendum." *S.T.*, I, q. 105, a. 5: "Si sint multa agentia ordinata, semper secundum agens agit in virtute primi: nam primum agens movet secundum ad agendum. Et secundum hoc omnia agunt in virtute ipsius Dei; et ita ipse est causa actionum omnium agentium." *S.T.*, I-II, q. 79, a. 2: "Omnis autem actio causatur ab aliquo existente in actu, quia nihil agit nisi secundum quod est actu. Omne autem ens actu reducitur in primum actum, scilicet Deum, sicut in causam, qui est per suam essentiam actus. Unde relinquitur quod Deus sit causa omnis actionis in quantum est actio."

[43]*In Metaph.*, L. 5, lect. 2: "Dicitur causa unde primum est principium permutationis et quietis; et haec est causa movens vel efficiens."

influence on the being (*esse*) of what is caused."[44] Where there is no becoming in the proper sense of the term, there is causality. Hence whatever is found in a being outside its own essence must be caused either by that essence's own principles, as the proper attributes that flow from the essence, or by an external principle. When the *esse* itself of a thing is really distinct from the essence, then it must be caused by an external cause or by the essential principles of that thing.[45] The notion of cause is applied in its highest degree to creation, for "to create is, properly speaking, to cause or produce the being of things."[46]

Aquinas' thought is therefore clear. He has recourse to efficient causality in the second way to account for the very being of the effect. Over and above the action of the secondary causes in the production of the effect, whether by change or otherwise, there is in the last analysis a creation. But, the starting point of his argument must be a fact of experience. What is that fact? The awareness of a series of efficient causes, each one contributing to the production of an effect, and the consideration that among those causes there is an order.

b. *The order of causes.*

i. One must consider in the first place the order of cause to effect and of effect to cause or causes. As Thomas says, "to make and to be made denote a relation of cause to effect, and imply change only as a consequence."[47] Moreover, "from each cause there results a certain order in its effects, for every cause is a principle."[48] The effect, on the other hand, necessarily implies a relation to its cause, for the effect cannot be its own cause. If a thing were its own efficient cause, it would be prior to itself, which is impossible. Hence nothing can give *esse* to itself, if it itself is

---

[44]*In Metaph.*, L. 5, lect. 1. The study of causes as such belongs properly to the metaphysician: "Considerare de causis in quantum huiusmodi, proprium est philosophi primi; nam causa in eo quod causa est, non dependet a materia secundum esse, eo quod in his etiam quae a materia sunt separata, invenitur ratio causae." *In Phys.*, L. 2, lect. 5, and *In Metaph.*, L. 5, lect. 1.

[45]*S.T.*, I, q. 3, a. 4. See also *Con. gent.*, I, c. 22 "Amplius..."; *De ente et essentia,* c. 5. The text from this latter work is particularly important because it contains in a nutshell the whole proof of the second way: "Omne autem quod convenit alicui vel est causatum ex principiis naturae suae, sicut risibile in homine, vel advenit ab aliquo principio extrinseco, sicut lumen in aëre ex influentia solis. Non autem potest esse quod ipsum esse sit causatum ab ipsa forma vel quidditate rei, dico sicut a causa efficiente: quia sic aliqua res esset causa sui ipsius, et aliqua res seipsam in esse produceret, quod est impossibile. Ergo oportet quod omnis talis res, cuius esse est aliud a natura sua, habeat esse ab alio. Et quia omne quod est per aliud reducitur ad id quod est per se, sicut ad causam primam, ideo oportet quod sit aliqua res quae sit causa essendi omnibus rebus, eo quod ipsa est esse tantum."

[46]*S.T.*, I, q. 45, a. 6.

[47]*S.T.*, I, q. 45, a. 2, ad 2.

[48]*S.T.*, I, q. 105, a. 6.

in need of receiving it: "Nothing can be the sufficient cause of its own being, if its being is caused."[49]

Where, then, is the reason to be found for the actual existence of an effect? That is the specific problem of the second way. The answer to the question is obvious. The reason for the existence of an effect must be found in its cause. The cause, in turn, cannot be held responsible for its effect, unless it somehow precontains it. "Whatever perfection exists in an effect must be found in the efficient cause."[50] It is plain that every effect pre-exists virtually in its efficient cause, and to pre-exist virtually in an efficient cause is to pre-exist not less but more perfectly.[51]

ii. In the second way Thomas speaks of a series of intermediate causes, or causes that exert their causality between the ultimate effect and the first cause. This series concerns an order of causes that are formally subordinated to one another precisely in their causation. In such a series, where the causes are linked together by virtue of their nature, an infinite regress is impossible, for the first among such causes is the cause of the intermediate and the intermediate is the cause of the last, no matter what the number of intermediate causes: "Because in all efficient causes following in order, the first is the cause of the intermediate cause, and the intermediate is the cause of the ultimate cause, whether the intermediate cause be several or one only."

On the other hand, Thomas continues, to suppress the cause is to suppress the effect. Hence if there is no first cause among the efficient causes, there will be no ultimate and no intermediate cause. But to go on to infinity in a series of efficient causes is to suppress the first efficient cause. Consequently, there will be neither an ultimate effect nor any intermediate efficient cause, all of which is plainly false. There must be therefore a first efficient cause.

Thomas' statement, "In all efficient causes following in order, the first is the cause of the intermediate cause, and the intermediate is the cause of the ultimate cause," could be misleading. For a correct interpretation of it certain other more explicit texts of his must be used. A valuable explanation can be found in his Commentary on Aristotle's *Metaphysics* and especially in his treatise *De potentia*. The text of this latter work is particularly enlightening: "Furthermore, we find that the order of effects follows the order of causes, and this must be so on account of the likeness

---

[49]*S.T.*, I, q. 3, a. 4.

[50]*S. T.*, I, q. 4, a. 2.

[51]*S. T.*, I, q. 4, a. 2: "Manifestum est enim quod effectus praeexistit virtute in causa agente: praeexistere autem in virtute causae agentis, non est praeexistere imperfectiori modo, sed perfectiori." See also *S.T.*, I, q. 19, a. 4 and *De pot.*, q. 3, a. 15.

of the effect to its cause." This is exactly the problem that concerns us: the order of causes as it is related to the order of effects.

Now in every natural thing we find that it is a being, a natural thing, and of this or that nature. The first is common to all beings, the second to all natural things, the third to all the members of a species, while a fourth, if we take accidents into account, is proper to this or that individual. Accordingly this or that individual thing cannot by its action produce another individual of the same species except as the instrument of that cause which includes in its scope the whole species and, besides, the whole being of the inferior creature. Wherefore no action in these lower bodies attains to the production of a species except through the power of the heavenly body, nor does anything produce being except by the power of God. For being is the most common first effect and more intimate than all other effects: wherefore it is an effect which it belongs to God alone to produce by his own power.[52]

Thus—and this is the meaning of Thomas' reasoning in his second way—the *ultimum,* that is, the ultimate determination of the effect, is due to an intermediate cause that produces such and such an effect or an effect that is proper to an individual within the species. A man generates a man, but no individual human being can be the cause of human nature as such, or else it could be its own cause.

A perfect thing participating any nature, makes a likeness to itself, not by absolutely producing that nature, but by applying it to something else. For an individual man cannot be the cause of human nature absolutely, because he would then be the cause of himself; but he is the cause that human nature exists in the man begotten.[53]

If we suppose that there is in nature a universal cause acting on the world of our inferior realities—a cause such as Thomas considered celestial bodies to be—this cause could intervene in the production of human

---

[52]*De pot.,* q. 3, a. 7. The parallel text from *Metaphysics,* L. 6, lect. 3, is also worth quoting: "Invenitur autem in rebus triplex causarum gradus. Est primo causa incorruptibilis et immutabilis, scilicet divina; sub hac secundo est causa incorruptibilis, sed mutabilis, scilicet corpus caeleste; sub hac tertio sunt causae corruptibiles et mutabiles. Hae igitur causae in tertio gradu existentes sunt particulares et ad proprios effectus secundum singulas species determinatae: ignis enim generat ignem, et homo generat hominem, et planta plantam.—Causa autem secundi gradus est quodammodo universalis et quodammodo particularis. Particularis quidem, quia se extendit ad aliquod genus entium determinatum, scilicet ad ea quae per motum in esse producuntur; est enim causa movens et mota. Universalis autem, quia non ad unam tantum speciem mobilium se extendit causalitas eius, sed ad omnia quae alterantur et generantur et corrumpuntur: illud enim quod est primo motum, oportet esse causam omnium consequenter mobilium.—Sed causa primi gradus est simpliciter universalis: eius enim effectus proprius est esse: unde quidquid est, et quocumque modo est, sub causalitate et ordinatione illius causae proprie continetur."
[53]*S.T.,* I, q. 45, a. 5, ad 1.

nature as such (except of course for the soul, which, for Aquinas, is created). But this intermediate cause (or causes) does not account for everything that is in the effect. Beyond this individual nature, and beyond nature itself, there is the fact that this reality is a being, and no intermediate cause can explain the production of being as such. The effect transcends the nature and hence the power of the cause. More specifically, the being of the intermediate causes, their very *esse*, cannot find its sufficient reason within the causes themselves, for it is not of their nature to be *ipsum esse* or being itself. And this is why they are called intermediate rather than first causes. These causes are themselves caused; they receive from the first being both their nature and their *esse*.

While the secondary intermediate causes explain the fact that such an individual and an individual of such nature is caused, they do not and cannot of themselves explain the fact that there is being. On the level of being, they are on a par with the ultimate effect itself. *Esse*, as the most universal of effects, demands a most universal cause for its production.

For the more universal effects must be reduced to the more universal and prior causes. Now among all effects the most universal is being itself: and hence it must be the proper effect of the first and most universal cause, and that is God.[54]

It is worth noting that, for Thomas, *esse* is not a simple "formality" common to all beings. Rather it is the actuality of every form or nature. *Esse* is the most perfect of all realities, because it plays the role of act with regard to everything else. Nothing is in act except in so far as it is or exists. That is why *esse* is the actuality of all things and even of all forms.

Existence (*ipsum esse*) is the most perfect of all things, for it is compared to all things as that by which they are made actual; for nothing has actuality except in so far as it exists. Hence existence is that which actuates all things, even their forms.[55]

Since *esse* is found in everything, God is the cause of everything, i.e., of everything that is in the ultimate effect and of everything that is in the intermediate causes: "That which is first must be the cause of what comes afterwards, namely, the medium and the ultimate."[56] The intermediate

---

[54]*S.T.*, I, q. 45, a. 5.

[55]*S.T.*, I, q. 4, a. 1, ad 3.

[56]*In Metaph.*, L. 2, lect. 3. Because of its importance, we shall quote the full text: "In omnibus his, quae sunt media inter duo extrema, quorum unum est ultimum et aliud primum, necesse est quod illud quod est primum, sit causa posteriorum, scilicet medii et ultimi...Non enim possumus dicere id quod est ultimum esse causam omnium, quia nullius est causa; alioquin non est ultimum, cum effectus sit posterior causa. Sed nec possumus dicere quod medium sit causa omnium; quia nec est causa nisi unius tantum, scilicet

causes produce their specific effect, which is thus sufficiently explained through them. But since in the production of their effect there is also a production of being, it is necessary to go back to the self-existent being, which is also the first cause, to explain whatever there is of being in the effect.

Since this is the case, the being of the ultimate effect and of the secondary causes must come from God. Hence, in the production of the effect, the secondary causes are no more than God's instrumental causes. Still the effect is attributed in its entirety to both the created cause and the divine power.

It is also apparent that the same effect is not attributed to a natural cause and to divine power in such a way that it is partly done by God, and partly by the natural agent; rather, it is wholly done by both, according to a different way, just as the same effect is wholly attributed to the instrument and also wholly to the principal agent.[57]

One last remark. The intermediary causes will never be able to be more than causes of becoming (fieri).[58] Consequently the second way leads to a doctrine of creation, which is presupposed by all becoming.[59] Just as the first way led to the first immovable mover, so here we are led to a first cause which is not included within the series of intermediary causes but transcends it completely and is responsible for all created being. This cause is both immanent and transcendent. With regard to its immanence, the following text is englightening.

Now since God is being itself by his own essence, created beings must be his proper effect. . . . God causes this effect in things not only when they first begin to be, but as long as they are preserved in being. . . . But being is innermost in each thing and most fundamentally inherent in all things. . . . Hence it must be that God is in all things, and innermostly.[60]

---

ultimi. . . Sic igitur, si causae moventes procedant in infinitum, nulla erit causa prima: sed causa prima erat causa omnium: ergo sequeretur quod totaliter omnes causae tollerentur: sublata enim causa tolluntur ea quorum est causa."

[57]Con. gent., III, c. 70 in fine.

[58]De pot., q. 3, a. 4; S.T., I, q. 45, a. 5, ad 1; I, q. 104, a. 2, ad 3.

[59]S.T., I, q. 44, a. 2; I, q. 45, a. 5.

[60]S.T., I, q. 8, a. 1 and De pot., q. 3, a. 7 in fine. In this text from De potentia Thomas admirably summarizes the first two ways in a few sentences: "Sic ergo Deus est causa actionis cuiuslibet in quantum dat virtutem agendi et in quantum conservat eam (second way), et in quantum applicat actioni, et in quantum eius virtute omnis alia virtus agit (first way). Et cum coniunxerimus his, quod Deus sit sua virtus et quod sit intra rem quamlibet non sicut pars essentiae sed sicut tenens rem in esse, sequitur quod ipse in quolibet operante immediate operetur, non exclusa operatione voluntatis et naturae."

God is present to all beings more intimately than they are to themselves, for it is he who makes them be what they are. God's presence is at once creative and conservative, and yet the first cause enjoys an absolute transcendence over creatures. A created being is indeed totally dependent on God as its source, while God has no real relation to a creature. The creator's relation to his creatures is only one of reason.

3. THE THIRD WAY

"The third way is taken from possibility and necessity."

The third way argues from the possible to the necessary.[61] Indeed we find in nature things that are possible to be and not to be *(possibilia esse et non esse)*. Proof of this is the fact that they are generated and do corrupt,[62] which means that they are indifferent to existing and not existing.[63]

a. The starting point of the third way is definitely within the domain of

---

[61]The third way cannot be correctly interpreted without referring to Thomas' Commentary on the first book of *De caelo et mundo*, especially lectures 24 to 29. The proof has often been mishandled or disfigured for want of consulting the texts indispensable for its understanding.

[62]When faced with the expression "generari et corrumpi," one should not forget to consult Thomas' Commentary on *De generatione et corruptione*. A reminder of the notion of generation and corruption is found also in lecture 24 of *De caelo et mundo*. Generation is one form of *motus:* "Generatio importat aliquid commune, quod est incipere esse; et etiam importat determinatum modum essendi, scilicet per transmutationem." Conversely: "Corruptio importat desitionem [esse] cum determinato modo, scilicet per transmutationem." Hence the notion of the corruptible and the generated: "Sicut enim corruptibile est quod cum prius fuerit, nunc non est, vel contingit non esse quandoque in futurum, ita genitum est quod nunc est, sed prius non fuit." *Ibid.,* lect 26. Also: "Hoc autem quod est aliquando non esse, sequitur ad corruptibile et genitum sicut quoddam communius." *Ibid.,* lect 26. And conversely: "Propriissime dicitur aliquid esse incorruptibile, quod non solum non potest corrumpi, sed nec etiam quocumque modo aliquando esse et postea non esse; et similiter ingenitum proprie dicitur quod est impossibile scilicet esse et non esse, et quod non potest fieri quocumque tali modo quod prius non sit et postea sit." *Ibid.,* lect. 25.

[63]*Possibile esse et non esse* is said in two different ways: 1) "Possibile et impossibile uno modo dicuntur absolute, quia scilicet tale est quod possit esse verum vel non possit esse verum propter habitudinem terminorum. 2) Alio modo dicitur possibile et impossibile alicui, quod scilicet potest esse vel non esse verum, vel secundum potentiam activam vel passivam. Et sic accipitur hic possibile et impossibile, scilicet quod aliquod agens aut patiens potest aut non potest: haec enim significatio maxime congruit rebus naturalibus." *De caelo et mundo,* lect. 25.

It is not a question, in the third way, of the *possibile esse vel non esse absolute,* but of the *possibile esse et non esse alicui* "secundum potentiam quae est in ipsis." In other words, we are not concerned here with the limitation of being in itself, for this limitation is common to all beings that are not the one and unique necessary being in itself, or the being that is the *esse per se subsistens;* we are rather concerned with the limitation of the power to be within the duration of existence. The non-limitation of this duration of existence is due to some sort of immutability: the immutability of the *esse formae.* Accordingly, subsistent forms are not subject to the privation of the *esse formae,* "quia esse consequitur formam, et nihil corrumpitur nisi per hoc quod amittit formam. Unde in ipsa forma non est potentia ad non esse." *S.T.,* I, q. 9, a. 2.

time. The experiential datum is constituted by corruptible beings, which are subject to birth and death. They appear and disappear, an evident sign of their fragility. They do not exist always: their duration is limited. It is no doubt possible to deny the substantial change that is here involved. But where shall that lead us? To some sort of pantheism, where all these changes would be merely superficial and accidental manifestations of a single necessary being. If the cat is *a* cat, a living being with his own particular kind of life, and if man is *a* man, an individual being which is in himself distinct from other men and has his own personality entirely to himself, one is bound to admit the reality of their birth and death and, consequently, of their substantial change.

Since there are beings which are born and die (*generantur et corrumpuntur*), it must be admitted that they have the capacity to be and not to be; otherwise we will have to deny them the possibility of generation and corruption. This capacity refers to duration and, more specifically, to a limited duration that is measured by time. To deny this is to run into a contradiction. In fact, if one holds that these beings can have an unlimited duration, he will have to accept one of two alternatives. Either these beings have the power or internal capability to exist forever, and then there is no reason why they should not do so since their constitution seems to demand it. This, however, is contrary to the nature of a being that is subject to generation and corruption. Or, and this is the second alternative, the beings in question have at one and the same time the power to exist for an unlimited time and the capability not to exist for an unlimited time, which again is a contradiction.[64]

The article of the *Summa* here referred to is also very important for the understanding of the third way. Once placed in existence, the separated substances cannot but continue to exist (in the sense above mentioned), no matter whether they have received existence from eternity or in time. See also in this connection *S.T.*, I, q. 46, a. 1, ad 2.

[64] Aquinas develops this argument at great length in lecture 26 of the first book of *De caelo et mundo*. Since it is obviously impossible to reproduce here the whole text, we shall quote only two characteristic passages: "Si ergo ponamus quod aliquid existens in infinito tempore sit corruptibile, sequitur ex hoc quod est corruptibile, quod habeat virtutem ad hoc quod quandoque non sit; quod quidem oportet intelligi respectu eiusdem temporis infiniti in quo est, vel respectu alicuius partis eius. Quia ergo est in infinito tempore, et tamen ponitur potens non esse, eo quod est corruptibile, sit existens quod potest non esse, idest ponatur non esse ex quo dicis quod potest non esse. Et quia poterat non esse respectu infiniti temporis vel alicuius partis eius, sequitur quod simul secundum actum sit et non sit: quia in infinito tempore ponebatur esse, et postea ponitur non esse respectu eiusdem temporis." Here is the other passage: "Sicut enim corruptibile est quod, cum prius fuerit, nunc non est, vel contingit non esse quandoque in futurum, ita genitum est quod nunc est, sed prius non fuit. Non est autem dare aliquod tempus in quo id quod semper est, possibile sit non esse, neque in tempore finito neque in tempore infinito: quia quod potest esse tempore infinito, sicut id quod semper est, potest esse quolibet tempore finito, quod includitur a tempore infinito; et ita sequetur, secundum praedictam deductionem, quod aliquid simul sit et non sit, quod est impossibile."

What is the ground of the contingency of the beings that are possible to be and not to be? It is the very nature of such beings, that is, their composition of matter and form. "Being can change because the form changes, for it is the form that receives the *esse.*" Hence "nothing corrupts except inasmuch as it loses its form."[65] A being's loss of form is due to matter, which, as pure potentiality, is not totally actualized by its present form and has the potentiality to receive other forms.

Possibility of being and non-being does not belong to a thing save by reason of its matter, which is pure potentiality. And matter, since it cannot exist without a form, cannot have a potentiality in respect of non-being, save as, while existing under some form, it retains the possibility of receiving another form.[66]

To have the potentiality to receive other forms is to be able to have them in act. But matter cannot have them in act unless the preceding form disappears and makes room for a new one.

Prime matter tends toward its perfection by actually acquiring a form to which it was previously in potency, even though it then ceases to have the other form which it actually possessed before, for this is the way that matter may receive in succession all the forms to which it is potential, so that its entire potentiality may be successively reduced to act, which could not be done all at once.[67]

---

[65]*S.T.*, I, q. 9, a. 2.

[66]*De pot.*, q. 5, a. 3. Also *In Phys.*, L. 1, lect. 15: "Nihil est igitur aliud appetitus naturalis quam ordinatio aliquorum secundum propriam naturam in finem suum. Non solum autem aliquod ens in actu per virtutem activam ordinatur in suum finem, sed etiam materia secundum quod est in potentia; nam forma est finis materiae. Nihil igitur est aliud materiam appetere formam quam eam ordinari ad formam ut formam ad actum. Et quia sub quacumque forma sit, adhuc remanet in potentia ad aliam formam, inest ei semper appetitus formae: non propter fastidium formae quam habet, nec propter hoc quod quaerat contraria esse simul; sed quia est in potentia ad alias formas, dum unam habet in actu." We thought it necessary to quote these texts—and we could quote more—because they help to dissipate many misunderstandings about Aquinas' concept of matter. Hence: 1) Primary matter is pure potentiality. 2) It is a reality that is totally related to the form, so that its being cannot even be conceived or defined apart from its relation to the form, i.e., to its act. Just as it cannot be conceived apart from its act, so primary matter cannot exist apart, or separated from, its act. 3) Hence the reciprocal causality of matter and form: "materia etiam dicitur causa formae, in quantum forma non est nisi in materia; et similiter forma est causa materiae, in quantum materia non habet esse in actu nisi per formam: materia enim et forma dicuntur relative ad invicem" (*De princ. natur.*, no. 10). 4) The relation of matter to form is that of potentiality to act. From this it follows that the concepts of matter and form are in themselves metaphysical concepts. 5) On the physical level, one is never confronted with pure or primary matter, but always with matter as it is actuated by a form and endowed with quantity and extension. Primary matter is the metaphysical basis of material substances, but it cannot purely and simply be identified with corporeal beings in nature. These are bodies, i.e., composites of form and matter, and their matter is subject to dimensional quantity whereby it is divided into parts.

[67]*Con. gent.*, III, c. 22.

The third way, then, takes as its starting point the fact of generation and corruption, which shows that certain beings are possible to be and not to be and therefore have a limited duration. This is a particular category of beings in the sensible order that are subject to a substantial change involving a temporal succession, a beginning and an end.

b. It is impossible that in the universe there should be only beings of this kind. If that were the case, there would be no universe at all. Why? Because a being that is possible not to be, at some time does not exist (*quod possibile est non esse, quandoque non est*). Indeed, what is capable of not existing does not have within itself the reason for its existence and much less for existing always; otherwise it would not only always exist but would also exist necessarily. Since in it potentiality of being precedes the act of existing, the being in question must have had a beginning.

If all beings had a beginning, before they began there was nothing. But no being can emerge from nothing and, consequently, if at one time there was nothing, no being would be in existence today, for that which does not exist cannot give existence to anything. It is plain in fact that nothing can begin to exist except through something that is already in existence. In Thomas' words,

> Therefore, if everything is possible not to be, then at one time there could have been nothing in existence. Now if this were true, even now there would be nothing in existence, because that which does not exist begins to exist only by something already existing. Therefore, if at one time nothing was in existence, it would have been impossible for anything to have begun to exist; and thus even now nothing would be in existence.

The statement "at one time there was nothing in existence" does not refer to a real time before the beginning of things, for time has no meaning except as a measure of an existing reality. Rather it refers to a duration that is the measure of a permanent reality, i.e., that which can be neither generated nor corrupted. Now if everything had a beginning, before it began there was nothing in existence that would have a stable and permanent nature. Hence nothing could have become or emerged into existence. We are bound therefore to admit that beyond the fragile veil of time there must be something permanent. To multiply the series of possible beings will not solve the problem of existence but only push it back. There can never be a case in which a being that is possible to be and not to be will, of itself, be a necessary being and have an unlimited duration.

> A thing whose nature contains the possibility of non-existence does not acquire from an external source the necessity of being so that this necessity be contained in its nature, since this would involve a contra-

diction, to wit the possibility of a nature's non-existence together with the necessity of its existence.[68]

Beyond the temporal series of possible beings there must be a necessary and immutable being.

c. "There must exist something whose existence is necessary." What kind of necessary being will that be? We shall study this problem on the basis of Thomas' texts.

The beginning *(inceptio)* of something, not unlike its corruption *(corruptio)*, presupposes a permanent reality that remains the same under all changes. But "in those things which contain a possibility of non-being the matter remains."[69] Matter is therefore the reality which remains unaltered under the different forms it assumes.

But adequately to explain change or becoming, Thomas adds, a preexisting agent is also required.

> Corruptible things cease to exist, in so far as their matter receives another form, with which its previous form was incompatible: wherefore their corruption requires the action of a certain agent, whereby the new form is educed from its potential state into actual existence.[70]

What kind of agent is required in the case under consideration? A necessary agent. Aquinas speaks of a necessary being whose necessity has been caused, such as an angel and the heavenly bodies. Both of these are immutable: the angel because it is a purely subsistent form, and the heavenly bodies because their form, by conferring upon them a perfect act, exhausts the potentiality of their matter.[71] Although we can no longer accept Thomas' view concerning the heavenly bodies, nevertheless, we consider this hypothesis because it is a part of Aquinas' thought that we are supposed to interpret. For him the incorruptible heavenly bodies exert their causality upon other bodies: "They [the celestial bodies] are the causes of others by the fact that they cause generation and corruption and other changes in these lower things."[72]

In his third way Aquinas is very concise and confines himself to saying that one cannot stop at beings whose necessity is caused, nor proceed to infinity in a series of necessary beings of that nature: "It is impossible to go on to infinity in necessary things which have their necessity caused by another." One must therefore reach a being that is necessary of itself *(per se necessarium)*, or such a being that not only does not have a cause for its

---

[68]*De pot.*, q. 5, a. 3, ad 8.
[69]*De pot.*, q. 5, a. 3, c.
[70]*De pot.*, q. 5, a. 3, ad 2.
[71]*S.T.*, I, q. 9, a. 2 and *Con. gent.*, II, c. 30.
[72]*Con. gent.*, III, c. 22.

necessity, but it itself is the cause of the necessity of other necessary beings. "Therefore we cannot but admit the existence of some being having of itself its own necessity, and not receiving it from another, but rather causing in others their necessity."

The third way must be completed with certain other considerations that are found elsewhere in St. Thomas. Thus one must attain a being that is necessary of itself not only so as to explain the necessity of other necessary beings, but also because these other beings cannot of themselves explain the emergence of corruptible beings in this world. To say that they have a cause of their necessity is to acknowledge that they are not eternal in the strict sense of the term. Only he who is identical with his own being is also identical with his own duration, even though, properly speaking, God does not have duration; he simply is, he is eternity itself.[73] Hence those beings "which are not," or the necessary beings which have a cause, cannot produce being. Further, the action of these necessary agents always presupposes a subject on which to act. In the case of generation and corruption, the subject is primary matter. But even if we assume that this matter is eternally existent, along with those eternal agents that supposedly pre-exist things that are possible to be and not to be, it will still be necessary to admit that matter is created. Now only a being that is necessary of itself can create primary matter, for it alone is being itself.[74] On the other hand, primary matter is never without a form,[75] and since it is the composite that exists, it must also be the composite that is created.[76] Again, an agent that is limited in its being can neither create nor be the instrument of creation. Thus, in the last analysis, one is bound to admit the intervention of God.[77]

Clearly, then, the third way, no matter how we approach it, leads to a being that is necessary of itself. Behind the perishable there is the imperishable, the immutable, and the necessary, which gives the former the

---

[73]*S.T.*, I, q. 10, a. 3, c and ad 3.

[74]*S.T.*, I, q. 44, a. 2: "Oportet ponere etiam materiam primam creatam ab universali causa entium."

[75]*S.T.*, I, q. 44, a. 2, ad 3: "Ratio illa non ostendit quod materia non sit creata, sed quod non sit creata sine forma. Licet enim omne creatum sit in actu, non tamen est actus purus. Unde oportet quod etiam illud quod se habet ex parte potentiae sit creatum, si totum quod ad esse ipsius pertinet, creatum est." *Con. gent.*, II, c. 43: "Materia autem prima non potest praefuisse per seipsam ante omnia corpora formata, cum non sit nisi potentia tantum; omne enim esse in actu est ab aliqua forma."

[76]*S.T.*, I, q. 45, a. 4: "Proprie vero creata sunt subsistentia." And ad 3: "Ratio illa non probat quod sola materia creetur, sed quod materia non sit nisi ex creatione. Nam creatio est productio totius esse, et non solum materiae."

[77]*Con. gent.*, II, c. 43 *per totum*. The following conclusion is worth noting: "Impossibile est igitur quod prima inductio formarum in materia sit ab aliquo creante formam tantum: sed [est] ab eo qui est creator totius compositi."

power to appear on the scene of the world within the boundary of time. It is not a being that becomes necessary once it has been brought into existence, but a being that is necessary of itself. Behind time, which is the measure of what is subject to substantial change and has a before and after, there is eviternity, the duration of that which has neither before nor after and is subject to no change in its substantial being. And beyond time and eviternity there is eternity, which, in addition to guaranteeing the reality of both time and eviternity, is, properly speaking, neither a measure nor a duration but self-existent being itself.

4. THE FOURTH WAY

"The fourth way is taken from the gradation to be found in things."

The fourth way has a very particular structure. It includes two distinct parts: one ascending, from the degrees to the highest in that category (*maxime tale*); one descending, from the highest in a particular category to the various degrees of that perfection. The reason for this distinction will become evident during the course of our exposition.

a. *From the degrees to the "maxime tale."*

The fourth way places us in the very heart of metaphysics. Yet the starting point is simple. The objects of our experience are multiple and limited; theirs is a limitation that affects not only their duration but also their being. These objects are more or less true, more or less good, more or less noble, and the like. These qualifications, it is worth noting, belong to every existing being. They are, in fact, common and universal aspects of being as such, which they manifest in different ways.[78] Every being, inasmuch as it is a being, is good,[79] and just as the good is convertible with being, so is the true.[80] These are primary notions of metaphysics: the concepts of being, truth, goodness, and so forth.

What is affirmed at the very outset of the fourth way is the actual existence, in the things of our experience, of a reality that we assert to contain goodness, truth, and consequently being. Nevertheless, this reality is found to be realized in things, not in the same way, but according to various degrees. Now *more* and *less*, Thomas tells us, are predicated of different things in so far as they resemble in their different ways something which is the maximum. This means that to account for the existence of the different degrees of a particular perfection, we must reach a maximum in that particular order of perfection or something that embodies that perfection to the supreme degree.

---

[78]*De ver.*, q. 1, a. 1: "Modus expressus [sit] modus generaliter consequens omne ens."
[79]*S.T.*, I, q. 5, a. 3: "Omne ens, in quantum est ens, est bonum."
[80]*S.T.*, I, q. 16, a. 3: "Sicut bonum convertitur cum ente, ita et verum."

What is at issue is not merely an idea, but an actual reality containing the maximum of that perfection.[81] How could it be otherwise? The greater or lesser degrees of a perfection can be said only in relation to their approximation to a maximum (*maxime tale*), which is not just one or more degrees more perfect than other beings, but such that it realizes within itself the fullness of the perfection discovered in limited degrees in the beings of our experience. The *maxime tale* is therefore beyond the series of degrees; in its unlimited, infinite perfection, it transcends them all.

> Whenever something is found to be in several things by participation in various degrees, it must be derived by those in which it exists imperfectly from that one in which it exists most perfectly: because where there are positive degrees of a thing so that we ascribe it to this one more and to that one less, this is in reference to one thing to which they approach, one nearer than another: for if each one were of itself competent to have it, there would be no reason why one should have it more than another.[82]

In fact, if in our search for the explanation of the different degrees of perfection in the beings of our experience we could stop, let us say, at the tenth degree, the reason for our stopping there would be that ten degrees would realize the very essence of that perfection. But if the essence of goodness, truth, and being were ten degrees, it would be impossible to find it anywhere existing to any greater or lesser degree. The perfection in question would of itself be limited; it would have a fixed, stable degree. Moreover, being determined and limited in its essence, it would be found to be the same always and everywhere.

> That in respect of which a thing receives its species, must be something fixed and stationary, and as it were indivisible....If, therefore, a form, or anything at all, receives its specific nature in respect of itself, or in respect of something belonging to it, it is necessary that, considered in itself, it be something of a definite nature, which can be neither more nor less.[83]

But because in the perfection under discussion there are degrees, we must conclude that of itself the perfection is unlimited and that it is in reference

---

[81]We are confronted here with realities of which truth, goodness, and being are predicated, but only analogically. Being, for example, is predicated of many things, but only in relation to one and the same being: "Sciendum quod illud unum ad quod diversae habitudines referuntur in analogicis, est unum numero, et non solum unum ratione, sicut est unum illud quod per nomen univocum designatur. Et ideo dicit quod ens etsi dicatur multipliciter, non tamen dicitur aequivoce, sed per respectum ad unum; non quidem ad unum quod sit solum ratione unum, sed quod est unum sicut una quaedam natura" (*In Metaph.*, L. 4, lect. 1).

[82]*De pot.*, q. 3, a. 5.

[83]*S.T.*, I-II, q. 52, a. 1.

to this unlimited perfection that we can speak of degrees. Furthermore, the perfection's limitation to such degrees has a definite meaning. We are not face to face with the perfection itself, with the good, the true and, to put it summarily, with absolute being. Perfection as such cannot take on any outside element that would limit it and prevent it from being perfectly itself. Perfection does not lend itself to be exploited, as it were, in that way; it necessarily remains in its splendid isolation. "Although every essence may have something superadded to it, this cannot apply to absolute being."[84] The *maxime tale* is goodness, truth, and being by its very nature. It encompasses the whole plenitude of perfection that makes up the good, the true, and being itself. If it did not possess the whole plenitude of perfection, it would belong to the class of beings with a limited degree of perfection. Thomas therefore concludes that something exists that is supremely true, supremely good, and supremely noble and, consequently, also supremely being. And that is God.

> God is existence itself, of itself subsistent. Consequently, he must contain within himself the whole perfection of being.... Since therefore God is subsistent being itself, nothing of the perfection of being can be wanting to him.[85]

Thus the first part of the fourth way already concludes to the existence of the supreme being which is God.

If the *maxime tale* did not exist, if it were a pure creation of our mind, we would find ourselves confronted with this open contradiction: there is in existence something that is good, true, and being, and yet there is neither goodness, truth, nor being as such. The good, the true, and being are realized but never according to their essence or what is required by their constitutive nature. Something would exist in reality that does not have that which makes it be what it is: a perfection that of itself admits of no limit and yet does not exist in itself but is found in things that are graded and limited! Hence when we think we have found this perfection, spread out as it is among different things, it is not really this perfection we have discovered, nor is it its nature that has become manifest to us. What we have found are but faint images, imperfect approximations, which are distinct from the perfection itself and which borrow their name from the

---

[84]*S.T.*, I, q. 3, a. 6. (This is a quotation from Boethius' *De hebdomadibus*). See also *De ente et essentia*, c. 5: "Si autem ponatur aliqua res quae sit esse tantum, ita ut ipsum esse sit subsistens, hoc esse non recipiet additionem differentiae, quia iam non esset esse tantum, sed esse, et praeter hoc forma aliqua; et multo minus recipiet additionem materiae, quia iam esset esse non subsistens sed materiale... unde relinquitur quod talis res quae sit suum esse, non potest esse nisi una. Unde oportet quod in qualibet alia re praeter eam, sit aliud esse suum et aliud quidditas vel natura seu forma sua."

[85]*S.T.*, I, q. 4, a. 2.

perfection they resemble. It is because of the obvious inconsistency that would result from its denial, that a *maxime tale* must be said to exist in the order of truth, goodness, and being itself. Thus the first part of the proof leads to the existence of God as being itself and the exemplary cause of all other beings.[86]

---

[86]For certain authors the argument of the first part of the fourth way is not conclusive; for, so they say, it leads only to a *maxime tale* in the ideal order and not to an actually existing being. Accordingly, the real proof is only to be found in the second part of the fourth way. Likewise, there are those who fear that, if we accepted the notion of an actually existing *maxime tale* as the conclusion of the first part of the proof, we might be implicitly accepting St. Anselm's ontological argument, that is, an a priori argument.

The following observations will help throw some light on this issue. 1) Anselm's argument takes as its starting point the idea of *aliquid quo maius cogitari non potest,* i.e., something than which nothing greater can be conceived (cf. *S.T.,* I, q. 2, a. 1, ad 2), whereas the fourth way argues from the degrees of perfection that are found in things *(in rebus),* and is therefore an a posteriori argument *(ex effectibus ad causam).*

2) A prejudice that seems to dominate the mind of certain authors is that the only way to argue to God is by way of efficient causality, whereas for St. Thomas it is also possible to argue from effects to their exemplary and final cause. Thus in the forty-fourth question of the *Summa,* he views God as the efficient, exemplary, and final cause of all creatures.

3) As regards the first part of the fourth way, the very structure of the argument and the expressions therein clearly indicate that Thomas had in mind an existing reality to be attained by reasoning from the degrees of perfection discovered in creatures: "Est igitur aliquid quod est verissimum...et per consequens maxime ens." There is then really a *maxime ens* in the order of existence. In fact, Thomas does not say, "we must conceive a *maxime ens,"* but "there is...a *maxime ens."* Furthermore, if the *maxime tale* were not conceived as existing at the end of the first part of the fourth way, the second part would become unintelligible. The *maxime tale* is indeed the *causa omnium....* How could the mere idea of a *maxime tale* be the cause of all things? And, lest we forget, the *maxime tale* is said to be the cause of all things precisely as the *maxime tale.*

4) We are told that Thomas refers the reader to his Commentary on Aristotle's *Metaphysics* for the transition from the *maxime verum et bonum* to the *maxime tale.* However, this reference does not change in any way our interpretation of Thomas' text. If one starts from the *verum* that is found in things *(de veritate quae est in rebus—S.T.,* I, q. 16, a. 6), as in the case at issue, one must end up with a *maxime verum* that is also a reality. And since *verum et ens convertuntur,* the *maxime verum* can be none other than the *maxime ens.* It is right to say that the true is convertible with being: "Unumquodque sicut se habet ad hoc quod sit, ita etiam se habet ad hoc quod habeat veritatem." Hence what is subject to change in being, must also be subject to change as regards its truth: "Ea enim quorum esse non semper eodem modo se habet, nec veritas eorum semper manet. Et ea quorum esse habet causam, etiam veritatis causam habent." Now the cause of truth and being can be none other than the *verissimum* and the *maxime ens.* What Thomas says in *Metaphysics,* L. 2, lect. 2, is correct, and so is what he says, although in slightly different words, in the second part of the fourth way. But this is no argument against our interpretation of the fourth way. Moreover, let us not forget that in *Metaphysics, loc. cit.,* Thomas already assumes that there is a cause of truth: "Quia illud quod est causa veritatis, est causa communicans cum effectu in nomine et ratione communi, sequitur quod illud, quod est posterioribus causa ut sint vera, sit verissimum."

5) Finally, we would like to point out that Aquinas develops the proof at issue in other contexts by relying on the first part of the fourth way and leaving out completely the second part. See, for example, *Con. gent.,* I, c. 13. See also, as regards truth and goodness, *S.T.,* I, q. 16, a. 6 and *Con. gent.,* I, c. 38, respectively.

b. *From the "maxime tale" to the degrees.*

Although the existence of God is already proved in the first part of the fourth way, the second part is not without point. Here, however, the problem is reversed: How can we explain that outside of Being there are degrees of being? The reason can be only that the *maxime tale* or being to the supreme degree is the cause of all the degrees of being. To put it another way, one must see why we can speak of degrees of being and maintain at the same time that they are not Being, and the explanation is found in the efficient causality of the *maxime tale* with regard to the degrees of being. "Therefore there must be something which is to all beings the cause of their being, goodness, and every other perfection."

i. As efficient cause, the *maxime tale* explains the *similarity* existing between itself and its effects.

> Since every agent reproduces itself so far as it is an agent, and everything acts according to the manner of its form, the effect must in some way resemble the form of the agent. . . . In this way all created things, so far as they are beings, are like God as the first and universal principle of all being.[87]

The degrees of being, truth, and goodness are what they are only analogically, inasmuch as they are a faint representation of their cause imprinting its similarity on them.

ii. As efficient cause, the *maxime tale* explains the *existence* of the degrees of being. If there is being, and consequently truth and goodness, in the existential order, it is because God, the *maxime tale,* produces it. Of itself, what is not being as such, is nothing.

> What has its being from another is nothing considered in itself, if it be distinct from the being that it receives from another. . . . That which is may have a mixed being: but being itself cannot.[88]

Participated being receives whatever it has of reality from that which is being by its very nature. While borrowing its reality from God to whom it is totally indebted as to its source, a finite being remains nevertheless essentially distinct from him.

Created being does not add anything to the being of God; it is rather like his perduring impress. Hence one cannot say that there is an infinite being plus something else. To be exact, one must say that there is an infinite being and, totally dependent on it, the finite being, which exists only because of God and to the extent that God gives it reality. All created be-

---

[87]*S.T.*, I, q. 4, a. 3.
[88]*De pot.*, q. 3, a. 13, ad 4.

ing is therefore relative; it must be conceived in terms of a relation of total and unceasing dependence on the absolute that is God.

iii. As efficient cause, the *maxime tale* explains the *multiplicity* and *diversity* of the degrees of being. The possibility of having diverse and multiple degrees in participated being is due to the fact that the *esse* is received by and contracted to a particular nature as act by potency. "Because a created form thus subsisting has being, and yet is not its own being, it follows that its being is received and contracted to a determinate nature."[89]

God creates participations of his own being by establishing in creatures a relation between *esse* and essence, as between actuality and potentiality. One should not conceive potentiality, i.e., nature or essence, as having some sort of being before existing, but only as a principle that determines the limit of the *esse*. It is wrong, in other words, to think of potentiality or essence as existing prior to the *esse*, for potentiality or essence exists only for the *esse*. Thomas writes in this connection that essence is created with existence: "God at the same time gives being and produces that which receives being."[90] And again:

> From the very fact that being is ascribed to a quiddity, not only is the quiddity said to be but also to be created: since before it had being it was nothing, except perhaps in the intellect of the creator, where it is not a creature but the creating essence.[91]

Here we are face to face with the mystery of created being. Since of itself it is nothing (*in se consideratum est non ens*), created being must receive everything from God and, first of all, its intelligibility. It is God who creates, so to speak, the intelligibility of a creature, its possibility of being, its relation to existence: *id quod potest esse*. Just as potentiality and actuality are correlative principles and mutually referential notions, so are essence and existence. The essence of a created being cannot be defined except in terms of its relation (possible or actual) to existence. Also, created being is not immediately related to the divine being as to its cause but rather to the creative intellect and will. First, to the intellect. The idea of things is God's essence, but in so far as this is contemplated by the divine mind: "God's essence is the idea of things, not indeed considered as an essence, but considered as it is known."[92] In God's relation to himself (of the knowing God to the known God), the divine mind knows the full

---

[89]*S.T.*, I, q. 7, a. 2, c *in fine*. See also *De ente et essentia*, c. 5.
[90]*De pot.*, q. 3, a. 1, ad 17.
[91]*De pot.*, q. 3, a. 5, ad 2.
[92]*De ver.*, q. 3, a. 2.

extent of the divine power and all that can be a participation of the divine being and involves no contradiction.

Thus far, in speaking of the divine mind, we have been concerned only with the possibility of created being. To reach the existential order, we must realize that God's knowledge by vision (*scientia visionis*) of all that comes into existence is the cause of things only in so far as his will is joined to it.[93] In God there is the idea of each thing, but the idea refers to a thing to be actualized: "An idea, properly speaking, is related to a thing in so far as it can be brought into existence."[94] The idea concerns the "practical" knowledge of God; it includes the divine will as deciding what a certain thing will be and what it will not be in the existential order. An object of wisdom and will, the real concrete being is created in its entirety, both as regards its essence and its existence. God is therefore the cause of the nature of things which he produces by an act of absolute generosity and freedom. In the existential order everything depends on the free will of God, the primary cause of all being and all the differences in being.[95]

A final note will help us to understand the difference between the conclusion of the second way and that of the fourth way. In the second way we were led to assert the production of the being of creatures by God, but that production did not exclude the intervention of intermediary causes as far as the quality or suchness of the effect was concerned. A secondary cause is said to intervene inasmuch as the effect contains a particular aspect which is proper to it. In the fourth way, where being, the true, and the good are considered precisely as such, we have been led to the conclusion that God operates immediately in all things and everywhere without the intervention of any secondary cause. It is God who creates the truth, the goodness, and the being of all things. Briefly stated, it is God who creates whatever a thing has of reality.[96]

---

[93]*S.T.*, I, q. 14, a. 8: "Necesse est quod sua [Dei] scientia sit causa rerum, secundum quod habet voluntatem coniunctam."

[94]*De ver.*, q. 3, a. 5. See also *ibid.*, a. 2: "Ipsa divina essentia, cointellectis diversis proportionibus rerum ad eam, est idea uniuscuiusque rei."

[95]*Peri Herm.*, L. 1, lect. 14: "Voluntas divina est intelligenda ut extra ordinem entium existens, velut causa quaedam profundens totum ens et omnes eius differentias."

[96]If we compare the fourth way with the second way, certain interesting features will emerge. The second way takes as its starting point the causality noticeable in a series of causes involved in the production of an effect. And this effect is known precisely because it becomes evident that, in the objects of our experience *(in istis sensibilibus)*, a series of causes contributed to its production. Next the argument proceeds to a first cause, which alone can furnish the ultimate, total reason of the effect. The fourth way, on the other hand, starts from the degrees of truth, goodness, and being and reaches out to the *maxime tale*, or that which is supreme in each of those perfections. If the *maxime tale* alone is such by its essence, it alone must possess the *esse* of and by itself. Consequently, other beings do not possess the *esse* in virtue of their nature but must receive it from the *maxime tale*, the *esse per essentiam*.

5. THE FIFTH WAY

"The fifth way is taken from the government of the world."

This way argues from the governance of the world to a first intelligent being by which all things in nature are ordained to their end. "Therefore some intelligent being exists by whom all natural things are directed to their end; and this being we call God."

The fifth way is by no means the easiest to understand. Really to penetrate the mind of its author, one must first clarify and understand several notions.

a. *The governance of the world.*

Among these notions, the first in need of clarification is "the governance of the world" from which the fifth way takes its start. Without prejudging in any way the validity of the proof, one is quite justified in asking Aquinas what he means by the governance of the world. Governance, he will tell us, is the carrying out of the decree of divine providence. Whereas providence is eternal, inasmuch as it is the plan in the divine mind directing all things to their end, governance is the execution in time of the order of providence, which presupposes creation and the existence of different kinds of things. To govern is to lead things to their end:

> We observe that in nature things happen always or nearly always for the best; which would not be the case unless some sort of providence directed nature towards good as an end. . . .Therefore it belongs [to the divine goodness] to lead [things] to their end, and this is to govern.[97]

Thus we argue to governance from the order observed in the things of the world: "The unfailing order we observe in things is a sign of their being

---

In the fourth way the efficient causality of the *maxime tale* follows upon the necessity of establishing a *maxime ens* in the order of existence. And it is precisely because it is the *maxime ens*, the *ens per essentiam tale*, that the *maxime tale* is the cause of all other beings. It is therefore an illusion to think that the fourth way proves the existence of God through efficient causality. The truth of the matter is that the efficient causality of God bearing on the beings mentioned in the second part of the fourth way is but a consequence of what has been proved in the first part, namely, the existence of a *maxime tale*. Hence to refuse to accept the validity of the proof contained in the first part of the fourth way is, for all practical purposes, to reject the whole proof. It is to reduce the fourth way to the second way, with the aggravating circumstance of a weak, if not faulty, start. When Thomas exploits the second part of the fourth way, as can be seen in *S.T.*, I, q. 44, a. 1, he does not do so in order to prove the existence of God. Rather, after having proved that there is a God, he wants to show that all other beings, no matter what their nature, must ultimately come from him: "Necesse est dicere omne quod quocumque modo est, a Deo esse." And this is a perfectly valid way of reasoning.

[97]For the notion of governance see *S.T.*, I, q. 103, a. 1 and a. 4. All texts quoted in this paragraph are taken from those two articles, the first of which matches quite well the fifth way: "Ipse ordo certus rerum manifeste demonstrat gubernationem mundi."

governed." In other words, from the actual carrying out of the governance we are led to the providence that has conceived the order in question.

But what are the effects of divine governance that make up, as it were, the structure of the fifth way? Thomas mentions one general effect and two particular effects. The general effect is derived from the end and consists in the assimilation of creatures to the supreme good (*assimilari summo bono*). The particular effects are those by which creatures are made similar to God and consist in the preservation of things in their goodness and in their movement toward the good.

> The effect of the government of the world may be considered on the part of those things by means of which the creature is made like to God. Thus there are, in general, two effects of the government...the preservation of things in their goodness, and the moving of things toward the good.

The preservation of beings belongs, properly speaking, to the second way. As for the moving of things toward the good, we may consider motion as such, and then we are within the confines of the first way. But we may also consider motion precisely as a tendency toward the good, that is, the direction of beings toward the good that is their end, and then we are within the fifth way.

b. *The idea of order.*

St. Thomas tells us that the unfailing order of things clearly manifests the governance of the world. The most general idea of order includes a proportion between two distinct things joined together as the perfectible and perfection, potentiality and actuality. More rigorously, order indicates a mode of priority and posteriority with regard to a principle. Since the first principle in all things is the final cause, order implies most specifically a relation of priority and posteriority with regard to the end.[98]

Order in the universe includes both the conservation and the movement of the different things of which the universe is composed. Actually the order found in creatures consists in this, that one thing moves another.[99] Hence there is, according to Aquinas, a twofold order: a static

---

[98]For the concept of order see the following texts: *In Phys.*, L. 8, lect. 3: "Omnis autem ordo proportio quaedam est"; *S.T.*, II-II, q. 26, a. 1: "Ordo autem includit in se aliquem modum prioris et posterioris. Unde oportet quod ubicumque est aliquod principium, sit etiam aliquis ordo." (See also *In Metaph.*, L. 5, lect. 13 and *S.T.*, I, q. 42, a. 3). Since the end is first among the causes, order is said primarily of the ordering of things to their end. *Con. gent.*, I, c. 1: "Tunc enim unaquaeque res optime disponitur, cum ad suum finem convenienter ordinatur."

[99]*S.T.*, I, q. 103, a. 4, ad 1: 'Ordo universi includit in se et conservationem rerum diversarum a Deo institutarum et motionem earum; quia secundum haec duo invenitur ordo in rebus, secundum scilicet quod una est melior alia, et secundum quod una ab alia movetur."

order determined by the hierarchy of beings according to their ontological value, and a dynamic order represented by the interaction of beings among themselves, so that inferior beings are ordered to the superior by which they are enriched and the totality of beings is ordered to the end.[100]

The foregoing notions will help us better to grasp the meaning of the fifth way, which may have either of two different forms. A shorter and less developed form is the one that is literally contained in Question 2 of the first part of the *Summa*; a longer and much more developed form is that which includes numerous texts from other works of Aquinas. This latter form appeals to the order in the world and involves a conception of the universe that leads to God as the universal good and ultimate end of everything, and finally, to divine providence.

c. *Here is how the fifth way is first presented to us.*

There are beings that lack knowledge and yet act in view of an end: "We see that things which lack knowledge, such as natural bodies, act for an end." This is evident from the fact that these beings act always, or nearly always, in the same way, so as to obtain the best result (*ut consequantur id quod est optimum*).

What does Thomas mean by "the best result" or *optimum*? This, he tells us, is the ultimate end.[101] The ultimate end, and therefore the best result, is the good of the order of the universe.[102] We can now relate this to what he says in the first article of Question 103: "The unfailing order we observe in things is a sign of their being governed"; and again: "The un-

---

[100]*De ver.*, q. 5, a. 1, ad 9: "In rebus potest considerari duplex ordo: unus secundum quod egrediuntur a principio; alius secundum quod ordinantur ad finem. Dispositio ergo pertinet ad illum ordinem quo res progrediuntur a principio...sed providentia importat illum ordinem qui est ad finem." In the arrangement of the beings of the universe, there is first of all an inner order in each of them: "Pars ignobilior est propter nobiliorem: sicut sensus propter intellectum....Omnes partes sunt propter perfectionem totius" (*S.T.*, I, q. 65, a. 2). When taken together, all beings are arranged in a hierarchical order: "Sunt ergo elementa propter corpora mixta; haec vero propter viventia; in quibus plantae sunt propter animalia; animalia vero propter hominem" (*Con. gent.*, III, c. 22. See also *In Metaph.*, L. 12, lect. 12). It is worth noting that among the various orders of beings there is a transition or *transitus*. Thus the animal's estimative power is a form of imperfect participation in human reason, just as there is some sort of affinity between man and angel. (See *S.T.*, I, q. 89, a. 1). In general, it can be said that "divina sapientia fines primorum coniungit principiis secundorum" *(De malo,* q. 16, a. 1, obj. 4, in a quotation from Dionysius' *De divin. nomin.,* c. 7), or that "supremum infimi est infimum supremi" (cf. *De ver,* q. 6, a. 2 and *De spirit. creat.*, a. 2 *in fine).* As far as dynamic order is concerned, creatures are so related to one another that, in their ordering to the end, the inferior ones are moved by the superior. *S.T.*, II-II, q. 2, a. 3: "In omnibus naturis ordinatis invenitur quod ad perfectionem naturae inferioris duo concurrunt: unum quidem quod est secundum propriam naturam, aliud autem quod est secundum motum superioris naturae." (See also *In II Sent.*, d. 1, q. 2, a. 3).

[101]*S.T.*, I-II, q. 34, a. 3: "Optimum autem in unaquaque re est ultimus finis."

[102]*S.T.*, I, q. 15, a. 2: "Illud autem quod est optimum in rebus existens, est bonum ordinis universi."

varying course of natural things which are without knowledge, shows
clearly that the world is governed by some reason." Thomas' thought can
be expressed in these terms: beings that lack knowledge tend to achieve,
in addition to their own perfection, what is best in the world, that is, the
order in the universe. Consequently, it is not by chance, but rather in virtue of an intention outside themselves, that they attain their end: "They
achieve their end, not fortuitously, but designedly." For "whatever lacks
knowledge cannot move toward an end, unless it be directed by some being endowed with knowledge and intelligence, as the arrow is directed by
the archer."

This tendency toward the end, which is determined by the very nature
of the beings that lack knowledge, manifests an intention, and this can
only be the act of an intelligent being.[103] Indeed, intention refers to the
end to be achieved by means that are proportioned to it, and only an intelligent being can know the proportion or exact relation between means and
end.

> Those things that lack reason tend to an end by natural inclination, as
> being moved by another and not by themselves, for they do not know
> the nature of an end as such. Consequently they cannot ordain any-
> thing to an end, but can be ordained to an end only by another.[104]

The conclusion is therefore reached: there is an intelligent being by whom
all natural things are directed to their end, and this being we call God.

One cannot possibly stop at an intelligent being that is not God, and
this for the following reasons:

i. The tendency toward an end is a fundamental orientation that is embedded in the very nature of beings that lack knowledge, and only the
author of their nature can have given it to them.

ii. The conclusion of the argument concerns all natural things (omnes
res naturales) and therefore the universe as a whole. Now the universe
tends to achieve the best result that is proper to it, that is, an order that
directs all natural beings toward a common, unique end. Such a direction
or ordination can only be the work of someone that is not part of the order
in question but transcends it. (The more developed form of the proof will
make this point clear.)

iii. Any intelligent being that is not intelligence itself is, first of all, a
nature, so that all intelligent beings must also be reckoned among res

---

[103]Intention is defined as "motus voluntatis qui fertur in finem secundum quod acquiri-
tur per ea quae sunt ad finem" (S.T., I-II, q. 12, a. 4, ad 3). Also: "Intendere finem est
moventis, prout scilicet ordinat motum alicuius in finem, vel sui vel alterius, quod est rationis tantum" (Ibid., a. 5).

[104]S.T., I-II, q. 1, a. 2 and In III Sent., d. 27, q. 1, a. 2.

naturales or natural things. Now at the basis of all knowledge and willing the very structure of intellect and will must be considered. This will reveal that just as the intellect is made to know truth, so the will is made to achieve the good. And the proportion between a power and its object can only be the work of a creating intelligence.

d. *The development of the fifth way from the viewpoint of the unity of order in the universe takes place in three main steps.*

i. The fact of the unity of the universe and its metaphysical import are set forth.

To avoid contradiction, one must admit that there is order, and therefore finality, in the universe. If, *per impossibile,* the world were but a puzzle, an assemblage of different and unrelated pieces, it would be chaos, characterized by mere chance.

It must also be maintained against pantheism that there is a multitude of beings joined together in varying types and degrees of unity. We are faced, that is, with a world that tends to a superior unity through all its multiple components which, although different among themselves, are hierarchically arranged and interdependent, one acting upon another. All the beings of the universe tend to achieve the good of the whole, namely, the unity of order. "For each thing in its nature is good, but all things together are very good, by reason of the order of the universe, which is the ultimate and noblest perfection in things."[105] Such an order cannot be merely the result of an artificial assemblage of beings, of a purely accidental and superficial union. The beings of the universe must be conceived as a whole, aiming to form, as it were, a single organic unity.[106] It is a profound unity that is due to the very nature of the beings in question, which are open to one another and mutually engaged in their activities.

No creature can be completely understood without its relation to the whole: "For it is characteristic of any being, whether material or immaterial, to have some reference to something else."[107] If the order existing in the universe were not the result of an ensemble constituted as a metaphysical whole, it would be inexplicable. Each being, taken individually, would tend toward its particular good. Having achieved it, it would have completely exhausted its capacity, with no further motive for action. Action is indeed possible because of a desire, and desire is the expression of love for a good or of a natural appetite. Consequently each

---

[105]*Con. gent.,* II, c. 45 *in fine.*

[106]St. Thomas compares the order of the universe to a form. See *In Metaph.,* L. 12, lect. 12: "Forma autem alicuius totius, quod est unum per ordinationem quandam partium, est ordo ipsius." *S.T.,* I, q. 49, a. 2: "Forma quam principaliter Deus intendit in rebus creatis, est bonum ordinis universi."

[107]*De ver.,* q. 23, a. 1.

nature would be enclosed within itself and only particular orders would be possible, or, at most, fortuitous encounters. There would be as many universes, or at least as many individual species, as individual beings.

Every being tends toward good, and by desiring the good it desires its own unity without which it could not exist. In fact, a being is or exists to the extent that it is one. Hence we observe that things resist division as far as they can, and that the dissolution of a thing arises from some defect within itself.[108] Thus every being strives for the best. This is, first, its own perfection, its complete individual good, and hence its unity; secondly, the good of the species or its formal perfection and unity; and thirdly, every being as part of the universe tends to achieve, together with other beings, the perfection of the universe as a whole.

ii. The end of the universe is the universal good, which is to be found outside the universe: *"Bonum universale est extra mundum."*

Unity of order cannot be explained by order alone. When Thomas says that order is the ultimate and highest perfection of things, one must not understand the good of the whole as though it were an entity in itself, or some sort of a suppositum that would integrate in itself all the perfections of the universe. Order is not a substance or an absolute; it is a relation.[109] The good of the whole is the sum total of particular goods, which are bound together very closely, but only inasmuch as they are related to a principle of order which, in our case, is the end. It is therefore necessary to discover, beyond order or the things so ordered, the principle of order, that is, the end, which is ontologically the reason for the order in question.

This principle must be found either within or without the universe. If it were within the universe, it could be only a particular good or a particular kind of order. But it is impossible that a particular good be the end of the universe as a whole and the adequate cause of the unity of order. In fact, a particular good is itself part of the whole; immersed within the ensemble, it does not emerge or stand up on its own. As part of the series of the goods of the universe, it does not transcend them, and even if it were the first and most perfect of the series, it would remain nevertheless a particular good. As such, it could only be a particular end and the principle of a particular order.

Nor can it be said that this good is not a part but rather the whole of the universe. This would be possible only if all other beings were ordained

---

[108]*S.T.*, q. 103, a. 3: "Sicut omnia desiderant bonum, ita desiderant unitatem, sine qua esse non possunt; nam unumquodque in tantum est, in quantum unum est. Unde videmus quod res repugnant suae divisioni quantum possunt, et quod dissolutio uniuscuiusque rei provenit ex defectu illius rei."

[109]*S.T.*, I, q. 116, a. 2, ad 3: "Dispositio designat ordinem, qui non est substantia sed relatio."

to it as parts of its own being by entering into a composition with it to form a single nature, or by letting themselves be absorbed into it. Whatever the case, the other beings would not be ordained to it except by losing their own autonomy or their identity as independent natures. Moreover, a being that would enrich itself at the expense of other beings would manifest its own weakness and fundamental deficiency, for it would not be able to achieve its complete perfection without the aid of other beings.

On the other hand, this particular good, precisely because it is particular, is necessarily ordained to something other than itself as to its end. Otherwise it would be its own end, its ultimate end, the absolute good or goodness itself. Now, if the particular good in question is itself ordained to an end, it becomes part of the order rather than its principle. The ordering principle of the universe must therefore be sought outside the universe itself, beyond the series of the multiple beings that make up the universe.[110]

Thus only the universal good (*bonum universale*) can be the principle of the unity of order in the universe. This unity of order must, in turn, be derived from a common end toward which all beings are directed: "Things that are diverse do not come together in the same order unless they are ordered thereto by some one being."[111] This common end, this one and only end, is the ultimate end or end as such (*simpliciter finis*). And since the good has the nature of end (*bonum habet rationem finis*), the ultimate end must also be a good that cannot be ordered to anything else, while everything else is necessarily ordered to it. It is the universal good (*bonum universale*), the good as such. This absolute good can be none other than God.

The good that is nothing but good cannot be ordered to anything else without changing its nature. Being the plenitude of perfection, it can neither acquire nor seek anything outside itself. Instead, all other beings are necessarily ordered to it. How is this possible?

The causality of the good consists in being the object of appetite and desire: "The influence...of a final cause consists in being sought or desired."[112] The supreme good is supremely desirable and on that account cannot but communicate its goodness to others. In doing so, it gives itself

---

[110]*S.T.*, I, q. 103, a. 2: "Manifestum est enim quod bonum habet rationem finis. Unde finis particularis alicuius rei est quoddam bonum particulare; finis autem universalis rerum omnium est quoddam bonum universale. Bonum autem universale est quod est per se et per suam essentiam bonum, quod est ipsa essentia bonitatis; bonum autem particulare est quod est participative bonum. Manifestum est autem quod in tota universitate creaturarum nullum est bonum quod non sit participative bonum. Unde illud bonum quod est finis totius universi, oportet quod sit extrinsecum a toto universo."

[111]*S.T.*, I, q. 11, a. 3.

[112]*De ver.*, q. 22, a. 2.

to others by an act of liberality and draws them to itself so that they may thereby be enriched.

God gives himself, in the first place, in the form of a participated good, which however is desirable only to the extent that it reflects the good as such, for it is the supreme good that pours itself out in the participated being.[113] Since outside of him there is nothing, God's liberality must be the creative cause of all good and, first of all, of the goodness inherent in all natures. Hence by desiring its own good, each individual being desires the divine good. That is why creatures love God, the universal good, by a natural love greater than the love they have for themselves.[114]

All natural or voluntary appetite tends toward the assimilation to divine goodness, and this tendency or desire would attain divine goodness itself, were it possible for anyone to possess it as his own essential perfection.[115]

If all beings in the universe tend ultimately to achieve unity of order, it is because they all strive to go beyond their particular good and attain a good that surpasses all others and truly brings all tendencies to unity. Now all creatures tend to be similar to God, each in its own way and according to its own possibilities. Unable to attain God himself, inferior creatures cling to something that is better than themselves by striving to come out, as it were, of their natural condition and climb to a superior one that is closer to God. Thus all bodily creatures are ordered to man as to

---

[113]S.T., I, q. 44, a. 4: "Primo agenti, qui est agens tantum, non convenit agere propter acquisitionem alicuius finis, sed intendit solum communicare suam perfectionem, quae est eius bonitas. Et unaquaeque creatura intendit consequi suam perfectionem, quae est similitudo perfectionis et bonitatis divinae. Sic ergo divina bonitas est finis rerum omnium." And ad 3: "Omnia appetunt Deum ut finem, appetendo quodcumque bonum, sive appetitu intelligibili, sive sensibili, sive naturali, qui est sine cognitione; quia nihil habet rationem boni et appetibilis, nisi secundum quod participat Dei similitudinem." The same doctrine is found in Metaph., L. 12, lect. 7 and lect. 12, where Thomas, following the lead of Aristotle, says that the primum movens immobile moves first as a good and hence as an end: "Primum movens movet sicut bonum et appetibile. Et quia appetibile habet rationem finis," it moves as an end, inasmuch as it is desired and loved: "movet quasi amatum." "Est enim aliquod bonum separatum, quod est primum movens, ex quo dependet caelum et tota natura, sicut ex fine et bono appetibili."

[114]S.T., I, q. 60, a. 5: "Quia igitur bonum universale est ipse Deus, et sub hoc bono continetur etiam angelus et homo et omnis creatura, quia omnis creatura naturaliter, secundum id quod est, Dei est, sequitur quod naturali dilectione etiam angelus et homo plus et principalius diligat Deum quam seipsum." Ibid., ad 1: "In illis quorum unum est tota ratio existendi et bonitatis alii, magis diligitur naturaliter tale alterum quam ipsum, sicut dictum est quod unaquaeque pars diligit naturaliter totum plus quam se. Et quodlibet singulare naturaliter diligit plus bonum suae speciei quam bonum suum singulare. Deus autem non solum est bonum unius speciei, sed est ipsum universale bonum simpliciter. Unde unumquodque suo modo naturaliter diligit Deum plus quam seipsum."

[115]In II Sent., d. 1, q. 2, a. 2: "Omnis appetitus naturae vel voluntatis tendit in assimilationem divinae bonitatis, et in ipsammet tenderet, si esset possibile haberi ut perfectio essentialis, quae est forma rei."

their immediate end.[116] Man, in turn, tends toward a perfect assimilation to God. He has the capacity or passive ability to attain God in himself by his own operation. Once God grants him his grace, he will be able to unite himself to the divine substance by the acts of his intellect and will.[117] In a future life man attains God himself, not only by his operation but also by his being. Here being is taken to mean, not *esse* or the act of the essence, because a creature cannot be changed into the divine nature, but rather the act of the hypostasis or person, as when a creature is elevated to a union with that person. This is the case with the humanity of Christ. It is for this reason that, in a Christian concept of the universe, Christ is at the summit of all creation. He is substantially united with God and recapitulates in himself the whole universe.[118]

iii. The transition is then made from the universal good, the one and only end of the universe, to divine providence.

The preceding steps of our dialectic have already led us to God as the universal good and ultimate end of the universe. Just as there is a metaphysical proof from formal exemplary causality (the fourth way), so there is a metaphysical proof from final causality. Similarly, just as in the fourth way we have been led to the conclusion that the supreme being as such (*maxime tale*) is the cause of all being, all true, and all good, so the fifth way leads us to a governance of the world adequate to the ultimate end and, beyond that, to an eternal providence. This final step thus comprises two stages.

α. *A governance of the world adequate to the end.* The starting point of the proof, it is worth recalling, was the governance of the world (*ex*

---

[116]*In II Sent.*, d. 1, q. 2, a. 3: "Sed quia optimo assimilatur aliquid per hoc quod simile fit meliori se, ideo omnis creatura corporalis tendit in assimilationem creaturae intellectualis quantum potest, quae altiori modo divinam bonitatem consequitur, et propter hoc etiam forma humana, scilicet anima rationalis, dicitur esse finis ultimus intentus a natura inferiori." See also *Con. gent.*, L. 3, c. 22: "Ultimus igitur finis generationis totius est anima humana, et in hanc tendit materia sicut in ultimam formam. . . . Homo igitur est finis totius generationis." Matter finds in man its ultimate perfection, its perfect form. By serving man and being useful to him, the material creation makes it possible for man to fulfill his special vocation, namely, to attain God in himself. The whole sensible universe is contained in man in two ways: first, inasmuch as man is a microcosm: "in homine est quaedam similitudo ordinis universi; unde et minor mundus dicitur: quia omnes naturae quasi in homine confluunt" (*In II Sent.*, d. 1, q. 2, a. 3); secondly, because all things can be contained in the soul in a superior way, i.e., by knowledge (cf. *Con. gent.*, III, c. 112 and *De ver.*, q. 2, a. 2).

[117]*S.T.*, I-II, q. 2, a. 8; q. 3, a. 7 and a. 8.

[118]*In I Sent.*, d. 37, q. 1, a. 2. Needless to say, this final consideration transcends the order of reason and is valid only in a context of faith and revelation. However, we felt the need of adding it here, because it sums up St. Thomas' thought on the creatures' assimilation to God and the communication that God makes to them of his own goodness. By the Incarnation, Thomas asserts (*S.T.*, III, q. 1, a. 1), God communicates himself in the highest manner (*summo modo*) to his creatures.

gubernatione mundi). Now, to govern is to direct, to move things toward their end. Accordingly, governance includes the intervention of an agent who by his motion leads things to their end.[119] This agent can only be God, who alone is adequate to the ultimate end, for "the end and the agent tending toward the end are always found to belong to one and the same order of reality."[120] God alone is therefore capable of moving toward the ultimate end the totality of the beings of the universe. Although this motion is formally the act of the divine will, ultimately it is traced back to the divine intellect.

The proper causality of the good as such consists in being desired, and to this effect there must be an order, a proportion, a connaturality between the good and the appetite. What is this proportion? It is the one that exists between potentiality and its proper act. Every being in effect tends toward its fulfillment, to the perfection that is its own act. If the good as object did not present itself as the fulfillment of the appetite, and the latter did not already have the object in potentiality, no desire could ever be aroused. Thus the fundamental source of all desire rests on the proportion that exists between potency and act. And this proportion between potency and act, between being and its end, is given by God himself to all beings along with their nature and its corresponding knowledge.

This apprehension [of the appetible thing by the natural appetite] is a prerequisite in the one who established the nature, who gave to each nature its own inclination to a thing in keeping with itself.[121]

---

[119]*S.T.*, I, q. 103, a. 3: "Gubernatio nihil aliud est quam directio gubernatorum ad finem, qui est aliquod bonum." *Ibid.*, a. 5, ad 2: "Gubernatio est quaedam mutatio gubernatorum a gubernante."

[120]*Con. gent.*, I, c. 72: "Finis et agens ad finem semper unius ordinis inveniuntur in rebus; unde et finis proximus, qui est proportionatus agenti, incidit in idem specie cum agente, tam in naturalibus quam in artificialibus....Deo autem nihil coordinatur quasi eiusdem ordinis nisi ipse: alias essent plura prima cuius contrarium supra ostensum est. Ipse est igitur primum agens propter finem, qui est ipsemet. Ipse igitur non solum est finis appetibilis, sed appetens, ut ita dicam, se finem, et appetitu intellectuali, cum sit intelligens, qui est voluntas." *S.T.*, I-II, q. 109, a. 6: "Necesse est enim, cum omne agens agat propter finem, quod omnis causa convertat suos effectus ad suum finem. Et ideo, cum secundum ordinem agentium sive moventium sit ordo finium, necesse est quod ad ultimum finem convertatur homo per motionem primi moventis....Sic igitur, cum Deus sit primum movens simpliciter, ex eius motione est quod omnia in ipsum convertantur secundum communem intentionem boni, per quam unumquodque intendit assimilari Deo secundum suum modum."

[121]*De ver.*, q. 25, a. 1. Also in *Metaph.*, L. 12, lect. 12: "Natura in rebus naturalibus est principium exequendi unicuique id quod competit sibi de ordine universi. Sicuti enim qui est in domo per praeceptum patrisfamilias ad aliquid inclinatur, ita aliqua res naturalis per naturam propriam. Et ipsa natura uniuscuiusque est quaedam inclinatio indita ei a primo movente, ordinans ipsam in debitum finem. Et ex hoc patet quod res naturales agunt propter finem, licet finem non cognoscant, quia a primo intelligente assequuntur inclinationem in finem."

This natural appetite is found in every being in nature. As a particular accidental nature or form, each faculty of the soul also has a natural inclination.[122] This is of course the case with the will, which is directly ordered to the universal good: *"Voluntas habet ordinem ad universale bonum."* Moreover, this ordering to the universal good which is embedded in the very nature of the will is the work of divine wisdom, just as it is God who gives to human will its primary inclination toward the good: "God moves man's will, as the universal mover, to the universal object of the will, which is the good."[123] Hence at the beginning of every act of appetition by the will toward the universal good, there is a first intelligent being that directs all things to their end. This end is none other than God himself.[124]

β. *From governance to providence.* As previously stated, the governance of the universe presupposes that things be constituted in their own nature, as well as in their distinction and inequality, and that they tend to their end in conformity with the plan established by God. The order of the universe is thus attributed to God as its author. This is so because he is the creative cause of the good (by diffusing his goodness through creation). Now God does not act out of natural necessity but rather by an act of his will, which, in turn, does not operate in an arbitrary way but always in accord with divine wisdom. There is then, in the first place, an order according to which creatures proceed from God as their creator. Secondly, they proceed from God as their final cause, that is, inasmuch as God orders them to himself as to their ultimate end. This is what is called the order of providence, which, far from being something exterior to the universe, is the very reason for its existence.

Thus we have a twofold order: the order of things coming from God (*exitus rerum a Deo*) and the order of things returning to God (*reditus rerum ad Deum*). The former is called disposition, the latter providence. The order of providence is prior in intention and hence the cause of the order of disposition. The end toward which creatures tend is in fact the reason for the ordering of things in the universe.[125] It is in providence that the ultimate reason must be found for the beings constituting a universe

---

[122]*S.T.*, I, q. 80, a. 1, ad 3: "Unaquaeque potentia animae est quaedam forma seu natura, et habet naturalem inclinationem in aliquid." See also *In III Sent.*, d. 27, q. 1, a. 2: "Omne autem quod est a Deo, accipit aliquam naturam qua in finem suum ultimum ordinetur. Unde oportet in omnibus creaturis habentibus aliquem finem inveniri appetitum naturalem, etiam in ipsa voluntate respectu ultimi finis. Unde naturali appetitu vult homo beatitudinem et ea quae ad naturam voluntatis spectant."

[123]*S.T.*, I-II, q. 9, a. 6, c and ad 3.

[124]*In Boeth. de Trinit.*, q. 1, a. 3, ad 4: "Quamvis Deus sit ultimus finis in consecutione, et primus in intentione appetitus naturalis, non tamen oportet quod sit primus in cognitione mentis humanae quae ordinatur in finem; sed in cognitione ordinantis, sicut et in aliis quae naturali appetitu tendunt in finem suum."

[125]*De ver.*, q. 5, a. 1, ad 9: "Sed quia ex fine artificii colligitur quidquid est in artifi-

that is one and perfectly ordered. It is providence that has conceived the universe as a whole and contains in itself the idea of its universal order. Accordingly, providence extends to all things and all particular events, so that nothing escapes its governance, for providence alone is adequate to the universal good (*bonum universale*), with which it is actually identified.[126]

The development of the fifth way here presented following Aquinas' thought shows very well how this way completes all the others.

All divine motion that necessarily intervenes in each of the operations of natural beings is for the purpose of helping them to achieve their destiny, that is, their resemblance to God.

All divine causality in the creation and conservation of beings, which represents the *exitus* of creatures, is the work of divine goodness that wants to give itself to creatures in the form of their own created perfection.

In their fragility, creatures subject to substantial change and to time rest on the immutable and the necessary. Sensible and inanimate beings, which have only an ephemeral existence, tend to God in their own particular way and manifest a progress in nature from the inferior forms to the human soul, toward which matter tends as to its ultimate form. The soul, which is immutable and incorruptible, tends in turn to participate, and makes the body participate, in the eternity of God.

The fourth way is completed by the fifth in the sense that the participation of created beings in the being of God is according to a universal order that makes it possible to define natures, not only as they are in themselves, but also in their relation to the universe. It is providence that bestows upon each nature all that belongs to it and what it needs to achieve its end as part of the entire universe.

Having reached this summit, we may say that creatures are in the first place ordered to divine providence, next to the knowledge and will of God, as presupposed by providence, and finally, through the mediation of divine knowledge and will, to the essence of God.[127]

---

ciato; ordo autem ad finem est fini propinquior quam ordo partium ad invicem, et quodam-modo causa eius; ideo providentia quodammodo est dispositionis causa et propter hoc dispositionis actus frequenter providentiae attribuitur."

[126]The whole dialectic of the fifth way is very well summed up in the concluding text of St. Thomas' Commentary on Aristotle's *Metaphysics*, L. 12, lect. 12: "Unde relinquitur quod totum universum est sicut unus principatus et unum regnum. Et ita oportet quod or-dinetur ab uno gubernatore. Et hoc est quod concludit, quod est unus princeps totius universi, scilicet primum movens, et primum intelligibile, et primum bonum, quod supra dixit Deum, qui est benedictus in saecula saeculorum. Amen."

[127]*De ver.*, q. 5, a. 2, ad 4: "Deus per essentiam suam est causa rerum; et ita ad aliquod simplex principium reducitur omnis rerum pluralitas. Sed essentia eius non est causa rerum nisi secundum quod est scita, et per consequens, secundum quod est volita communicari

In concluding this chapter, we are aware of the imperfection and limitations of our work. A complete study of the five ways would have called for further developments, for additional research into Aquinas' own sources and a comparison between them and his original thought. Furthermore, it would have called for a confrontation of Aquinas' way of thinking with modern thought, as well as for an analysis of the objections raised against the proofs in question. These points are obviously beyond the limits of our original plan. We are confident, however, that the chief objective of this study, namely, the presentation of the metaphysical structure of the five ways without betraying the thought of their author, has been substantially achieved.[128]

---

creaturae per viam assimilationis; unde res ab essentia divina per ordinem scientiae et voluntatis procedunt; et ita per providentiam."

[128]We have endeavored to interpret St. Thomas through his own texts and follow him as closely as possible in the dialectic of the five ways. We are convinced that, by eliminating from the Thomistic proofs certain non-essential elements—such as the intervention of the celestial bodies and the like—it is possible to develop the five ways by taking the human activity of intellect and will as starting point without betraying the metaphysical principles adopted by the Angelic Doctor in each of his proofs. The following reflections based on the activity of the intellect suggest the line of thought to be followed in such an attempt.

1. All intellectual activity requires the intervention of God, the first immovable mover (first way). "Ad cognitionem cuiusque veri, homo indiget auxilio divino ut intellectus a Deo moveatur ad suum actum" (S.T., I-II, q. 109, a. 1.—See note 31 above).

2. God is not only the cause of the moveri (operation), but also of the very esse of the intellect and of all principles of operation (second way). "Non solum autem a Deo est omnis motio sicut a primo movente, sed etiam ab ipso est omnis formalis perfectio sicut a primo actu. Sic igitur actio intellectus et cuiuslibet entis creati dependet a Deo quantum ad duo: uno modo, in quantum ab ipso habet formam per quam agit; alio modo, in quantum ab ipso movetur ad agendum" (S.T., I-II, q. 109, a. 1). "Ipsum enim lumen intellectuale quod est in nobis, nihil est aliud quam quaedam participata similitudo increati" (S.T., I, q. 84, a. 5).

3. The act by which man knows is a contingent act (possibile esse et non esse), subject to a twofold mutability: first, man can know or not know: "intellectus noster non est aeternus, nec veritas enuntiabilium quae a nobis formantur est aeterna, sed quandoque incoepit"; secondly, man can pass from truth to falsity and vice versa: "mutatur de veritate in falsitatem" (S.T., I, q. 16, a. 7, ad 4 and a. 8). Moreover, it is clear that truth is formally in the intellect. Hence, if there were only contingent activities by an intellect that is subject to time in its operation, there would be no necessary and eternal truth: "Unde si nullus intellectus esset aeternus, nulla veritas esset aeterna. Sed quia solus intellectus divinus est aeternus, in ipso solo veritas aeternitatis habet" (S.T., I, q. 16, a 7, c and ad 4. See also Con. gent., II, c. 84," Quod vero"—third way).

4. The human intellect is true when it is adequate to, or in conformity with, reality (adaequatio intellectus ad rem). Now things are more or less true according to their greater or lesser degree of ontological truth: "Unumquodque autem in quantum habet de esse, in tantum est cognoscibile" (S.T., I, q. 16, a. 3). This truth, which is found in things in varying and multiple degrees, is so called in relation to a maxime verum: "Si vero loquamur de veritate secundum quod est in rebus, sic omnes sunt verae una prima veritate, cui unumquodque assimilatur secundum suam entitatem" (S.T., I, q. 16, a. 6—fourth way). Consequently God, who is truth by his very essence, is the cause of the truth of things: "Adaequatio rei ad intellectum divinum" (see the end of our exposition of the fourth way). The same conclusion can be drawn from the analysis of the human intellect itself, which is a participation

We willingly concede that the five ways are not accessible to minds lacking adequate training in the vocabulary and intricacies of Thomistic metaphysics. We likewise acknowledge that no one should attempt to penetrate Aquinas' thought and its highly technical articulation without adequate preparation. But, after all, is not this the case with the writings of most geniuses and original thinkers? And among them Aquinas is unquestionably one of the greatest.

BIBLIOGRAPHY

For the benefit of the reader, we indicate here the sources referred to by Louis Charlier in his presentation of St. Thomas' Five Ways.

Works by Thomas Aquinas

A. GENERAL EDITIONS:
> *Opera omnia.* 25 vols. Parma: Fiaccadori, 1852-1873. Photographic reproduction by Musurgia Publishers in New York, 1948-1950.
> *Opera omnia.* 34 vols. Paris: Vivès, 1871-1880.
> *Opera omnia.* 24 vols. (to date). Rome: Leonine Edition, 1882-1976. When completed, the Leonine Edition will comprise 50 volumes.

B. INDIVIDUAL EDITIONS:
> *Summa theologiae.* 4 vols. Ed. by P. Caramello. Turin-Rome: Marietti, 1948-1950.
> *Summa contra gentiles.* Editio Leonina Manualis. Turin-Rome: Marietti, 1946.
> *Scriptum super libros Sententiarum.* 4 vols. Ed. by P. Mandonnet (vols. 1 and 2) and M. F. Moos (vols. 3 and 4). Paris: Lethielleux, 1929-1947.

---

of the divine intellect. "Semper enim quod participat aliquid, et quod est mobile, et quod est imperfectum, praeexigit ante se aliquid quod est per essentiam suam tale, et quod est immobile et perfectum. Anima autem humana intellectiva dicitur per participationem intellectualis virtutis.... Unde ab ipso [Deo] anima humana lumen intellectuale participat" *(S. T.,* I, q. 79, a. 4).

5. Fundamentally, the ordering of the intellect to its good, which is also the true, calls for the intervention of a first intelligent being who has established a proportion of nature between a faculty and its object. This object, in turn, is identified with the universal good, which the intellect is capable of attaining on a level that is immediately accessible to it: "Sola autem natura rationalis creata habet immediatum ordinem ad Deum. Quia ceterae creaturae non attingunt ad aliquid universale, sed solum ad aliquid particulare, participantes divinam bonitatem vel in essendo tantum, sicut inanimata, vel etiam in vivendo et cognoscendo singularia, sicut plantae et animalia: natura autem rationalis, in quantum cognoscit universalem boni et entis rationem, habet immediatum ordinem ad universale essendi principium" *(S. T.,* II-II, q. 2, a. 3). Thus, starting from the intellect and its operation, it is possible to argue to a universal good and to a first intelligent being *(fifth way).*

Expositio super librum Boethii De Trinitate. Ed. by Bruno Decker. Leiden:
 E. J. Brill, 1955.

Opuscula philosophica. Ed. by R. M. Spiazzi, O.P. Turin-Rome: Marietti,
 1954. It contains *De ente et essentia, De principiis naturae, De substan-
 tiis separatis, De unitate intellectus, De aeternitate mundi,* and several
 other treatises. See also the Leonine Edition, vol. 43 (1976), for some of
 the above treatises.

Quaestiones disputatae. 2 vols. Ed. by R. M. Spiazzi, O.P. Turin-Rome:
 Marietti, 1949. Vol. I contains *De veritate.* Vol. II contains, among other
 treatises, *De potentia, De anima, De spiritualibus creaturis,* and *De
 malo.* See also the Leonine Edition, vol. 22 (3 fasc.; 1970–1976), for *De
 veritate.*

In Aristotelis libros Peri Hermeneias et Posteriorum Analyticorum expositio.
 Ed. by R. M. Spiazzi, O.P. Turin-Rome: Marietti, 1964.

In VIII libros Physicorum Aristotelis expositio. Ed. by M. Maggiolo, O.P.
 Turin-Rome: Marietti, 1954.

In XII libros Metaphysicorum Aristotelis expositio. Ed. by R. M. Spiazzi,
 O.P. Turin-Rome: Marietti, 1950.

*In libros de caelo et mundo, in libros de generatione et corruptione...exposi-
 tio.* Ed. by R. M. Spiazzi, O.P. Turin-Rome: Marietti, 1952.

Expositio in evangelium Ioannis. Ed. by R. Cai, O.P. Turin-Rome: Marietti,
 1952.

CHAPTER V

DUNS SCOTUS' PROOF FOR
THE EXISTENCE OF GOD

John Duns Scotus has developed a proof for the existence of God that for depth, thoroughness, and logical rigor has no parallel in the history of philosophy. He began work on it early in his academic career and continued to revise the original draft until the end of his life. As a result, more than one version of the proof has come down to us. The final version, although substantially the same as those preceding it, took the form of *A Treatise about the First Principle*, a work of great complexity and originality that contains much of what can be known about God by the light of natural reason.

In the formulation of this proof, hailed as one of the greatest achievements of the human mind,[1] Scotus spared no effort to analyze and evaluate previous attempts by philosophers, scholastic or other, to reach God by strictly philosophical reasoning. In fact, he took into consideration all the positive elements of the classic theistic arguments from Plato and Aristotle to Augustine, Avicenna, Anselm, and Aquinas and incorporated the best of them into his unique, comprehensive proof which rises like a monolithic structure with many different faces, each one contributing to its completeness and variety. The Scotistic proof is a single piece of extended metaphysical reasoning that, by means of an impeccable logic, leads man to and over the threshhold of the divinity.

The purpose of this chapter is to follow Scotus in his rational ascent to God. It would be difficult, however, fully to grasp the meaning and value of his proof for the existence of God without first knowing some of the epistemological and metaphysical positions that characterize his system of philosophy. Scotus' proof is in effect the culmination of all his metaphysical thinking, which in turn presupposes the solution of certain epistemological problems fundamental to any realistic philosophy. We shall therefore introduce our discussion of Scotus' approach to God by presenting his teaching on the proper object of the human intellect and on being as the

---

[1]This is the view of Thomas Merton, who wrote: "It is getting to be rather generally admitted that, for accuracy and depth and scope, this [Scotus'] is the most perfect and complete and thorough proof for the existence of God that has ever been worked out by any man." *The Seven Storey Mountain* (New York: Harcourt, Brace and Co., 1948), p. 94. For a comprehensive bibliography on Scotus' proof for the existence of God see Donald A. Cress, "Toward a Bibliography on Duns Scotus on the Existence of God," *Franciscan Studies,* 35 (1975), 45-65.

object of metaphysics. A comparison between his view and that of other medieval schoolmen will enable us better to understand his position on man's ability to know God.

I. THE PROPER OBJECT OF THE HUMAN INTELLECT

Long before Kant, Scotus realized that the question of man's knowledge of God depends to a great extent on the solution to the problem of the proper object of the human intellect. If our mind were so constituted that its only object of investigation were the sensible data of experience or a reality directly connected with the physical world, it would be useless to attempt to prove by reason the existence of a being that is supposedly beyond all empirical evidence. The mind would not only be unable to prove the existence of such a being, but any discussion of it would be meaningless. We would have to agree with Hume and his present-day followers, the logical positivists and most analysts, that God is not a subject of philosophy. Or we would have to accept the thesis of some modern and contemporary theologians that God is beyond the reach of the human mind and that the only approach to him is by faith.

In anticipation of these difficulties, and because of his concern about certain theories of knowledge of his own day, Scotus felt the need to discuss the possibility of man's knowledge of God by the light of natural reason, and in so doing he took up the question of the proper object of the human intellect. The fact that he raised this issue in all his major works, from the *Quaestiones subtilissimae super libros metaphysicorum Aristotelis* to the *Lectura I*, the *Opus Oxoniense*, the *Quaestiones super libros Aristotelis de anima*, and the *Quaestiones quodlibetales*, not to mention the *Reportata Parisiensia*, is an indication of the importance he attached to the problem under consideration. On the other hand, the large number of pertinent texts and the lack of a consistent and well-defined terminology have contributed to the confusion that exists among Scotistic commentators on the subject. Here an attempt will be made to present Scotus' thought as clearly as possible by relying primarily on his latest and most dependable works.[2]

---

[2]Scotus' works will be quoted as follows. The first book and distinctions 1-3 of the second book of the *Opus Oxoniense* will be quoted from the Vatican edition (vols. I to VII; 1950-1973) under the title *Ordinatio* I or II, followed by distinction, number, volume, and page; and so will the *Lectura* I (vols. XVI-XVII; 1960-1966). The remaining distinctions of the second book, as well as Books III and IV of the *Opus Oxoniense* and other Scotus' works —except the *De primo principio*—will be quoted from the Wadding-Vivès edition in the same way as the first two books of the *Ordinatio,* with the addition of the question after the distinction and the page column (a or b) after the volume number. The *De primo principio,* unless otherwise specified, will be quoted from the Latin text contained in Allan B. Wolter's

There are three ways in which an object can be said to enjoy primacy with regard to the intellect: first, from the point of view of the origin or actual genesis of our concepts (*ordo originis sive secundum generationem*); second, from the point of view of its perfection (*ordo perfectionis*); and third, from the standpoint of its adequation to the human mind *(ordo adaequationis)*.[3] The *ordo originis* concerns the process by which man acquires intellectual cognition in the present state of union of soul and body; it involves a transition from what Scotus calls confused knowledge to clear and distinct knowledge. The *ordo perfectionis* may refer either to the perfection of the object known or to the perfection of the cognitional act. However, our immediate concern is the third kind of primacy, the *ordo adaequationis*, which builds on the two preceding orders of knowledge and goes beyond them. At this stage we have knowledge through judgment and not merely that kind of conceptual knowledge that characterizes the two previous stages in the cognitive process. Scotus makes this third level of knowledge the object of a whole question in his *Ordinatio*: "Whether God is the first natural object that is adequate to the intellect of man in his present state."[4]

The first and adequate object of a power, Scotus writes, is that which is proportionate to that power considered precisely as a power (*ex natura potentiae*), and not as it exists in a particular situation.[5] Thus the first and adequate object of sight is not that which can be seen by the light of a candle, but rather that which can be seen under the most favorable conditions.[6] In fact the object is what specifies a power. Whether we call it formal object, as some schoolmen do, or first and natural object, as Scotus' texts indicate, is unimportant. The idea conveyed by these terms is that the proper object of a power is that toward which the power is primarily directed by its nature. Because of the perfect proportion that must exist between object and power, we may also speak in terms of adequate object, and that quite independently of the particular conditions that may limit the exercise of the power in question. There is no need, however, that object and power be similar to one another in their mode of being, since they are related as moving and movable and differ in the same way as act and

---

translation and edition, *A Treatise on God as First Principle* (Chicago, Ill.: Franciscan Herald Press, 1966).

[3]Cf. *Ord.* I, d. 3, no. 69; III, 48.

[4]*Ord.* I, d. 3, q. 3; III, 68.

[5]*Ibid.*, no. 186; III, 112: "Obiectum primum potentiae assignatur illud quod adaequatum est potentiae ex natura potentiae, non autem quod adaequatur potentiae in aliquo statu."

[6]*Ibid.*

potency do.[7] A relation of proportionality between object and power is sufficient.

With regard to human cognition, it must be said that whatever the intellect knows must fall within the area of its natural and adequate object, since it is toward it that the intellect is primarily directed. Moreover, the adequate object is also the viewpoint from which the human mind knows all things. Scotus had this in mind when he wrote:

> There is a twofold adequation of the object, one according to its virtuality (*secundum virtutem*) and the other according to its predication (*secundum praedicationem*). From the point of view of its virtuality, that object is adequate to its power which alone can move the intellect to the knowledge of itself and other things, just as the divine essence is the first and adequate object of the divine intellect. . . . From the point of view of its predication, that object is adequate [to its power] which can be predicated *per se* and essentially of all things knowable to the power in question, just as light or color or what is common to both of them can be predicated of all visible things.[8]

Clearly, then, for Scotus the proper and adequate object of the human intellect is that which makes all things intelligible and is the very reason for their intelligibility. It is also that which moves the intellect to know, since it is of the nature of an object to actuate the power to which it is primarily and naturally ordained.[9]

Having established the nature and characteristics of the proper object of the human intellect, Scotus proceeds to analyze the solutions to the problem at issue offered by the two principal schools of thought in his own day. The first theory is that of the Aristotelian-Thomistic school, which maintains that the proper formal object of the human intellect is the quiddity of material things. Since the human intellect exists only in conjunction with the body, it is argued, the proper object of its knowledge can only be an essence that is abstracted from matter.[10] This reasoning rests on the principle that between a faculty and its proper object there must be a strict proportion in being (*in essendo*). Aquinas, the chief representative

---

[7]*Ibid.*, no. 120; III, 74: "Potentiam enim et obiectum non oportet assimilari in modo essendi: se habent enim ut motivum et mobile, et ista se habent ut dissimilia, quia ut actus et potentia."

[8]*Quaestiones super libro Aristotelis de anima* (henceforth to be referred to as *De anima*), q. 21, no. 2; III, 612-613a. See also *Ord.* I, d. 3, nos. 117-118; III, 72-73.

[9]*Ibid.*, no. 126; III, 79.

[10]*Ibid.*, nos. 110-112; III, 69-70. See also *De anima*, q. 19, no. 2; III, 599ab. In a note to the *Ordinatio* Scotus mentions Thomas as the defender of this view. Cf. *Ord.* I, d. 3, no. 24; III, 16, under *Adnotatio Duns Scoti*. For Aquinas' view on the subject see *Sum. theol.* I, q. 84, a. 7 c; q. 85, a. 1 c.

of this view, does not deny that the human intellect can attain to the knowledge of immaterial things and of being as such, which for him is the most common object of our understanding and that to which all other concepts can be reduced. But he holds that this kind of knowledge does not fall within the realm of the proper formal object of the human intellect, precisely because it transcends—in a way that neither he nor his later interpreters made quite clear—the nature of an intellect that is incarnated, as it were, in a material body.

Scotus objects to this view on several counts. As a Christian theologian, he argues that if one limits the proper object of the intellect to sensible quiddities, he cannot explain how the human soul can enjoy the vision of God in a future life without changing the nature of the intellect itself. This difficulty cannot be avoided by introducing a special light (*lumen gloriae*) enabling the intellect to know an object that transcends its natural grasp, for an accidental quality can only perfect the capacity of a power already existing but cannot change its basic nature.[11]

There are other considerations that compel Scotus to depart from the preceding view. If the proper object of the intellect *ex natura potentiae*, and not merely in its present state, is only an essence abstracted from the phantasm, then how can the intellect know the ultimate causes of things by a clear and distinct knowledge and not only in a confused manner? That the intellect should be able to obtain the knowledge toward which it has a natural desire, as in the case at hand, no one can deny without questioning the very reason for that desire.[12]

Moreover, no power can attain to a knowledge that is beyond the sphere of its proper object, or else the object in question is not adequate to it. But the intellect can transcend mere material things and know being in general, which is the object of metaphysics, not to mention God, the soul, etc. Hence, unless we want to reduce metaphysics to the study of physical reality, we must admit that the proper object of the human intellect is not confined to sensible quiddity. Nor is it necessary, as previously stated, that the object known and the intellect be in the same order of being. As moving and movable (*motivum* and *mobile*), no greater proportion or similarity is required between them than the one based on the natural relationship of one to the other.[13]

---

[11]*Ord.* I, d. 3, nos. 113–114; III, 70–71. See also *Quaestiones quodlibetales* (henceforth to be referred to as *Quodlib.*), q. 14, no. 12; XXVI, 46b; *De anima*, q. 19, nos. 2–3; III, 599b–600a. While admitting that the human intellect, when separated from the body, has the capacity to see God directly, Scotus does not intend to say that the divine essence is its natural object. It is rather a "voluntary" object, in the sense that the vision of God is contingent upon an act of the divine will. Cf. *Ord.* I, d. 3, no. 57; III, 39.

[12]*Ord.* I, d. 3, nos. 115–116; III, 71–72; *De anima*, q. 19, no. 3; III, 600a.

[13]*Ord.*, nos. 117–122; III, 72–75; *De anima*, q. 19, no. 4; III, 600ab.

Having disposed, at least to his own satisfaction, of the Aristotelian-Thomistic theory, Scotus turns to that of Henry of Ghent, who was at the time the chief exponent of the Augustinian school. Henry taught that God, as the first and most perfect being in the order of existence, is also the first and proper object in the order of knowledge. Just as God is the cause of all things and no other reality is conceivable except insofar as it participates in the divine nature, so, Henry argues, the idea of God is also the cause of all our knowledge and the light through which we understand all other things.[14]

Scotus, who is generally well disposed toward the Augustinian school, objects to Henry's solution of the problem at issue for two principal reasons. First, God is not naturally ordained to our intellect as a moving cause of its intellection, except perhaps under the general concept of being, which, by its very nature, includes all reality and not only the being of God.[15] Thus Henry's solution fails to meet one of the requirements for the proper object of the intellect, namely, that the object be naturally ordained to the intellect *sub ratione motivi*.[16] There is another reason why Henry's view must be rejected. God is not the primary and adequate object of our intellect whether from the point of view of its commonness (*primitate adaequationis propter communitatem*) or of its virtuality (*primitate adaequationis propter virtualitatem*). Not from the point of view of its commonness, because the concept of God is not predicated of all cognizable objects; not from the viewpoint of its virtuality, because in this life our intellect does not have a direct knowledge of the divine essence which would lead to the knowledge of other things. Rather than being the cause of our knowledge of other things, God is the goal or terminus at which we arrive by a process of inference from the objects of our expe-

---

[14]*Ord.* I, d. 3, nos. 108-109; III, 68-69; *ibid.*, no. 125; III, 78.

[15]The general concept of being here referred to is that which the intellect attains in its grasp of the sensible quiddity and which, because of its universal nature, can be predicated of all beings, including God. (Cf. references to Scotus' texts in notes 30-34 below.) It is wrong, therefore, to say that for Scotus "the unlimited being is the naturally motivating object of the created intellect." This view, which is held by Cyril L. Shircel in his doctoral thesis, *The Univocity of the Concept of Being in the Philosophy of John Duns Scotus* (Washington, D.C.: The Catholic University of America Press, 1942), pp. 49-50 and n. 18, is based on a text from the *Quaestiones quodlibetales* that represents an objection to Scotus' position rather than his own thought. Scotus writes in effect in *Quodlib.*, q. 14, no. 11; XXVI, 40a: "Pro quocumque statu, cuiuscumque intellectus creati praecise, ens limitatum est objectum adaequatum, quia praecise illud potest attingi virtute causae naturaliter motivae intellectus."

[16]Scotus teaches that the human intellect has a natural tendency to know God just as it has to know any other being, but that the divine essence does not naturally move our intellect. Cf. *Ord.*, Prologus, no. 57; I, 35; *ibid.*, no. 60; I, 37; *Quodlib.*, q. 14, no. 11; XXVI, 40a.

rience. Briefly, the concept of God does not fulfill the requirements that have been set out for the proper and adequate object of our intellect. Nor does substance in general, Scotus adds, meet such requirements. For, on the one hand, accidents have their own power to move our mind, and, on the other, substance is not the primary cause of our knowledge of itself and of other intelligible objects.[17]

If neither the sensible quiddity of material things, nor God, nor substance in general is the proper object of our intellect, then, Scotus argues, we must either say that there is no such object or we must find it elsewhere. That the intellect must have its proper and adequate object seems to be beyond dispute. A power cannot exist without a specific purpose, and this it achieves by the attainment of the object for which it has been primarily made. Since the proposed solutions are unsatisfactory, Scotus advances his own theory. He suggests that the proper and adequate object of the human intellect is being. It is only in being that we can find the twofold primacy of community and virtuality which is characteristic of such an object. In fact, whatever is of itself intelligible—and this extends to everything that is not pure nothing—either includes essentially the concept of being or is contained virtually or essentially in that which includes essentially the concept of being.[18]

This calls for an explanation, and we can best provide it by using Scotus' analogy from the sense of sight. The proper object of the sense of sight is color, so that whatever the eye sees, it sees it from the point of view of its color. Color is in effect that to which our vision is primarily directed. There are, however, different kinds and shades of color. These too are perceived by the eye, but they cannot be considered as the proper object of the sense of sight, because they are merely accidental qualities. More specifically, they do not represent color as such but only such and such a color. A distinction must therefore be made between color as the proper object of sight without which vision is impossible, and the different kinds and shades of color which, although different from one another, contain color as their fundamental ground.[19]

The same thing is true of being. Its notion is included quidditatively in the essential concept of each and every thing, and even in the concept of

---

[17]*Ord.* I, d. 3, nos. 126-128; III, 79-80. See also *Quodlib.*, q. 14, no. 17; III, 62b-63a.

[18]*Ord.* I, d. 3, no. 137; III, 85: "Dico quod primum obiectum intellectus nostri est ens, quia in ipso concurrit duplex primitas, scilicet communitatis et virtualitatis, nam omne per se intelligibile aut includit essentialiter rationem entis, vel continetur virtualiter vel essentialiter in includente essentialiter rationem entis." As for the extension of the concept of being, Scotus says in *Quodlib.*, q. 3, no. 2; XXV, 114a: "Communissime [est ens] prout se extendit ad quodcumque quod non est nihil."

[19]*Ord.* I, d. 3, no. 151; III, 93.

the uncreated being, God. Being is in effect a most simple concept (*conceptus simpliciter simplex*) which cannot be reduced to any other concept, while all other concepts in some way presuppose it. On the other hand, the ultimate differences or intrinsic modes of being, such as finite and infinite, contingent and necessary, are contained essentially in that which includes being essentially—e.g., genus, species, the individual—since they pertain to the very essence of a thing. As for the proper attributes of being, or what in scholastic terminology are called *passiones entis*, such as unity, truth, and goodness, they are said to be contained in being and its inferiors virtually but not essentially, since they do not enter the formal definition of an essence.[20] In this sense, Scotus says, being fulfills the requirements of the first and adequate object of the human intellect and can be predicated univocally of everything that is intelligible, including God. Furthermore, only in this way can we attain to a real, quidditative knowledge of God.[21]

Brief mention must be made of Scotus' doctrine of univocity, since it is important for an understanding of his metaphysics and natural theology. Scotus teaches that even in this life man can form a concept that is univocal to God and creatures, and not merely analogous, as both the Augustinian and the Thomistic schools maintain. To avoid misunderstanding, he explains that by a univocal concept he means one that possesses such unity that to affirm and deny it of one and the same thing is contradictory. A univocal concept can also serve as the middle term of a valid syllogism, whereas an analogous or equivocal concept cannot.[22]

On the basis of this doctrine, which he applies to being and its transcendental attributes, such as unity, truth, and goodness, Scotus maintains that man can attain to a quidditative knowledge of God even in this life.

---

[20]*Ibid.*, no. 137; III, 85: "Omnia enim genera et species et individua, et omnes partes essentiales generum, et ens increatum includunt ens quiditative; omnes autem differentiae ultimae includuntur in aliquibus istorum essentialiter, et omnes passiones entis includuntur in ente et in suis inferioribus virtualiter." For a discussion of being and its transcendentals, see Allan B. Wolter, *The Transcendentals and Their Function in the Metaphysics of Duns Scotus* (Washington, D.C.: The Catholic University of America Press, 1946), especially pp. 77-97. See also Robert Prentice, "The Fundamental Metaphysics of Scotus Presumed by *De primo principio* (1)," *Antonianum*, XLIV (1969), 67-83.

[21]*Ibid.*, no. 139; III, 87: "Deus non est cognoscibilis a nobis naturaliter nisi ens sit univocum creato et increato." See also *ibid.*, no. 25; III, 16-17: "Dico ergo primo quod non tantum haberi potest conceptus naturaliter in quo quasi per accidens concipitur Deus, puta in aliquo attributo, sed etiam aliquis conceptus in quo per se et quiditative concipitur Deus."

[22]*Ibid.*, no. 26; III, 18. For a short presentation of the historical background of the doctrine of univocity and analogy see Timotheus A. Barth, "Being, Univocity, and Analogy according to Duns Scotus," in *Studies in Philosophy and the History of Philosophy*, vol. 3: *John Duns Scotus, 1265-1965*, ed. John K. Ryan and Bernardine M. Bonansea (Washington, D.C.: The Catholic University of America Press, 1965), pp. 250-55.

Thus our intellect can at first doubt whether God is finite or infinite, created or uncreated, but, as will be explained later, it can know with certainty that he is a being,[23] i.e., that to which existence is not repugnant, which is Scotus' notion of being.[24] Scotus agrees with Aristotle and Aquinas that in this life our knowledge can begin only with sense perception through the interaction of the intellect and the phantasm or the object manifested in the phantasm. But he argues that if all our concepts of God and creatures were merely analogous, then it would be impossible for us to arrive at any proper knowledge of God, since no created object contains God either essentially or virtually. Nor is it possible to avoid this conclusion by appealing to discursive reasoning, for such reasoning is valid only in terms of univocal concepts applicable to both creatures and God. It is therefore imperative that the concepts of being and its transcendental attributes, as well as those of all other simple perfections, be applied to God in exactly the same way as they are applied to creatures.[25]

An observation is in order. When Scotus teaches that the concept of being as applied both to God and to creatures is univocal, he does not consider being merely from the point of view of a logician concerned with being as a reflex concept or what Scholastics call a second intention (*intentio secunda*). He rather sees it as a metaphysician who considers being in its actual reality.[26] Yet Scotus does not identify God and creatures, and it would be wrong to accuse him of pantheism. On the contrary, he affirms categorically that while certain concepts are predicated of God and creatures univocally, the reality of God and the reality of creatures taken as a whole are totally different.[27] Scotus' position becomes understandable in the light of his notion of the proper object of the human intellect and his

---

[23]*Ord.* I, d.3, no. 27; III, 18: "Omnis intellectus, certus de uno conceptu et dubius de diversis, habet conceptum de quo est certus alium a conceptibus de quibus est dubius; subiectum includit praedicatum. Sed intellectus viatoris potest esse certus de Deo quod sit ens, dubitando de ente finito vel infinito, creato vel increato; ergo conceptus entis de Deo est alius a conceptu isto et illo, et ita neuter ex se et in utroque illorum includitur; igitur univocus." While Scotus' concept of being is primarily a quidditative concept, it nevertheless includes a relation to existence, or, more specifically, a tendency or aptitude to exist. This is particularly true when Scotus speaks of being as *effectivum* or *effectibile,* as will be seen in connection with his proof for God's existence. For a detailed discussion of Scotus' concept of being cf. Timotheus Barth, "De fundamento univocationis apud Ioannem Duns Scotum," *Antonianum,* XIV (1939), 277–87.

[24]*Op. Oxon.* IV, d. 8, q. 1, no. 2; XVII, 7b: "Ens, hoc est, cui non repugnat esse."

[25]*Ord.* I, d. 3, nos. 35–40; Ill, 21–27.

[26]This is clear from Scotus' statement in the *Lectura* I, d. 3, no. 126; XVI, 273, where he affirms: "Dicendum quod conceptus entis communis Deo et creaturae sit conceptus realis." See also Scotus' addition to *Ord.* I, d. 3, no. 124; III, 77: "Ens enim in quantum ens, communius est quocumque alio conceptu primae intentionis (secunda intentio non est primum obiectum [intellectus])." For a discussion of this point cf. Barth, "Being, Univocity, and Analogy according to Duns Scotus," *art. cit.,* pp. 246–50.

[27]*Ord.* I, d. 8, no. 82; IV, 190: "Deus et creatura non sunt primo diversa in conceptibus;

doctrine of formalities, whereby it is possible formally to distinguish in God between being and the intrinsic modes or perfections that characterize his essence, such as infinity, unity, truth, and the like. Whether or not Scotistic univocity does away with the traditional doctrine of analogy may be disputed, but some of Scotus' texts clearly indicate that for him univocity and analogy are in no way incompatible. In fact univocity provides the *analogia entis* with a logical and epistemological foundation.[28] In the words of one of his interpreters,

> according to Scotus the univocation of being is not opposed to the analogy of being; it rather accompanies it and strives to make it really possible inasmuch as it brings the transcendental commonness and ultimate identity of being into sharp relief.[29]

It will be helpful to elaborate further on Scotus' notion of being as the proper object of the human intellect and its application to our knowledge of God. As we have previously indicated, when Scotus discusses the proper object of the human intellect, he considers it from the point of view of its adequation or proportion to the intellect precisely as a knowing faculty (*ex natura potentiae*). It is in this sense, and only in this sense, that he maintains that being, rather than the sensible quiddity, fulfills that role. However, Scotus agrees with the Aristotelian-Thomistic school that in the present state of union of soul and body the sensible quiddity is the first object that naturally moves our intellect to know; i.e., it is the first object *in ratione motivi*.[30]

---

sunt tamen primo diversa in realitate, quia in nulla realitate conveniunt." Gilson writes in this connection: "Thus the Scotist univocity is a radical negation of pantheism, since the common attribution of the concept of being to God and creatures requires precisely that it should not be extended to that which makes the being of God to be God; but at the same time it unifies the whole order of human knowledge in affirming the essential unity of its object throughout all the diversity of the states through which it may pass." Etienne Gilson, *The Spirit of Mediaeval Philosophy*, trans. A. H. C. Downes (New York: Charles Scribner's Sons, 1940), p. 266.

[28]Thus Scotus can write in *Op. Oxon.* II, d. 12, q. 2, no. 8; XII, 604a: "Nulla enim maior est analogia, quam sit creaturae ad Deum in ratione essendi, et tamen sic esse, primo et principaliter convenit Deo, quod tamen realiter et univoce convenit creaturae; simile est de bonitate et sapientia et huiusmodi."

[29]Cf. Barth, "Being, Univocity, and Analogy according to Duns Scotus," pp. 260-61, who refers to the following sources for his interpretation: *Ord.* I, d. 3, nos. 152-157; III, 94-95; *ibid.*, nos. 162-166; III, 100-103; *Lect.* I, d. 3, nos. 105-123; XVI, 264-273.

[30]*Ord.* I, d. 3, no. 186; III, 113. Scotus suggests that the reason why in its present state the human intellect can acquire knowledge only through a sensible quiddity is either a decree of the divine wisdom in punishment of man's original sin, or the natural harmony that exists among the soul's powers and their operations. *Ibid.*, no. 187; III, 113. Whatever the cause of man's present inability to know without the phantasm, the proper and adequate object of the human intellect *ex natura potentiae* is for Scotus the same as that of the angelic intellect, because their cognitive power is basically the same. *Ord.* II, d. 1, no. 319; VII, 155:

In an addition to the text of the *Ordinatio* appearing for the first time in its Vatican edition and representing Scotus' latest thought on the subject,[31] the Subtle Doctor makes it clear that our intellect, by grasping the sensible quiddity, attains also to the knowledge of whatever is essentially or virtually included in the sensible, such as being and the relations inherent in the sensible.[32] Moreover, the being which is thus known through the sensible quiddity is not only the *ens terminativum* but also the moving cause of our intellection.[33] Clearly, then, for Scotus the proper object of the human intellect is the being abstracted from the sensible quiddity which, because of its primacy of commonness and virtuality, can be predicated univocally of all beings, including God.

In this way Scotus is able to establish metaphysics, the science of being as being, on a real basis and maintain that even in this life man can attain to a quidditative knowledge of God.[34] It is of course an imperfect knowledge because of the indirect way in which we attain it; but it is real and positive knowledge derived by reasoning from the perfections we dis-

---

"Intellectualitas angeli, in quantum intellectualitas, non differt specie ab intellectualitate animae in quantum intellectualitas." See also *Quodlib.*, q. 14, no. 12; XXVI, 47a: "Obiectum adaequatum intellectui nostro ex natura potentiae non est aliquid specialius obiecto intellectus angelici."

[31]Cf. Carolus Balić, "Circa positiones fundamentales I. Duns Scoti," *Antonianum.* XXVIII (1953), 274.

[32]*Ord.* I, d. 3, no. 123; III, 76. The same idea is found in *Quodlib.*, q. 14, no. 12; XXVI, 46b–47a.

[33]*Ord.* I, d. 3, no. 123; III, 76: "Nec oportet hic distinguere quod solum sensibile est obiectum motivum: ens terminativum—quia inclusum in sensibili sic vel sic—non tantum terminat sed movet, saltem intelligentiam per propriam speciem in memoria, sive a se genitam sive ab alio."

[34]Care must be taken not to confuse the problem of the first and adequate object of the intellect with the problem of being as the object of metaphysics. On Scotus' premises, a fully satisfactory solution to the first problem involves the knowledge of some data of revelation, whereas the solution to the second problem is completely independent of revelation. By failing to distinguish between these two problems, Etienne Gilson drew the unwarranted conclusion that according to the *Opus Oxoniense* "the human intellect would not be able, naturally and without the aid of revelation, to rise to the true notion of being, which is the object of metaphysics." Cf. "Les seize premiers Theoremata et la pensée de Duns Scot," *Archives d'histoire doctrinale et littéraire du Moyen Age,* XII–XIII (1937-38), 82. A similar mistake has been made by Joseph Owens, C.SS.R., in his article, "The Special Characteristic of the Scotistic Proof that God Exists," *Analecta Gregoriana,* LXVII (1954), where he states: "Duns Scotus maintains that the intellect in the present state of fallen nature does not know by natural means what its own first object is." *Ibid.,* pp. 325-26. For an appraisal of Gilson's view in the light of the critical edition of the *Opus Oxoniense (Ordinatio),* cf. Balić, *art. cit.,* pp. 268-78. See also Camille Bérubé, "Jean Duns Scot: Critique de l'Avicennisme Augustinisant," in *De doctrina Ioannis Duns Scoti, Acta Secundi Congressus Scholastici Internationalis Oxonii et Edimburgi diebus 11–17 Sept. 1966 celebrati,* I, 207-243, where the author takes issue with Gilson's interpretation of Scotus' teaching on the natural object that moves the created intellect, as though this were something interior to the mind rather than an external reality.

cover in creatures.[35] Accordingly, we can form concepts which are proper only to the divine essence, such as the concepts of simple perfections in the highest possible degree. Furthermore, we can form the concept of God as an infinite being which, in addition to including all the other pure perfections to the supreme degree, is also the conclusion of all arguments for the existence of God.[36] There should be no doubt, therefore, that Scotus' solution to the problem of the proper object of the human intellect, coupled with his doctrine of the univocity of the concept of being and other transcendental concepts, plays a fundamental role in his metaphysical theory and in his approach to God. It is to this latter issue that we shall now turn our attention.

II. DEMONSTRABILITY OF GOD'S EXISTENCE

In his attempt to prove the existence of God by the light of natural reason, a philosopher can start from a concept that in his view best represents the divine nature. This need not be a complete and exhaustive concept, which in any case is impossible, but it should be such as can serve as a provisional definition of God. Because of God's absolute simplicity, any of his attributes could, theoretically speaking, serve as a starting point for a theistic proof, for each attribute is God himself considered from a particular point of view. There are, however, certain attributes or perfections in God which, from our viewpoint, seem to be more fundamental than others. In addition, they seem better to distinguish God from all other beings and to serve as a source from which all other divine attributes can be logically derived.

While this is a commonly accepted teaching in traditional scholastic circles, the question of which among the divine attributes can best fulfill the functions above mentioned is open to discussion. This question has often been identified with the problem of the metaphysical essence of God, a problem that has received different solutions in the course of history. Whatever the relationship between the two issues here involved, namely, the provisional definition of God to the effect of a theistic proof and the definition of God from a strictly metaphysical viewpoint, it is a fact that in Scotus' theodicy the two issues are closely related, and that the concept of infinity plays the central role in both of them. Whether we call it a positive perfection or an intrinsic mode of being, infinity is for Scotus the fundamental attribute that best characterizes God and is at the root of all other divine perfections. "Just as being includes virtually in itself the

---

[35]*Ord.* I, d. 3, no. 61; III, 42. See also *Quodlib.*, q. 14, no. 3; XXVI, 5b-6a.

[36]*Ord.* I, d. 3, nos. 58-59; III, 40-41; *ibid.*, no. 61, under *Adnotatio interpolata;* III, 42-43; *Quodlib.*, q. 14, no. 3; XXVI, 5b-6a.

good and the true, so an infinite being includes infinite truth and infinite goodness and all simple perfections *sub ratione infiniti.* "[37] In other words, "the infinite contains in itself really and by way of identity all simple perfections."[38]

The Scotistic concept of infinity is thus richer and much more complex than the traditional notion of extensive and intensive infinity, one standing for the sum-total of divine perfections and the other for the infinite degree in which all simple perfections exist in God. The metaphysical essence of God is for Scotus "radical" infinity, or the exigency that God has for all perfections to the supreme degree. Radical infinity includes both extensive and intensive infinity but is deeper and more fundamental than both of them; it is like the root from which all other divine perfections spring forth, including aseity and perseity.[39] The fact that infinity can be proved from God's aseity, which for some Scholastics is the metaphysical constituent of the divine essence, does not indicate that the latter is a more fundamental attribute than the former; it means only that in our present state, where knowledge begins with creatures, aseity is easier to prove than infinity. On the other hand, all the other divine attributes can be more easily derived from radical infinity, which is one of the characteristics of the metaphysical essence of God, than from aseity or any other attribute. This is particularly true with regard to unicity, intelligence, and will, as will be seen in the exposition of Scotus' proof.

Given such a notion of the infinite, it is little wonder that, in approaching the problem of God's existence, Scotus should introduce the question by asking, "Whether among beings something exists that is actually infinite."[40] Having formulated the question in these terms, he proceeds in

---

[37] *Ord.* I, d. 3, no. 59; III, 41.

[38] *Quodlib.*, q. 5, no. 7; XXV, 210b.

[39] Cf. *Op. Oxon.* IV, d. 13, q. 1, no. 32; XVII, 689a: "Quaelibet enim [perfectio divina] habet suam perfectionem formalem ab infinitate essentiae tamquam a radice et fundamento."

[40] Ord. I, d. 2, no. 1; II, 125: "Utrum in entibus sit aliquid existens actu infinitum." The same question, with a slightly different wording, is asked in the *Lectura in I Sententiarum,* which contains the notes used by Scotus for his commentary on the first book of the Sentences at Oxford and served as one of the sources for his compilation of the *Ordinatio.* Cf. *Lectura* I, d. 2, no. 1; XVI, p. 111. While the *Ordinatio* will be the main source of our study, we shall make use of Scotus' other pertinent works, such as the *Quaestiones subtilissimae super libros metaphysicorum Aristotelis,* the *Reportata Parisiensia,* and the still unedited *Reportatio examinata.* This latter work was approved and revised by Scotus himself who used it, along with the *Lectura* I, for the compilation of the *Ordinatio.* Special use will be made of the treatise, *De primo principio,* where the Scotistic proof receives its most complete treatment. The reason for our choice of the *Ordinatio* over the *De primo principio* is not only that the text of the *Ordinatio* has been critically edited and constitutes the most reliable source for Scotus' thought, but also because it is easier to follow without getting involved in the complexities of the *De primo principio.* A substantial portion of this treatise has at any rate been taken almost verbatim from the *Ordinatio.*

scholastic fashion to state a few arguments against the possibility of an actually infinite being, which he then counters with arguments favoring such a possibility. But before taking up the issue specifically and presenting his own viewpoint, he feels the need to discuss a preliminary question whose solution could somewhat influence the issue at hand. He asks whether the proposition "An infinite being exists" or "God exists" is self-evident.[41]

The reason for raising such an issue as a preamble to his theistic proof is obvious. If an affirmative answer is given to the question, there is no need to go any further in the search for a proof of God's existence. What is self-evident needs no demonstration. All one can do is to show the reasons for the evidence in question. If, on the contrary, the question is answered negatively, then the problem of the existence of God must be solved in terms of an a posteriori proof, which is undoubtedly what Scotus had in mind in the formulation of his first question.

There is another advantage in prefacing an a posteriori proof with the discussion of what has come to be known as Anselm's ontological argument, and this too must have been foreseen by Scotus. Even if the argument were to be found weak and unconvincing, there might be a way to show that it is not completely useless. Perhaps the *ratio Anselmi* could be worked out in such a way as to make it more appealing to a critical and unprejudiced mind and be used as a supporting argument for the actual demonstration of God's existence. This is precisely what Scotus will do.

In his approach to the Anselmian argument, he shows, first, the noncontradiction of the concept of a supreme conceivable being—or of an infinite being for that matter—and therefore the possibility that such a being exist in actual reality. Next he shows the real contradiction that would follow from denying the existence of a supreme conceivable being, which, as previously shown, is possible, and yet would never be able to exist. It is indeed of the very nature of such a being not to depend on an outside cause for its existence.[42]

Yet, despite some "persuasive reasons" in support of the Anselmian

---

[41]*Ord.* I, d. 2, no. 10; II, 128: "Utrum aliquod infinitum esse sit per se notum, ut Deum esse."

[42]For a complete presentation of Scotus' position on the Anselmian argument, the reader is referred to the pertinent section in chapter III of this volume. For the sake of completeness, we would like to mention the fact that, in addition to the Anselmian argument, Scotus discusses very briefly three other views favoring the self-evidence of God's existence. They are as follows: (1) the theory of St. John Damascene that the knowledge of God's existence is naturally implanted in man like the first principles of metaphysics; (2) the Augustinian argument that just as the existence of truth is self-evident, so is the existence of God who is truth itself; and finally, (3) the view that the proposition "God exists" is self-evident, for as soon as our intellect understands the two terms, it knows that one is necessarily related to the other. Cf. *Ord.* I, d. 2, nos. 10, 12-13; II, 128-30; nos. 34, 37-38; II, 145-48.

argument, Scotus refrains from endorsing it as a demonstrative proof of God's existence. It is only by an argument a posteriori that such a proof is possible. This is what he means when, in introducing his answer to the question, "Whether among beings something exists that is actually infinite," he says that, although it is not possible to demonstrate the existence of an infinite being by a demonstration a priori (*propter quid*), it is necessary and altogether possible to demonstrate it by a demonstration a posteriori (*quia*) beginning with creatures.[43]

The distinction and value of the two kinds of demonstration is worth considering and to this effect we wish to refer to an important text of the *Quaestiones quodlibetales*, one of Scotus' latest and most reliable works.[44] In his preface to the solution of question seven, where he discusses the demonstration of God's omnipotence, Scotus makes a twofold distinction, one with regard to the term *demonstration* and the other with regard to the concept of omnipotence. The first distinction—the only one that interests us here—is taken from Aristotle's *Posterior Analytics*, and it is between a demonstration *propter quid*, i.e., from the cause, and a demonstration *quia*, i.e., from the effect.[45]

The adequacy of this distinction is proved as follows. Every proposition that is necessarily true but whose evidence is from the terms of another proposition with which it is necessarily connected, can be demonstrated by means of this latter. The truth of the proposition in question can be derived from the cause or from the effect, for truths about the cause can entail truths about the effect and vice versa. Thus a true proposition can be demonstrated by means of another true and evident proposition derived either from the cause, in which case it is a demonstration *propter quid*, or from the effect, and this is a demonstration *quia*.

Having described the two kinds of demonstration, which correspond roughly to what are commonly called demonstration a priori and demonstration a posteriori or, more recently, demonstration of the reasoned fact and demonstration of the simple fact, Scotus goes on to explain further the two kinds of truth involved in them. While there are certain propositions that are evident from their terms and admit of no *quia* demonstra-

---

[43]*Ord.* I, d. 2, no. 39; II, 148: "Ad primam quaestionem sic procedo, quia de ente infinito sic non potest demonstrari esse demonstratione propter quid quantum ad nos, licet ex natura terminorum propositio est demonstrabilis propter quid. Sed quantum ad nos bene propositio est demonstrabilis demonstratione quia ex creaturis."

[44]The importance of the *Quaestiones quodlibetales* or *De quolibet* for Scotus' thought is stressed by Charles Balić in his article, "The Life and Works of John Duns Scotus," vol. 3 of *Studies in Philosophy and the History of Philosophy*, pp. 24–27. The work has been translated into English by Felix Alluntis and Allan B. Wolter under the title, *God and Creatures* (Princeton, N.J.: The Princeton University Press, 1975).

[45]Cf. *Posterior Analytics* I, chaps. 13–14 (78a 22–79a 33).

tion, there are others that are intermediate between the first or primary truths and the last conclusions. The latter admit of a *quia* demonstration through the first and evident truths. As for the reason why a truth derived from the effect can be evident whereas a truth taken from the cause is not so, Scotus quotes once more Aristotle to the effect that this is the way scientific knowledge is acquired, namely, from experience.[46] It is a fact that we know an effect to occur from the repetition of many individual instances perceived by the senses, and yet we do not know immediately the reason for such an occurrence. In fact the reason is not given us through sense perception but can only be obtained by further investigation.[47]

Scotus' position on the value of a *quia* demonstration is of paramount importance for his approach to God. Having sided against Henry of Ghent's theory that God is the first natural object of the human intellect and questioned at the same time the value of Anselm's a priori argument, he is left with the only way open for a rational justification of God's existence, namely, that by way of creatures. This, as previously indicated, is exactly what he says at the outset of his theistic proof. Does this mean that his proof is deficient by failing to meet the requirements of a strict metaphysical demonstration based on the nature of the being in question? The answer is "No," but with a qualification. If by metaphysical demonstration is meant an ideally perfect demonstration that comes close to the evidence of the first principles of knowledge and metaphysics, then a *propter quid* demonstration is superior to a *quia* demonstration. But if by metaphysical demonstration is meant a rational process whereby from the nature of an effect known to us by experience we argue to the existence of its proper and adequate cause on the basis of the first metaphysical principles and following the laws of strict syllogistic reasoning, then an a posteriori proof, although less evident, is just as valid as its a priori counterpart. That this is the mind of Scotus is clear from the above text of the *Quaestiones quodlibetales* which paves the way for a rational justification of his ascent to God.

There are other texts to support this view. Thus in his *Prologus* to the *Reportata Parisiensia* Scotus discusses the requirements for scientific knowledge, and, quoting Aristotle's definition of science as certain knowledge of a necessary truth derived by syllogism from a previously evident truth or principle,[48] he emphasizes the fact that the way we acquire such knowledge manifests the imperfection of our intellect, which has to reason

---

[46]Cf. Aristotle, *Metaphysics* I, ch. 1 (980b 27-981a 3); *Post. Anal.* II, ch. 19 (100a 4-11).
[47]*Quodlib.*, q. 7, no. 3; XXV, 283-84.
[48]Cf. *Post. Anal.* I, ch. 2 (71b 17-22).

from the known to the unknown—precisely as in the case of a theistic proof. Yet this imperfection does not diminish the value of the conclusions, as long as the conditions of scientific knowledge are fulfilled.[49] Likewise, in a lengthy question of the *Ordinatio* dealing with man's knowledge of God, Scotus discusses the nature of scientific knowledge obtained by induction from the objects of our experience and affirms that such a knowledge is perfectly valid.[50] He explains: whenever a large number of instances indicate that an effect always follows upon a cause that is not free, our mind is justified in concluding that the effect is the natural outcome of that cause, even though the knowledge of the sequence of cause and effect is obtainable only through sense perception.[51] The knowledge of the effect, he adds, may sometimes lead to the knowledge of the cause itself. But the case may also be that, despite the fact that the existence of the cause is conclusively proved by a *quia* demonstration, the nature of the cause remains unknown.[52] In either case, the inductive process is valid, and consequently it can be used for a metaphysical proof of God's existence.

How is it possible, Scotus asks in an earlier work, that metaphysics, whose object is being as being, should be a *propter quid* science, while the science about God, who is the supreme being, is only a *quia* science? His answer is that the whole of metaphysics is actually ordained to God.[53] However, since in our present state we cannot have a direct knowledge of him, God is only an indirect object of metaphysics, inasmuch as we come to know him by a *quia* demonstration from the properties of the beings of our experience.[54] This is the way Scotus approaches the problem of God, convinced as he is that God's existence, along with his unicity and infinity, can be established on truly rational grounds.[55]

---

[49]*Rep. Par.*, Prologus, q. 1, no. 4; XXII, 7-8.

[50]*Ord.* I, d. 3, no. 235; III, 141: "De secundis cognoscibilibus, scilicet de cognitis per experientiam, dico quod licet experientia non habeatur de omnibus singularibus sed de pluribus, neque quod semper sed quod pluries, tamen expertus *infallibiliter novit* quia ita est et semper et in omnibus." (Italics ours.)

[51]*Ibid.*, p. 142: " 'Quidquid evenit ut in pluribus ab aliqua causa non libera, est effectus naturalis illius causae'; quae propositio nota est intellectui licet accepisset terminos eius a sensu errante, quia causa non libera non potest producere 'ut in pluribus' effectum non libere ad cuius oppositum ordinatur, vel ad quem ex sua forma non ordinatur."

[52]*Ibid.*, nos. 236-37; III, 143-44.

[53]Cf. *Quaestiones subtilissimae super libros metaphysicorum Aristotelis* I, q. 1, no. 45; Wadding-Vivès ed., VII, 34: "Respondeo, quod tota illa scientia *propter quid,* quae est de ente, inquantum ens, ordinatur ad *quia* de Deo." See also *ibid.*, VI, q. 4, no. 1; Vol. VII, 348: "Deum esse probatur hic [in Metaphysica]."

[54]*Ibid.*, I, q. 1, no. 45; VII, 34-35.

[55]See, for example, *Ord.* I, d. 2, no. 165; II, 226, where Scotus says of God's unicity: "Videtur tamen quod illa unitas posset naturali ratione ostendi." Again in *De primo principio*, p. 147, he affirms: "Ad quod ostendendum [quod scilicet unus Deus sis] non puto

If this is the case, how can we explain the apparently contradictory statements in the *Theoremata*, an opuscule that has been traditionally ascribed to Scotus?[56] In fact the author of this opuscule seems not only to deny the ability of the human mind to prove the existence of God but also to question some of the fundamental principles that underlie such a proof. He states, for example, that it would be difficult, if not impossible, for unaided reason to prove that in essentially ordered beings or causes there is a first which is unique and coexistent with the series. He states further that it is not easy to prove that an essential order is needed at the foundation of all series of causes, and consequently, that it cannot be established that God is actually in existence now, even though he may be the first efficient cause in a particular series.[57] These and other even more shocking statements throughout *Theoremata* XIV-XVI—a special section entitled *Tractatus de creditis (Treatise on Things Believed)*—give the impression that their author challenges most of the theses established by Scotus in the *Opus Oxoniense*, in the *De primo principio*, and in some other previous works concerning the demonstrability of God's existence.

It is little wonder that, because of these seeming contradictions, some authors (De Basly, Longpré, Ciganotto) have either questioned or denied the authenticity of the *Theoremata*. However, since their studies were made in the first quarter of this century, it is questionable whether such authors would uphold the same conclusions today after the discovery of new manuscript codices and documents supporting the authenticity of the opuscule.[58] It is mainly on the basis of this newly discovered material that Father Balić, former president of the commission for the critical edition of Scotus' works, decided to side with "all editors of Scotus' works from the fifteenth century on" and place the *Theoremata* among Scotus' authentic works. He cautioned, however, that his decision was based principally on what the critics call *criteria externa*, that is, reasons or motives that lie

---

deficere rationem." The *Reportatio examinata*, Mert. cod. 59, f. 24r; Balliol, cod. 205, f. 23v contains a similar statement: "Credo quod conclusio ista potest demonstrari, scilicet quod sit unicum ens primum unitate numerali."

[56]The authenticity of the *Theoremata* has been affirmed very strongly by Wadding: "Nulli dubium opusculum hoc Scoti esse." Cf. *Theoremata subtilissima*, Wadding-Vivès ed., V, 1: "R.P.F. Lucae Waddingi censura." Wadding's view reflects also the opinion of Scotus' most faithful interpreter, Maurice of Port, who published the *Theoremata* for the first time with his own preface and annotations, and of Hugh Cavellus, who added the *Scholia* and his own notes to the text.

[57]*Theoremata*, XV, nos. 1-3; Wadding-Vivès ed., V, 51-52.

[58]For a survey of the views concerning the authenticity of the *Theoremata* the reader is referred to the study of Gedeon Gál, "De J. Duns Scoti 'Theorematum' authenticitate ex ultima parte operis confirmata," *Collectanea Franciscana*, XX (1950), 5-17, where pertinent sources are indicated. See also Efrem Bettoni, *L'ascesa a Dio in Duns Scoto* (Milano: Vita e Pensiero, 1943), pp. 104-121, for a lengthy discussion of the same problem.

outside the work itself and have no reference to its contents. Hence, because of its controversial nature, the *Theoremata* ought to be considered as one of the least reliable sources for the knowledge of Scotus' genuine thought.[59]

Whereas Balić approached the problem of the authenticity of the *Theoremata* from the point of view of external criticism, Gilson went directly to its text—that of the first sixteen theorems, to be precise, including the controversial *Tractatus de creditis*[60]—and after comparing its content with that of Scotus' works of unquestionable authenticity, he reversed his previous position and claimed that no evident contradiction exists between them. The reason for the apparent discrepancy between Scotus' solution to the problem of man's knowledge of God and his position on the demonstrability of God's existence lies in the different approaches he takes to the issue at hand. Whereas in the *Opus Oxoniense* and the *De primo principio* Scotus approaches God primarily as a theologian enlightened by revelation, in the *Theoremata* he attempts to reach God purely as a philosopher, i.e., by the light of natural reason alone. That explains why Scotus can hold, on the one hand, that man can prove the existence of God by a *quia* demonstration, and maintain, on the other, that such a proof is questionable.[61]

How does Gilson prove his new position? In the first place, he says, the Scotistic proof of God's existence rests on being and its transcendental properties. Now since for Scotus the concept of being as the first object of our intellect and the object of metaphysics cannot be attained without the aid of revelation, the human intellect will never be able to produce a proof of God's existence by relying exclusively on its own power. This is Scotus' attitude toward God reflected in the *Theoremata*, a work that is different from, but not opposed to, his other works of a more theological nature.[62]

There is another reason, continues Gilson, that may help us understand Scotus' twofold approach to God. Accepting the Aristotelian notion of demonstration as a syllogism productive of scientific knowledge (*scientia*),[63] Scotus maintains that, strictly speaking, only a *propter quid* demonstration can fulfill the requirement of the syllogism in question.

[59] See Charles Balić, "The Life and Works of John Duns Scotus," pp. 26–27.

[60] Cf. "Les seize premiers Theoremata et la pensée de Duns Scot," pp. 5–86.

[61] *Ibid.*, p. 82: "Les *Theoremata* ne contredisent pas l'*Opus Oxoniense* s'ils disent que l'on ne peut prouver l'existence de Dieu dans des conditions où l'*Opus Oxoniense* lui-même enseigne qu'il devient impossible de la prouver. Tout au contraire, s'il en était ainsi, ces deux oeuvres se confirmeraient mutuellement."

[62] *Ibid.*, pp. 82–83.

[63] *Super universalia Porphyrii quaestiones*, q. 1, no. 2; Wadding-Vivès ed., I, 51: "Demonstratio est syllogismus faciens scire."

Scientia is, in fact, certain knowledge of a necessary truth derived by syllogistic reasoning from previously known principles that are both necessary and evident.[64] Since for Scotus, as well as for most Scholastics, no a priori knowledge of God is possible, neither is a demonstration possible of God's existence from cause to effect, which is really what a strict demonstration amounts to. Hence the a posteriori proof of God's existence that Scotus develops in his certainly authentic works is not a strict metaphysical demonstration; it is only a proof that, from the point of view of a metaphysician, is probably valid but not necessarily so. This, Gilson believes, is what Scotus had in mind when he wrote in the *Theoremata*, and more specifically in theorem XV, that in a series of essentially ordered causes one cannot demonstrate the coexistence of a First Cause by a proof that is simply necessary (*simpliciter necessaria*) and based merely on natural reason (*ratione mere naturali*). The proof has only a probable value. On the other hand, when Scotus speaks of this same proof in some of his other works and calls it necessary, he is right, because his proof is really such. However, the necessity in question becomes known to him as a theologian rather than as a philosopher. And even in that capacity, Gilson concludes, he does not make evident the necessity of the proof; he achieves only the conclusion of a *quia* demonstration and not that of a demonstration in the strict sense of the term.[65]

Gilson's interpretation of the *Theoremata*, if correct, has the advantage of solving one of the centuries-old puzzles that has worried Scotists of different trends. Whether authentic or not—a question that Gilson leaves up to historical criticism to decide—the *Theoremata* would not present any inconsistency with Scotus' genuine teaching. As for the demonstrability of God's existence, which is our main concern here, theorems XIV–XVI would say nothing that is not already implied in the *Opus Oxoniense*. In this sense the two works, far from being contradictory, would complement each other.[66]

It is true that Gilson's position is not altogether new, as he explicitly admits. He depends to a great extent on Maurice of Port and Hugh Cavellus, two Irish commentators who defended a similar view long before him.[67] However, because of his many new insights and his widely recognized authority on medieval thought, Gilson's study became soon the object of serious criticism by scholars who felt the need to take issue with his

---

[64]*Rep. Par.*, Prologus, q. 1, no. 4; Wadding-Vivès ed., XXII, 7–8.
[65]See the whole section on Theoremata XV and XVI in Gilson, *art. cit.*, pp. 54–80.
[66]*Ibid.*, p. 82.
[67]See, for example, pp. 46, 62 and 83 of his study.

conclusions.[68] In view of the position adopted in this study with regard to Scotus' teaching on the demonstrability of God's existence, the following observations are in order.

First of all, Gilson's thesis rests on the erroneous assumption, which we did not fail to point out,[69] that for Scotus "being" as the first and adequate object of the human intellect and "being" as the object of metaphysics are one and the same. If we keep the two concepts of being distinct, as Scotus' texts indicate should be done, we shall see that the human intellect can, even in this life, attain to the knowledge of God in virtue of its own power and without the aid of revelation. This is particularly true in light of Scotus' doctrine of univocity, according to which man can attain to a quidditative knowledge of the divine essence. Thus the distinction between Scotus as a philosopher (*Theoremata*) and Scotus as a theologian (*Opus Oxoniense,* etc.), which serves as a basis for Gilson's thesis, is seen to be altogether groundless.

A second assumption on which Gilson builds his theory, is that Scotus does not consider a *quia* demonstration to be a genuine metaphysical proof, since it fails to meet the requirements of necessity and evidence that are proper to a demonstration in the strict sense of the term. This assumption, no less than the preceding one, is also unwarranted and goes against Scotus' texts which point to the opposite conclusion. Since the nature and value of the Scotistic demonstration have already been dealt with earlier in this section, we refer the reader to that discussion.[70] We wish only to point out in this connection that one of the key passages for Gilson's thesis, namely, that for Scotus no demonstration from effect to cause is a demonstration in the strict sense of the term (*demonstratio simpliciter*), is not an authentic text.[71]

Given the unsatisfactory nature of Gilson's solution to the problem of

---

[68]Reference is made here especially to the study of Efrem Bettoni, *L'ascesa a Dio in Duns Scoto,* pp. 104-121, and to that of Allan B. Wolter, "The 'Theologism' of Duns Scotus," *Franciscan Studies,* VII (1947), 257-73 and 367-98.

[69]Cf. n. 34 above.

[70]See especially our commentary on the text from the seventh question of the *Quaestiones quodlibetales* referred to in n. 47 above, where Scotus' teaching on the nature of a *quia* demonstration as certain and evident proof is clearly indicated.

[71]Although the text which reads, "Nulla demonstratio, quae est ab effectu ad causam, est demonstratio simpliciter," is not found in Gilson's article on the *Theoremata* but rather in his book, *La philosophie au Moyen Age* (Paris: Payot, 1925), p. 228, there is no doubt that it exerted a considerable weight on his interpretation of Scotus' thought, just as it did on other interpreters of Scotus. (See, e.g., Parthenius Minges, O.F.M., *Ioannis Duns Scoti doctrina philosophica et theologica* [Ad Claras Aquas: Collegium S. Bonaventurae, 1930], II, 29-30). The original source of the text is a commentary *In librum primum Posteriorum Analyticorum Aristotelis,* q. 11, no. 7; Wadding-Vivès ed., II, 227b-228a, which Wadding wrongly attributes to Scotus.

the *Theoremata* and the obvious differences between Scotus' approach to God in that opuscule and that of his other certainly authentic works, one is left with the following options.

1) One may deny the authenticity of the opuscule because of its contradictions of Scotus' genuine thought. As we have seen, this view has been held by several prominent Scotists in the past, but it is questionable whether it can be sustained today in light of Father Balić's recent discoveries.

2) One may admit the authenticity of the opuscule as a whole and repudiate its controversial and somewhat independent section, *Tractatus de creditis,* as the work of an author other than Scotus. This solution would undoubtedly cut at the root of the whole problem, but, among other things, it seems to run against Scotus' reference to the above *Tractatus* in the *De primo principio.* [72]

3) One may hold with Scotus' commentators, Maurice of Port and Hugh Cavellus, that in the *Tractatus de creditis* Scotus does not necessarily express his own viewpoint but that of "some ancient theologians" who had little use for reason in their approach to God.[73] This explanation may be true of many passages, but, as Father Minges observes,[74] there are many other passages in this *Tractatus* where Scotus states clearly and unequivocally his own personal opinion, and this seems to conflict with the hypothesis—for that is what it is—advanced by the two Scotus' commentators.

4) In a slight revision of the aforesaid hypothesis and in response to its ensuing criticism, a recent author has put forth the view that in the *Theoremata* Scotus speaks sometimes in the name of others and sometimes in his own name. He would speak in the name of others when in his reasoning he proceeds by way of causality and analogy; he would speak in his own name when he shows the inadequacy of the way of analogy to demon-

---

[72]"Licet igitur omnipotentiam proprie dictam, secundum intellectum Catholicorum, usque ad *tractatum de creditis* distulerim...," *De primo principio,* p. 131. This reference has led Balić to conclude that the *Theoremata* is one of Scotus' latest works, even though its actual compilation may have been made by others who, following Scotus' general plan of the work, took most of the material from the *Opus Oxoniense.* Cf. Carolus Balić, "De critica textuali Scholasticorum scriptis accommodata," *Antonianum,* XX (1945), 289–96. For a critical appraisal of Scotus' reference to the *Tractatus de creditis* in the *De primo principio,* see Wolter, "The 'Theologism' of Duns Scotus," and his introduction to *A Treatise on God as First Principle,* pp. xiii–xvii. Wolter believes that, until evidence to the contrary is forthcoming, the work referred to by Scotus in the *De primo principio* is not the *Tractatus de creditis* of the *Theoremata.*

[73]Cf. *Theorema XIV,* Scholium I; Wadding-Vivès ed., V, 38; also "Annotationes" to *Theorema XIV,* no. 9; V, 43.

[74]*Op. cit.,* II, 28–29.

strate the existence of God and his attributes by a proof that is "simply necessary and based on purely natural reason." It is because of this inadequacy, the author argues, that Scotus expresses the need for a new approach to God based on the doctrine of univocity. This interpretation, we are told, can be sustained even if Scotus already held firmly to the doctrine of univocity at the time he wrote the *Theoremata*.[75] By way of comment, it can be said that while this reformulation of the hypothesis of the two Scotistic commentators previously mentioned is a plausible attempt to solve the enigma of the *Theoremata,* its proponent does not seem to derive much support from the text itself. There is indeed little evidence in the opuscule that the doctrine of univocity is a very important factor in the author's approach to God, even though we know from other works that that was Scotus' conviction. Moreover, the hypothesis assumes that the *Theoremata* is one of Scotus' earliest works, an assumption which is far from certain.

5) Another and perhaps easier way out of the impasse caused by the *Theoremata* is to admit a gradual development in Scotus' thought, so that he would have rejected at a later date what he had defended in his earlier writings. The difficulty involved in this opinion is that, in addition to assuming as settled the issue of an early date of the *Theoremata,* it does not take into account the fact that Scotus maintained more or less the same position on man's ability to know God at all periods of his life, from his early questions on Aristotle's *Metaphysics* to his latest writings.

6) There is one more option, which has been advanced as a possible alternative to their own view by the previously mentioned Scotists, Maurice of Port and Hugh Cavellus.[76] It consists in saying that when Scotus speaks in the *Theoremata,* and especially in the *Tractatus de creditis,* of certain doctrines that cannot be proved by "a simply necessary and purely natural reason,"[77] he takes the term *proof* in the strict Aristotelian sense of a *propter quid* demonstration.[78]

It is well known that Scotus was an extremely competent logician, and that he had a great esteem for Aristotle, whom he frequently quotes in his works. It is also a fact that the Oxford school was at his time under the influence of men like Robert of Grosseteste and Roger Bacon, who placed

---

[75]Cf. Gedeon Gál, *art. cit.,* p. 14.

[76]See *Theorema XIV,* Scholium I; Wadding-Vivès ed., V, 38; also "Annotationes" to *Theorema XIV,* no. 9; V, 43.

[77]*Theorema XV,* no. 1; V, 51: "simpliciter necessaria ratione, et mere naturali probare."

[78]Cf. Aristotle, *Post. Anal.* I, ch. 24 (85b 22): "Demonstration is syllogism that proves the cause, i.e., the reasoned fact."

great emphasis on the mathematical method in philosophy.[79] It is possible, then, that in writing the *Theoremata* Scotus wanted to meet the demands of those contemporary schoolmen who had little use for a demonstration that was not along strictly logical and mathematical lines. This is not to say that in his other works, like the *De primo principio*, the *Opus Oxoniense*, and the *Quaestiones quodlibetales*, he abandoned that method and adopted a more theological approach to God in the sense mentioned by Gilson. Rather he broadened his view and tried to show that even an a posteriori demonstration can meet the requirements of necessity and evidence demanded by the rules of the Aristotelian syllogism, without thereby denying that, ideally speaking, an a priori demonstration is the best way to attain strictly scientific knowledge in the Aristotelian sense of the term. Scotus' preoccupation, as clearly seen in the *Opus Oxoniense* and the *De primo principio*, was to work out a theistic proof that takes its starting point from premises that are evident and necessary and assume the truth of the doctrine of univocity, as will be seen presently. And this fact may serve to confirm the viewpoint here expressed.

Whatever the case, the problem of the *Theoremata* still awaits a satisfactory solution that is not likely to come until a critical edition of its text is available and a comparative study is made of all Scotus' pertinent texts. However, the uncertainty about the nature of the forthcoming solution in no way weakens the value of Scotus' proof developed in his certainly authentic and more mature works, which are the primary sources of our study.

III. DEMONSTRATION OF GOD'S EXISTENCE

The long digression on the demonstrability of God's existence has had two main advantages: first, it has shown Scotus' precise position on the issue at hand; and secondly, it has obviated any objection that might be suggested because of the *Theoremata*. With the assurance from Scotus' certainly authentic works that the demonstration of God's existence by human reason is a definite possibility, we shall now turn directly to his proof which, as previously stated, takes the form of an answer to the question, "Whether among beings something exists that is actually infinite."

An infinite being has two kinds of properties, says Scotus: relative and absolute. Relative properties refer to creatures and are therefore more

---

[79]Cf. Paul Vignaux, *Philosophy in the Middle Ages*, trans. E. C. Hall (New York: Meridian Books, 1959), pp. 95–97, for quotations from Robert Grosseteste and Roger Bacon to the effect that only a strictly *propter quid* demonstration is considered as valid.

easily demonstrated, since the existence of one term or being of the relation implies immediately and necessarily the existence of its correlative. Absolute properties, on the other hand, have no direct reference to creatures; they can be established only by reflecting upon the logical implications of the relative properties that have been shown to belong to the infinite being. Hence Scotus' proof includes two major parts, each with several sections, and concludes with an additional discussion of the unicity of God. The following schema based on the *Ordinatio* will help the reader to follow the logic of Scotus' ascent to God.[80]

SCOTUS' PROOF OF GOD'S EXISTENCE

A. *The Relative Properties of God*
  1. The Triple Primacy
     a. A First Efficient Cause
        i. Its possibility
        ii. Its uncausability
        iii. Its existence
     b. An Ultimate Final Cause
        i. Its possibility
        ii. Its uncausability
        iii. Its existence
     c. A Most Perfect Nature
        i. Its possibility
        ii. Its uncausability
        iii. Its existence
  2. Interrelation of the Three Primacies
  3. The Triple Primacy of Efficiency, Finality, and Eminence Belongs to One Nature

B. *The Absolute Properties of God*
  1. The Infinity of the First Being
     a. Preliminary Theses
        i. The First Being is endowed with intellect and will
        ii. Self-knowledge and self-volition of the First Being are the same as its essence
        iii. Knowledge and volition of other things are also the same as the First Being's essence
        iv. Distinct and necessary knowledge of all intelligibles by the First Being

---

[80]*Ord.* I, d. 2, nos. 39–181; II, 148–236.

b. Proofs of the Infinity of the First Being
   i. From its infinite power
   ii. From its infinite knowledge
   iii. From its infinite goodness
   iv. From its infinite perfection
2. The Unicity of God
   Proofs from:
   i. The infinite intellect
   ii. The infinite will
   iii. The infinite goodness
   iv. The infinite power
   v. The notion of absolute infinity
   vi. The nature of necessary being
   vii. The notion of omnipotence

The relative properties of the infinite being are those of efficient and final causality and of eminence. The exemplary cause, Scotus observes, does not represent a distinct kind of causality.[81] If it did, we would have five causes instead of the traditional four. The exemplary cause is the idea that an intelligent agent has in mind in his production of the effect and is therefore a form of efficient causality. Since there are only three relative properties of the infinite being, the first step will be to show that for each term of the relation in question there is a correlative term or being that is simply first in its particular order and is such that it includes no imperfection.[82] This will lead to the affirmation of an absolutely first being in the orders of efficient causality, final causality, and eminence. Once this is done, the next step will be to show that the three kinds of primacy are interrelated in such a way that the first being in one order is also the first being in the other two. From this the conclusion will be drawn that the triple primacy belongs to one and the same nature.[83] This will mark the end of the first part of the proof.

---

[81]The opposite view, which is the object of Scotus' criticism, was held by Henry of Ghent. Cf. his *Summa quaestionum ordinariarum*, a. 22, q. 4 in corp.

[82]*Ord.* I, d. 2, no. 41; II, pp. 149-50: "Primo ergo ostendam quod aliquid est in effectu inter entia quod est simpliciter primum secundum efficientiam, et aliquid est quod etiam est simpliciter primum secundum rationem finis, et aliquid quod est simpliciter primum secundum eminentiam." The expression "simpliciter primum" means that the primacy in question admits of no imperfection. Cf. *ibid.*, *Textus interpolatus*, p. 149.

[83]*Ibid.*, p. 150.

A. The Relative Properties of God

1. THE TRIPLE PRIMACY

a. *The Existence of a First Efficient Cause.*

"Some being is producible" (*aliquod ens est effectibile*). This is possible only in terms of the being itself, of nothing, or of another being. It cannot be from nothing, for nothing is the absence of being and no one can give what he does not have. To use Scotus' expression, nothing can be the cause only of nothing. The production of a being cannot be by the being itself either, for it is absurd to think of something that makes or begets itself. It would have to act before existing, which is an evident contradiction. Hence, since the two other alternatives are inconceivable, one must conclude that if a being is producible, it can be produced only by another being.[84]

Before we proceed further in the exposition of Scotus' thought, a few observations are in order. First of all, the starting point of the Scotistic proof is not the immediate object of our experience, as in St. Thomas and many other scholastic philosophers. The Subtle Doctor does not build his proof on an empirical fact, such as physical motion or change, but rather on the possibility of such a fact. Motion and change are in effect contingent events, whereas the possibility of such events, once they have been ascertained beyond doubt, is a metaphysical and necessary truth. This is true in virtue of the principle that *ab esse ad posse valet illatio,* whereas the reverse is not always the case. Scotus writes in this connection:

> I could argue in terms of the actual. . . . But I prefer to propose conclusions and premises about the possible. For once those about the actual are granted, those about the possible are also conceded, but not vice versa.[85]

There is another reason why Scotus prefers to argue from the possible or quidditative order rather than from actual existence, and that is his concern to formulate a proof that meets the requirements of a strict Aristotelian demonstration. This, as we have already shown in the preceding section, demands that the premises of the syllogism be both evident and necessary. An argument based on an experimental fact, such as the fact of our existence or the existence of other things around us, is valid. Scotus himself had used it in the first draft of his proof in the *Lectura* I, where he also defended it against objections. It must be said, however, that, follow-

---

[84]*Ibid.,* no. 43; II, 151.
[85]*De primo principio,* p. 43.

ing the pattern of Richard of St. Victor, Scotus raised the argument of the *Lectura* from the physical order of motion and change to the metaphysical level of being and showed that the contingent calls for the necessary as its only possible explanation. So obvious is this premise, according to Scotus, that anyone who denies it is not only unrealistic but needs senses and punishment (*indiget sensu et poena*)![86]

Yet, despite the fact that he did not find any fault in the traditional argument from contingency, Scotus was not completely satisfied with it. A strict demonstration calls in fact for a premise that is not only evident but also necessary. This consideration had already led him to develop in the *Lectura* a new and original proof that takes its lead, no more from the contingent fact of our existence or the existence of other things around us, but from the possibility of existence. The following statement is enlightening:

> I say that although beings other than God are actually contingent with regard to their actual existence, they are not so with respect to potential existence. Hence those things which are said to be contingent as regards their actual existence, are necessary with reference to potential existence.[87]

Thus reformulated, the proof for God's existence—which Scotus develops fully in the *Opus Oxoniense* and the *De primo principio*—proceeds from premises that are both evident and necessary and meet all the requirements of a strict metaphysical demonstration.[88] The proof remains an a posteriori demonstration, for the possibility of existence is not a purely mental construct but has its foundation in reality. In this sense Scotus is consistent with his constant teaching that only an a posteriori proof of God's existence is possible. Yet, since the immediate premise of the argument is the possibility of existence rather than existence itself, the proof moves within the quidditative order and is not entirely a posteriori.[89]

Having clarified this important feature of Scotus' proof, we shall now resume the dialectic of its reasoning. A producible being (*ens effectibile*) can be produced or brought into existence only by another being, for it has been shown that it can neither come from nothing nor be its own effect.

---

[86]*Lectura* I, d. 2, no. 41; XVI, 126; *ibid.*, no. 56; XVI, 131. See also *Ord.* I, d. 2, no. 56; II, 161-62.

[87]*Lectura* I, d. 2, no. 57; XVI, 131.

[88]For an appraisal of Scotus' proof in the *Lectura* I and its background and originality see P. Herman Leo Van Breda, O.F.M., "La preuve de l'existence de Dieu dans la 'Lectura'," in *De doctrina Ioannis Duns Scoti*, ed. by the Scotistic Commission (Rome, 1968), II, 363-75.

[89]See Ephrem Bettoni, O.F.M., "De argumentatione Doctoris Subtilis quoad existentiam Dei," *Antonianum*, XXVIII (1953), 53, where he takes a stand both against Séraphin Belmond who holds that Scotus' proof is simply a posteriori, and against Léonard Puech, who claims that the proof is based only on a concept.

Let us now assume, Scotus continues, that this other being is simply first in the sense that it can neither be produced by another being, nor depend upon it for its production. If such is the case, then we have achieved the purpose of our inquiry.

But if the being in question is not first in the sense specified, then it is a posterior agent (*posterius effectivum*), either because it can be produced by another being, or because it depends on it for its own causal activity. Assuming that this other being is not the first either, then we must ask the same question about it as we did with regard to the preceding one. Now, either this process will go on to infinity, so that every being is posterior to that which precedes it, or we shall reach a being that has nothing prior to itself. But, since an infinite series in an ascending order, i.e., from posterior to prior, is impossible, one must admit the existence of a first being. Moreover, whatever has nothing prior to itself, is posterior to nothing posterior to itself, for a circle in causes is inadmissible. In a circle of causes there would be a cause that is prior and posterior, cause and effect, at one and the same time, and this is an evident contradiction.[90]

Two main objections have been raised against this argument. First, not everyone agrees that an infinite series of causes in an ascending order is impossible, and at any rate no circle in causes is being assumed. Thus there seems to be no contradiction in an infinitely extended process of generation where no single member of the species is first but each is second to some other. Secondly, the argument fails to meet one of the requirements of a demonstration because it proceeds from contingent premises. Scotus takes notice of these objections and answers them in order.

As far as the first objection is concerned, a distinction is necessary. Those philosophers who admit the possibility of an infinite series of causes, do so only with regard to accidentally ordered causes, not with regard to those causes which are ordered to one another essentially or by their very nature. The two orders of causes are quite distinct from one another. In essentially ordered causes, the second depends on the first in its very act of causation. In accidentally ordered causes, on the other hand, the second cause may depend on the first for its existence or in some other way, but not for the exercise of its causality. Thus a son begets a child without his father, even though he could not come into existence without him. Another difference between the two orders of causes concerns the nature and order of causality. In essentially ordered causes, the higher cause is more perfect and exerts a different and superior form of causality than the lower; in accidentally ordered causes, there is no such

---

[90]*Ord.*, I, d. 2, no. 43; II, 151-52. See also *De primo principio*, p. 45.

distinction. Finally, all essentially ordered causes are required to act simultaneously for the achievement of a particular effect, whereas accidentally ordered causes can achieve their effect by acting in succession, since none of them depends on the others for the exercise of its causality.[91]

On the basis of this distinction, Scotus suggests three conclusions, which he then goes on to prove separately. First, an infinity of essentially ordered causes is impossible; second, an infinity of accidentally ordered causes is likewise impossible unless it rest on an essentially ordered series; third, if an essential order is denied, no infinite series of any kind is possible. Whatever the case, a being is needed that is simply first in the order of efficient causality.[92]

To prove the first proposition, Scotus advances five arguments. This in itself is an indication of the importance he attaches to it. And rightly so, for the other two propositions and, to a certain extent, the whole issue concerning the need for a first efficient cause, depends on the solidity of this first proposition. An analysis of the five arguments is therefore indispensable for an understanding of Scotus' proof, especially because, in addition to the *Ordinatio*, they are found with minimal variations in all his other pertinent works. These are the arguments.

1) A series of essentially ordered causes, in which each member depends on the preceding one for its causation, calls for a cause outside the series itself, or else the series is either groundless or self-contradictory. In fact, all the causes of that series are also effects with respect to the preceding causes. If there is no outside cause that is not in turn the effect of anything else, then the series either depends on an effect without a cause, which is no dependence at all, or on a cause that is its own effect, which is a definite contradiction. The question of whether the series is finite or infinite—assuming that an infinite series of essentially ordered causes is possible—is irrelevant. The issue concerns the nature of the causes that make up the series, not their number or lack of it, which is purely accidental to the effect of the series.

2) One of the characteristics of a series of essentially ordered causes is that all the causes involved must act simultaneously in the production of a particular effect. If the series is infinite, we would have an actual infinity of causes acting at one and the same time and no first cause to begin with. This is something that no philosopher is willing to admit.

3) According to Aristotle,[93] whatever is prior is nearer to the beginning. But where there is no beginning, as in the case of an infinite series of causes, nothing is essentially prior to anything else.

---

[91]*Ord.,* I, d. 2, nos. 44–51; II, 152–55; *De primo principio,* pp. 45–47.
[92]Ord. I, d. 2, no. 52; II, 156–57; *De primo principio,* p. 47.
[93]*Metaph.* V, ch. 11, (1018b 9–11).

4) As previously indicated, in a series of essentially ordered causes, the higher cause is more perfect in its causality than the lower. Hence an infinitely higher cause must also be infinitely more perfect both in itself and in its causality. But that is impossible with regard to a cause that acts only in virtue of another. Therefore a cause is needed that is not part of the series and is simply first.

5) The ability to produce something (*effectivitas*) does not, of itself, involve any imperfection. There is no reason, then, why it could not be found somewhere or in someone without imperfection. But if all causes depend on others for their activity, there is no agent without imperfection. Hence an independent power to produce something must be able to exist in some nature, and this nature is simply first. This shows that an absolutely first causing power is possible, which is precisely what the argument is supposed to prove. Later it will be shown that the possibility of this power includes also its actual existence.[94]

Having proved the impossibility of an infinite series of essentially ordered causes, Scotus takes up the question of an infinity of accidentally ordered causes and this too he shows to be impossible unless it is grounded in the essential order. Indeed, in an infinity of accidentally ordered causes, assuming that that is possible, the causes in question do not act simultaneously but only in succession, so that the activity of one cause flows, as it were, from the activity of the other. Yet there is no dependence among the causes as such, for each succeeding cause exerts its own activity without the actual concurrence of the preceding one, as a son begets a child regardless of whether his father is alive or dead.

Now an infinite series of such causes is not possible unless there is something on which it depends and which is equally infinite in duration. A succession of new beings or new forms of being is indeed conceivable only in terms of something permanent that is not part of the succession. The reason is simple. All the components of that succession are of the same nature, and since none of them can be coexistent with the entire succession without changing its temporal character, then something must exist that is prior to the succession itself. It is not a question of a merely accidental priority, such as that which exists in a series of accidentally ordered causes; involved here is a priority of a different order. The whole series of accidentally ordered causes so depends on an outside and superior cause that without it no causality, and consequently no series, is possible. The proposition is therefore established that no infinite series of accidentally

---

[94]*Ord.* I, d. 2, no. 53; II, 157–59; *De primo principio*, pp. 47–49. See also *Rep. Par.* I, d. 2, q. 2, no. 5; XXII, 65, where Scotus calls the third and fifth arguments "persuasiones" rather than arguments in the strict sense of the term.

ordered causes is possible unless an essentially ordered cause exists that serves as its foundation.[95]

Coming to the last of the three propositions advanced to counteract the objection that an infinite series of causes in an ascending order is not impossible, Scotus stresses once more the necessity of a first efficient cause and shows that this conclusion is inescapable even if an essential order of causes is denied. The discussion of this point may seem redundant, but it is not so for Scotus. In his concern to refute all possible arguments against his thesis, he feels obliged to answer the objection of those who "pertinaciously" insist that a particular cause can produce an effect of the same nature and just as well as a total cause, as a son is begotten by a father, and so on *in infinitum*. [96]

To this objection, which is based on the self-sufficiency of an infinite series of accidentally ordered causes, Scotus answers, first, by restating a conclusion already established, namely, that since nothing can come from nothing and something is now in existence, a nature capable of causing effectively is possible. Now if we deny an essential order of agents, we must say that this nature acts in virtue of itself. And even granted that in some individual cases the nature in question could be caused, it remains true that at least in one case it is not caused. Otherwise, how could we explain causality at all? But if this is the case, we have proved our original thesis, i.e., that a causing nature (*natura effectiva*) is simply first. This conclusion can also be confirmed with an argument *ab absurdo*. In fact, if we assume that in every individual case the causing nature is in turn caused, then we run into the previously mentioned contradiction that results from the denial of an essential order in causes. It is indeed inconceivable that a nature that is caused in every individual case and is therefore included within an accidental order of causes, be not itself dependent on a superior and essentially different cause.[97]

With this observation Scotus concludes his answer to the first objection against the possibility of a first efficient cause. Next he takes up the second objection, namely, that his argument is not a strict demonstration because it rests on contingent premises. Since we have already dealt with this problem in the beginning of this section, we shall proceed to his second statement, namely, that the first efficient cause or *primum effectivum* is not only uncaused but also uncausable.

This conclusion is not difficult to understand, for it follows logically from the preceding discussion. A being that can produce but cannot be

---

[95]*Ord.* I, d. 2, no. 54; II, 159-60; *De primo principio,* p. 49; *Rep. Par.* I, d. 2, q. 2, no. 6; XXII, 65.

[96]*Rep. Par.* I, d. 2, q. 2, no. 6; XXII, 65.

[97]*Ord.* I, d. 2, no. 55; II, 160-61; *De primo principio,* p. 51.

part of any series of causes, whether essentially or accidentally ordered, must be able to produce by itself and without the concurrence of any other being. If not, we would have either an infinite series of causes without a first and independent cause to support it, or a circle of causes none of which can account for its original causality. These obvious contradictions show the need for a first efficient cause that is not only independent in its causation but is itself neither actually nor possibly the effect of any other cause. In Scotus' words, it is proved that the *primum effectivum* cannot be an *effectibile* without denying its very nature.

If this is true with regard to efficient causality, what about the other types of causality? Is this being so independent as to exclude also any kind of final, formal, or material cause? This is the next question asked by Scotus, and his answer is of course in the affirmative. A being that cannot be produced, cannot have a final cause either (*quod est ineffectible, ergo est infinibile*). A final cause is the end that moves the efficient cause to act. It is not a question of a real motion, since the end does not cause any real change in the agent; it is rather a metaphorical kind of motion that takes place within the intentional order. Now a being that has no efficient cause because it itself is the first *effectivum,* cannot have a final cause. To think otherwise, is not only to invert the order of causality, but also to conceive of a being that is at the same time its own cause and effect in the intentional order.

Just as a first producing being does not have a final cause, so it does not have a material or formal cause. The reason for this inference is that material and formal causes are the intrinsic principles of a physical entity and as such are inferior to, and dependent upon, the extrinsic causes (efficient and final). In fact, while the notion of extrinsic causation implies no imperfection, or else it could not be found in the first producing being, an intrinsic cause is necessarily imperfect, for it becomes part of the composite that it constitutes. An extrinsic cause therefore enjoys a natural priority over an intrinsic cause. To affirm that a being is not subject to the former, as is the case with a first producing being, is to affirm that it is not subject to the latter. This is even more evident if we consider that the intrinsic causes depend on the efficient and final causes either for their being, for the constitution of the composite, or for both, since of themselves they are unable to join together to form a new reality. Thus the conclusion is proved that the *primum effectivum,* in addition to being uncaused, is also absolutely uncausable.[98]

The transition from the possibility and uncausability of a first efficient cause to its actual existence is the third and last conclusion of Scotus'

---

[98]*Ord.* I, d. 2, no. 57; II, 162-64; *De primo principio,* p. 51.

dialectic about the absolute primacy in efficient causality. This conclusion is, like the preceding one, based on strictly logical reasoning which, it is worth recalling, is not merely a priori, for it rests on premises that have their ultimate foundation in existing reality. Scotus' argumentation is as follows. A being to whose nature it is repugnant to receive existence from another, if it is able to exist, can exist of itself. But it has already been shown, on the one hand, that the nature of a first producing being excludes the possibility of receiving existence from another; and on the other hand, it has also been shown that such a being is possible.[99] Therefore a first producing being can exist of itself.

The possibility of self-existence is an immediate inference from the argument's premises; it is also the least that can be said of a being that is both possible and uncausable. But mere possibility of self-existence is no guarantee as yet that the being in question does actually exist. To prove this latter point, Scotus makes use once more of an argument *ab absurdo*. He writes: "What does not exist of itself, cannot exist of itself; otherwise a nonbeing would cause something to exist, which is impossible."[100] This implies that if the *primum effectivum* were not self-existent, it could never exist at all unless it came from nothing, since no other being can bring it into existence. Hence, since from nothing nothing comes, such a being would be possible but unable to exist, which is a contradiction. Furthermore, to cause itself, if that were at all possible, is still to be caused, and this is against the nature of a being that has been proved to be absolutely uncausable. To avoid all such inconsistencies, Scotus draws the argument to its logical conclusion and states categorically that if the first efficient cause can exist of itself, then it does exist of itself.[101]

Before moving further, we wish to observe that with this last statement the Subtle Doctor would have concluded what, after Kant, has been called the cosmological argument, which in turn corresponds basically to Aquinas' first three ways of proving God's existence. All the elements of the arguments from change, causality, and contingency are there, although interpreted in a somewhat different manner in order to meet the requirements of strict logic and of a metaphysics of being in the quidditative order. Since the argument is an attempt to explain an actual reality in

---

[99]Reference is made by Scotus to his fifth argument for the impossibility of an infinite series of essentially ordered causes (see text referred to in n. 94 above). The argument rests on the idea that *effectivitas* as such implies no imperfection; it is therefore the concept of a possible activity and, by derivation, of a *primum effectivum* which personifies, as it were, such activity. Reference is also made in this connection to the preceding four arguments (see references in note 94) which, Scotus adds, can be worked out from contingent but manifest premises based on existence, or from necessary premises based on essence or the possibility of existence. *Ord.* I, d. 2, no. 58; II, 164.

[100]*Ibid.*, pp. 164–65.

[101]*Ibid.*, p. 165; *De primo principio*, p. 53.

terms of its ultimate efficient cause, Scotus could very well have concluded it by saying with Aquinas, "and this is what everyone understands by God."[102] But he did not do so. The reason is not that he felt the argument inconclusive, but rather that the aim of his proof is to demonstrate the existence of an infinite being rather than the existence merely of a first being. This explains why the term *God* appears only at the end of a lengthy process that, despite the complexities of its dialectic, helps us to obtain a much greater insight into the nature of the being whose existence it is supposed to prove.

b. *The Existence of an Ultimate Final Cause.*

Once the existence of a first being in the order of efficient causality has been established, it is not difficult to prove that there is also a first being in the order of final causality and of eminence—roughly, the fourth and fifth ways of St. Thomas. The three issues are closely related and the same arguments used for the first can also be used, with proper adaptation, for the other two. This is what Scotus does in his approach to the second and third primacies of being, where he not only refers to the arguments used for the first, but also proposes for each one of them three similar conclusions. We shall discuss them briefly, beginning with final causality.

"Some being is simply first in the order of finality," Scotus asserts, for among beings there must be one that cannot be ordained to any other or exert its finality in virtue of anything else than itself. Indeed, if something is producible, as previously shown, something must also be able to be directed to an end, for production is possible only in view of an end. This is what Aristotle means when he states that every agent acts for an end and explains that the principle is valid in every instance, even though it is more manifest in the case of an intelligent being.[103] It is impossible, however, that there should be a series of ends with none to which they are ultimately referred, and this for the same reason for which an infinite series of essentially ordered causes in efficient causality has been rejected. Hence an ultimate final cause or, which amounts to the same thing, a first being in the order of finality, is possible.

Such a being is also uncausable, just as a first producing being is uncausable, for, as the ultimate end, it cannot be ordained to any further being. Obviously, it cannot have an efficient cause, since, as we have already indicated, an agent acts only for an end, and where no further end is possible, no production is possible either. If this is true with regard to a *per se* cause, it is even more so when an incidental cause, such as chance

---

[102]*Sum theol.* I, q. 2, a. 3 c.
[103] Aristotle, *Physics* II, ch. 5 (196b 17-22).

or fortune, is involved. In fact an incidental cause can never be first in any given order of causes and is ultimately reducible to a *per se* cause.[104] Since the *primum finitivum* admits of no efficient cause, it will admit of no material and formal cause either, for these two depend on the efficient cause for their actualization. Having thus proved, on the one hand, that the *primum finitivum* is possible and, on the other, that it cannot be caused by any other being, Scotus concludes that the being in question must exist of itself; otherwise, it would be possible and impossible at one and the same time.[105]

c. *The Existence of a Most Perfect Nature.*

The proof of the existence of a first being in the order of eminence follows along the same lines as the two preceding ones. But whereas the first two primacies have to do with the extrinsic causes of being, the primacy of eminence is concerned with the essence of the being itself. As Aristotle says,[106] forms or essences are like numbers. Hence there is a necessary order among essences, and this calls for an ultimate nature that is also the most perfect for the same reasons for which a first efficient cause and an ultimate final cause are proved to be necessary. Moreover, the most perfect nature cannot be caused, or else it could be ordained to an end, since causality is always exercised for an end. But whatever is so ordained, is surpassed in goodness, and hence in perfection, by the end to which it is ordained. Now a most perfect nature admits of no further perfection, and consequently of no further end. On the other hand, since an efficient cause can act only in view of an end, it is evident that a most perfect nature cannot be the effect of such a cause. Nor can it be the product of a material or formal cause, for both of these depend upon the efficient cause. Briefly, a most perfect nature is uncausable.

This conclusion is further strengthened by the consideration that production or effectibility is necessarily related to a cause that is prior and superior to its effect. A most perfect nature excludes any such relationship. One must therefore conclude that the most perfect nature, which is possible but uncausable, exists of itself.[107]

2. INTERRELATION OF THE THREE PRIMACIES

Having proved separately the existence of a first cause in each of the three orders of causality, Scotus proceeds to show, first, the interrelation

---

[104]Scotus supports his statement once more with Aristotle's *Physics* II, ch. 6 (198a 5-13).

[105]*Ord.* I, d. 2, nos. 60-62; II, 165-67; *De primo principio.* pp. 59-61.

[106]*Metaph.* VIII, ch. 3 (1043b 33).

[107]*Ord.* I, d. 2, nos. 64-66; II, 167-68; *De primo principio.* pp. 61-63.

of the three primacies, and secondly, their identification with one and the same nature.

The first efficient cause is also the ultimate end, for the end is proportioned to the cause. Just as a prior cause acts for a prior end, so an absolutely first cause must act for an absolutely first end which, in the intentional order, coincides with the ultimate end or that to which all other ends are ordained. But the first efficient cause cannot act primarily and ultimately except for itself, since there is nothing prior to it that could constitute the object of its activity. Hence the first efficient cause is also the ultimate end. It is likewise the most perfect nature, for it is not a univocal but an equivocal cause with respect to the other efficient causes. Consequently, it is more eminent and nobler than all other causes; it is indeed the most eminent cause.[108]

3. THE TRIPLE PRIMACY BELONGS TO ONE NATURE

From the interrelation of the three primacies it seems to follow logically that they all pertain to one and the same nature, and that any further proof to this effect would be redundant. Scotus had no doubt about this point. But in his concern to answer the objection of those philosophers who, under the influence of Aristotle's theory of separate intelligences, might conceive the possibility of some other natures that would enjoy one or the other kind of primacy, although not all of them together,[109] he felt the need of establishing his doctrine on even more solid grounds. Accordingly, he goes on to prove the unity of the first nature with regard to the triple primacy, but not before showing that the first efficient cause is of itself necessarily existent. There is no need, of course, to pursue the same line of thought with regard to the other two primacies, since both of them can be actualized only in the first efficient cause.

That the first efficient cause is of itself necessarily existent can be shown from the fact that its nature excludes any kind of causality, whether efficient, final, or otherwise. Proof of this has already been offered. Once this is admitted, it remains to be seen whether there is any reason why the cause in question should not exist, or would not be able to exist, since possibility of existence is all that is needed for the actual existence of an uncausable being. Such reasons can be only in terms of an intrinsic contradiction within the being itself that would make its existence or continuation in existence impossible. But there is nothing contradictory in the notion of a self-existent, and hence totally uncaused, being. Were there

---

[108]*Ord.* I, d. 2, nos. 68-69; II, 168-69.

[109]This is clear from Scotus' statement in *De primo principio*, p. 69, where he alludes to Aristotle's doctrine on intelligences and characterizes the objector as "quis protervus."

any contradiction, it would be due to the presence of an incompatible entity within the being itself.

Now this entity, Scotus argues, can either exist of itself or in virtue of some other being. If it can exist of itself, then it does actually exist of itself on the same ground that a first efficient cause exists. In such a case, two incompatible entities would exist at one and the same time within the same being. But this is impossible, since one would destroy the other. How can, in fact, one and the same being have two different reasons for being precisely what it is, i.e., a self-existent being? If, on the other hand, the entity in question is caused by another being, then we are faced with another contradiction. Indeed no agent can destroy a being by producing an entity that is incompatible with the being to be destroyed, unless it is able to confer a more perfect and intense existence upon that entity than that which the being to be destroyed possesses. But no caused existence will ever equal the perfection of a self-existent being, since to be caused is to depend, whereas to exist of itself is to be independent. Hence no being can destroy the first efficient cause.[110] This conclusion paves the way for Scotus' thesis of the unicity of the first nature, which is the main point of his discussion.

To show that the first nature can be only one, Scotus advances three arguments, the first of which is a direct inference from the property of necessary existence that characterizes the first efficient cause. He reasons this way. If there were two necessarily existing natures, each one would be distinguished from the other by virtue of a proper and individual entity. Now each of these two entities is either formally necessary or not. If it is not formally necessary, then it cannot be the reason for the necessary existence of a being, since it need not belong to it. In fact, a merely possible or contingent reality can never be an essential constituent of a necessary being. If, on the contrary, the distinguishing entity is necessary, then each necessarily existing nature will include two formal reasons for its necessary existence, one which it shares with the other and one which is proper to itself. However, this is impossible. Since neither of the two reasons includes the other, if either were eliminated, a being would still exist necessarily by virtue of the other. Thus we would have a being whose intrinsic necessity of existence is determined by something that is not part of its necessary structure after all. This is plain contradiction.[111] It might be added that, as previously shown, the very idea of two natures, each one having a different reason for its necessary existence, is a pure assumption.

---

[110]*Ord.* I, d. 2, no. 70; II, 169-70; *De primo principio,* pp. 53-55; 69.
[111]*Ord.* I, d. 2, no. 71; II, 171-72. The *De primo principio* does not follow the same order of discussion as the *Ordinatio.*

It is indeed inconceivable that one and the same perfection, such as necessary existence, should be due to two entirely different reasons.

The second argument for the unicity of the first nature is based on the impossibility that there should be two most perfect natures in the universe, and hence two first efficient causes. To this effect, Scotus quotes once more Aristotle's principle[112] that species or natures are like numbers, no two of which can occur in the same order. So much the less is it possible that two first and most perfect natures should be in existence at the same time.[113]

The third and last argument stems from the nature of the ultimate final cause, which, no less than the first efficient cause and the most eminent nature, can be only one. If there were two ultimate ends, there would also be two distinct groups of coordinated beings, each one tending to its own end independently of the other. This is so because what is ordered to one ultimate end cannot be ordered to another. We would then have more than one universe, which is obviously not the case, since the universe embraces all existing reality apart from the first being.

The preceding arguments can be confirmed by the consideration that no two beings can be the terminus of a total dependence of one and the same thing. For if one of the two beings were removed, the thing in question would still be totally dependent on the other, so that its dependence on the former would be useless or no dependence at all. Now all things depend essentially on the first efficient cause, which in turn is also their ultimate end and the most perfect nature. Consequently, there cannot be two different natures on which things depend according to the triple primacy. The thesis of one and unique nature enjoying the triple primacy is thus established.[114]

B. The Absolute Properties of God

1. THE INFINITY OF THE FIRST BEING

Consistently with his original plan for a theistic proof that, while taking its lead from the beings of our experience, reaches up, as it were, into the very nature of God, Scotus proceeds to the analysis of what he calls God's absolute properties, and chief among them, his infinity. By proper inference from the notion of the triple primacy that has been established

---

[112]*Metaph.* VIII, ch. 3 (1043b 33).

[113]*Ord.* I, d. 2, no. 72; II, 172.

[114]*Ibid.,* no. 73; II, 172-73. In the *De primo principio* Scotus concludes the chapter on "The Triple Primacy of the First Principle" with a prayerful address to the Lord in which he says: "You are the unique first, and everything besides you comes after you by reason of a threefold order, as I have explained to the best of my ability." *Ibid.,* p. 71.

in connection with the first being, he goes on to show that such a being is infinite and must exist. However, before proving these main points, he feels the need to establish some preliminary theses.

a. *Preliminary Theses.*

First among these theses is that the first agent is endowed with intellect and will. Referring to Aristotle's statement that no incidental cause can be prior to a *per se* cause,[115] Scotus argues that there must be an agent that acts *per se* and is first among all agents. Moreover, since every agent acts for an end that it wills and loves, and this in turn presupposes knowledge, it follows that the first agent is endowed with intellect and will.

To say that a natural agent acts of necessity in virtue of its physical laws and structure is no argument against the above reasoning. Scotus does indeed anticipate this objection, which is also being raised by some contemporary philosophers in support of their atheistic view of the universe, and here is his answer. Granted that a natural agent would act just as well if it acted independently of any other agent—which of course is not conceivable in a realistic philosophy—the agent in question would still act for an end, for action is possible only in terms of a purpose or object to be achieved. Hence the necessity of action on the part of a natural agent, or of the whole of nature for that matter, does not eliminate its teleological character; rather it calls for an agent distinct from the physical entity itself, which knows and loves the end. Ultimately, it calls for a first and independent agent endowed with intellect and will.

This same conclusion can be reached from an analysis of the action of the first agent. Since the first agent acts for an end, as previously established, Scotus argues that this end moves the agent either because it is loved by an act of the will or because it is loved naturally. In the former case, the conclusion follows that the first agent is both intelligent and willing, for love presupposes knowledge. In the latter case, we run into a contradiction, since the first agent can have nothing but itself as the object of its natural love. If it had a different object or end, it would be directed toward it and hence depend on it, which is against the nature of a first agent. However, if it loves itself as its own end and in virtue of its own nature, then we simply affirm the first agent's self-identity.

There is another and perhaps better reason to support the thesis under discussion, and this involves a peculiar aspect of Scotus' metaphysics of causality. Starting from the empirical observation that something is caused contingently, he argues that on the basis of the principle of proportionality between cause and effect, the first cause must also cause con-

---

[115]*Physics* II, ch. 6 (198a 8–9).

tingently, and hence voluntarily. In fact, every secondary cause can cause only insofar as it is moved by the first cause—a principle that Scotus holds in common with all scholastic philosophers. If the first cause moved necessarily, all other causes would also move necessarily, for it is out of necessity that they would be moved to act. But if any secondary cause moves contingently, the first cause also moves contingently. And since the principle of a contingent action can only be the will because of its inherent freedom, the first agent must be free and endowed with intellect and will.[116]

Scotus' second preliminary thesis to the proof of the first being's infinity is that self-knowledge and self-volition are identical with the very essence of the first being. This can be shown as follows. According to Avicenna, the causality of the final cause is absolutely first, for it precedes all other causality, including that of the efficient cause which it moves to act.[117] Being first, the causality of the ultimate end cannot be caused in any way whatsoever. Actually the ultimate end moves the first efficient cause by making itself loved, and since an object is loved only to the extent that a will loves it, the love by which the first efficient cause loves the ultimate end is equally necessary as, and identical with, the first nature. From this it follows that the knowledge by which the first being knows itself is also, and even more so, identical with its nature, since love presupposes knowledge.[118]

Scotus' third preliminary thesis is that the first being's knowledge and volition of other things are also the same as its essence. It is enough to reflect on the meaning and implications of the first efficient cause, which is but one aspect of the first nature, to see that none of its acts can be accidental. To have the ability to produce all producible things independently of any other cause, as the notion of a first efficient cause implies, is also to be able to know and to will the things to be produced. But the first cause admits of no other source of knowledge or volition except itself, since everything else must come from it. Hence the knowledge and volition of all things must also be identified with the first nature. To think otherwise, it may be added, is to attribute to the first being contradictory properties, such as we find in all pantheistic and panentheistic theories.

There are other considerations that, in Scotus' view, support his doctrine. The following two are worth mentioning. All acts of intellection have the same relationship to the intellect concerned, so that they all are

---

[116]*Ord.* I, d. 2, nos. 75-81; II, 175-77. Following the exposition of his third argument, Scotus discusses certain objections stemming mainly from an Aristotelian conception of the universe, to the effect that contingent causality in lower beings does not necessarily imply contingent causality in the first agent. The discussion is too involved to be dealt with here.

[117]Cf. Avicenna, *Metaph.* VI, ch. 5 (94va).

[118]*Ord.* I, d. 2, no. 89; II, 180-81.

either essentially or accidentally identified with it. In the case of our intellect, whose knowledge comes from external objects, there is only an accidental relationship between the intellect and the object known. But in the case of the first being the situation is reversed. Since its self-knowledge cannot be an accident, neither can any other kind of knowledge it possesses be accidental. Furthermore, and this is an even better argument, the same act of intellection can embrace a plurality of interrelated objects; and the more perfect the act, the greater the number of objects known. Hence a most perfect act of knowledge, or one than which no greater can be conceived, must embrace at one and the same time all that is knowable. Such is the knowledge of the first being. Now since it has already been proved that the first being's knowledge of itself is the same as its essence, it may rightly be concluded that its knowledge of other things is also identical with its essence. The same conclusion holds true with regard to the act of volition.[119]

The fourth and last preliminary thesis to the proof of the first being's infinity is that such a being has from all eternity an actual, distinct, and necessary knowledge of all intelligibles, which is prior by nature to the existence of the things in themselves. Maintaining that the first being has the capacity to know all intelligibles, since it is from it that they ultimately derive their reality, Scotus argues that it is a mark of perfection for an intellect to be able to grasp actually and distinctly everything that is knowable. This ability is indeed demanded by the very nature of the intellect whose object is being in its most universal sense. But since it has already been shown that all knowledge possessed by the first being is identical with itself, it follows that the first being knows all intelligibles actually and distinctly and by a knowledge that is equally eternal and necessary as its own essence.

The priority of such knowledge over things in their actual existence should not be difficult to understand, since none of those things is necessary, and what does not exist necessarily is posterior by nature to a self-existent and necessary being. Moreover, every being other than the first depends upon the latter as upon its cause. But no causality is possible without the knowledge of the being to be caused. Hence the knowledge of the first being is naturally prior to the existence of the things known.[120]

---

[119]*Ibid.*, nos. 98–101; II, 184–86.

[120]*Ibid.*, nos. 105–108; II, 187–88. For a discussion of the four preliminary theses in the *De primo principio* cf. pp. 81–103 of the treatise, where the theses are arranged in a somewhat different order.

b. *Proofs of the Infinity of the First Being.*

Having established the foregoing preliminary theses, Scotus is now ready to prove the infinity of the first being. He will do this in four different ways, namely, from the first being's infinite power, infinite knowledge, infinite goodness, and infinite perfection. This fourfold approach to the infinite, or what might be called the establishment of the four properties that characterize an infinite being, is of paramount importance for Scotus, for it represents the summit of his theistic proof. It is infinity that for him best represents God in his unique, transcendent nature. An infinite being, he says, is that which excels every finite being, not merely in a limited manner, but in a way that transcends all limits and proportions.[121] Infinity is, in fact, more like an intrinsic mode of the divine essence than a mere attribute.[122] It is because of this notion of infinity that Scotus would not settle for any argument for an infinite being that did not meet the demands of a strictly metaphysical proof. Aristotle's way to the infinite from efficient causality is a case in point.

i. *Proof from Efficient Causality.* As is well known, Aristotle argues to the infinite power of the first being from the endless movement by which it moves the world.[123] The argument would perhaps be valid if it could be shown that the world has been in existence from all eternity and will continue to exist forever under the impetus of the first mover. But this thesis, in addition to being in conflict with Christian doctrine, has the support of neither science nor revelation. Moreover, even if proved correct, it would not lead necessarily to the existence of an infinite being in the strict sense of the term or even to a being endowed with infinite power. At most, it would prove that the First Mover has an infinite duration, which is but one aspect of infinity.

While these considerations have led Scotus to question the value of the Aristotelian thesis, still, because of the Stagirite's high reputation, he does not reject the doctrine altogether; rather he tries to strengthen its reasoning by establishing it on a more metaphysical basis. The weakness of Aristotle's reasoning consists in the gratuitousness of its premise, namely, that the first being is the cause of an endless motion. If instead of building an argument on a questionable fact, as Aristotle did, we argue from the possibility that the first being caused an infinite movement, then we can

---

[121]*Quodlib.*, q. 5, no. 4; XXV, 200a: "Ens infinitum est quod excedit quodcumque ens finitum, non secundum aliquam determinatam proportionem, sed ultra omnem determinatam proportionem vel determinabilem."

[122]*Ibid.*, 200b: "ergo ipsa infinitas est magis modus intrinsecus essentiae, quam aliquod attributum."

[123]Cf. Aristotle, *Physics* VIII, ch. 10 (266a 10-24); *Metaph.* XII, ch. 7 (1073a 3-13).

logically conclude to the existence of an infinite power. The possibility of causing an infinite movement calls in fact for the existence of an infinite power just as well as does the actual causation of such movement. Since the first being has the ability to cause an endless movement because of its self-existence and absolute independence, the argument is valid even if the being in question did not actually cause such a movement.[124]

But even in this new formulation, the argument is not free from criticism. All it proves is the existence of a power with infinite duration that can produce successively an indefinite number of beings. This is not the kind of agent Scotus is seeking. The agent in question must possess an intensive as well as an extensive infinity, or such that it includes all perfections in the highest possible degree. To prove the existence of such an agent, one must show that there is a being that has the power to produce an infinity of effects all at once. This is no longer Aristotle's argument, except in its conclusion; it is, however, the only way to make the argument effective. Accordingly, Scotus formulates his proof of infinity in the following terms. If the first being had formally the power to produce at once an infinite multitude of things, even if such things could not be so produced for reasons extrinsic to the power itself, then the being in question must be infinite. That the first being has such a power is clear from the preceding discussion, for no limit can be imposed on an agent that is self-existent and totally independent in his causality. The first being is, therefore, infinite.

Scotus warns us, however, that the infinite power to which reason can argue from the nature of the first being is not the same as omnipotence in the proper sense of the term as theologians understand it. He refers in this connection to his discussion of the subject elsewhere,[125] where he distinguishes between omnipotence as an article of faith, meaning that God can cause all effects immediately, and infinite power, which also means that God can cause all effects but, at least with regard to some of them, only through the mediation of secondary causes. Natural reason can prove only the latter, not the former. Yet the value of the proof of infinity is not thereby diminished, for the first cause must contain eminently all the causal perfection of the secondary causes. And this is even better than if the first cause had the causality of the secondary causes formally, were that possible.[126]

Before concluding his first proof of infinity, Scotus takes up the question of creation which, in the mind of some scholastic philosophers, is in

---

[126]*Ord.* I, d. 2, nos. 117–20; II, 192–97.
[125]*Ord.* I, d. 42, q. unica; VI, 341–49; *Quodlib.*, q. 7; XXV, 282–341.
[126]*Ord.* I, d. 2, nos. 117–20; II, pp. 192–97.

itself a proof of the first being's infinite power because of the infinite distance that separates being from nonbeing.[127] Scotus rejects such an argument on the ground that creation, whether understood as implying a sequence in time between cause and effect, as Christian revelation teaches, or simply a sequence in nature, as Avicenna taught,[128] does not involve an infinite distance between two extremes, being and nothing. To have an infinite distance between two extremes, Scotus argues, one of the extremes must be infinite, as is the case between God and even the highest possible creature. But between creature and nothing the distance, if we can use that term at all, is necessarily limited, because the more perfect of the two extremes, the creature, is itself limited. Stated otherwise, the distance between two extremes is determined by the greater degree of perfection of one of the two. When one of the extremes is nothing and the other is a finite being, the distance between them is measured by the degree of perfection of the latter.[129]

ii. *Proof from the Knowledge of the First Being*. A being that is infinitely powerful must also be able to know an infinity of things, for power presupposes knowledge. Thus the proof of an infinite being from efficient causality leads logically to the proof of the same kind of being from the point of view of its distinct knowledge of all possible things. Here is how the argument can be formulated. There is no limit to the number of things that can be known, just as there is no limit to the number of things that can be made. But all intelligibles must be known actually, and not merely potentially, by an all-knowing intellect. Therefore such an intellect is infinite, and that is the intellect of the first being.[130]

That the first being has an actual knowledge of all possible things is proved by Scotus in the following way. In a potentially infinite series of beings where one follows the other in an endless succession, the beings are such that, if they all existed at one and the same time, they would be actually infinite in number, or, more precisely, constitute an infinite multi-

---

[127]See, for example, St. Thomas, *Sum theol.* I, q. 45, a. 5 ad 3; Henry of Ghent, *Summa,* a. 35, q. 6 c; *Quodlib.* IV, q. 37 c.

[128]*Metaph.* VI, ch. 2.

[129]*Ord.* I, d. 2, nos. 121-24; II, 198-201. The proof from efficient causality is treated in the *De primo principio* as the last and seventh way to infinity. *Ibid.*, pp. 125-33. This does not mean that Scotus attaches less value to it than to the other proofs, for he states clearly that "infinita potentia [as distinct from "omnipotentia"] *probatur* quae simul ex se habet eminenter omnem causalitatem" *(ibid.,* p. 131). The rearrangement of the proofs is simply the result of a new approach to infinity which includes seven ways rather than the four ways of the *Ordinatio.*

[130]*Ord.* I, d. 2, no. 125; II, 202: "intelligibilia sunt infinita, et hoc actu, in intellectu omnia intelligente; ergo intellectus ista simul actu intelligens est infinitus. Talis est intellectus primi."

tude. While our created intellect, because of its obvious limitations, has the capacity to know the beings of such a series only successively, the divine intellect must be able to know them all in act and simultaneously. Hence the divine intellect has an actual knowledge of an infinite multitude of beings, or, which amounts to the same thing, of an infinity of possible objects.

The major of the syllogism, Scotus observes, should present no difficulty. The beings of a potentially infinite series, once they are conceived as existing all at once—whether they actually so exist or not is irrelevant to our purpose—are either actually finite or infinite. If they are finite, then our mind, by taking one after the other, will be able to know them all and in act. But if that is not possible, as is obviously the case with our limited intellect, then the beings in question must be actually infinite or such that only an infinite mind can know them all and at once.

This conclusion is further proved by the principle that a proportion must exist between cause and effect, so that a larger number of effects demands a greater perfection in the cause. Hence just as in the physical order a greater strength is needed to carry ten objects than to carry five, so in the intellectual order a greater perfection is required to know distinctly two objects rather than one alone, unless the same act of knowledge includes eminently the perfections of both objects. The same is true with regard to three or more objects and so on to infinity.[131]

A similar line of reasoning can be pursued from the point of view of the *ratio intelligendi* or the reason for which the intellect of the first being knows all possible objects. The greater the number of objects known distinctly, the more perfect is the act of knowledge, for this must include in an eminent way the perfections that are proper to each cognitive act. When the acts of knowledge are infinite, the perfection of the intellect must also be infinite.

To better understand this argument, one must keep in mind that for Scotus, as previously stated, the intelligibles exist in the intellect of the first being prior to, and even apart from, their actualization in concrete reality. This is so because the first being cannot, without contradicting itself, depend in any way on secondary causes. Thus the intellect of the first being, by the mere act of contemplating the first nature (*natura prima*), produces all intelligibles without the concurrence of any finite object. This amounts to saying that the knowledge of the first being is infin-

---

[131] Scotus' reasoning is based on his theory of the principle of individuation, whereby each being contains an individual perfection that distinguishes it from all other beings of the same species. Thus the interpolated text mentioned in the critical edition, "differentia numeralis non infert aliquam perfectionem aliam" (*ibid.*, no. 127; II, 203), should be disregarded. For the discussion of this point cf. *De primo principio*, pp. 105–107.

ite, because no finite object can add any intelligibility to it. Moreover, since cognoscibility presupposes reality,[132] the first nature, as the source of all possible knowledge, must also be infinite.[133]

iii. *Proof from Finality*. There is another way of arguing to the infinity of the first being, and this is taken from the natural desire that our will has for an infinite good as its ultimate end. Our will, like our intellect, can never be satisfied with a limited object, no matter how good or perfect it may be. In its craving for love, it seeks always something greater and more perfect than any finite being can offer it. Moreover, the will seems to have a natural inclination to love an infinite good to the highest possible degree, because, as a free power, it does so spontaneously and with a certain delight rather than by force of an acquired disposition or habit. This is the reason why the will is never fully satisfied with the possession of a limited good. If this is the case, then it can hardly be explained how an infinite good could involve any contradiction or be opposed to the natural object of the will, since the latter naturally hates whatever is against its tendency, just as it naturally hates nonbeing. The conclusion is therefore established that an infinite good is not only possible but is the only object that can fully satisfy man's natural aspirations. To hold the contrary is to say that a power has been given to man for frustration rather than for fulfillment.

Here Scotus refers to a similar argument based on the object of the intellect, which seems to indicate, among other things, that he attached the same value to both arguments. Although he considered them to be valid proofs, it is questionable whether he thought of them as "strictly philosophical arguments" in the sense Gilson maintains he did.[134] The fact that the argument from the object of the intellect referred to by Scotus falls under the same general heading of persuasive arguments (*item suadetur*) as those which precede it, seems to imply that neither of the two arguments in question was held by him to be a strictly philosophical proof.[135]

iv. *Proof from Eminence*. A fourth way of arguing to infinity is by analyzing the logical, as well as ontological, implications of the notion of a most perfect being. As previously seen, it is of the nature of such a being to be supreme in every respect, so that no other being can excel it in perfection. But this cannot be true of a finite being, whose nature admits of a possible addition to its perfection. Therefore, a most perfect being

---

[132]Cf. Aristotle, *Metaph.* II, ch. 1 (993b 30–31).

[133]*Ord.* I, d. 2, nos. 125–29; II, 201–205; *De primo principio,* pp. 103–107.

[134]Cf. *Jean Duns Scot,* p. 164.

[135]The argument from finality is presented in *Ord.* I, d. 2, no. 130; II, 205–206; *De primo principio,* p. 125.

must be infinite. The validity of this syllogism rests on the premise, to be dealt with promptly, that infinity is not incompatible with the concept of being, and consequently, that an infinite being, if possible, is greater than any conceivable finite being.

The same argument, says Scotus, can be formulated in a slightly different way starting from the notion of intensive infinity. A being to which intensive infinity is not repugnant cannot be absolutely perfect unless it be infinite, for a finite being can be exceeded in perfection. But infinity is not repugnant to being. Therefore, the most perfect being is infinite.

The validity of this form of the argument depends, like that of the other form, on the premise that infinity is not repugnant to being. Scotus is aware of the need to prove that this is the case; it is a problem he has already met in connection with the argument from finality and the object of the will. He takes this opportunity, then, to make a critical analysis of the statement in question.

There is no way, he affirms, of proving a priori the non-repugnance, and consequently the positive compatibility, of the two terms, *being* and *infinite*. For, on the one hand, being is a most simple concept that cannot be explained in terms of anything better known to us, and, on the other hand, the infinite can be understood only by means of the finite. It can be shown, however, that no manifest incompatibility exists between the two concepts, just as it can be shown that two contradictory terms are by their nature mutually incompatible.

The infinite can be defined in rather general terms as that which exceeds the finite, precisely not by reason of any finite measure, but rather in excess of any conceivable measure. Once this notion is accepted, there appears to be no definite contradiction between the concept of being and that of infinity. If these two concepts were mutually incompatible, it could only be either because it is of the nature of being to be finite or because finiteness is an attribute coextensive with being. But neither of these assumptions is true. It must therefore be concluded that, since the incompatibility between *being* and *infinite* is not manifest, and since, on the other hand, whatever does not contain incompatible notes is possible, an infinite being or, which amounts to the same thing, a most perfect being is possible. This conclusion is further strengthened by the consideration that the intellect, whose object is being, does not seem to find any repugnance in the notion of an infinite being. On the contrary, the intellect seems to rest in it as in its most perfect object, an object that fully satisfies its craving for knowledge.[136]

---

[136]For the complete discussion of the proof from eminence cf. *Ord.* I, d. 2, nos. 131-39; II, 206-211; *De primo principio.* pp. 121-23.

With this consideration, which Scotus characterizes once more as a "persuasive" argument rather than a strict metaphysical demonstration, the proof from eminence comes to an end. Scotus next proceeds to evaluate the *ratio Anselmi* mentioned in the preliminary question of his approach to God. Since the Anselmian argument and Scotus' evaluation of it have already been discussed elsewhere, we shall turn to the next and final issue involved in the Scotistic proof, namely, whether there is only one first being or whether there can be many. But, following Scotus' lead, we shall first summarize the results thus far achieved in this study.[137]

By arguing from those of God's properties which have a direct reference to creatures inasmuch as they show the creatures' dependence on God, it has been established, in the first place, that there is a being that is simply first by the triple primacy of efficiency, finality, and eminence. The priority of this being is so perfect and absolute that it makes it impossible for any other being to precede it in any conceivable way. Next, by a process of conceptual analysis and proper inference, it has been shown that the first being is infinite because it is the first efficient cause, it knows all intelligibles, is the last end, and is most eminent. This is what Scotus calls a proof from God's absolute properties, infinity in this case, in contrast with the preceding proof from God's relative properties. To synthesize the conclusions thus far reached, the answer to the original question can be formulated as follows: "In the realm of beings there actually exists one being which has a triple primacy, and this being is infinite. Therefore an infinite being does actually exist."[138]

Since the concept of infinite being, Scotus adds, is the most perfect concept that one can have of God, it has therefore been proved that God exists in terms of the most perfect concept of him attainable by human reason in this life.[139]

2. THE UNICITY OF GOD

With the proof of the existence of an infinite being enjoying the triple primacy of efficiency, finality, and eminence, there seems to be no question that this being must be numerically one and that even the thought of

---

[137] Before taking up the question of the unicity of God, and even before summarizing the conclusion of the preceding question, Scotus discusses a fifth way of arguing to the infinity of the first being, namely, from the absence of any material, and therefore limiting, principle in an immaterial being. Since Scotus considers this way to be ineffective, we shall omit it. Cf. *Ord.* I, d. 2, nos. 140–44; II, 211–13.

[138] *Ibid.*, no. 147; II, 214.

[139] *Ibid.*, no. 147; II, 215: "Et sic probatum est Deum esse quantum ad conceptum vel esse eius, perfectissimum conceptibilem vel possibilem haberi a nobis de Deo."

a plurality of such beings is unthinkable. Scotus was undoubtedly convinced of this doctrine, as well as of the fact that, for all practical purposes, his proof for the existence of God was completed with the preceding discussion. But because not all philosophers were of one mind as to the ability of human reason to prove the unicity of God,[140] and more specifically, because of the statement of Moses Maimonides that in the view of some Arabian theologians this doctrine can be known only by revelation,[141] he felt the need to devote a special question of his *Ordinatio* to this problem. This takes the form of a corollary to the proof of God's existence.[142]

Taking a positive stand on the issue, Scotus argues for the unicity of God on purely rational grounds and advances to this effect no less than seven different arguments, all but one based on the notion of infinity. This is one more indication of the central role that the concept of infinity plays in Scotus' theodicy. Let us follow him in his dialectic, which contains a most effective refutation of all forms of polytheism and confirms the accord that exists between reason and faith on one of the most fundamental doctrines of the Judeo-Christian religion.

The first argument for God's unicity is based on the nature of the infinite intellect. Such an intellect must know whatever is knowable and in the most perfect manner, i.e., to the extent that the knowable object is intelligible in itself. Its knowledge must also be independent of any other cause or being. If we suppose that there were two gods, A and B, each with a most perfect knowledge, A would know B as perfectly as this can be known, that is, to the supreme degree of its intelligibility. But this is impossible. Indeed, either A will know B through this latter's essence or not. If not, then A will not know B in the most perfect manner, since nothing can be better known than through its essence if this is knowable in itself, as is clearly the case with B. If, on the other hand, A knows B through the latter's essence, then A's cognitive act is not supremely perfect either, because it is posterior to, and hence dependent upon, the essence of B. In neither case, therefore, is the nature of the infinite intellect preserved. And even if we assume that, because of the great similarity between the two, A knows B through its own essence, the perfection of divine cognition

---

[140]See, for example, William of Ware (held by some historians to have been the teacher of Scotus) who in the question, "Utrum Deum esse tantum unum possit probari ratione demonstrativa vel sola fide teneatur" (ed. by Petrus Muscat in *Antonianum*, II [1927], 344-50), defends the view that the rational arguments for the unicity of God are not convincing "nisi praesupposita fide" *(ibid.*, p. 344).

[141]Cf. *The Guide for the Perplexed*, trans. M. Friedländer (2nd ed. rev.; New York: Dover Publications, 1956), p. 141.

[142]*Ord.* I, d. 2, q. 3, no. 157; II, 222: "Quaero utrum sit tantum unus Deus."

is not thereby preserved. Knowledge through similarity is far too general to be called perfect or intuitive knowledge, as the cognition of an infinite intellect is supposed to be.

There is a further difficulty involved in the hypothesis of two gods or two infinite intellects. One and the same act of intellection can have only one adequate object. But if A is its own adequate object, as the essence of an infinite being must be with regard to an equally infinite intellect, then the essence of B becomes redundant to the perfection of A's knowledge. Worse still, it contradicts the very nature of an adequate object, which would be such regardless of whether or not there is another infinite being in existence. Briefly, an infinite intellect can have only one perfect and adequate object. This so exhausts intelligibility that it makes the existence and consequent knowability of another God altogether inconceivable.[143]

The same procedure followed in the argument for the unicity of God from the nature of the infinite intellect is also used by Scotus in the related argument from the infinite will. The only difference is that instead of arguing from the infinite perfection of the cognitive act and of the object known, as in the preceding case, he argues now from the infinite perfection of the volitive act and of the object loved, as well as from the infinite happiness resulting from the possession of the latter. The argument leads to the conclusion that, just as there can be only one infinite object of the divine intellect, so there can be only one infinite object of the divine will. This object so completely satisfies the infinite will's desire for happiness, that the hypothesis of another God becomes untenable.[144]

A similar argument, Scotus' third way, is derived from the notion of the infinite good. By its nature a will tends to seek and love a greater good whenever this is available. But if more than one infinite good were possible, then together they would contain a greater amount of goodness than one infinite good alone. A perfectly ordered will would therefore find greater satisfaction in the possession of more than one infinite good, and consequently not be fully satisfied with only one such good. This, however, is against the very nature of the infinite good, which must be such as to be able to satisfy the desire of any will whatsoever. The existence of more than one infinite good is therefore altogether impossible.[145]

There is a fourth way of showing the unicity of God, and this is based on the idea of infinite power. The argument runs as follows. It is impossible that each of two causes be totally responsible for the same effect and within the same order of causality. But an infinite power is the total and

---

[143]*Ibid.*, nos. 166-68; II, 226-28; *De primo principio*, p. 149.
[144]*Ord.* I, d. 2, nos. 169-70; II, 228-30; *De primo principio*, p. 149.
[145]*Ord.* I, d. 2, no. 171; II, 230; *De primo principio*, p. 151.

primary cause of all existing beings. Therefore no other power can be the total and primary cause of any being, or, which is the same thing, no other cause can be infinite in power. That no two causes can be totally responsible for the same effect is proved by the absurd consequence that would otherwise result: a thing would be the cause of an effect which does not depend on it in any conceivable way. In fact, nothing depends essentially on anything the absence of which is irrelevant to its own existence. But if an effect had two total primary causes, it would be possible for it to exist even if either one of the two causes in question were nonexistent, since each cause would of itself be capable of producing the whole effect.

This argument, Scotus points out, can be used to establish the unicity of any of the three primacies previously discussed, namely, efficiency, finality, and eminence. Hence, just as it has been proved that there can be only one infinite power, so it can also be proved that there can be only one ultimate end and one most perfect being.[146]

The next step in Scotus' argumentation for God's unicity is to the effect that two infinite beings are impossible, since the infinite can in no way be excelled. This argument, which is Scotus' fifth way, synthesizes, as it were, all the preceding ones, inasmuch as they all take their lead from a particular aspect of infinity. In fact, the very notion of an infinite being or, for that matter, of an infinite perfection, makes it impossible for any additional perfection to exist either in the infinite being itself or in some other being. If two or more beings could share in the same perfection—except, of course, in the sense of the Platonic doctrine of participation—none of them would be absolutely infinite. The unicity of the infinite being, whose existence has already been proved, is thus once more confirmed.[147]

The sixth way to God's unicity is of particular interest because it represents a new and, in our opinion, very effective approach to the problem at issue. It takes its lead from the notion of necessary existence, one of the perfections of the first being. Here is how Scotus formulates the argument. Whenever it is possible to have a plurality of individuals within the same species, no limit can be set to the number of such individuals, for a species can be multiplied to infinity. A species of corruptible beings is a case in point. But if necessity of existence (*necesse esse*) were a perfection that can be multiplied like individuals within the species, there is nothing that could prevent it from being multiplied to infinity, since no numerical restriction can be set to the number of individuals sharing in the same perfection. However, in the case of an infinity of necessary beings, there

---

[146]*Ord.* I, d. 2, nos. 172-74; II, 230-32; *De primo principio,* p. 151.

[147]*Ord.* I, d. 2, no. 175; II, 232. There is no mention of this argument in the *De primo principio.*

arises a unique and insolvable problem. These beings must either exist in act or they are neither necessary nor possible. They are not necessary, for they can be conceived as nonexistent without contradiction; they are not possible, for a necessary being can exist only by and of itself, and no being can bring itself into existence. One must therefore conclude that since an infinity of actually existing beings is impossible—Scotus has no doubt about this point—two or more necessary beings are also impossible. *Necesse esse*, in other words, is not a perfection comparable to a species of perishable beings that can be multiplied in more than one individual.

The same conclusion can be reached from the analysis of the entity or perfection that would distinguish one necessary being from another, in the supposition that a plurality of necessary beings existed. Since this argument is substantially the same as the one used by Scotus to prove the unity of the first nature,[148] the reader is referred to it for a detailed discussion.[149]

The seventh and final way of proving the unicity of God is not considered by Scotus as a strictly philosophical argument, for it is based on the notion of omnipotence, which for him is something distinct from infinite power and is known by faith alone.[150] He feels, however, that once the theological concept of omnipotence is accepted, an argument can be worked out in the following way. An omnipotent being, let us say A, has absolute power over every other being to the extent that it can bring it into existence and then destroy it completely once it has been in existence. Accordingly, A can destroy B and thus deprive it of all power. This goes to prove that B is not God for, if it were, it would be able to resist its own destruction.

To the objection that the object of omnipotence can only be a contingent being and not a necessary one, as is assumed in the case of B,[151] Scotus answers by restating the argument—which he admittedly took from Richard of St. Victor—in a slightly different way. Just as an omnipotent being can by an act of its will produce whatever is possible, so it can by an opposite act prevent a possible being from coming into existence or destroy it once it is existing. Now if A is omnipotent, it can will all beings other than itself and thus cause them to exist. But it is not necessary for B to will the same thing that A does, for if the two beings are equal, their wills are only contingently related to each other. Thus if B wills that none of those things willed by A should exist, then none will exist. Conse-

---

[148]Cf. n. 111 above for reference to Scotus' text and pertinent discussion.

[149]*Ord.* I, d. 2, nos. 176-77; II, 232-34; *De primo principio,* p. 151.

[150]See references to Scotus' discussion of this question in n. 125 above and our explanation of his view in the same context.

[151]Cf. St. Bonaventure, *Sent.* I, d. 2, a. un., q. 1 ad 4; William of Ware, *Sent.* I, d. 2, q. 2 in corp.

quently, in the hypothesis of two omnipotent beings, each would render the other impotent, not by destroying it, but rather by preventing that the things willed by it should come into existence.

Nor can the contradiction involved in the hypothesis of two omnipotent beings be avoided by suggesting, sophistically, that the two beings could reach some sort of agreement between themselves, even though there is no real necessity that they do so. The contradiction, Scotus says, is unavoidable even in such a far-fetched hypothesis. If A is omnipotent, it can by an act of its will produce whatever is producible. Consequently, B will be unable to produce anything, since there will be nothing left to be produced. Hence B cannot be omnipotent.

The correctness of this reasoning can be confirmed by the previous conclusion that no two total causes can produce one and the same effect. The unicity of the first being is therefore established even on the basis of the theological concept of omnipotence.[152]

CONCLUSION

As we followed Duns Scotus through the various steps of his rational ascent to God, we could not help noticing the power and rigor of his dialectic and the thoroughness with which he achieved the objective he had set before himself. He wanted to construct a proof of the existence of an infinite, and therefore unique and transcendent, being that would meet all the requirements of a strict philosophical demonstration and answer all the objections that were likely to be raised against it on the strength of past and contemporary philosophies. He did so by showing, first, the possibility of a first efficient cause, which is also the ultimate final cause and the most eminent nature. Next, he showed the impossibility that a being enjoying that triple primacy should itself be the effect of a cause in that triple order of causality. Then he went on to prove by an argument *ab absurdo* that the being in question, which he had shown to be possible but uncausable, can and must exist, or else it would be a contradictory concept. Proceeding further in his dialectic, Scotus showed that the triple primacy of efficiency, finality, and eminence can only belong to one and the same nature. Finally, by a series of arguments derived from power,

---

[152]*Ord.* I, d. 2, nos. 178-81; II, 234-36. The *De primo principio* does not mention the argument for God's unicity from the concept of omnipotence. Scotus' discussion of God's unicity in that treatise ends with the following prayerful address to the Lord, which is also the conclusion of the entire treatise: "O Lord our God! You are one in nature. Truly have you said that besides you there is no God. For though many may be called gods or thought to be gods, you alone are by nature God. You are the true God from whom, in whom and through whom all things are; you are blessed forever. Amen!" *Ibid.*, p. 151.

knowledge, goodness, and perfection, he argued to the infinity of the being possessing such a nature. Since infinity is for Scotus the attribute or mode of being that best characterizes God in his unique and transcendent reality, the existence of God has thus been established. The ensuing question about God's unicity has further strengthened the conclusion of his theistic proof and shown the perfect agreement between reason and faith on an important point of Christian doctrine.

One may question the value or effectiveness of certain minor points of Scotus' proof or disagree with some of the fundamental positions on which the proof is based, but once its epistemological and metaphysical premises have been accepted, it will be difficult to find fault with the proof as a whole. We are confident that our presentation has made this point clear and that no further discussion is needed. Rather, by way of conclusion, we would like to emphasize the particular features that distinguish Scotus' proof from other similar attempts before him and the advantages and disadvantages that characterize his original and unique approach to God.

A comparison that suggests itself immediately to the reader acquainted with scholastic philosophy is the relationship between Scotus' proof and St. Thomas' "five ways." This comparison is all the more important because the five ways have traditionally been given great prominence by the manuals of scholastic philosophy and considered as the classic arguments for God's existence. They have also been the subject of innumerable commentaries by philosophers of different persuasions. One thing, however, must be made clear from the outset, namely, that any attempt to compare the approach to God of the two schoolmen is bound to be somewhat inadequate, simply because Aquinas, in contrast with Scotus, never took upon himself the task of working out a complete and original theistic proof. In Thomas' words, the five ways are basically "the arguments by which both philosophers and Catholic teachers have proved that God exists."[153] While Thomas did not claim any originality for his *quinque viae,* which, ironically enough, have become perhaps the most celebrated page of his *Summa theologiae,* he must be given due credit for his ability to synthesize them so clearly and systematically that even an individual of average educational background can follow the logic of their reasoning. This is unquestionably an advantage for the understanding and practicality of the *quinque viae.* Yet their very conciseness and simplicity have made them an easy target of attacks, not only by critics outside the school, but even by some Thomistic philosophers.[154]

---

[153]*Con. gent.* I, ch. 13.

[154]Thus, in his discussion of "The Problem of the Five Ways," Fernand Van Steenberghen can affirm that "the deficiencies and imperfections of that celebrated page [of Aquinas' *Summa theologiae* containing the *quinque viae]* are recognized, implicitly at least,

Having clarified the different perspectives from which the two proofs in question must be approached, we are now in a position to see how one relates to the other. Both proofs, it must be admitted, are demonstrations a posteriori, inasmuch as they both argue from effect to cause, and ultimately to a first or ultimate cause as the explanation of the existence, nature, and scope of the beings of our experience. The vehicle used for the ascent to God is likewise the same in both proofs, namely, the principle of causality, which is but an application of the principle of sufficient reason or of the intelligibility of being. This, in turn, is based on the principle of noncontradiction. Neither Aquinas nor Scotus had any doubt as to the ontological validity of such principles, just as they both agreed that it is impossible to have an infinite series of essentially subordinated causes in a vertical order. The impossibility of such series plays an important role in the dialectic of both proofs.

These are the points of agreement between the two proofs. But there are also noticeable differences which distinguish one from the other. First among them is the structure of the proof itself, which for Thomas takes the form of five ways, each one independent of the other, whereas for Scotus it involves only three ways. Moreover, the three ways are so arranged that the second presupposes the first and the third presupposes the first two, even though their order could be inverted without jeopardizing the value of the proof. Further, Scotus' first way is a complex argument that includes basically the first three ways of Aquinas and corresponds roughly to what Kant has termed the cosmological argument. His other two ways correspond in turn to Aquinas' fourth and fifth ways but in an inverted order, so that the teleological argument comes first while the henological argument based on the degrees of being is next. It must also be observed that, whereas the Thomistic five ways are for all practical purposes five distinct proofs, Scotus' is a unique but comprehensive proof that moves along three different paths.

A second feature that distinguishes the two proofs is that, whereas Aquinas starts with a fact and arrives at an actual being as the ultimate explanation of that particular fact, Scotus starts with a possibility and arrives directly at the possibility of a first being in the triple order of primacy, and then, by a dialectic similar to that of Anselm's ontological argument, moves on to prove the actuality of the being in question. This is not to say that Scotus' proof is merely an a priori proof—Scotus would be the first to reject such an inference. It means simply that, while Scotus

---

by all exegetes, who affix explanations and additions which, by any standards, exceed the literal meaning of the text." *Hidden God,* trans. Theodore Crowley, O.F.M. (St. Louis: Herder, 1966), p. 144.

bases his proof on the actual existence of the objects of our experience, i.e., the production or *effectivitas* of certain effects, he goes further in his dialectic and, by a legitimate inference from the actual to the possible, he builds his argument on the possibility or *effectibilitas* of those very same effects. By this procedure, which combines in an unprecedented fashion Aristotle's logic and Avicenna's metaphysics, Scotus is able to devise a theistic proof that enjoys the character of a scientific demonstration in the Aristotelian sense of the term and has the value of rigorous metaphysical reasoning.

This leads to the question of the nature and ontological content, if any, of the *esse quidditativum,* the immediate starting point of Scotus' ascent to God. By implication, the question may also be raised whether Scotus' proof reflects basically an essentialist approach to reality in contrast to the so-called existentialist approach of Thomistic philosophy, whose advantages and superiority have been greatly extolled by some of Aquinas' followers in recent times. The nature of this study does not allow for a detailed discussion of this complex and controversial issue, but it may suffice to point out that, since for Scotus no real distinction exists between essence and existence in concrete reality, much of the controversy between essentialism and existentialism does not affect his philosophy. Hence the attacks directed against his so-called essentialism may miss the point entirely. It remains true, however, that Scotus' approach to reality is from the point of view of its essential content rather than its act of existing, as some contemporary Thomists like to interpret Aquinas' philosophy.[155] This brings us directly to the question of the nature of the *esse quidditativum.*

As previously explained, Scotus' *esse quidditativum* denotes being as abstracted from an actual reality or object of our experience and is by no means a mere product of the human mind or what is known as a logical being (*ens secundae intentionis*). On the other hand, the being that serves as the immediate starting point of Scotus' proof is not exactly the actual, physical being from which its concept has been derived and to which the mind has been intentionally directed through its perceiving power. Rather, the *esse quidditativum* stands for the intelligible entity that represents the essence of an individual object, and has therefore the characteristics of a universal concept grounded in reality, but considered not precisely as representing that particular object. It stands for the reality of an

---

[155]For a new and original interpretation of Aquinas' thought and an evaluation of some other contemporary views see our translation of Cornelio Fabro, "The Intensive Hermeneutics of Thomistic Philosophy: The Notion of Participation," *The Review of Metaphysics,* 27 (March, 1974), 449–91.

essence in the order of intelligibility or, more specifically, for a possible being with an aptitude for existence.[156] In fact, the starting point of Scotus' proof is neither the production (*effectivitas*) nor the possibility of production of an individual being (*effectibilitas huius entis*), but rather the possibility of production of *some* being (*aliquod ens est effectibile*). This is what makes Scotus' proof a real scientific demonstration, in the sense that science (*scientia*) was understood by Aristotle. At the same time, the proof goes beyond Aristotle's physics so noticeable in Aquinas' first way and moves onto the higher level of Avicenna's metaphysics.

Next, one may go on to ask, what is the difference between Scotus' proof and the so-called ideological argument of Augustinian origin or, for that matter, Anselm's ontological argument? The answer is not difficult. Yet much of what is to be said depends on the way one understands the two arguments in question. If by ideological argument is meant an attempt to prove the existence of God from the nature of the intelligibles or possible essences whose concept is derived from actual reality, then the ideological argument and the Scotistic proof have much in common. However, their principle of demonstration is different. Whereas the ideological argument is based on the principle of sufficient reason, Scotus' proof rests primarily on the principle of causality. So understood, both proofs are a posteriori demonstrations and therefore valid approaches to God, although the validity and effectiveness of the Scotistic proof are much more evident than those of its counterpart. But if by ideological argument is meant an approach to God on purely logical or conceptual grounds and with no reference to the actual world, then the two arguments are a world apart and their similarity is merely accidental.[157]

The difference between Scotus' proof and the ontological argument is even more obvious, since Anselm's starting point is a concept of God rather than the concept of a possible being abstracted from creatures, as is the case with Scotus. Yet the transition from the possibility of a first being in the triple order of causality to its actual existence, is effected by Scotus through a logical process that comes close to the *ratio Anselmi*. It is in this sense that a contemporary Scotist has been able to affirm that Scotus' proof is a synthesis of St. Thomas and St. Anselm and that herein lies to a great extent the originality of the Scotistic demonstration.[158]

---

[156]We believe that Gilson is substantially correct when he describes Scotus' notion of essence (in the context of his theistic proof) in the following terms: "l'entité de l'essence n'est pas une doublure abstraite de l'existence mais bien la réalité de l'intelligible en tant que tel." *Jean Duns Scot*, p. 180.

[157]For a discussion of the ideological argument in its literary and historical context see chapter II above.

[158]See Bettoni, *Duns Scotus: The Basic Principles of His Philosophy*, p. 144. For further information on Scotus' position on the ontological argument, the reader is referred to Section IV of the preceding chapter III.

But, to return to and complete our presentation of the differences between Scotus' and Aquinas' proofs, we must emphasize that the Subtle
Doctor is not completely satisfied with the proof of the existence of a first
being in the triple order of causality, which is substantially what Aquinas'
five ways amount to. He goes further and, after showing that the threefold
primacy belongs to one and the same nature, takes great pains to prove
the infinity of the first being. Thus the conclusion of Scotus' proof extends, as it were, to the very nature of God. It shows that God is not only
the first efficient and final cause, as well as a most eminent nature, but
also an infinite and absolutely perfect being. If, in addition to what has
been said, we set Scotus' proof within the context of his doctrine of univocity, we see even better its positive aspect as compared with Aquinas'
proof based exclusively on the doctrine of analogy.

The question has been asked whether, despite the obvious difference
between their approaches to God, Aquinas would subscribe to Scotus'
proof, either partially or in its entirety. We believe that, apart from the
dóctrine·of univocity, which is not really an indispensable element of
Scotus' rational ascent to God, Aquinas would have no difficulty in accepting Scotus' proof in the terms here presented. However, with regard to
the related issue of whether Aquinas, had he known Scotus' proof, would
have revised his own presentation of the *quinque viae,* the answer must be
in the negative. Scotus' proof, it must be admitted, is not an easy one.
Written primarily for well-trained philosophers and theologians or, we
might say, an elite,[159] it could hardly find its way into "a manual for begin-
ners in theology," as Aquinas calls his *Summa theologiae.* The two proofs
are equally valid and effective, each one in its own right and according to
the particular objective of its author. However, if we may offer a suggestion to the reader who is metaphysically inclined and wants to find a rational justification of his theistic belief, we would advise him to study first
Thomas' five ways, both in their text and context, and then approach
Scotus' proof either in the *Ordinatio* or in the *De primo principio.* The
journey will be long and perhaps tiresome, but, we may assure him, the reward is worth the effort.

---

[159]In the words of William of Vorillong, "eius [Scoti] dicta communem transcendunt
facultatem." *Opus super IV libros Sententiarum,* 1. IV, epilogus (Lyons, 1489), f. 291va.
Quoted in Balić, "Circa positiones fundamentales I. Duns Scoti," p. 299 and n. 3. Gilson
writes in this connection: "Duns Scot écrit pour exprimer sa pensée plutôt que pour la faire
comprendre." *Jean Duns Scot,* p. 9.

BIBLIOGRAPHY

Aristotle. *The Basic Works of Aristotle.* Edited and with an Introduction by Richard McKeon. 3d printing; New York: Random House, 1941.

Balić, Carolus. "De critica textuali Scholasticorum scriptis accommodata," *Antonianum*, XX (1945), 267-308.

————. "Circa positiones fundamentales I. Duns Scoti," *Antonianum,* XXVIII (1953), 261-306.

————. "The Life and Works of John Duns Scotus." In *John Duns Scotus, 1265-1965,* pp. 1-27. Ed. by John K. Ryan and Bernardine M. Bonansea. Washington, D.C.: The Catholic University of America Press, 1965.

Barth, Timotheus A. "Being, Univocity, and Analogy according to Duns Scotus." In *John Duns Scotus, 1265-1965,* pp. 210-62. Ed. by John K. Ryan and Bernardine M. Bonansea. Washington, D.C.: The Catholic University of America Press, 1965.

————. "De fundamento univocationis apud Ioannem Duns Scotum," *Antonianum,* XIV (1939), 181-206; 277-98; 373-92.

Bérubé, Camille. "Jean Duns Scot: Critique de l'Avicennisme Augustinisant." In *Acta Secundi Congressus Scholastici Internationalis Oxonii et Edimburgi diebus 11-17 Sept. 1966 celebrati.* Vol. I, pp. 207-243.

Bettoni, Efrem. *L'ascesa a Dio in Duns Scoto.* Milano: Vita e Pensiero, 1943.

————. "De argumentatione Doctoris Subtilis quoad existentiam Dei," *Antonianum,* XXVIII (1953), 39-58.

————. *Duns Scotus: The Basic Principles of His Philosophy.* Trans. and ed. by Bernardine Bonansea, O.F.M. Washington, D.C.: The Catholic University of America Press, 1961. This is admittedly the best and most widely used introduction to Scotus' thought in English. A reprint by Greenwood Press, Westport, Conn., is forthcoming.

Bonansea, Bernardine M., and Ryan, John K., eds. *John Duns Scotus, 1265-1965.* Vol. III of "Studies in Philosophy and the History of Philosophy." Washington, D.C.: The Catholic University of America Press, 1965. Symposium of 15 articles by outstanding Scotists throughout the world.

Bonaventure, St. "In I Sententiarum." *Opera omnia,* vol. I. Quaracchi: Typographia Collegii S. Bonaventurae, 1882.

Cress, Donald A. "Toward a Bibliography on Duns Scotus on the Existence of God," *Franciscan Studies,* 35 (1975), 45-65.

Duns Scotus, John. *Opera omnia.* Editio nova iuxta editionem Waddingi. 26 vols. Paris: Vivès, 1891-1895.

————. *Opera omnia.* Studio et cura Commissionis Scotisticae ad fidem codicum edita. Vols. I to VII of the *Ordinatio* published. Civitas Vaticana: Typis polyglottis Vaticanis, 1950-1973. When finished, the *Ordinatio* will comprise 15 volumes. Also published by the Vatican Press is Scotus' *Lectura in I Sententiarum,* vols. XVI-XVII, 1960-1966.

————. *A Treatise on God as First Principle.* Translation and edition of Duns Scotus' *De primo principio* by Allan B. Wolter, O.F.M. Chicago, Ill.: Franciscan Herald Press, 1966.

————. *God and Creatures.* Translation of Duns Scotus' *Quaestiones quodlibetales* by Felix Alluntis and Allan B. Wolter. Princeton, N.J.: The Princeton University Press, 1975.

Fabro, Cornelio. "The Intensive Hermeneutics of Thomistic Philosophy: The Notion of Participation," *The Review of Metaphysics*, 27 (March, 1974), 449-91. Trans. by B. M. Bonansea.

Gál, Gedeon. "De J. Duns Scoti 'Theorematum' authenticitate ex ultima parte operis confirmata," *Collectanea Franciscana*, XX (1950), 5-50.

Gilson, Etienne. *The Spirit of Medieval Philosophy*. Trans. by A. H. C. Downes. New York: Charles Scribner's Sons, 1940.

_____. "Les seize premiers Theoremata et la pensée de Duns Scot," *Archives d'histoire doctrinale et littéraire du Moyen Age*, XII-XIII (1937-1938), 5-86.

_____. *La philosophie au Moyen Age*. Paris: Payot, 1925.

_____. *Jean Duns Scot. Introduction à ses positions fondamentales*. Paris: Vrin, 1952. An important work on Duns Scotus' fundamental philosophical doctrines as understood by an eminent medieval scholar.

Henry of Ghent. *Summa quaestionum ordinariarum*. Paris, 1520; Ferrara 1646.

_____. *15 Quaestiones quodlibetales*. Paris, 1518; Venice, 1613.

Maimonides, Moses. *The Guide for the Perplexed*. 2d ed. rev. Trans. by M. Friedländer. New York: Dover Publications, 1956.

Merton, Thomas. *The Seven Storey Mountain*. New York: Harcourt, Brace and Co., 1948.

Minges, Parthenius, O.F.M. *Ioannis Duns Scoti doctrina philosophica et theologica*. 2 vols. Quaracchi: Typographia Collegii S. Bonaventurae, 1930. An extremely valuable work by a leading twentieth-century Scotist.

Owens, Joseph, C.SS.R. "The Special Characteristic of the Scotistic Proof that God Exists," *Analecta Gregoriana*, LXVII (1954), 311-27.

Prentice, Robert, O.F.M. "The Fundamental Metaphysics of Scotus Presumed by *De primo principio*," *Antonianum*, XLIV (1969), 67-83.

Shircel, Cyril L., O.F.M. *The Univocity of the Concept of Being in the Philosophy of John Duns Scotus*. Washington, D.C.: The Catholic University of America Press, 1942.

Van Breda, Herman Leo, O.F.M. "La preuve de l'existence de Dieu dans la 'Lectura'." In *De doctrina Ioannis Duns Scoti*, II, 363-75. Ed. by the Scotistic Commission. Rome, 1968.

Van Steenberghen, Fernand. *Hidden God*. Trans. by Theodore Crowley, O.F.M. St. Louis, Mo.: Herder, 1966.

Vignaux, Paul. *Philosophy in the Middle Ages*. Trans. by E.C. Hall. New York: The World Publishing Company "Meridian Books," 1959.

William of Vorillong. *Opus super IV libros Sententiarum*. Lyons, 1489.

William of Ware. "Utrum Deum esse tantum unum possit probari ratione demonstrativa vel sola fide teneatur," *Antonianum*, II (1927), 344-50. Ed. by Petrus Muscat.

Wolter, Allan B. *The Transcendentals and Their Function in the Metaphysics of Duns Scotus*. Washington, D.C.: The Catholic University of America Press, 1946.

_____. "The 'Theologism' of Duns Scotus," *Franciscan Studies*, VII (1947), 257-73; 367-98.

CHAPTER VI
MAURICE BLONDEL'S APPROACH TO GOD*

Maurice Blondel was, until quite recently, little known to the English-speaking world, even within the limited circle of philosophers. Few of his works have even now been translated into English, no comprehensive study has been made of his thought by our scholars, relatively few articles have been written on him in our periodicals, and even his name is seldom mentioned in our manuals of the history of philosophy.

Yet Blondel has been the object of many studies, especially in France and Italy, where he became the center of a heated controversy upon the publication in 1893 of his famous thesis, *L'action; essai d'une critique de la vie et d'une science de la pratique.* While some attacked him for his new ideas, which they closely associated with the insidious error of modernism, others praised him for his courage to stand up and defend Christian doctrine against the widespread rationalism and positivism of his day.

There seems to be no question today as to either the orthodoxy or the profundity of Blondel's thought, which has won the admiration of many outstanding scholars who see in the French philosopher a leading figure in the intellectual movement of the twentieth century. Thus Michele F. Sciacca, former professor of philosophy at the university of Genoa and an enthusiastic admirer of Blondel, calls him "the greatest contemporary Catholic thinker."[1] Père Auguste Valensin, Blondel's intimate friend and disciple, praises his master for having given a new orientation to philosophical thinking.[2] Henri Bouillard, S.J., professor at the Institut Catholique in Paris and a recognized authority in Blondelian studies, says that no work has exercised so profound an influence upon the French theology of the first part of the twentieth century as that of Blondel. He adds further that perhaps no other work has so helped contemporary Christian philoso-

---

*Reprinted, with some minor changes, from *Twentieth-Century Thinkers,* ed. John K. Ryan (Staten Island, N.Y.: Alba House, 1965). In a personal communication to this writer, Mlle N. Panis, who for many years had been Blondel's private Secretary, made the following comment on our essay on Blondel. "I have read your essay with great interest and want to congratulate you for having grasped and expressed so well in a few pages the essence of Blondel's method and the major themes of his philosophy."

[1]Cf. *Il problema di Dio e della religione nella filosofia attuale* (3d ed. rev.; Brescia: Morcelliana, 1953), p. 322.

[2]"Maurice Blondel et la dialectique de l'action," *Études,* 263 (Oct.-Dec., 1949), 145.

phers to harmonize their convictions with their faith.[3] Charles Moeller
goes so far as to compare Blondel with St. Augustine and St. Thomas
Aquinas, and says that with them "he is one of the three great Christian
minds called to reaffirm the meaning of humanism and of the supernatural in our world sickened from atheism and lies." Moeller expresses
the belief that Blondel "will become more and more the great dominating
figure of our unfortunate twentieth century."[4]

To these testimonies of appreciation for Blondel's philosophy it may be
added that when the Archbishop of Aix, Monseigneur Bonnefoy, was
prompted by attacks on Blondel to inquire of Pope Pius X what he
thought of his philosophy, the Pope replied: "I am sure of Blondel's orthodoxy, and I charge you to tell him so."[5] Pope Pius XI received Blondel in a
special audience and expressed to him the hope that his students might be
inspired by his spirit.[6] Pope Pius XII, in a letter written by Msgr. G. B.
Montini, the late Pope Paul VI, also commended Blondel's work.[7] These
authoritative documents should be enough to dispel any doubt as to
Blondel's orthodoxy.

I. LIFE AND WORKS

Blondel was born at Dijon, France, on November 2, 1861. After preliminary studies in his own town, he obtained his licentiate in literature
and his baccalaureate in science and law. In 1881 he entered the École
Normale Supérieure of Paris where Henri Bergson had just completed his
studies. His masters, Léon Ollé Laprune and Émile Boutroux, two well-
known figures in the history of nineteenth-century French philosophy, exercised a considerable influence on the formation of his thought. It was
during the second year at the École Normale that he decided on action as
the topic for his doctoral thesis. Reportedly, when one of his classmates
heard of the choice of the topic, he exclaimed: "A thesis on action: my
God, what could that be? The word 'action' does not even appear in
Franck's dictionary of philosophy."[8] As a matter of fact, when Blondel went

---

[3]Cf. *Blondel et le christianisme* (Paris: Éditions du Seuil, 1961), p. 16.

[4]Cf. *Au seuil du christianisme*, Cahiers de "Lumen Vitae," IV (Bruxelles: Éditions universelles, XVI, 1952), p. 97.

[5]Katherine Gilbert, *Maurice Blondel's Philosophy of Action* (Chapel Hill, N.C.: University of North Carolina, 1924), p. 4.

[6]Fiammetta Vanni Bourbon di Petrella, *Il pensiero di Maurice Blondel* (Florence: L'Arte della Stampa, 1950), p. 21.

[7]As reported by M. de Solages in the *Bulletin de littérature ecclésiastique* and quoted by Paul E. McKeever, "Maurice Blondel: Figure of Controversy," *American Ecclesiastical Review*, 126 (Jan.-June, 1952), 444.

[8]Fiammetta Vanni, *op. cit.*, p. 10. Adolphe Franck's *Dictionnaire des sciences philosophiques* was a popular philosophical dictionary in France at that time.

to the Sorbonne and asked for approval of his topic, he was told by the secretary that there would not be sufficient material for such a thesis. As things turned out, Blondel found enough to write several hundred pages!

It took Blondel ten years of hard work to complete his thesis, which he presented to the Sorbonne in 1893. After reading the manuscript, Boutroux, under whose guidance the thesis had been written and who would be on the presiding board of examiners, suggested that Blondel go and see the other members of the board, who, in his own words, had been deeply upset by the novelty of the topic and especially by his notion of Christian philosophy. In this way, Boutroux told Blondel, "they will have a chance to blow up before they do so in public."[9] The defense of the thesis took place before a packed auditorium on June 7, 1893, in a memorable session full of emotion and heated discussion, that lasted from three o'clock in the afternoon until seven fifteen in the evening. It was an historical event, for, as one writer puts it, not without a little sarcasm:

> ...the great pontiffs of the Sorbonne presiding at the defense of the thesis had the clear but painful sensation that a revolution was taking shape. This revolution was going to shake the very foundations of that spiritual rationalism which they so well represented. They felt that their power was coming to an end.[10]

Blondel defended himself so well in the course of the debate that the thesis was unanimously approved and accorded the marked distinction of the right of publication.

As previously stated, the publication of the thesis, which was completely sold out in fifteen months, caused a great stir among philosophers and theologians, both in France and abroad. Blondel had to defend himself against the attacks of those Catholics who saw in him a supporter of modernism and against rationalists who thought he had compromised the rights of human reason. For the rationalists, says Prof. Sciacca, Blondel was too much of a Christian; for the Catholics, he was not Christian enough.[11] As a result of these attacks, Blondel was refused a professorship at the Sorbonne. But through the good offices of his former teacher, Émile Boutroux, he was appointed "Maître de conference" at the

---

[9]*Ibid.*, p. 11.

[10]Eugène Masure, "Le témoignage d'un théologien," *Les études philosophiques,* new series, 1 (1950), 54–55. Blondel reports that after the defense of his thesis one of the board members asked him whether his "manifesto" was the work of a "savage" or the beginning of a campaign against an independent and secularized philosophy. "It is the work of a 'savage'," he answered, "but against barbarians of a new type and for the defense of civilization." Cf. Maurice Blondel, *Le problème de la philosophie catholique* (Paris: Bloud and Gay, 1932), p. 18, n. 1.

[11]Sciacca, *op. cit.,* p. 323.

University of Lille, and later ordinary professor at the University of Aix-Marseille, where he remained until his retirement in 1927. The gradual loss of his sight, which eventually led to complete blindness, forced him to return to private life. From then on he dictated his works and had philosophical publications read to him.

It was only after forty-one years of intense meditation and profound thinking that he published his second major work. This is the first of a five-volume series which appeared between 1934 and 1937 and includes *La pensée* (in 2 volumes), *L'Être et les êtres* (in 1 volume), and *L'action* (in 2 volumes, the first of which is entirely new, while the second is a partial recasting of the 1893 thesis). The five volumes constitute what Blondel calls his "trilogy" and represent a synthesis of his entire philosophical system. *L'action* (in both editions) remains, however, Blondel's most original and perhaps most important work. Between 1944 and 1946 Blondel published two volumes of *La philosophie et l'esprit chrétien*, a treatise on Christian philosophy which may be taken as his spiritual testament.[12] He died on June 4, 1949, at the age of 88, without having been able to complete a third volume.[13]

It is our purpose in this chapter to present the general theme of Blondel's philosophy, with special emphasis on his approach to God as found in *L'action* and in the other works of his trilogy.

II. *L'ACTION* (1893)

The basic idea of Blondel's philosophy was suggested to him by the atmosphere of religious indifference he found at the École Normale Supérieure when he was a student there. He noticed with great concern the almost total lack of interest on the part of his teachers and his schoolmates in all matters pertaining to religion. Is it possible, he asked himself, that a chasm has been opened between philosophy and religion, and that religion has come to be of so little importance to the philosopher that he can completely ignore it and even boast of such an attitude? The way in

---

[12]The two volumes of *La philosophie et l'esprit chrétien* have been published in Paris by the Presses Universitaires de France in the following order: vol. I, *Autonomie essentielle et connexion indéclinable*, 1944; vol. II, *Conditions de la symbiose seule normale et salutaire*, 1946.

[13]Blondel is the author of numerous articles and several other works, in addition to those already mentioned. In the bibliography accompanying this chapter, the reader will find several technical essays of particular interest to the professional philosopher. It is noteworthy that Father André Hayen's Blondelian bibliography, compiled in 1951, includes 1090 entries, and that many other works on Blondel have been written since then, mostly in French and Italian. The bibliography compiled for this chapter, then, gives only a small indication of the literature available on Maurice Blondel.

which Blondel would confront and attempt to solve this problem was to consist in concrete study and analysis of the fundamental issue of human destiny.

A. The Method of Immanence

Accepting St. Thomas' principle that the best way to refute an error is to use the very arguments advanced by its defenders,[14] Blondel takes the principle of immanence as the starting point for his dialectic, since immanentism was a current philosophical trend in his day. In doing so, he uses what later became known as the "method of immanence," which may be defined as the psychological process of posing all philosophical and religious problems by starting from the self. It differs from the "theory of immanence" in that the source of philosophical and religious truth is held to be internal observation rather than consciousness or subconsciousness. The theory of immanence confines its study to the subject and denies or ignores all transcendent reality; the method of immanence, while studying the subject, goes beyond the subject and admits the existence of other realities than the self, and especially the supreme reality of God.[15]

In Blondel's view, the infinite disproportion that we observe between the exigencies and the ideals in our lives makes us realize our deficiencies and our need for a transcendent and necessary being. Thus the questions posed by nature find their answer in the supernatural order of grace and revelation as manifested in Christian religion. The method of immanence is therefore, in Blondel's words, the denial of, and the antidote against, immanentism in the strict sense of the term.[16] It is also the best possible method, for traditional metaphysics "is impotent when it is a question of bringing modern minds to Christianity."[17] He writes in this connection:

> Modern thought considers with jealous pride the notion of immanence as the very condition of philosophy.... If there is one conclusion to

---

[14]*Contra gentiles,* Book I, chap. 2, no. 3.

[15]"L'immanentisme est un système qui nie ou néglige toute réalité transcendante, qui aboutit à enfermer le sujet en lui-même. Or M. Blondel a affirmé très fortement la nécessité pour le sujet de sortir de son immanence, de reconnaître des réalités differentes de la sienne et en particulier celle de Dieu." Joseph de Tonquedec, *Immanence; essai critique sur la doctrine de M. Blondel* (Paris: Beauchesne, 1913), p. 8.

[16]Cf. André Lalande, *Vocabulaire technique et critique de la philosophy* (Paris: Presses Universitaires de France, 1960), p. 469. It is worth mentioning that Blondel has contributed several articles to this classical dictionary of philosophy, which is thus a valuable source for the understanding of some Blondelian terms.

[17]Maurice Blondel, "Lettre sur les exigences de la pensée contemporaine," as reported in *Les premiers écrits de Maurice Blondel* (Paris: Presses Universitaires de France, 1956), pp. 5–6.

which modern philosophy attaches itself as to a certainty, it is the idea, basically justifiable, that nothing can enter into a man which does not come from him, and does not correspond in some fashion to a need for expansion.... There is no truth for him which really matters and no acceptable precept that is not in some way autonomous and autochtonous.[18]

And a little further on, we read:

If the meaning of modern philosophy fails to be grasped by many people, who in our very own time have lived, as it were, in the past, and if so many current doctrines appear to them enigmatic and vague, it is no doubt because of their failure to show the least appreciation for the principle of this method, a principle that has become and is going to be more and more the soul of philosophy.[19]

Blondel believes that his method of immanence contains a positive affirmation leading to faith. Yet he does not pose as an apologist of the Christian religion, as he is often alleged to have done, despite his explicit statement to the contrary. He is and wants to be essentially a philosopher. The purpose of his dialectic is to show to the intellectualists of his own day that a philosopher cannot be indifferent to the problem of religion, and that Christianity, more specifically Catholicism, is the only answer to the fundamental problem of human destiny.[20] It is important to keep this in mind if one is to avoid a tendentious interpretation of Blondel's system.

B.   Dialectic of Action

Yes or no [Blondel asks in his introduction to *L'action*], has human life a meaning, has man a destiny? I act, but I do not know what action is. I have not wished to live, and I do not know exactly who I am or

---

[18]*Ibid.*, p. 34.

[19]*Ibid.*, p. 39.

[20]Blondel affirms explicitly the agreement of philosophy with Catholicism: "....la philosophie essentielle 'convient' pleinement et librement avec le catholicisme, dont elle peut même, dans le sens que nous avons dit, épouser le nom, sans perdre le sien; à ce prix seulement, la philosophie réelle et réaliste peut coopérer, sans présomption ni hybridation, à cette oeuvre indivise et distincte foncièrement dont nous parlèrent saint Bernard et saint Bonaventure avant Deschamps, et qui, parce qu'elle forme une vivante trame de deux tissus allogènes mais anastomosés, semble en effet comporter une double appellation quelque peu hybride." *Le problème de la philosophie catholique,* pp. 175–76. Hence Duméry's pertinent observation: "Pour Blondel il ne peut y avoir une métaphysique du bouddhisme au même titre que du christianisme. La philosophie de la religion est nécessairement et intrinsèquement philosophie de la religion chrétienne. Il faut même dire, d'après Blondel, que *la* philosophie est essentiellement *catholique,* car en toute rigueur elle n'a place dans son registre rationnel que pour une notion du surnaturel expressément et littéralement définie au sens catholique." *Les études philosophiques,* new series, 1 (1950), 37, n. 2.

even whether I am.... And yet my actions carry within themselves an eternal responsibility.... Shall I say, then, that I have been condemned to live, condemned to die, condemned to eternity! How is that possible, and by what right, since I neither knew it nor willed it?... The problem is inevitable; man inevitably resolves it; and his solution, right or wrong, each one carries out in his own actions. That is why one must study *action*. [21]

For Blondel *action* is a complex term that stands for the entire human experience conceived within the framework of man's basic needs and tendencies; it is the synthesis of thought, will, and being itself, the activity of the whole man. The greater and the nobler is man's activity, the greater and the nobler is his action. In this sense Blondel can say with St. John of the Cross that to think of God and to contemplate him is the supreme form of action. [22] Action is the most universal fact in human life, and no one can avoid it. Suicide itself is an act. Action is also a personal obligation that may demand a hard choice, a sacrifice, and even death.

Blondel's dialectic of action is a description of the real logic that governs each human destiny. In his own words, "it is the role of the logic of action to determine the chain of necessities that compose the drama of life and lead it inevitably to its denouement."[23] Today, as one author puts it, we would call such an enterprise a philosophy of existence.[24]

Just as Freud was later to devise a method by which one can bring to the level of consciousness what is hidden in the deep subconscious, so Blondel has devised a method of revealing to man what he wills without being aware of it. Freud calls his procedure "psychoanalysis," to distinguish it from the ordinary observation of the psychologists; one could perhaps, with Auguste Valensin, call Blondel's procedure "a metapsychological analysis."[25] It consists not so much in cataloguing the contents of consciousness as in bringing forth the contents of the will as manifested in action or activity in which it is incarnated.

The dialectic of action is an important feature of Blondel's thought. It has a characteristic of its own which it derives from the very nature of the problem it aims to solve, namely, the problem of human destiny. Action is essentially an act of the will. There is only one way to make sure that the need of the supernatural towards which the dialectic tends is found in the will as will and not merely in the will of some individual persons: one must

---

[21]*L'action (1893)* (reprint; Paris: Presses Universitaires de France, 1950), pp. vii–viii.
[22]Lalande, *op. cit.*, pp. 20–21.
[23]*L'action*, p. 473.
[24]Henri Bouillard, S.J., "The Thought of Maurice Blondel: A Synoptic Vision," *International Philosophical Quarterly*, 3 (1963), 396.
[25]"Maurice Blondel et la dialectique de l'action," p. 149.

start from the most basic and limited act of the will, show that this act inevitably implies another act, this other a third one, and so on, until one arrives at an act of the will that attains the object desired and fully satisfies man's aspirations. This transition from one act of willing to another is Blondel's dialectic of action. It would be impossible to follow him step by step in such a dialectic, since to do so would amount to condensing into a few pages the substance of a 495-page volume. An attempt will be made, however, to give a general idea of its process and its terminus.

We have already seen that for Blondel action is a necessity and an obligation, and that even to refuse to act, or to do away with one's own life, is an action. This same principle must be applied to human willing, which is a characteristic of human activity. The most simple act of willing, no matter how limited its object may be, is still too rich and too involved to serve as a starting point for the metapsychological analysis of the will and its contents. One can always think of willing something less than he actually does. For example, one can think of not willing at all, of making no choice and no decision. Yet to do this is to will something, for any refusal to will is possible only in terms of an act of willing. To refuse to choose is to make a choice.

To show that man cannot live without willing is not enough. One must also show that he actually wills something, for otherwise his act of willing would be a purely negative one. We would have no starting point for our analysis which must lead inevitably to something positive, a definite end. Now the minimum object we can assign to the will, after it has been proved that it is impossible for the will not to will, is to will nothing or nothingness (*le néant*). This is what Blondel calls the attitude of the pessimist, while in the former case, namely, in the case of a man who refuses to will altogether and makes no decision as to the purpose of his life, we have the attitude of the dilettante or amateur.

But is it possible to will nothing or to make nothingness, i.e., nonbeing, the term of our act of willing? Evidently not, answers Blondel, because a negation is conceivable only in terms of an affirmation. As Schopenhauer had already remarked, even the man who takes his own life does so only because he would like to enjoy a better life. It is the love of an ideal being that makes one hate his present being. Blondel therefore concludes the first phase of his dialectic of action by saying that the human will always tends toward *being,* and any statement to the contrary is a contradiction.[26]

Blondel then goes on to study human activity in all its aspects. He notices everywhere a contrast between action and its realization, between the

---

[26]*L'action,* p. 38.

object willed and the primitive *élan,* the impetus of the will; or, in his own terminology, between the *volonté voulue* (the willed will) and the *volonté voulante* (the willing will). This contrast constitutes the permanent dissatisfaction of human life, and provides the incentive for further action. When a man has reached the extreme limit of what can be willed and desired in the natural order, he soon realizes that his willing power is far from being exhausted. On the contrary, it craves something more, something that cannot be found in the natural order where all goods are finite. It is at this stage that the idea of the infinite comes to man's mind and, with it, the idea of God as the "unique necessary" which can completely satisfy his aspirations. This idea impresses on action a character of transcendence. Man wishes to possess God who is somehow present to him; he wants to become similar to him. But this he cannot do by himself. Hence he is inevitably confronted with an option, a decision that concerns the meaning and value of his whole life.

> Yes or no [Blondel asks at this point], is man going to will to live, and even to die, as it were, by consenting to be supplanted by God? Or will he pretend to get along without Him, profiting by His necessary presence without making it voluntary, borrowing from Him the power to get along without Him, and infinitely willing without willing the infinite?[27]

Blondel is aware, and states explicitly, that not all men are confronted with this tragic dilemma in the same exacting terms. However, he remarks that once the thought is suggested to a person, in one form or another, that he must do something with his own life, even the rudest and least educated of men realizes that he is called upon to resolve this most important problem, the only really necessary concern in his life.

It is at this point that Blondel proposes his theory of the supernatural as the necessary fulfillment of the natural order and thus introduces the most crucial and controversial issue of his entire philosophy. He realizes the challenging and provocative character of his doctrine, but he does not retreat. He writes:

> Action is not completely achieved in the natural order. But is not the very term "supernatural" a scandal to human reason? When a philosopher is confronted with such an unknown [term or reality], is it not true that his attitude is simply to ignore it, or, more resolutely and more frankly, to deny it? No. To deny or to ignore it is against the spirit of philosophy. Far from invading a reserved domain [i.e., the domain of theology or revelation], one must show that any such invasion

---

[27]*Ibid.,* pp. 354-55.

is impossible, and that it is precisely because of this impossibility that a necessary relation exists [between the natural and the supernatural order]. It is the task of rational science to study the absolute independence as well as the necessity of the supernatural order.[28]

These statements contain the theme of Blondel's concluding treatment of action, namely, the relationship between the natural and the supernatural order. We shall return to this theme later.

III. THE TRILOGY

The dialectic of action, whose main outlines have just been described, is to a great extent a phenomenology of action. The trilogy, on the contrary, contains what may be called Blondel's ontology. While still retaining the basic ideas of his previous work, in the trilogy Blondel feels that the title "philosophy of action" no longer provides an adequate description of his system. Action presupposes being, and being is intelligible. To be complete a philosophical system must include the study of thought and being. This is what Blondel proposes to furnish in *La pensée* and *L'Être et les êtres*, which, together with the new version of *L'action*, constitute what has rightly been called "Blondel's integral realism."

A. *La pensée*

The two volumes of *La pensée* make it clear that Blondel is interested, not so much in thought as representation, as in the intrinsic act of thinking, the very reality and possibility of thinking.[29] He does not present a critique of knowledge, nor does he discuss the value of knowledge as such. Rather, he studies the dynamism of thought: its origin, its development, and the necessary conditions for its fulfillment. In his analysis, he begins with *cosmic* thought, or thought as represented by the inorganic world. It has often been said that the world is a thought that does not think itself. This statement acquires a special meaning in Blondel, for whom the world is just as intelligible as it is real. Does the world derive its intelligibility merely from the divine mind on which it depends or from our mind which apprehends it? Evidently not. The world has an intelligibility of its own; it is a subsistent, although incomplete, thought.[30] The world has the characteristics of the one and the many, which are proper to thought. It is

---

[28]*Ibid.*, p. 389.
[29]*La pensée,* I: *La genèse de la pensée et les paliers de son ascension spontanée* (Paris: Presses Universitaires de France, 1948), p. 3.
[30]*Ibid.*, p. 34.

in effect a permanent whole, with mutually dependent parts, in a continuous becoming that gives rise to multiplicity and variety. As a result, cosmic thought presents two different aspects: the *noetic,* which stands for the universal and the rational in the universe; and the *pneumatic,* which represents the singular, the unique, and the ineffable. These two different aspects of the universe have their counterpart in man's perception of it.

Blondel extends his analysis to *organic* thought and *psychic* thought, and finds in them the same characteristics of unity and multiplicity which belong to cosmic thought but on a proportionately higher level. The principle of unity in organic beings is life, an active and original power that organizes the manifold material into a new reality, an architectonic perfection that makes up for the inadequacy observable in the inorganic world. The characteristics of life are unity, spontaneity, and "perennity," or a tendency to continue in existence, as manifested in the preservation of the species. These characteristics are even more noticeable in psychic life, which represents a further step in the ascending process of the many towards the one. Psychic thought, roughly called animal consciousness, paves the way for *human* thought, in which Blondel distinguishes again between noetic and pneumatic thought, a duality corresponding to the relationship between the one and the many in the structure of the universe. Noetic thought is simply abstract thought dealing with the universal and the rational; pneumatic thought is concrete thought representing the singular and the unique. Both noetic and pneumatic thought coexist in one and the same *pensée pensante* (thinking thought) of which they are but different forms or aspects. Besides, they are so intimately related to one another that they cannot be separated. They are, to use Blondel's expression, "two thoughts in one thought."[31] Yet pneumatic thought is superior to noetic thought because it reveals to us the real in its concreteness rather than by morcellation, i.e., piecemeal, as noetic thought does. In pneumatic thought we have real knowledge; in noetic thought we have purely notional knowledge.

By applying to thought the dialectic of action, Blondel proves the radical inequality between the *pensée pensante* (thinking thought) and the *pensée pensée* (thought that is thought). He discovers at the very heart of thought a drama similar to the one that takes place in action, namely, that the more man comes to know, the more he wants to know; and this vital desire for knowledge and truth cannot be satisfied within the limits of his temporal life or by the objects of a finite world. This is not merely an em-

---

[31]*La pensée,* II: *Les responsabilités de la pensée et la possibilité de son achèvement* (Paris: Presses Universitaires de France, 1954), p. 13.

pirical fact; it is something essential and intrinsic to human nature. It is not merely an accidental wound that can be cured with time, but a constitutional disease. Death itself, Blondel says, is the best proof of the inadequacy of human thought, for death is something against man's nature; it is both antiphysical and antimetaphysical.[32] The very idea of death is meaningless and unreal without the implicit certitude that we possess within us something that is immortal. Blondel calls this a sort of ontological argument for the immortality of the soul.

In fact, Blondel argues, our thought cannot know itself except by understanding a truth that is independent of all transitory accidents. And this act of understanding essentially transcends time, for truth has the characteristics of universality and eternity. Hence the thinking soul belongs to a world superior to that characterized by simple duration, becoming, and decay, and an incompatibility exists between the life of thought and the inevitable disappearance of the thinking subject. It is from this incompatibility that arises the scandal of human reason, the instinctive revolt of our consciousness, the strange ease with which, although certain of our impending death, we still look at it as something hypothetical, unreal, uncertain, and foreign to our concrete preoccupations.[33]

Whatever one may think of this argument, Blondel goes on to show that the dialectic of thought imposes on us an option. Shall human thought be confined to knowing and organizing the finite world, or shall it open itself to a perfection that it can find neither in itself nor in any object in this world? This again leads man to God and the supernatural as the only solution to his critical dilemma.

B.   L'Être et les êtres

The same conclusion is reached by Blondel in his dialectic of being, which he develops in *L'Être et les êtres,* or *An Essay on Concrete and Integral Ontology,* as the subtitle indicates. Here, however, as one author points out, the drama of human destiny is enlarged to become a drama of the universe.[34] *Being* is a most common term that has its equivalent in every language and seems to convey the most simple meaning to everyone who uses it. But is being really so simple as to make all explanation and analysis useless? Despite its apparent clarity, Blondel observes, *being* is one of the most confusing and equivocal terms of our everyday usage. Its

---

[32]*Ibid.,* p. 179.
[33]*Ibid.,* pp. 178–79.
[34]Bouillard, *art. cit.,* p. 401.

meaning is so obscure that it borders on mystery. Yet it is impossible, even mentally, to deny being, for to think is to think something. The idea of nothing is but a nothingness of an idea; it is a pseudo-idea, a fiction.[35] But while we know that being is, we do not know what it actually is; we believe in being.[36] Hence an analysis of being is necessary.

In his analysis, Blondel attempts to prove that none of the beings of our experience fully instantiates the concept of being in the strict sense of the term. Being is not a mere abstraction but a concrete presence; it is not something that is most universal and common (*ens generalissimum et commune*), but an irreducible singularity. The term *being* is a proper, incommunicable, and substantial name.[37] The beings of our experience have an objective reality—Blondel was not an idealist—and to this extent they have some sort of being, but they never completely realize in themselves the notion of being as such. There is only one being, he concludes, that fully realizes this notion, so that we can say of it without any qualification, "it is." That being is *l'Être en soi et par soi* (Being in itself and by itself), God.[38]

The dialectic of being leads once more to the crucial alternative of an option for God or against God. As a rational being, man has the power to divert himself from his end. However, his refusal to possess Being becomes for him a positive privation, since the universal order from which he excludes himself continues to subsist against him. By failing to choose God, he fails to achieve his eternal destiny.

C. *L'action* (new version)

This same theme is restated in the new version of *L'action,* the third part of the trilogy, where the problem of action is approached from the metaphysical viewpoint of the relationship between the secondary causes and God as pure act. Action, by its very nature, tends toward an end which is also a good, or toward goodness itself. The study of action, even in its lowest form of physical operations, shows that the intimate dynamism of nature is but a progressive realization of the metaphysical principle that all beings tend to be similar to God (*omnia intendunt assimilari Deo*). It is only to the extent that this tendency and aspiration is freely accepted and effectively carried out by spiritual beings, that we can properly

---

[35]*L'Être et les êtres* (new ed.; Paris: Presses Universitaires de France, 1963), pp. 43–44.
[36]*Ibid.,* pp. 35, 325, 359 and 455.
[37]*Ibid.,* pp. 46, 48, 54 and 387.
[38]*Ibid.,* pp. 45, 46, 60 and 67.

speak of them as free agents and true secondary causes participating in the sovereignty of the unique primary cause.[39]

The action of secondary causes is essentially a becoming, a transient reality, a movement from the imperfect to the perfect. However, becoming does not exclude a determinate orientation, an internal finality, a rigorous judgment. That is why a critical study of secondary causes and transient actions can and must lead to the idea, the affirmation, the absolute and necessary truth of a pure act. In it alone are to be found the perfect intelligibility and the subsistent specification of a permanent and immutable action, an action with no stagnation, inertia, or sterility. In pure act alone action receives its formal specification precisely because, in it, determination of action is inseparable from its exercise, which is always actual and fecund. On the contrary, the specification of the action of secondary causes is determined only by the end they are supposed to attain, an end that is not merely their cause, but can become their life and their reward as well.[40]

It would be wrong, therefore, to look for a true and complete manifestation of action in the immanent series of secondary causes, whether taken separately or seen in the totality of the universal order. The essence of action can only be found in an absolute being, in a being in which transcendence is fully immanent to itself. This is so true that if, by a pure hypothesis, the only kind of action were a becoming, there would be, properly speaking, no action. If our acts are in effect always of a transitory nature, as we know them to be by experience, it is precisely because we are constantly tending towards the eternal and pure act, in which being, knowledge, and will are joined together in a perfect unity.[41]

The tragic dilemma that confronts man in his desire to become similar to God and in the realization of his own inadequacy are reasserted by Blondel in the second volume of *L'action* in essentially the same terms as in his 1893 dissertation.

The directive idea and unifying principle of the entire trilogy is best summarized in Blondel's own assertion that everywhere, in thought, being, and action, we are confronted with a duality that becomes known to us only because of a natural tendency towards unity. Everywhere we meet, at the heart of all contingent reality, an imbalance which, far from discouraging, opens up a new vista and stimulates us to further action in view of a superior end. Thus in all we are and in all we know, will, and do an in-

---

[39]*L'action,* I: *Le problème des causes secondes et le pur agir* (Paris: Presses Universitaires de France, 1949), p. 200.

[40]*Ibid.,* pp. 202-203.

[41]*Ibid.,* pp. 192-94.

finite is everywhere present which we must acknowledge in our mind and accept in our actions.[42]

A philosopher, it has been said, expresses only one idea in his lifetime. Blondel did not think otherwise. He writes: "All philosophical endeavor only translates a primitive and permanent idea and intention which would seem to be locked up in one word, but which many assembled books do not exhaust."[43] The idea that Blondel tried to convey to the intellectuals of his own day was in answer to a question raised at the École Normale Supérieure in Paris by one of his schoolmates: "Why should I be obliged," his friend asked him, "to investigate and to pay attention to an event which happened 1900 years ago in an obscure corner of the Roman empire, when I glory in ignoring so many other important historical events?"[44] Blondel's answer to his friend is that Christianity is not merely a thing of the past but an actual reality that concerns every man, and the philosopher perhaps more than any other. He proves this, or at least he attempts to do so, by showing that in our thought there is more than our thought, that in our being there is more than our being, and that in our action there is more than our action. In his analysis of thought, being, and action he arrives at one and the same conclusion, namely, that in the very immanence of our own spontaneous life a transcendent being is revealed, for the relative and contingent is not intelligible except in terms of the necessary and absolute.[45]

IV. NATURAL AND SUPERNATURAL ORDER

Before concluding this chapter, we must state very briefly what seems to be Blondel's position on the relationship between the natural and the supernatural order, since a clear understanding of his teaching on this delicate subject is necessary for a proper grasp of his entire philosophy.

According to Blondel, the existence of the supernatural order is a fact that is known to us exclusively by faith in revelation. The supernatural order is in no way due to man: it is absolutely gratuitous on the part of God. This is Blondel's firm belief as a Catholic—all agree in saying that he was a sincere and devout Catholic—and the teaching that can be

---

[42]*L'action*, II: *L'action humaine et les conditions de son aboutissement* (new ed.; Paris: Presses Universitaires de France, 1963), p. 14.

[43]*Une énigme historique: le "Vinculum substantiale" d'après Leibniz et l'ébauche d'un réalisme supérieur* (Paris: Beauchesne, 1930), p. 116.

[44]*Le problème de la philosophie catholique*, p. 11, n. 1.

[45]Paul Archambault, *Initiation à la philosophie blondélienne en forme de court traité de métaphysique* (Paris: Bloud and Gay, 1941), pp. 77-79.

gathered from his writings, especially those of a later date, when he felt the need to defend his own position against the attacks of some theologians.[46] Yet, in Blondel's view, a philosopher can arrive at the idea of a supernatural order even without the help of revelation, inasmuch as this order may appear to him as the necessary fulfillment of the order of nature.

Contrary to what has been affirmed by some of his critics, Blondel does not study the relations existing between pure nature or nature in the theological sense of the term, which is a pure abstraction, and the supernatural order. He always considers nature as found in concrete and actual reality, a nature which has *de facto* been raised to the supernatural order. For Blondel, therefore, the supernatural is something that must be reckoned with even by a philosopher. To refuse to accept the supernatural is not the same thing as to reduce oneself to the order of pure nature, just as any attempt to build up a philosophical system that prescinds from the supernatural is not the same thing as to deny the existence of the supernatural as such.

The exact point of demarcation between the natural and the supernatural order is not clearly stated by Blondel, who on the other hand is very explicit in his teaching that once the supernatural is presented to our mind we have no choice but to accept it. To reject it, or even to refuse to decide either way, is to renounce the divine call and expose ourselves to the most serious consequences for having failed to achieve our eternal destiny, the very purpose of our earthly existence.[47] It is in the light of these principles that Blondel advances his theory of the hypothetical necessity of the supernatural and claims for Christian philosophy the exclusive right to be called a true and genuine philosophy.[48]

---

[46]See, for example, *L'action*, I, p. 190, n. 1, where Blondel explains his thought concerning man's exigency for the supernatural order: "Qu'on ne prenne pas à rebours ce terme d'*exigence*. L'absolue et inaliénable transcendance de Dieu exige que cette incommensurabilité métaphysique demeure ontologiquement intacte et moralement inviolable. Bref, elle exige que, dans ses plus extrêmes condescendances, rien ne soit exigible d'elle. Loin donc d'interpréter nos assertions comme si l'hypothèse que nous examinons ici pouvait être réalisée par nous, ou même requise de notre part, nous voulons signifier expressément ce qu'il y a d'innaturalisable en elle. Dès lors que l'on comprend cette hypothèse telle qu'elle est, on est prémuni contre tout danger de semi-rationalisme, de modernisme et de naturalisme immanentiste." To make his mind even more clear as to the absolute gratuitousness of the supernatural order, he states further: "Il est donc nécessaire de maintenir que, pour une si merveilleuse élévation, l'initiative vient absolument et totalement de Dieu qui, par une grâce prévenante, donne à l'être contingent de quoi donner le nécessaire et naître à nouveau, *dat nobis Deus gratis id quod illi dare debemus necessario ad salutem.*" *Ibid.*, p. 191.

[47]Cf. Yves de Montcheuil, *Maurice Blondel: Pages religieuses* (Paris: Aubier, 1942), Introduction, pp. 40-43 and 55. See also McKeever, *art. cit.*, p. 444.

[48]Cf. *Le problème de la philosophie catholique*, pp. 31-39, where Blondel speaks of the hypothetical necessity of the supernatural order, and pp. 136-57, where his notion of Chris-

One may question the correctness of some of Blondel's statements, especially in his early writings, which taken out of context may give the impression of a systematically antagonistic attitude toward traditional scholastic philosophy and even of an open rejection of some of its fundamental tenets. However, when such statements are considered in their proper context and within the general framework of his entire system, they lose much of their polemic character and become more acceptable. They can, at any rate, be corrected and made to harmonize with Christian teaching in the light of his later declarations.

It is our conviction that despite its inevitable inaccuracies and shortcomings Blondel's system stands out as a landmark in the history of human thought.[49] It represents a vigorous and original attempt to rethink man's basic philosophical problems from the point of view of his concrete life, his inner desires and aspirations, his many failures and disappointments, and the evident but painful realization of his own inability to solve the problem of human destiny. The value and constructive nature of Blondel's system appears even more evident when compared to certain contemporary philosophies that have captured the imagination of the public and won acceptance among various groups of people but are purely negative in their approach to reality and the basic problems of man. Whereas the anguish and anxieties that beset twentieth-century man have often led thinkers to a philosophy of despair and of the absurd, these very anxieties and basic inadequacies become for Blondel the starting point and springboard for his ascent to God by calling man's attention to the perennial and vital truth of the Augustinian saying, "You have made us for yourself, and our heart is restless until it rests in you."[50] This is Blondel's message to his twentieth-century fellow men, who in the midst of the most confusing ideologies often lose sight of the fact that man has a fundamental tendency towards the infinite. It is hoped that his message

---

tian philosophy is discussed and defended. Blondel's teaching on the relationship between the natural and the supernatural order is the object of a special study by Bouillard: *Blondel et le christianisme,* pp. 67-131. For a critical evaluation of Blondel's doctrine cf. Paolo Valori, S.J., *M. Blondel e il problema d'una filosofia cristiana* (Rome: "La Civiltà Cattolica," 1950), pp. 225-34.

[49]Sciacca calls Blondel's "integral realism" the most original, organic, and complete system of Catholic philosophy that has been devised since Antonio Rosmini. Cf. *op. cit.,* p. 337. Valori speaks of Blondel's system as of "a kind of modern *Summa Theologiae,*" *op. cit.,* pp. 232-33, while Carlo Giacon praises it as one of the most forceful invitations to contemporary philosophy to retrace the way to the rational acceptance of Christian ideals. *Attualità filosofiche,* "Atti del III Convegno di studi filosofici cristiani, Gallarate 1947" (Padua: Editoria Liviana, 1948), p. 324.

[50]St. Augustine, *The Confessions,* translated, with an Introduction and Notes, by John K. Ryan (Garden City, N.Y.: Doubleday "Image Books," 1960), Bk. I, chap. 1, no. 1, p. 43.

will not go unheeded and that history will assign him that place among the great minds which a thinker of his stature rightly deserves.

BIBLIOGRAPHY

This bibliography has been updated so as to include the principal publications since the writing of our original essay on Blondel in 1965.

A. WORKS BY BLONDEL

—*De vinculo substantiali et de substantia composita apud Leibnitium.* Paris: Alcan, 1893.
—*L'action (1893)*; reprint. Paris: Presses Universitaires de France, 1950.
—"Lettre sur les exigences de la penseé contemporaine en matière d'apologétique et sur la méthode de la philosophie dans l'étude du problème religieux," *Annales de philosophie chrétienne*, Jan.-July, 1896.
—*Principe élémentaire d'une logique de la vie morale.* Paris: Colin, 1903.
—"Le point de départ de la recherche philosophique," *Annales de philosophie chrétienne*, Jan.-June, 1906.
—*Le procès de l'intelligence.* Paris: Bloud and Gay, 1922.
—"Le problème de Dieu et de la philosophie," *Bulletin de la Société Française de Philosophie*, Jan. 1930.
—*Une énigme historique: le "Vinculum substantiale" d'après Leibniz et l'ébauche d'un réalisme supérieur.* Paris: Beauchesne, 1930.
—"Ya-t-il une philosophie chrétienne?", *Revue de métaphysique et de morale*, Nov. 1931.
—*Le problème de la philosophie catholique.* Paris: Bloud and Gay, 1932.
—"Pour la philosophie intégrale," *Revue néoscolastique de philosophie*, May, 1934.
—*La philosophie et l'esprit chrétien.* 2 vols. Paris: Presses Universitaires de France, 1944-1946.
—*La pensée.* 2 vols. Paris: Presses Universitaires de France, 1948-1954.
—*L'action.* 2 vols.; new ed. Paris: Presses Universitaires de France, 1949-1963.
—*Exigences philosophiques du christianisme.* Paris: Presses Universitaires de France, 1950.
—*Études blondéliennes.* 3 vols. Paris: Presses Universitaires de France, 1951-1954.
—"Lettre sur les exigences de la pensée contemporaine." In *Les premiers écrits de Maurice Blondel*, pp. 5-95. Paris: Presses Universitaires de France, 1956.
—*Lettres philosophiques.* Paris: Aubier, 1961.
—*L'Être et les êtres.* New ed. Paris: Presses Universitaires de France, 1963.

B. ENGLISH TRANSLATIONS

Brantl, George. "The Unity of the Christian Spirit," translation of chapters 4 and 5 of *Exigences philosophiques du Christianisme, Cross Currents* (Spring, 1951), 1-12.
Dru, Alexander, and Trethowan, Illtyd. *Maurice Blondel: "The Letter on Apologetics" and "History and Dogma."* New York: Holt, Rinehart and Winston, 1965. The book contains a very good introduction to Blondel's method and thought.

Somerville, James. "The Theory and Practice of Action," translation of the introduction to *L'action (1893)*, *Cross Currents* (Spring-Summer, 1954), 251-61.

C. WORKS ON BLONDEL AND OTHER PERTINENT STUDIES

Archambault, Paul. *Vers un réalisme intégral: L'oeuvre philosophique de M. Blondel*. Paris: Bloud and Gay, 1928.

————. *Initiation à la philosophie blondélienne en forme de court traité de métaphysique*. Paris: Bloud and Gay, 1941.

Augustine, St. *The Confessions*. Translated, with an Introduction and Notes, by John K. Ryan. Garden City, N.Y.: Doubleday "Image Books," 1960.

Bonansea, Bernardino M. "Maurice Blondel: The Method of Immanence as an Approach to God." In *Twentieth-Century Thinkers*, pp. 37-58. Ed. by John K. Ryan. Staten Island, N.Y.: Alba House, 1965.

Bouillard, Henri, S.J. *Blondel et le christianisme*. Paris: Éditions du Seuil, 1961. English translation by James M. Somerville as *Blondel and Christianity*. Washington, D.C.: Corpus Books, 1970. This is unquestionably one of the best studies of Blondel's thought.

————. "The Thought of Maurice Blondel: A Synoptic Vision," *International Philosophical Quarterly*, 3 (1963), 392-402.

Cartier, Albert, S.J. *Existence et vérité; philosophie blondélienne de l'action et problématique existentielle*. Paris: Presses Universitaires de France, 1955.

Crippa, Romeo. *Il realismo integrale di M. Blondel*. Milan-Rome: Bocca, 1954.

De Lubac, Henri. *Blondel et Teilhard de Chardin: Correspondance Commentée*. Paris: Beauchesne, 1965. English translation by William Whitman as *Correspondence: Pierre Teilhard de Chardin—Maurice Blondel*, with notes and commentary. New York: Herder and Herder, 1967. An important documentary for the understanding of two great contemporary thinkers.

De Montcheuil, Yves. *Maurice Blondel: Pages religieuses*. Paris: Aubier, 1942.

De Tonquédec, Joseph. *Immanence; essai critique sur la doctrine de M. Blondel*. Paris: Beauchesne, 1913.

Dru, Alexander. "The Importance of Maurice Blondel," *The Downside Review*, 80 (April, 1962), 118-29.

————. "From the *Action Française* to the Second Vatican Council: Blondel's *La Semaine Sociale de Bordeaux*," *The Downside Review*, 81 (July, 1965), 226-45.

Duméry, Henry. *La philosophie de l'action*. Paris: Aubier, 1948.

————. "Pour une philosophie de la religion," *Les études philosophiques*, new series, 1 (1950), 34-42.

————. *Blondel et la religion*. Paris: Presses Universitaires de France, 1954.

Garrigou-Lagrange, Reginald, O.P. *God: His Existence and His Nature*. 2 vols. Trans. by Dom Bede from the 5th French ed. St. Louis, Mo.: Herder, 1948-1949.

Gilbert, Katherine. *Maurice Blondel's Philosophy of Action*. Chapel Hill, N.C.: University of North Carolina, 1924.

Lacroix, Jean. *Maurice Blondel: An Introduction to the Man and His Philosophy*. Trans. by John C. Guinness. New York: Sheed and Ward, 1968.

Lalande, André. *Vocabulaire technique et critique de la philosophie*. Paris: Presses Universitaires de France, 1960.

Lefèvre, Frédéric. *L'itinéraire philosophique de Maurice Blondel*. Paris: Spes, 1928.

Masure, Eugène. "Le témoignage d'un théologien," *Les études philosophiques*, new series, 1 (1950), 53-56.

McKeever, Paul E. "Maurice Blondel: Figure of Controversy," *American Ecclesiastical Review*, 126 (Jan.-June, 1952), 432-47.

McNeill, John J. *The Blondelian Synthesis. A Study of the Influence of German Philosophical Sources on the Formation of Blondel's Method and Thought.* Leiden: Brill, 1966.

Moeller, Charles. *Au seuil du christianisme.* Cahiers de "Lumen Vitae," IV. Brussels: Éditions universelles, XVI, 1952.

Mooney, Christopher F. "Blondel and Teilhard de Chardin," *Thought*, 37 (1962), 543-62.

Poncelet, Albert. "The Christian Philosophy of Maurice Blondel," *International Philosophical Quarterly*, 5 (Dec., 1965), 564-93.

Ritz, Maria. *Le problème de l'être dans l'ontologie de Maurice Blondel.* Fribourg, Switz.: Éditions Universitaires, 1958.

Roig, Gironella, J. *Filosofía blondeliana.* Barcelona: Ed. Balmesiana, 1944.

Romeyer, Blaise. *La philosophie religieuse de M. Blondel.* Paris: Aubier, 1943.

Sartori, Aloisius. *Teoresi*, 5 (1950). Commemorative volume dedicated to M. Blondel.

Sciacca, Michele F. *Il problema di Dio e della religione nella filosofia attuale.* 3d ed. rev. Brescia: Morcelliana, 1953. French translation by J. Chaix-Ruy as *Le problème de Dieu et de la religion dans la philosophie contemporaine.* Paris: Aubier, 1950.

Scott, William A. "The Notion of Tradition in Maurice Blondel," *Theological Studies*, 27 (Sept., 1966), 384-400.

Somerville, James. "Maurice Blondel: 1861-1949," *Thought*, 36 (1961), 371-410.

————. "Action and the Silence of Being." In *A Modern Introduction to Metaphysics*, pp. 420-31. Ed. by D. Drennen. New York: Free Press of Glencoe, 1962.

————. *Total Commitment: Blondel's L'action.* Washington, D.C.: Corpus Books, 1968. An excellent interpretation of Blondel's most important and controversial book.

Taymans d'Eypernon, Fr., S.J. *Le blondélisme.* Louvain: Museum Lessianum, 1933.

Thomas Aquinas, St. *Summa contra gentiles.* Editio Leonina Manualis. Turin-Rome: Marietti, 1946.

Valensin, Auguste. "Maurice Blondel et la dialectique de l'action," *Études*, 263 (Oct.-Dec., 1949), 145-63.

————. "Maurice Blondel: A Study of His Achievement," *Dublin Review*, 114 (1950), 90-105.

Valensin, Auguste, and De Montcheuil, Yves. *Maurice Blondel.* Paris: Gabalda, 1934.

Valori, Paolo, S.J. *M. Blondel e il problema d'una filosofia cristiana.* Rome: "La Civiltà Cattolica," 1950.

Vanni Bourbon di Petrella, Fiammetta. *Il pensiero di Maurice Blondel.* Florence: L'Arte della Stampa, 1950.

Various Authors. "Il pensiero filosofico di Maurizio Blondel." In *Attualità filosofiche*, Atti del III Convegno di studi filosofici cristiani, pp. 251-368. Gallarate, 1947.

Various Authors. "En hommage à Maurice Blondel," *Les études philosophiques,*
    new series, 1 (1950), 5–104.
Various Authors. *Teoresi,* 5 (1950). Commemorative volume dedicated to M.
    Blondel.
Zonneveld, Leo J., C.I.C.M. *Maurice Blondel's Approach to God.* Washington,
    D.C.: The Catholic University of America, 1960. Unpublished M. A. Thesis.
    _____. "Maurice Blondel: Action and the Concept of Christian Philosophy."
    In *Studies in Philosophy and the History of Philosophy,* vol. V, pp. 242–340.
    Ed. by John K. Ryan. The Catholic University of America Press, 1970. This is
    the substance of a doctoral thesis written for the School of Philosophy of The
    Catholic University of America in 1968.

Chapter VII

The Theistic Proof And Some Contemporary Philosophical Trends*

The title of this chapter calls for an explanation and a justification. It is not our purpose to discuss the arguments for the existence of God and show that they have value and cogency even for the twentieth-century man. Such a discussion is precluded both by the extremely broad scope it would involve and by the fact that there is little to be said on the subject that is not already known to most philosophers and students of philosophy.

Nor is it our intention to engage in a dialogue with the exponents of those philosophical systems which challenge the position of classical theism. Here again, the issue is too complex and involved to admit of more than a superficial and summary treatment.

What we propose to do is to analyze the nature of what is considered to be a theistic proof, to show both its value and its limitations, and to point out the untenable position to which a philosopher is reduced when he denies or questions the existence of God.

The possibility of a rational demonstration of God's existence has increasingly become a subject of discussion in various philosophical circles. Hence it is appropriate to re-examine the essential features of the theistic proof and to see why, despite the apparent cogency of its reasoning, it fails to convince many present-day thinkers. Our first step will be negative, namely, to indicate what the theistic proof is not meant to be.

I. NATURE, VALUE, AND LIMITATIONS OF A THEISTIC PROOF

There are many misunderstandings concerning the nature and value of a theistic proof. It is sometimes thought that for a proof to be a genuine and valid argument for the existence of God, it must be able to convince everyone, including the agnostic and the professed atheist. There is here a failure to see the difference between the validity of an argument in itself and conviction of its validity. While this distinction holds for arguments in

---

*This chapter is a development of a paper read at the Fourteenth International Congress of Philosophy held at Vienna in 1968 and published in *Akten des XIV Internationalen Kongresses für Philosophie, Wien, 2–9 September 1968*, VI (Vienna: Herder, 1971), 173–80.

general, it is especially important as regards the theistic arguments because of the consequences that follow upon their acceptance. For a man to believe in God—here we assume that the God in question is basically the God of Judeo-Christian religion—is to accept his dependence on a supreme legislator and judge to whom he is responsible for his actions and operations. Thus the acceptance of God should affect a man's entire life and behavior; in no way can it be compared to the acceptance of a mere theoretical or mathematical truth. Francis Bacon's statement that no one believes there is no God, except him for whom it is expedient that God should not exist,[1] contains a certain amount of truth even for the man of today.

The arguments for the existence of God, it is worth recalling, are not self-evident truths. No matter what their value and cogency, they are offered as proofs and they always remain so. A proof—a metaphysical proof in this case—is valid and cogent only to the extent that it represents a rational inference from firmly established premises. If the conclusion of the theistic arguments were a self-evident truth, no reasonable man would be able to deny it. But since God's existence is not self-evident to us and cannot be inferred merely from an analysis of the concept of God otherwise known to us, as is commonly held to be the case with St. Anselm's ontological argument, we must argue to God from the existence of the beings of our experience. The arguments so developed may be absolutely valid from the logical and metaphysical points of view and yet fail to convince an agnostic or professed atheist, because they still lack the evidence that is proper, for example, to truths in the mathematical order.

Another misunderstanding concerning the nature and value of a theistic proof is that it must appeal also to those philosophers whose system precludes all rational approach to a transcendent being. Thus a proof that fails to convince, for instance, a dialectical materialist, a logical positivist, or a linguistic analyst, is thought to be useless and devoid of any intrinsic value. This way of thinking seems to imply that a doctrine, to be true, must be able to win the assent of all men, even those who might be most prejudiced against it. It is not our intention to discuss such prejudices here; the subject will come up later. We wish only to point out that arguments which have appealed to many great minds, both in the past and in the present, do not lose their validity simply because a new and different approach to philosophy may hold them to be useless.

---

[1] "Nemo *Deos* non esse credit, nisi cui *Deos* non esse expedit." *Sermones fideles,* XVI, "De atheismo." For the English translation of Bacon's excellent essay on atheism, see Francis Bacon, *Works,* collected and edited by James Spedding, Robert Leslie Ellis, and Douglas Denon Heath (New York: Hurd and Houghton, 1869), vol. XII, pp. 131-35.

A similar but more widespread misconception about the theistic arguments is that they have become meaningless to the twentieth-century man. It is asserted that they rest on an outmoded philosophy that has now been transcended by more mature ways of thought. This assertion is a very common objection and a serious challenge, pragmatically if not theoretically, to the theistic position today. In reply, it must be said that the theistic arguments involve profound metaphysical thinking, and will never appeal to philosophers who in principle reject all metaphysical thinking as idle speculation. Given such an attitude toward philosophy, and especially toward metaphysics, it is not surprising that the classic theistic arguments, which are essentially metaphysical in nature, should fail to appeal to many present-day thinkers. Again, however, this situation does not affect the intrinsic validity of the arguments any more than it affects their appeal to those who are genuinely interested in the specific task of philosophy, which is the discovery of truth in its most universal sense and the ultimate explanation of reality.

To judge the validity of an argument merely from the effect it has on others, especially those who have a different cast of mind, is to confuse philosophy with apologetics. It is true that the theistic arguments are often used for apologetic purposes, but their effectiveness in convincing others can never be considered as a criterion of their validity; it can be a criterion only of their expediency. This may explain, for example, why many theistic philosophers in recent and contemporary times have adopted a somewhat antagonistic attitude toward the classical arguments for the existence of God. Their reason is not so much that they feel the arguments have completely lost their value, but rather that they think they have no value for the contemporary man. The arguments, they often say, serve only to convince those who already believe in God and therefore have no need of them. Effectively to answer this objection, we must discuss the relation between faith and reason in man's approach to God.

That human reason has the ability to prove the existence of God without the aid of revelation was an accepted doctrine until the rise of modern philosophy. This doctrine, which claims the support of the book of Wisdom and St. Paul's letter to the Romans and has been affirmed in many church documents, amounts to the rejection of fideism and traditionalism, i.e., the views of those who claim that the existence of God can be known only by faith in revelation, and the theory of Kant according to which the basic theistic arguments from reason are invalid. God's existence, Kant claims, must be accepted as a postulate of practical reason. The traditional doctrine is also an implicit refutation of more recent theories that claim the inability of the human mind to attain on its own to any knowledge of God (Barth, Brunner, Bultmann), or reduce such knowledge either to feeling and experience (Modernism and Neo-modernism) or to consciousness of the divine presence (Immanentism).

Yet while asserting the capacity of human reason to attain to the knowledge of God, scholastic philosophers have generally held that revelation is morally necessary for a firm assent by all persons to truths concerning the Supreme Being and for the preservation of such truths from distortion or error. We cannot explore here the issue whether it is possible to have a purely natural theology or whether natural theology should be integrated with the teaching of Judeo-Christian religion. This issue has been discussed exhaustively and at times passionately in the last forty years by men like Emile Bréhier, Etienne Gilson, and Maurice Blondel. It is a fact, however, that revelation has proved to be an indispensable aid to reason in the discussion of God. The approach to God of such thinkers as Augustine, Anselm, Thomas Aquinas, and John Duns Scotus has always been within a theological context. Their arguments for God's existence are the arguments of believers who seek rational justification of their faith. We must therefore ask at this point whether faith is a necessary requirement for the conviction of the validity of those arguments, or whether the arguments in question are so cogent as to be able to convince everyone even aside from faith in revelation.

It is our conviction that the basic theistic proofs which argue to God from the radical insufficiency of the beings of our experience, and hence from their contingent nature and essential dependence, retain their value independently of faith in revelation. As such, they should be able to convince everyone who approaches them with complete impartiality and objectivity and is not predisposed against them. However, since the conclusion still lacks the clarity proper to self-evident truths, as we have said, the proofs cannot as it were compel the assent of the intellect. Hence their acceptance is possible only through the joint cooperation of intellect and will and the concurrence of many factors in the psychological, moral, intellectual, and social orders that would take too long to discuss here. What we do want to discuss, however, is the embarassing and somewhat unreasonable position to which a philosopher is reduced by refusing to accept the validity of any argument leading to the recognition of a supreme and transcendent being.

II. ATHEISTIC TRENDS

There are two schools of thought today that, either directly or indirectly, make theism a target of their attacks, namely, atheistic existentialism and dialectical materialism. These schools, which we discussed in the first chapter of this volume, deserve additional consideration here, both for the completeness of this chapter and because of their extensive influence upon many people in our age.

A commonly held position among atheistic existentialists is, as we have seen, that the existence of the world must be accepted as a fact and that no explanation of it is possible. Indeed, any attempt at an explanation leads to contradictions. The existence of the world is an absurdity, and so is man, who has been cast into existence and must solve for himself the tragedy of life which fills him with nausea and despair.[2]

This negative and pessimistic view of reality is unworthy of a philosopher, whose task is precisely to find out the ultimate reasons of things and of human life in particular. There must be a reason for the world to exist rather than not, just as there must be a reason for the existence of each individual being in the world, and especially for the existence of a being endowed with intelligence and freedom.

Without contradiction I can think of myself, and of any other individual human being, as nonexistent, just as my thought extends to innumerable potential human beings who will never have actual existence. Why such a distinction between me and them? Why do I exist and why do they not? I know, of course, the immediate causes of my existence, but they are not its full explanation. My mind cannot be satisfied with only half an answer, especially in matters of such importance as those concerning the very purpose of human life. I want the full answer. The mind is made to know and wants to know all things without any arbitrary restraint.

To make this point clearer, let us compare a philosophical approach to reality with the approach of positive science. No one can blind himself to the fact that there are reasons for the ordinary occurrences of everyday life and for the larger events in the world in which we live. One of the tasks of a scientist is to discover the causes of such occurrences and events, whether in the physical, biological, or psychological order. The greater the knowledge of the causes in question, the greater the scientific progress. If this is true as regards the proximate causes of things, which are the direct concern of a scientist, why should not a philosopher be able to reach out and discover their remote and ultimate causes? Our reason tells us that since there is no event without an adequate cause in the world of our immediate experience, there must no doubt also be an adequate cause of the existence of the world itself, even though we cannot have direct knowledge

---

[2]Reference is made here to Jean-Paul Sartre, who may be considered the chief representative of contemporary atheistic existentialism. In *Being and Nothingness*, trans. by Hazel E. Barnes (New York: The Philosophical Library, 1956), Sartre claims that the idea of God is contradictory.

of that cause. From the nature of an effect our reason can infer the nature, or at least the existence, of its cause. This may be proximate or remote according to the case, but it must always be such as to be the proper and adequate cause of that particular effect.

Briefly, the principle that being is intelligible—which means that it must have a reason for being what it is—must be applied in the field of philosophy as well as in the area of positive sciences, and in an even more profound way. To refuse to admit this fact is to reject man's ability to know and to accept a philosophy of the absurd. This is precisely the position into which atheistic existentialists have been forced by their systematic denial of God.

Another antitheistic view that is even more widespread than the preceding one is that of the dialectical materialists. Their claim is not that the existence of the world is a patent absurdity, as atheistic existentialists maintain. It is rather that we need not go beyond the world itself for its explanation, if an explanation is possible, since matter and its movement are the only reality.[3] Although by movement they mean all types of change, physical, chemical, biological, and even social processes that take place in the history of mankind, the dialectical materialists always speak of movement as an essential attribute or existential form of matter, and never as something really distinct from it.[4] Just as there is no matter without movement, so, they say, there is no movement without matter. For the world, that is, the totality of existing things, is one,[5] and there is nothing in it that is not matter in motion or a product of matter in motion.

To defend this position, they are forced to admit, first, that matter is eternal, necessary, and unlimited, and at the same time that each individual thing exists in time and space, is constantly changing, and has a limited nature; secondly, that life, sensation, and even consciousness evolve through some mysterious process and without the aid of any extrinsic agent from the potentialities of matter, and yet that matter, at least in its former state, was inanimate, senseless, and unconscious; thirdly, that universal evolution follows definite laws and patterns which are the object of perpetual wonder to the scientist, and yet that there is no lawgiver and no

---

[3]Cf. J. M. Bochenski, *The Dogmatic Principles of Soviet Philosophy* (Dordrecht, Holland: D. Reidel Publishing Company, 1963), p. 9, 4.44: "In the world there is nothing and there never will be anything which is not matter in motion or a product of matter in motion. Therein lies the unity of the world."

[4]*Ibid.*, p. 7, 4.22: "Movement is not accidental. It is an eternal attribute, an existential form, of matter."

[5]*Ibid.*, p. 9, 4.41: "Contrary to the view that, in addition to the material world there is yet a second, 'spiritual,' world, science has step by step proved that there are not two worlds. The world is one."

mind behind such a marvelous evolution. The internally contradictory movement of matter—the expression is theirs[6]—is solely responsible for it. Fourthly, the entire plan of the universe, which includes the organized movement of millions and millions of stars and galaxies, is merely the product of blind mechanical forces of matter, since, let us repeat, for a dialectical materialist matter and its movement are the only reality. Finally, the fundamental issue of how such wonderful and mysterious matter happens to exist is simply dismissed by the dialectical materialist on the ground that since man came after matter he has no way of knowing its origin.[7] The existence of an eternal and all-powerful matter is therefore taken for granted.[8]

It is because of these inadequacies and contradictions that one must question whether dialectical materialism is really a challenge to theism. However, one should not forget that materialism today, under one form or another, pervades the culture of many highly civilized countries. That is why the need was felt to discuss it here, along with atheistic existentialism, so as to show that neither of the two philosophies can be a substitute for traditional theism.

III. AGNOSTIC TRENDS

The major threat to theism is not so much atheism with its fundamental weaknesses and manifest contradictions, such as those indicated above, as it is the more subtle attitude or philosophical movement known as agnosticism. It is to this movement and its various ramifications that we shall now direct our attention.[9]

The term "agnosticism" means literally a stand or outlook maintaining lack of knowledge, and was coined by Thomas H. Huxley in 1869 to describe the attitude of a person who asserts the inability of the human mind to know the ultimate realities, especially the existence and nature of

---

[6]*Ibid.*, p. 8, 4.27: "Movement is internally contradictory; it is absolute and relative; it is a change which contains a moment of immutability; it contains moments of continuity and discontinuity."

[7]*Ibid.*, p. 7, 4.11: "Science has indisputably established that the world existed long before man and life; and that the sun and earth, and so on, exist independently of any human consciousness. For this reason, since there neither is nor can be any other consciousness, matter is primary and knowledge is secondary"; *ibid.*, 4.13: "Matter exists outside of our knowledge."

[8]For a comprehensive study of dialectical materialism see Gustav A. Wetter, *Dialectical Materialism*, trans. by Peter Heath (3d printing; New York and London: Frederick A. Praeger, 1963). The contradictions of an eternally self-sufficient matter are discussed in the last chapter of this book.

[9]A portion of this section has been taken from this writer's article, "Existence of God in Philosophy," *New Catholic Encyclopedia*, VI, 547-52.

God.[10] The more rigid form of agnosticism considers knowledge about God to be entirely beyond the reach of human intelligence, so that man can know absolutely nothing about God, not even whether he exists or not. Moderate agnosticism may accept the existence of God on faith, but it denies any rational foundation for such belief. As far as the nature of God is concerned, moderate agnosticism agrees with rigid agnosticism in professing complete ignorance.

Two antimetaphysical trends of thought have contributed to the affirmation and spreading of modern agnosticism, namely, Comte's positivism and Kant's criticism. Although the two doctrines differ widely from one another, both are indebted to Hume's subjective empiricism and attempt to reduce the notion of knowledge to scientific knowledge. Since God is not the object of empirical observation, it follows that in their view man cannot have any concept of him. But whereas for Comte belief in God is useless and even harmful to mankind, inasmuch as it hampers the natural development of human reason, for Kant it is simply an act of faith for which no rational justification can be given. Comte is a pure agnostic; Kant a moderate agnostic.

The impact of these two philosophies is manifest in Herbert Spencer's theory of the Unknowable. Spencer admits the existence of the Absolute as a necessary postulate for the intelligibility of the relative objects of human experience, but he denies any knowledge of the Absolute. The mentality created by Spencer and his predecessors influenced the religious theory of William James. Following the pragmatic principle that an idea is true if it works and produces good results, James maintains that belief in God, which is largely a matter of feeling, is true because it has a real value in concrete life. The empirical study of such belief shows, in fact, that it expresses confidence in the promise of the future and has beneficial results for one's life, both as an individual and as a member of society. James spurns the traditional proofs of God's existence and settles for the "hypothesis of God" as more satisfactory than any alternative hypothesis. Truth is thus sacrificed to expediency, and belief in God, whom James prefers to consider as a finite being with limited power, is deprived of any metaphysical foundation.

The intellectual movement known as Modernism was influenced by similar ideas. Because of their fundamental phenomenalism, the Modernists hold that human reason cannot attain any supersensible and transcendent reality. While eliminating all rational demonstration of God's ex-

---

[10]Cf. Thomas H. Huxley, "Agnosticism," in *Collected Essays*, V (New York: Appleton and Company, 1894), 239.

istence, they also attempt to discredit the historical fact of God's actual intervention in the world.

A more recent form of agnosticism is logical positivism, a movement that began in Vienna in 1922, when a group of philosophers, mathematicians, logicians, and scientists joined around Moritz Schlick to form the "Vienna Circle," whose first organized International Congress was held in Prague in 1929. Although the Vienna Circle has long been defunct and few philosophers today would like to be called logical positivists, still some of the principles laid down by the Circle's manifesto, under the title *Wissenschaftliche Weltaufassung: Der Wiene Kreise*, are very much alive within the movement known as linguistic analysis and deserve careful consideration.

Logical positivism is the contemporary form of British empiricism. Generally speaking, logical positivists agree on the following points: 1) they hold Hume's view on causality, which amounts to the denial of any ontological nexus between cause and effect; 2) they insist on the tautological nature of logical and mathematical truths; 3) they conceive of philosophy as logical analysis, i.e., as a clarification of the language which we all speak in everyday life; 4) they maintain that such an analysis leads to the rejection of metaphysics, and consequently, of natural theology.[11]

The most popular and influential book, at least in the English-speaking world, expounding the tenets of logical positivism, is Alfred J. Ayer's *Language, Truth and Logic*, first published in 1936 and reprinted in 1946 with a new introduction. While in the introduction to this latter edition certain explanations are offered by the author in answer to his critics, there is no indication of a substantial departure from his previous position. Starting from Wittgenstein's premise that "a philosophical work consists essentially of elucidations" or "clarifications of propositions,"[12] Ayer divides all genuine propositions into two classes. There are, first, analytical propositions, such as those of logic and mathematics, which are necessary and certain because they are tautologies. Since they have no factual content, their validity depends solely on the definition of the symbols they contain. There are, in the second place, synthetic propositions, which are concerned with facts and whose validity can be determined by the principle of verification. These are the propositions of science, which alone provide us with new information about the world and any empirical situation, although analytic propositions may also be useful for a better

---

[11]Cf. Gustav Bergmann, "Logical Positivism," in *A History of Philosophical Systems,* ed. by Vergilius Ferm (New York: The Philosophical Library, 1950), p. 472.

[12]Ludwig Wittgenstein, *Tractatus Logico-philosophicus,* Prop. 4.112.

understanding of the use of certain symbols.[13] Propositions not reducible
to these two types are not genuine propositions at all, and are therefore
meaningless, since they can neither be proved to be true or false, like synthetic propositions, nor can they be called mere tautologies, like analytic
propositions. To the category of meaningless propositions belong all statements of metaphysics, ethics, and theology.

While ethical judgments are purely "emotive" expressions devoid of
any meaningful content,[14] all statements referring to a "reality" transcending the limits of sense experience have no literal significance. "From
which it must follow that the labors of those who have striven to describe
such a reality [i.e., the production of twenty-five centuries of thinking by
the greatest philosophical minds from Plato and Aristotle down to the present time] have all been devoted to the production of nonsense."[15]

Having ruled out metaphysics as meaningless, and therefore as a
pseudo-science—"The Elimination of Metaphysics" is the title of the first
chapter—and reduced philosophy to "the logic of science,"[16] Ayer feels
that any discussion about God is useless. Yet because of philosophers'
considerable interest in the subject, he takes up the issue in a special
chapter entitled "Critique of Ethics and Theology" and makes some pertinent observations.

No demonstrative proof of God's existence is possible, Ayer says,
because the premises from which the existence of God is deduced are
either empirical propositions, and therefore at most probable, or *a priori*
propositions, that is, mere tautologies. In either case, the conclusion of a
theistic argument shares the same weakness as the premises. But even the
probability of God's existence is ruled out by Ayer, for "God" is a metaphysical term, and as such devoid of any meaning.[17]

This attitude toward God and religious knowledge in general is not to
be confused, Ayer warns us, with the view adopted by atheists, or even
agnostics. "For if the assertion that there is a god is nonsensical, then the
atheist's assertion that there is no god is equally nonsensical."[18]

There is no need to proceed further in our analysis of Ayer's work,
which is but an attempt to draw the logical consequences from a pre-

---

[13]Cf. Alfred Jules Ayer, *Language, Truth and Logic* (New York: Dover Publications,
[1957], pp. 31, 78–79.
[14]*Ibid.*, pp. 107–108.
[15]*Ibid.*, p. 34.
[16]*Ibid.*, p. 153.
[17]*Ibid.*, p. 115: "If 'god' is a metaphysical term, then it cannot even be probable that a
god exists. For to say that 'God exists' is to make a metaphysical utterance which cannot be
either true or false."
[18]*Ibid.*

established position, namely, that the principle of [empirical] verification is the ultimate test and criterion of knowledge and truth. We shall rather confine ourselves to making a few observations on the principle in question and the implications it has for Ayer's entire system of philosophy.

1) Ayer's "verification principle" is self-defeating, for all attempts at its demonstration result in its denial. The principle does not admit of empirical verification and fails to pass its own test. To call the criterion of verifiability a methodological principle, as Ayer does in the introduction to the second edition of his work,[19] is no way out of the impasse. A methodological principle for which no rational justification can be offered except in terms of the principle itself, which is far from being self-evident (as is the case, for example, with the principle of contradiction), will never win the assent of a genuine philosopher.

2) On Ayer's premises, the verification principle can be classified neither as an analytic nor as a synthetic principle; it must therefore be considered a *meaningless* statement.

3) Ayer's assertion that all meaningful propositions must be empirically verifiable is not only a contradictory statement but also a *gratuitous* assumption. It fails to consider the human mind's power of abstraction and its ability to form universal ideas and the principles that lie at the foundation of all sciences, including the empirical sciences. On Ayer's premises, physical laws would become impossible.

4) To deny the human mind the power to attain any knowledge of spiritual substances, such as the human soul and God, on the ground that they are not empirically verifiable, is merely to affirm the consequences of a prejudicial principle.

5) Ayer's verification principle reflects a short-sighted view of reality which is characteristic of British empiricism of the Humean type and identifies the real with the material and the sensible. While it may be considered methodologically valid in the field of positive sciences, the principle can never become a rule of philosophical thinking. The failure to distinguish between philosophy and science is a serious flaw in Ayer's system, as well as in the system of logical positivism in general.

6) Although Ayer refuses to be identified as either atheist or agnostic on the ground that for him any talk about God is meaningless, his position is no better than that of those who deny or question the existence of God. Atheists and agnostics admit at least the conceivability of God; Ayer excludes even that. For all practical purposes, and no matter what his personal belief, Ayer's must be reckoned among the agnostic systems, since for him the human mind can know nothing about God.

---

[19]*Ibid.*, p. 16.

By way of general appraisal of modern and contemporary agnosticism, it may be said that this philosophical movement, under whatever form, amounts to a distrust of the power of human reason. Such a distrust is based on an erroneous conception of the limits and value of knowledge in general and of inferential knowledge in particular. Thus in the last analysis agnosticism is the consequence of a false epistemology.

This conclusion is borne out by the fact that, although human knowledge starts with the particular data of sense experience, man can form ideas that abstract from all individuating notes and represent the nature of a thing as it is in itself. These ideas have the characteristic of universality, which is in direct contrast with the datum of sense experience. And just as man can form ideas of the essence of sensible things, so he can form ideas of spiritual substances, such as the soul and God. The existence of these substances is proved by rational inference from the nature of their effects. Since every effect demands an adequate cause, from the nature of an effect one can infer the nature of its cause. The fundamental principle of positivism, as well as of Kantian criticism, namely, that the sensible alone is knowable, is a gratuitous assumption that is neither demonstrated nor demonstrable. It is in fact, as already observed with regard to Ayer's requirement of verifiability, a self-defeating principle.

To conclude, we would like to reaffirm our original conviction that the theistic proof retains its value despite the many attempts by philosophers to undermine it and do away with the very idea of a Supreme Being, the provident Creator of the universe. To help revive this idea and show its rational justification has been the primary concern of this entire volume, but more particularly of this chapter elucidating the essential features of the theistic proof.[20]

BIBLIOGRAPHY

Ayer, Alfred Jules. *Language, Truth and Logic*. New York: Dover Publications, [1957].

Bacon, Francis. "Of Atheism." In *Works*, vol. XII, pp. 131–35. Collected and edited by James Spedding, Robert Leslie Ellis, and Douglas Denon Heath. New York: Hurd and Houghton, 1869.

Bergmann, Gustav. "Logical Positivism." In *History of Philosophical Systems*, pp. 471–82. Ed. by Vergilius Ferm. New York: The Philosophical Library, 1950.

Bochenski, J. M. *The Dogmatic Principles of Soviet Philosophy*. Dordrecht, Holland: D. Reidel Publishing Company, 1963.

---

[20]See, in this connection, the Appendix to this volume, where we present a distillation of Thomistic and Scotistic insights which combine to illustrate the essential nature of a theistic proof with maximum economy.

Bonansea, Bernardino M. "Existence of God in Philosophy," *New Catholic Encyclopedia,* VI, 547-52.

Huxley, Thomas H. "Agnosticism." In *Collected Essays*, vol. V, pp. 209-262. New York: Appleton and Company, 1894.

Sartre, Jean-Paul. *Being and Nothingness: An Essay on Phenomenological Ontology*. Trans. by Hazel E. Barnes. New York: The Philosophical Library, 1956.

Wetter, Gustav A. *Dialectical Materialism*. Translated from the German by Peter Heath. 3d printing. New York and London: Frederick A. Praeger, 1963.

Wittgenstein, Ludwig. *Tractatus Logico-philosophicus*. London: Routledge and Kegan Paul, 1961.

PART THREE

SPECIFIC ISSUES CONCERNING
GOD AND THE WORLD

CHAPTER VIII

THE IMPOSSIBILITY OF CREATION FROM ETERNITY ACCORDING TO ST. BONAVENTURE*

The question of whether or not the world could have been created from eternity was discussed by medieval schoolmen with considerable interest and, to judge from their writings, not without some emotional overtones.[1] Confronted with an apparent conflict between the Aristotelian and Averroistic thesis of an eternal world and the revealed doctrine of the world's temporal creation, the school of thought headed by Aquinas approached the subject on strictly philosophical grounds and adopted an attitude of cautious reservation in the controversy by admitting the theoretical possibility of an eternally created world. In contrast, the school of thought represented by St. Bonaventure defended not only the absolute incompatibility of Christian teaching with the Aristotelian-Averroistic theory but also the impossibility of an eternal world as well as of an eternal creation.

I. IMPORTANCE AND COMPLEXITY OF THE PROBLEM

The controversy has not lost its appeal to the contemporary man, and even today it has more than an academic or historical value. Its solution— if a solution will ever be reached—involves some of the most fundamental issues of natural theology, metaphysics, and cosmology. It involves, first of all, the question of whether it is possible to conceive without contradiction a totally contingent world that would be limited in all respects but one, the extent of its duration. If a positive answer is given to this question, a further issue arises, and the possibility must be considered of an infinite multitude of actually existing beings, despite the obvious fact that each individual being exists separately and therefore has its own distinct and in-

---

*Reprinted from *Franciscan Studies,* 34 (1974), 7–33, where it appeared under the title, "The Question of an Eternal World in the Teaching of St. Bonaventure." The essay is a development of a paper read at the National Convention of the American Catholic Philosophical Association in 1974 and published in a volume dedicated to Thomas and Bonaventure. See *Proceedings of the American Catholic Philosophical Association,* XLVIII (1974), 121–35.

[1] In the words of D. E. Sharp, the possibility of an eternal creation was "one of the most important questions of the thirteenth century." See her *Franciscan Philosophy at Oxford in the Thirteenth Century* (London: Oxford University Press, 1930), p. 107.

dividual nature. The controversy involves the additional problem of whether it is possible to think of creation in the traditional sense of pro-duction of a being from nothing (*ex nihilo*) and admit at the same time that there would never have been a situation in which nothing, i.e., no creature, was in existence.

There are more far-reaching implications in the question at issue. Chief among them is our understanding of one of the most fundamental and yet mysterious attributes of God, the nature and extent of divine om-nipotence. Is God so powerful that he can create a world, although not necessarily the present one, from all eternity, despite the world's radical contingency and successive duration? Or is an eternal creation impossible even to an omnipotent Being simply because the very notion of it involves a contradiction?

These are only some of the problems involved in the issue under con-sideration. We may add that if we adopt the negative position in the con-troversy, we open the way to a refutation of those systems of philosophy that either identify God with the world or pretend to do away with God altogether and conceive the world as an eternally self-existent and self-sufficient reality. In other words, once the impossibility of an eternal world is accepted, much of what pantheism, materialism, or any atheistic philosophy stands for will appear to be either groundless or inconsistent.[2]

Coming now to the substance of the present discussion, we shall pre-sent the position of St. Bonaventure on the impossibility of creation *ab aeterno* as it emerges from its literary and historical context and compare it to the opposite view of St. Thomas. In the course of this presentation, we shall feel free to add our own reflections on the matter with a view to clarifying certain points that have been left obscure, or at least did not receive sufficient consideration, by the debating parties. The chapter will conclude with our personal evaluation of the whole controversy and a brief analysis of the latest literature on the subject.

II.   BONAVENTURE'S POSITION AND ITS
HISTORICAL BACKGROUND

Bonaventure discusses the problem of the eternity of the world in a special question of his *Commentary on the Sentences* of Peter Lombard

---

[2]It should be obvious to everyone that once the temporal nature of the world, any kind of world, has been established, it is no longer possible to identify it with God, an eternal and immutable Being, as pantheism does. Nor is it possible to maintain with materialists that matter is the only reality, since it would have to depend on another Being for its existence. It is indeed a truism that no being can give existence to itself, just as no being can come from nothing. For the contradictions involved in an atheistic philosophy see the preceding chapter of this volume.

where he asks, "Whether the world has been produced from eternity or in time."[3] Following the scholastic tripartite method, he lists first the arguments favoring an eternal production, and then refutes them one by one, but not before counteracting them with as many arguments supporting the opposite view, namely, that the world was produced in time and that creation from eternity is not only theologically untrue but also a contradictory, and therefore philosophically untenable, concept.

For a better understanding of Bonaventure's position, we should like to present the historical background of the controversy. We know from revelation that the world was created in time. The question is asked by philosophers whether God could have created the world or any creature from all eternity. Plato taught in the *Timaeus* that this order of the world had a beginning; but he admitted on the other hand the existence of an eternal matter in a chaotic state. Aristotle maintained the eternity of the world, and went as far as to say that the world could not have had a beginning. Yet these two great philosophers did not discuss specifically the question of the absolute beginning of things, since they did not have a proper notion of creation from nothing; rather they discussed the problem of whether or not the actual process of the world had a beginning.

While the possibility of an eternal creation was not a matter of discussion among the Fathers of the Church, Origen seems to have admitted an eternal creation, and Boethius did not find any contradiction in it. The controversy about the eternity of the world was raised in the Middle Ages. On the one side, we have the Jewish Neo-Platonists of the tradition of Proclus and the Arabian commentators on Aristotle, such as Avicenna and Averroes, who admit the eternity of the world; on the other side, we have the Jewish theologians and the Mohammedans who defend not only the fact of creation in time but also the impossibility of an eternal creation. Moses Maimonides, whose contribution to the understanding of the problem at issue is of primary importance, attempted to show that while the fact of creation is a matter of faith, a philosopher can demonstrate with absolute certainty neither the necessity nor the repugnance of an eternal origin of the world.[4] This is basically the view that was adopted later by Aquinas, who departed on this matter from the position of his teacher, Albert the Great, while Robert Grosseteste, Bishop of Lincoln, and the

---

[3]Cf. *II Sent.*, d. 1, pt. 1, a. 1, q. 2; *Opera omnia* (Quaracchi: Typographia Collegii S. Bonaventurae, 1885), II, 19.

[4]See Moses Maimonides, *The Guide for the Perplexed*, trans. M. Friedländer (2d ed. rev.; New York: Dover Publications, 1956), pp. 171-200, where ample treatment is given to the controversy and most of the arguments used later by scholastic philosophers on both sides of the issue, including Bonaventure and Aquinas, are discussed and evaluated.

Franciscans, Thomas of York,[5] Roger Bacon, and Alexander of Hales affirmed the impossibility of an eternal creation.

It is against this background that Bonaventure took his position in the controversy and rejected both the theory of an eternal world and the possibility of an eternal creation. "This notion is so much against reason," he states categorically, "that I can hardly imagine how any philosopher with but a little understanding could ever have maintained it."[6] Bonaventure is quite willing to admit that if matter had existed from eternity, as Aristotle and his followers taught, it is not unreasonable nor unintelligible to hold the view of an eternal world. Indeed, such a view is even more consistent with its hypothetical premise, and certainly more logical than Plato's idea of an eternal matter deprived of its form. Quoting a text from Augustine,[7] Bonaventure says that creation can be compared to a footprint in the dust, inasmuch as creatures carry within themselves the vestige of God. If the foot is eternal, and the dust on which it is imprinted existed also from eternity, the footprint will likewise be eternal. Similarly, creatures proceed from God like a shadow, while the Son proceeds from him as his splendor. As soon as there is light, there is splendor, and, given an opaque body, the shadow appears at one and the same time. Hence, once the existence of an eternal matter is admitted, the notion of an eternal world, far from being contradictory, is more reasonable than the opposite view. But is an eternal matter possible?

To avoid any misunderstanding, it must be made clear that when Bonaventure speaks of the impossibility of an eternal creation, he does not refer to the act by which God decides to create, or what in scholastic terminology is called *active* creation. Such an act, Bonaventure maintains with all other medieval schoolmen, must be eternal just as God himself is eternal, because of his absolute simplicity and perfection. The question concerns only *passive* creation, or creation looked at from the point of view of the world as the effect of the eternal decree of God that the world exist.

Likewise, when Bonaventure uses the expression "creation in time," he does not mean that creation took place at a particular moment of time,

---

[5]Thomas of York's discussion of the problem deserves special consideration because it contains many principles and arguments used by succeeding Franciscans, including Bonaventure, in support of their thesis. Cf. *Sapientiale*, ed. E. Longpré, *Archives d'histoire doctrinale et littéraire du Moyen Age*, I (1926), 273-93.

[6]*II Sent.*, d. 1, pt. 1, a. 1, q. 2; II, 22: "Dicendum, quod ponere, mundum aeternum esse sive aeternaliter productum, ponendo res omnes ex nihilo productas, omnino est contra veritatem et rationem . . . ; et adeo contra rationem, ut nullum philosophorum quantumcumque parvi intellectus crediderim hoc posuisse. Hoc enim implicat in se manifestam contradictionem."

[7]*De civitate Dei*, Book X, chap. 31. The analogy of the footprint in the dust is attributed by Augustine to the Platonists.

as though time preceded creation. There was no time when there was no creation, for time, according to the then commonly accepted teaching of Aristotle, is the measure of motion in a changeable being, and before creation there was no such a being. The proper expression for temporal creation is therefore "creation with time," although this expression is not of common usage.[8] Thus the problem under discussion concerns the possibility or not of a creation that would extend time itself, as it were, to infinity. More precisely, the question is being asked whether it is possible to conceive the world or any contingent being in such a way that the duration of its existence, while actually determinate here and now, would have had no beginning and would therefore be infinitely distant from the present moment. It is to this question that Bonaventure addresses himself, and these are the arguments he uses to support his thesis.

III. BONAVENTURE'S ARGUMENTS AGAINST AN ETERNAL WORLD

1. It is impossible to add to the infinite,[9] for any addition to it would make the infinite greater, and this is against the very nature of the infinite. Consequently, if the world had no beginning but existed from all eternity, it would admit of no additional duration. This is obviously wrong, for each new day represents a unit added to the number of days already gone. Anticipating Aquinas' objection that the infinite in question concerns only the past and not the present,[10] which is actually limited and therefore capable of further additions, Bonaventure argues that that is not true, for an eternal world implies an addition to the past as well as to the present. Indeed, for every solar revolution there would have been twelve revolutions of the moon, and since the revolutions of the sun are supposedly infinite, the lunar revolutions would be twelve times as many as those of the sun or twelve times as infinite. This is sheer contradiction.[11]

It may be added that an infinite duration in the past (*a parte ante*) involves an even greater contradiction than a similar duration in the future (*a parte post*). In the former case, we are in effect confronted with an ac-

---

[8]*II Sent.*, d. 2, pt. 1, dub. 2; II, 69-70.
[9]See Aristotle, *De caelo*, I, 12, 283 a 9.
[10]Cf. *Contra gentiles*, II, 38, ad *Quod etiam Quarto*.
[11]*II Sent.*, d. 1, pt. 1, a. 1, q. 2; II, 20-21. This argument had already been proposed by the Islamic theologian Algazel. Cf. Averroes, *Destructio destructionum philosophiae Algazelis*, disp. 1, dub. 5, as quoted in M. Gierens, S.J., *Controversia de aeternitate mundi*, "Textus et Documenta," Series phil., fasc. 6 (Rome: Universitas Gregoriana, 1933), p. 45, no. 33. The same argument is also found in the works of other Franciscans, such as Thomas of York (cf. *Sapientiale*, ed. Longpré, *Archives d'histoire doctrinale*, I, 290) and Matthew of Aquasparta (cf. *Quaestiones disputatae*, ed. Longpré, *ibid.*, p. 297).

tual infinity, or an infinite series of events that has already been actualized; whereas, in the latter case, there can only be a question of potential infinity or such that it will never be actualized.[12]

Moreover, since, of its very nature, a series of successive future events will always be limited, one may infer by analogy that the same ought to be true with regard to a series of successive past events. Thus, just as it is absurd to think of a line that would extend to infinity on one side with no possibility of any further addition to it, so it is difficult, to say the least, to conceive of a line that would reach out to infinity on the opposite side. But that is what an infinite series of successive events amounts to, for each event in the series is like a dot in a line. Briefly, an infinite duration in the past is just as inconceivable as is an infinite line or a line without a beginning.

The objection to be raised later by Durandus[13] and Suarez,[14] that this line of reasoning applies only to movable and changeable beings, and not to spiritual substances like the human soul and the angels, is irrelevant. For spiritual substances are at least capable of intellectual acts which are distinct from one another and constitute a series of limited units that is essentially the same as that of the material and changeable beings previously mentioned.

It is interesting to see how the defenders of the possibility of an eternal world react to Bonaventure's argument. According to one of their best exponents, a recognized authority on Aquinas' thought, Bonaventure would have fallen victim to a basic misunderstanding by assuming that the past is something *real*, whereas the truth of the matter is that it is only an idea in our minds. This idea may refer to a particular day, month, or year, or any other determined duration, in which case it is always possible to think of an addition to it. But if the idea refers to an infinite past taken as a whole, then the argument is nothing but a begging of the question, since the past cannot be considered as a whole except by determining and limiting it. Thus the argument assumes as true what is to be proved.[15]

Speaking for Bonaventure, we would say that such a criticism is not warranted. First of all, we cannot share the author's view that the past, even though specified as definite periods of time such as days, months, or years, is merely an idea in our minds. The measurement of the past in

---

[12]This is the observation made by Matthew of Aquasparta. Cf. *Quaestiones disputatae,* ed. Longpré, *ibid.,* p. 306.

[13]Cf. Gierens, *op. cit.,* pp. 80–86.

[14]*Ibid.,* pp. 90–100.

[15]See A. D. Sertillanges, O.P., "La preuve de l'existence de Dieu et l'éternité du monde," *Revue thomiste,* 5 (Nov., 1897), 623. See also his book, *L'idée de création et ses retentissements en philosophie* (Paris: Aubier, 1945), pp. 32–33, where he reaffirms his view even more forcefully than in his previous article.

terms of time units is, we agree, the product of our own thinking, but the basis for that measurement is not and cannot be a mere fiction. There have been *real* events, which took place within *real,* definite periods of time. It is wrong, therefore, to compare the past to the future and regard both as purely mental constructs. Secondly, with regard to the author's accusation that by conceiving the past as a determinate whole Bonaventure and his followers are begging the question, we think one could just as well reverse the charge and say: To hold that the past as a whole cannot be conceived because it transcends all limits and measurements, is precisely to accept as true what the argument is supposed to prove, namely, the infinite nature of the past. But more of this later.

2. It is impossible for an infinity of things to be ordered. In fact, all order involves a beginning, a middle term, and an end. Where there is no beginning, there can be no middle term and no end, and hence no order, at least as far as a whole series of events is concerned. So if the duration of the world, and consequently the revolutions of the heavenly bodies, were infinite, these revolutions would have no starting point,[16] nor would they follow one another, which is plainly false. There must therefore be a first term in the series of heavenly revolutions and hence a beginning of the world.[17]

If it is objected that in Aristotelian,[18] as well as Thomistic,[19] terms an infinite series is impossible only in essentially subordinated causes, Bonaventure disagrees and asks, "Why is not an infinite series of other causes equally impossible?" Aristotle teaches that there has never been a revolution of the stars around the earth without an animal being generated by another animal. Now it is obvious that animals are ordered among themselves by a causal relationship. If then, according to Aristotle, an order among causes is necessary, it does not seem possible to avoid the conclusion that there must have been a first animal and hence a beginning of the world.

To understand Bonaventure's reasoning, one must keep in mind that for him a series of causes in which one depends on another for its existence as a cause, although not for its own causality, is *de facto* a necessary series. For him, therefore, Aquinas' distinction between essentially and accidentally related causes does not hold, for, even though the causes in question do not act simultaneously, they are all needed for the final effect. What is accidental about the series, Bonaventure would say, is the fact

---

[16]Reference is made here to Aristotle's statement, "Infinitorum enim nihil est primum." *Phys.* VIII, 5, 256 a. 19.

[17]*II Sent.,* d. 1, pt. 1, a. 1, q. 2; II, 21.

[18]Aristotle, *Phys.* VIII, 5; *Metaph.* I, 2, 994 a 1 ff.

[19]*Sum. theol.,* I, q. 46, a. 2, ad 7.

that its members act in succession and within the same order of causality, rather than simultaneously and on a different level. Looked at from this point of view, the generation of an animal from another animal or of a man from another man is not merely accidental. Indeed, it is so essential that if any member of the series is missing, no final effect is possible. This goes to show, Bonaventure would insist, that without a first man there would be no men in existence today.[20]

Aquinas, as is well known, met Bonaventure's objection to an eternal world based on the impossibility of order in an infinite series of successive causes or events by denying the need for a first term in such a series.[21] This answer, if proved valid, would solve one of the most controversial issues that underlie our discussion: whether it is possible to conceive an infinite series of events and avoid at the same time the contradiction, admitted by both Aquinas and Bonaventure, that would result from the acceptance of the idea of an infinite number. This point will be discussed in connection with Bonaventure's third argument, which in many ways resembles the present one.

3. It is impossible to traverse the infinite.[22] But if the world had no beginning, an infinite number of celestial revolutions must have taken place and made it impossible to reach our present day.[23] Here again Bonaventure foresees Aquinas' objection[24] that this is a false problem, because in an eternal world no infinite distance is being traversed, since there is no first revolution to begin with. To this Bonaventure replies: either one revolution, or let us say one day, has preceded the present day infinitely, or none. If none, then all anterior days are at a limited distance from the present one, which means that they all had a beginning. If, on the contrary, one day stands at an infinite distance from the present one, then what about the day that immediately followed it? Would that day be infinitely removed from the present day or not? If it is not infinitely removed, then neither is the preceding day, for the distance between them is limited. If, on the other hand, it is infinitely removed, the same question must be asked about the third, the fourth, and all succeeding days indefinitely. This amounts to saying that the present day is at no further distance from any one day in the past than it is from another. All days are

---

[20]The idea that in the process of generation the causes are essentially related to one another is already found in Thomas of York (cf. *Sapientiale,* in Longpré, *art. cit.,* p. 291) and was later developed by Matthew of Aquasparta (cf. *Quaest. disp., ibid.,* p. 299).

[21]*Con. gent.,* II, 38, *Quod etiam Tertio; Sum. theol.,* I, q. 46, a. 2, ad 6.

[22]Aristotle, *Post. Anal.* I, 22; 82 b 38; *Metaph.* X, 10; 1066 a 35.

[23]*II Sent.,* d. 1, pt. 1, a. 1, q. 2; II, 21.

[24]*Sum theol.,* I, q. 46, a. 2, ad 6.

then simultaneous and no sequence of days is possible, which is obviously not the case.[25]

This argument, like the preceding ones, aims to show the absurd consequences that follow from the acceptance of an infinite series of past events. The argument is not to be taken lightly, for it involves one of the most critical issues in the present controversy and may well serve as a testing ground for Bonaventure's thesis. To understand his reasoning more clearly and appreciate the difference between his view and that of Aquinas, we now need a brief presentation of the latter's position.

In his attempt to show the possibility of an eternal creation, or at least its lack of evident self-contradiction, Thomas consistently maintains that it is possible to conceive of an infinite series of accidentally subordinated causes as long as the causes involved act only in succession. This he calls a potentially infinite series or multitude to distinguish it from an actually infinite multitude, whether this is taken absolutely, e.g., the act of the will, the movement of the hand and a hammer in the work of an artisan, or accidentally, as for example, an infinite multitude of hammers, one independent of the other.[26] To avoid the apparent contradiction of what might be construed as the acceptance of an infinite number, Thomas adopts Aristotle's distinction between number and multitude and claims that number adds to multitude the idea of measurement: "Number is multitude measured by one."[27] This distinction enables him to acknowledge the validity of the Aristotelian principle that the infinite admits of no addition, cannot be ordained, cannot be traversed, and the like, and still maintain his own view of the possibility of an eternal world.[28]

Bonaventure objects to Aquinas' position on this score, even though there is no evidence that Thomas was the direct target of his attack, and tries to refute it by a series of arguments *ad absurdum*. The third argument is a case in point.

---

[25]*II Sent.*, d. 1, pt. 1, a. 1, q. 2; II, 21.

[26]*Sum. theol.* I, q. 7, a. 4; q. 46, a. 2, ad 7.

[27]*Ibid.*, I, q. 7, a. 4. See also *In III Phys.*, lect. 8, where Thomas explains that while number is a species of discrete quantity, multitude is like a transcendental: "est enim numerus multitudo mensurata per unum, ut dicitur in decimo Metaphysicae; et propter hoc numerus ponitur species quantitatis discretae, non autem multitudo, sed est de transcendentibus."

[28]For a discussion of the notion of an infinite series of causes and related problems see Hildebrand Fleischmann, O.S.B., "De processu in infinitum in causis efficientibus," *Ephemerides theologicae Lovanienses*, III (1926), 5–28; Paolo Carosi, "La serie infinita di cause efficienti subordinate," *Divus Thomas*, 46 (1943), 29–77; 159–75; P. M. Périer, "A propos du nombre infini," *Revue pratique d'apologétique*, 27 (1919), 739–57. For an extensive and sympathetic treatment of Aquinas' doctrine of creation see James F. Anderson, *The Cause of Being* (St. Louis: Herder, 1952).

It would be impossible, it has been noted,[29] to disprove directly the theory of an infinite series of past events, for, being unthinkable, the theory does not lend itself to direct refutation. Yet it is not difficult to point out the absurd consequences to which the theory leads. This is precisely what Bonaventure attempts to do.

Aquinas' position seems to imply that an infinite series of causes is possible as long as the members of the series are not acting or existing simultaneously or actually required for a particular effect. Thus it is not impossible to conceive of an infinite series of hammers, as long as they are used successively for a particular work, just as it is not impossible for a man to be generated by man to infinity.[30] Accordingly, the successive or actual existence of the causes in question becomes the criterion of the possibility of an infinite series. But if this is the case, one may ask, why make a distinction between multitude and number—a distinction, incidentally, that is far from convincing—which is completely irrelevant to the problem at issue? Whether or not the causes are actually in existence, we are confronted in both cases with a series of distinct, determinate, and therefore measurable, units that has already been actualized and can in no way be called merely potential. The fact that some of the causes, e.g., hammers or men, are not in existence now is purely accidental to the effect of the series.[31] This is so true that the possibility of their being kept in existence by God from all eternity, provided an infinite series of such causes is conceivable, should be obvious to everyone. This point will become clearer when Bonaventure's fifth argument is discussed.

4. The fourth argument is based once more on an Aristotelian principle, namely, that it is impossible for a finite power to understand the infinite.[32] But that would be the case, Bonaventure says, if the world had no beginning. For if we admit with Aristotle that no celestial revolution is possible that is not being caused, or at least known, by a finite spiritual substance, and grant further that a pure intelligence does not forget what it knows, then we are bound to say that a finite power knows the infinite. It would be an actual, comprehensive knowledge of an infinite number of revolutions, since, in Aristotle's conception of the world, such revolutions would have been going on from all eternity. Nor can it be said, adds Bonaventure, that the knowledge of the revolutions in question could be obtained by a single idea on account of their similarity, for that knowledge

---

[29]Cf. Fernand Van Steenberghen, *Hidden God,* trans. Theodore Crowley (St. Louis: Herder, 1966), p. 175.

[30]*Sum theol.,* I, q. 46, a. 2, ad 7.

[31]For a discussion of this point cf. Fleischmann, *art. cit.,* pp. 62–63.

[32]Aristotle, *Metaph.* II, 4, 999 a 27.

extends also to the effects of the revolutions which would be both diverse and infinite. The conclusion is therefore inescapable: a finite intelligence would have an actual and comprehensive knowledge of the infinite.[33]

Needless to say, this argument is but another attempt on the part of Bonaventure to show the absurd consequences that follow from the notion of an eternal world. The fact that Bonaventure makes use of Aristotle's unscientific astronomy, incidentally, does not compromise his argument's validity. In fact, it is at least conceivable that in an eternally existing world a created intelligence—whether human or angelic is irrelevant—would be there to know the infinite number of actual or possible changes and events that would have taken place in it. Thus the only question to be solved is whether or not an infinite series of past events that have been actualized in succession can be present to a finite intelligence as a simultaneous and distinct whole on account of its intuitive grasp and unfailing memory. Bonaventure answers this question in the negative, and his answer is in complete agreement with his previous position.

5. The fifth argument is not only the culmination and logical conclusion of the preceding ones, but it also constitutes the most serious objection to the theory of an eternal world. Thomas himself felt very strongly the weight of this objection, and, as we shall see presently, he was never able to answer it to his complete satisfaction. Here is how Bonaventure frames the argument. It is impossible that an infinity of beings exist at one and the same time.[34] But if the world is eternal and, as Aristotle says, everything that exists is somehow related to man,[35] the world would never have been without man. Since, however, a man has only a temporal existence, there would then have been by now an infinite number of men. We know, on the other hand, that for each man there is a rational soul, and that the soul as a spiritual substance is immortal. Consequently, just as there would have been an infinite number of men, so there would have been an infinite number of souls, which, because of their incorruptible nature, would all be actually existing today. This is against the principle stated above of the impossibility of an actual infinity of beings. The theory of an eternal world must therefore be wrong.[36]

This conclusion cannot be evaded, continues Bonaventure, by the theory of a cyclic existence of the souls, whereby one soul could pass through an infinite number of bodies, for, according to Aristotle, each

---

[33]*II Sent.*, d. 1, pt. 1, a. 1, q. 2; II, 21.
[34]Aristotle, *Phys.* III, 5; *Metaph.* X, 10, 1066 b 11.
[35]Aristotle, *Phys.* II, 2, 194 a 34.
[36]*II Sent.*, d. 1, pt. 1, a. 1, q. 2; II, 21.

soul is the proper act of a determinate matter.[37] Nor can it be evaded by saying that a single soul or intellect is sufficient for the entire human race, since this is even a greater error than the preceding one. The conclusion is therefore unassailable.[38]

As previously stated, Thomas took this argument very seriously, and in both the *Summa contra gentiles*[39] and the treatise *De aeternitate mundi*[40] he acknowledges the particular difficulty it presents to his own thesis. This should not surprise anyone who is acquainted with his persistent denial of the possibility of an infinite number of actually existing beings. What may be a surprise is the way in which he tries to evade the issue by saying that God could have created a world without man, in which case the problem of an infinite number of souls would not even have arisen. Furthermore, in a statement that seems to reverse his previous position, he adds that "it has not yet been demonstrated that God could not make [a world] in which there would be an infinity of actually existing beings."[41]

In the words of one of his commentators,[42] this is Thomas' easy way out of the impasse in which he found himself. But did he really answer Bonaventure's objection? It does not seem so. First of all, the difficulty involved in the possibility of an infinite number of men, and therefore of an actual infinity of souls, cannot be dismissed simply by saying that God could have created a world without man. To be sure, God did not have to create man or any other being, in which case there would be no question to ask. But the fact is that God did create a world and did create man to live in it. The question is therefore whether in the hypothesis of an eternal world, which Aquinas accepts as a possibility, a man could have been created along with it, that is, from all eternity, and be endowed with a soul

---

[37] Aristotle, *De anima* II, 2, 414 a 25.

[38] *II Sent.*, d. 1, pt. 1, a. 1, q. 2; II, 21–22.

[39] Book II, chap. 38, ad *Quod autem*.

[40] The complete title of the treatise is *De aeternitate mundi contra murmurantes*. This will be quoted from the collection of St. Thomas' *Opuscula philosophica* edited by Raymundus M. Spiazzi, O.P. (Turin-Rome: Marietti, 1954). Here is how Thomas expresses himself in connection with the objection at issue: "Adducunt etiam pro se rationes quas etiam Philosophi tetigerunt et eas solverunt; inter quas illa est difficilior quae est de infinitate animarum: quia si mundus semper fuit, necesse est modo infinitas animas esse." *Ibid.*, p. 108, no. 310. See also for the same objection *Sum. theol.*, I, q. 46, a. 2, ad 8. For an English translation of all Aquinas' and Bonaventure's texts on the question of the eternity of the world see St. Thomas Aquinas, Siger of Brabant, St. Bonaventure, *On the Eternity of the World*, trans. from the Latin with an Introduction by Cyril Vollert, Lottie H. Kendzierski, and Paul M. Byrne (Milwaukee, Wis.: Marquette University Press, 1964).

[41] *De aeternitate mundi*, ed. cit., p. 108, no. 310. See also *Con. gent.*, II, chap. 38, ad *Quod autem*, where the same idea is suggested indirectly.

[42] Etienne Gilson, *The Christian Philosophy of St. Thomas Aquinas*, trans. L. K. Shook, C.S.B. (New York: Random House, 1956), p. 150.

that could go on in existence forever. This is the point at issue, and this, we believe, is a perfectly legitimate question to ask.

Nor can the issue be evaded, as Aquinas seems to suggest, by the supposition that the infinity in question might concern only spiritual substances, like angels and the human souls. The reason is obvious. An actual infinity of angels or souls is just as inconceivable as is an infinite number of individual men or bodies, for each member of either series is equally limited, determinate, and therefore measurable. Besides, if the Thomistic theory is held that the separated soul is individuated by its transcendental relationship to the matter of the body, then it is hardly understandable how a distinction could be made between spiritual and material substance as far as the series or multitude is concerned. There would have to be just as many bodies as there are souls, and this again goes to disprove Aquinas' thesis that only a potential infinite multitude is possible but not an actual one, whether absolute or accidental.[43]

Clearly, then, Thomas did not find it easy to cope with Bonaventure's argument based on the impossibility of an infinite number of souls. His suggestion that God might after all be able to create a world with an infinity of actually existing beings, which by some is considered as Thomas' last word on the matter, is also an indication that toward the end of his life he might have had doubts about the validity of his previous distinction between actual and successive infinity.[44] The problematic here involved is how to admit either of these two kinds of infinity and yet avoid the contradiction that would result from the existence of an infinite number of beings. Thomas' recourse to Aristotle's distinction between number and multitude is no doubt an ingenious device, but, as previously indicated, it is not absolutely convincing.[45] For one thing, it failed to convince Bonaventure, who appears certain of the impossibility of an actual infinite multitude of beings. It is in fact on precisely this impossibility that he bases his fifth argument.[46]

If an opinion can be expressed on this matter, we must say that we find it difficult to accept the idea of a multitude of distinct, individualized, and

---

[43]*Sum theol.* I, q. 7, a. 4. See also *ibid.*, q. 46, a. 2, ad 8, where Aquinas confirms the view expressed in q. 7, a. 4. For some of the difficulties involved in Aquinas' thesis see H. Pinard, "Création," in *Dictionnaire de théologie catholique.* III, 2, cols. 2178-2179.

[44]For Thomas' possible change of attitude toward the problem at issue see Iosephus Hontheim, S.J., *Institutiones theodicaeae* (Freiburg i. Br.: Herder, 1893), p. 713, n. 1.

[45]For a defense of Aquinas' view see Périer, *art. cit.*, pp. 739-57.

[46]Cf. Pius M. a Mondreganes, O.M.Cap., "De impossibilitate aeternae mundi creationis ad mentem S. Bonaventurae," *Collectanea Franciscana.* 5 (1935), 560. This article, which runs from p. 529 to p. 570, is a very good presentation of Bonaventure's thought on the eternity of the world and its philosophical background.

therefore determinate beings, that could not be measured in terms of numerical units. If an infinite material body cannot exist because its constitutive elements are all limited and determinate and the resulting compound cannot be of a different nature than the elements themselves—an idea with which Aquinas seems to agree, even if he does so for different reasons[47]—then we fail to see how an infinite multitude of equally limited and distinct beings (whether material or spiritual is irrelevant) could possibly exist in concrete reality.

6. Whereas the five arguments thus far considered are intended to show the impossibility of an eternal creation from the nature of the effect of God's creative act, the sixth and last of Bonaventure's arguments is based on the nature of creation itself. This argument deserves special consideration because, in Bonaventure's view, it is probably the strongest and most compelling one, and also because it is the one that has been most misunderstood. It runs as follows.

It is impossible for something that has being after non-being to exist from all eternity, for that implies a contradiction. But the world has being after non-being. Hence the world cannot be eternal. That the world has being after non-being is proved by the fact that it is produced by God totally, i.e., in its entire substance, and this can be only in terms of a production from nothing. It is not produced from nothing materially, as though there had been some kind of pre-existent matter, but only originally, inasmuch as the production of the world marks the beginning of its existence. This is a true production *ex nihilo*, since neither matter nor form was pre-existing. Moreover, matter could not come from any source outside of God, and God possesses no matter within himself. Thus to say that the world is eternal, or that it has been produced from eternity, and to hold at the same time that it has been produced from nothing, is entirely against truth and reason.[48]

The principal idea contained in this argument is that creation is not only the production of a thing in its totality, i.e., from no pre-existent principle or element, but that it also involves a transition, as it were, from non-being to being, and consequently, the emergence into existence of a new reality, the beginning of a new existence outside God. The two concepts of "total production" and "production *ex nihilo*" are linked together by Bonaventure in such a way that one cannot be separated from the other and both demand an initial emergence of being from an original nothing. This amounts to saying that if the being in question existed from

---

[47]Cf. *Sum. theol.*, I, q. 7, a. 3: "It is manifest that a natural body cannot be actually infinite."

[48]*II Sent.*, d. 1, pt. 1, a. 1, q. 2; II, 22.

all eternity, it could not have been produced from nothing, since there would never have been an original nothingness to begin with.

It would be wrong to interpret Bonaventure's expression of "being after non-being" (*esse post non-esse*) as meaning a sequence in time, as though creation would have taken place at a particular moment of time. No one was more aware than Bonaventure of Augustine's explanation that time began *with* creation: a doctrine that he made his own.[49] Thus when he says that being comes after nonbeing, he means simply that the world must have had a beginning, as the following text clearly indicates: "When [the world] is said to be made (*fieri*), it means that it has a beginning (*principium*). When it is said to be *eternal,* it means that it has no beginning."[50] Hence, to ask whether the world could have been created from eternity, is tantamount to asking whether the world could have had a beginning without having a beginning, which is a plain contradiction.[51]

Bonaventure therefore agrees with Aquinas in saying that creation does not involve a sequence in time or duration,[52] but he parts company with him when he draws the conclusion that creation involves only a sequence in nature between nothing and being.[53] There is of course a sequence in nature in the sense explained by Aquinas, namely, that a creature, left to itself, is nothing, and whatever of reality it has, comes to it from another being.[54] But this sequence does not explain the actual emergence of being from nothing, or, if we may so speak, the newness of being. As a matter of fact, if a mere sequence in nature in the sense ex-

---

[49]*Ibid.,* d. 2, pt. 1, dub. 2; II, 69-70: "Dicendum, quod differt dicere, secundum Augustinum, aliquid fieri *ex* tempore, et *in* tempore, et *cum* tempore. *Ex* enim importat ordinem, *in* importat continentiam, *cum* importat simultatem; et ideo nihil est factum *in* tempore, nec *ex* tempore, nisi quod exceditur a tempore. Quia igitur tempus et ea, quae in primordio temporis creata sunt, a tempore non excluduntur, ideo dicit, ea esse creata *cum* tempore, non *in* tempore, nec *ex* tempore."

[50]*I Sent.,* d. 44, a. 1, q. 4; I, 788.

[51]*Ibid.* See also *Comment. in Ecclesiasten,* chap. 3, q. 1; VI, 28, where Bonaventure says that time in creatures means "the measure of their exit from non-being to being *(mensuram exitus de non-esse ad esse).* "

[52]Sertillanges, like many others, is therefore wrong when he presents Bonaventure's notion of creation *ex nihilo* as implying the idea of duration prior to the actual existence of the world. He is also wrong, as will be seen later, when he states that Bonaventure considers the *nihilum* prior to creation as a positive point of departure. See *L'idée de création,* p. 26. Van Steenberghen is not very helpful either when he states that "St. Bonaventure confused creation *ex nihilo* with creation *post nihilum* " and gives the impression that the preposition *post* refers to a sequence in time. Cf. *Hidden God,* p. 172.

[53]*De aeternitate mundi,* p. 107, no. 304. "Sed ordo multiplex est: scilicet durationis et naturae. Si igitur ex communi et universali non sequitur proprium et particulare, non erit necessarium ut propter hoc quod creaturam esse post nihil dicitur, prius duratione fuerit nihil, et postea fuerit aliquid: sed sufficit, si prius natura sit nihil quam ens."

[54]*Ibid.:* "Esse autem non habet creatura nisi ab alio; sibi autem relicta in se considerata nihil est: unde prius naturaliter inest sibi nihil quam esse."

plained above exists between being and non-being, the whole idea of creation as production from nothing seems to be ruled out. This apparently is
what worries Bonaventure, who conceives creation as an event, and even a
change or *mutatio*. However, he takes care to explain, the term *change*
does not refer here to an actual transition to being or *esse* from *nihilum* as
a real *terminus a quo*. This would be a contradiction, for *nihilum* is the
negation of every reality whatsoever. The term is taken in the broader
sense of emergence of a new reality, the beginning of a new *esse*.[55]

To explain his thought more clearly, Bonaventure contrasts creation
ex nihilo to the process occurring in the Holy Trinity whereby the Son is
generated by the Father. In both cases there is a production, and in both
cases the production is due to an equally infinite power. But, whereas in
the generation of the Son by the Father there is an identity of substance
that excludes any change or transition from nothing to being, as well as
any beginning of *esse,* in creation there is a production *ex nihilo* by which
esse comes after *non-esse,* in the sense previously explained. This is what
is meant by the expression *fieri ex nihilo*: to be made from nothing, to
begin to exist. Briefly, production as such is indifferent to time and eternity; production *ex nihilo* involves necessarily the notion of time and
change, the beginning of something that did not exist before.[56] Once the
concept of production *ex nihilo* is explained in these terms, the question
of the possibility of an eternal creation does not even arise.

These, then, are the arguments used by Bonaventure to prove the impossibility of an eternal creation. Having stated his own position, he takes
up the objections raised by the defenders of the Aristotelian-Averroistic
theory of an eternal world mentioned at the beginning of the question and
answers them one by one. Since these objections have no direct bearing on
the subject of our discussion, we omit them and continue with a brief
evaluation of Bonaventure's position as compared to that of Aquinas.

IV. BONAVENTURE AND AQUINAS

From the foregoing exposition, it is evident that Bonaventure cannot
accept the idea of an eternal creation, both because of his understanding
of the nature of a creature and because of his notion of creation itself. For

---

[55]The following text is very enlightening: "Si ergo quaeratur, quae sit habitudo, quae
importatur in comparatione ad *non-esse;* dicendum, quod illa habitudo dicitur
mutatio.—Et si quaeras, quid sit illa mutatio; dico, quod non est aliud quam ipsa res.—Et
hoc patet, quia est mutatio *ad esse,* et mutatio *ab esse,* et mutatio *in esse.* Mutatio *ad esse*
nihil ponit nisi a parte termini;...et ideo *mutari* primo modo nihil aliud est, quam nunc
primo esse." II Sent., d. 1, pt. 1, a. 3, q. 2; II, 34.

[56]*Ibid.,* q. 1; II, 33.

Bonaventure, as for Aquinas and all the other medieval schoolmen, the question involves not extrinsic but intrinsic possibility. That is, as we have seen, it is a question, not of any lack in the divine power, but rather of the inner consistency of the very notion of eternal creation. Here is where Bonaventure parts company with Aquinas. While both schoolmen agree in their understanding of creation as the production of a being from absolute nothingness, Aquinas maintains that creation is essentially a relation of total dependence of the creature on its Creator, whereas Bonaventure holds that, in addition to the creature's dependence on God, creation necessarily implies also the beginning of the creature's existence. Furthermore, Bonaventure lays greater emphasis than Aquinas does on the positive aspect of creation as a production from nothing. Indeed, in the latter's view, creation is conceived in terms of a simple predicamental relation or, to use his own word, "an accident" that follows logically upon the thing created;[57] whereas for Bonaventure, "to be created (creari) is by nature, although not by duration, prior to the esse [of the creature]."[58] In this latter conception, the expressions inceptio essendi (the beginning of being) and novitas essendi (the newness of being), used by Aquinas to explain the creature's relation to God by creation,[59] acquire a more positive meaning. Creation becomes an event, the "exit" of esse from non-esse,[60] the beginning of a new reality. Hence Bonaventure's persistent refusal to accept the idea of an eternal creation that would do away with the very notion of creation in the sense that has just been explained.

Although Bonaventure does not make Thomas' concept of creation the direct target of his criticism, we feel the need to implement his teaching with a personal observation. To conceive creation as a relation of total dependence of the creature on its Creator is undoubtedly correct, for a creature has no reality of its own, and whatever reality it has, must come to it from God. But is such dependence really what makes a creature to be

---

[57]De potentia, q. 3, a. 3, Ad Tertium, in Quaestiones disputatae, II (8th ed. rev.; Turin-Rome: Marietti, 1949), p. 43: "Dicendum quod illa relatio accidens est, et secundum esse suum considerata, prout inhaeret subiecto, posterius est quam res creata." Many scholastic philosophers, following the lead of John Duns Scotus and John of St. Thomas, have accepted the view that creation involves a transcendental relation rather than merely a predicamental relation.

[58]II Sent., d. 1, pt. 1, a. 3, q. 2; II, 35: "Et ideo concedendum, quod creatio non est aliud secundum rem a creatura, nec medium inter ipsam et Deum secundum essentiam, sed secundum rationen et habitudinem; unde est prius natura creari quam esse, non duratione."

[59]De potentia, q. 3, a. 3, in Quaest. disput., II, 43: "in ipsa creatione...importatur...solummodo inceptio essendi, et relatio ad creatorem a quo esse habet; et sic creatio nihil est aliud realiter quam relatio quaedam ad Deum cum novitate essendi."

[60]II Sent., d. 1, pt. 1, a. 3, q. 2; II, 34: "Creari enim non significat esse principaliter, sed exire de non-esse in esse, et hoc ab aliquo."

a creature? or is not dependence something that follows logically, to say the least, upon creation? After all, in order to depend, one must first exist. Again, how does the notion of dependence convey the idea of production from nothing, which is what creation is all about? We would submit, therefore, that the relation of dependence can perhaps be better explained as an implication or logical sequel of creation, while creation itself as the actual production of a being from nothing takes precedence over that relation. Creation, in other words, is the production of a being as a being, and from this it follows that the being so produced is totally dependent on its Creator. This explanation, it seems to us, makes more sense than the one given by a previously mentioned Thomist commentator who, after saying that creation is "nothing but a unilateral relation of dependence," draws the following conclusion: "For a creature to be in relation to God, it must first exist. If creation is this relation, creation comes then after the creature in the order of being. This is truly the world upside down!"[61] We would agree with this last statement, if the author's notion of creation were correct. But is this really what creation amounts to? Can we really say that creation comes after the creature in the order of being? In the light of our preceding observations, the answer to these questions can only be in the negative.

In addition to the difficulty arising from the notion of creation, Bonaventure's other main source of objection to Aquinas' theory of a possible eternal world is the nature of the world itself. The Seraphic Doctor cannot visualize a world, or any created being for that matter, that could exist from all eternity and still retain its nature as a contingent, changeable, and therefore limited being. We have seen his arguments to this effect, and there is no need to repeat them. We would like, nevertheless, to add a final observation, to show that Bonaventure's view of the impossibility of an eternally created being is perhaps not as far-fetched as it may first appear to be.

By its nature, a contingent being—whether temporal or eternal does not matter—depends on its Creator for the entire length of its existence. Thus it is conceivable that God could annihilate it at any given moment of its existence by simply withdrawing his conservative act from it. If that is the case, how can we then account for such a possibility and still retain the idea of an eternal contingent being? Destruction or annihilation, let us keep in mind, is not a process; it is an instantaneous act, just as creation is. The only difference between the two is that creation demands a positive act on the part of God, whereas annihilation is effected through a negative act. Should we say, then, that there is an eternal instant in which the be-

---

[61] Sertillanges, *L'idée de création.* p. 47.

ing can be destroyed? That is obviously a contradiction. Hence the only other possible answer, it seems to us, is either that an eternal contingent being is not eternally destructible, which seems to conflict with the very nature of a contingent being, or that it is eternally destructible but can never be actually destroyed, in which case the infinite power of God is questioned. Whatever the answer, this is a problem that is at least worth considering.

V. RECENT LITERATURE ON THE SUBJECT

We would like now to compare the position adopted in this chapter with that of a renowned contemporary philosopher and medievalist, Fernand Van Steenberghen, who in a recent article[62] has reaffirmed and developed some of the ideas expressed in his earlier works.[63] Van Steenberghen introduces his study with a review of the latest writings on the subject, such as those by Pius a Mondreganes,[64] Etienne Gilson,[65] Georges H. Tavard,[66] Joseph Ratzinger,[67] and Vincenzo C. Bigi.[68] In the author's view, the article by Pius a Mondreganes is, despite some minor defects, a most valuable source of information not only for Bonaventure's doctrine, which is fully endorsed, but also for the thought of the Church Fathers and scholastic philosophers, both ancient and modern. Gilson's treatment of the theory of creation, Van Steenberghen continues, is confined to an objective presentation of Bonaventure's thought with no attempt to evaluate it critically. So is the presentation of Ratzinger, who discusses the problem of the origin of the world within the framework of Bonaventure's theology of history. The study of Tavard, says Van Steenberghen, is of an entirely different nature. Arguing on the basis of a passage from Bonaventure's treatise *De Trinitate*, Tavard takes a stand

---

[62]Cf. Fernand Van Steenberghen, "Saint Bonaventure contre l'éternité du monde," in *S. Bonaventura. 1274-1974*. III (Grottaferrata [Rome]: Collegio S. Bonaventura, 1973), 259-78.

[63]See, for example, *Hidden God*. pp. 171-75; *Ontology*. trans. Martin J. Flynn (New York: Wagner, 1952), pp. 240-44; *La philosophie au XIIIᵉ siècle* (Louvain: Publications Universitaires, 1966), pp. 225-26, 245, 291, 328, 345-46, 404-410, 428, 458-64, 472, 511, 542; "La controversie sur l'éternité du monde au XIIIᵉ siècle," *Bulletin de la Classe des Lettres* (de l'Académie Royale de Belgique), 1972 (5ᵉ serie, 68), 243-63.

[64]Cf. n. 46 above.

[65]*La philosophie de saint Bonaventure* (2d ed. rev.; Paris: Vrin, 1943), pp. 154-59.

[66]"On a Misreading of St. Bonaventure's Doctrine of Creation," *Downside Review*. 69 (1951), 276-88.

[67]*Die Geschichtstheologie des heiligen Bonaventura* (Munich: Schnell und Steiner, 1959), pp. 140-47.

[68]"La dottrina della temporalità e del tempo in San Bonaventura," *Antonianum*. 39 (1964), 437-88; 40 (1965), 96-151.

against all preceding historians and claims that according to Bonaventure the world has had a beginning only "because God willed it." This amounts to saying that, if God had willed otherwise, he could have created a world from all eternity. To the objection that for Bonaventure an eternally created world implies a contradiction, Tavard answers that the contradiction for the Seraphic Doctor lies only in the notion of an eternal world *created ex nihilo,* not in that of a world that would have been created from eternity but not *ex nihilo.* Accordingly, the arguments advanced by Bonaventure against the possibility of an eternal world do not represent his own thought.

Van Steenberghen sharply criticizes Tavard's position, calling it "totally indefensible." It is based, he says, on a faulty interpretation of Bonaventure's text and contradicts the constant teaching of the Franciscan Master.[69]

The treatment of Bonaventure's notion of creation and time by Father Bigi is in direct opposition to Tavard's view. Calling it "a solid and profound study," Van Steenberghen commends Bigi for a penetrating analysis of Bonaventure's concept of the temporality of the world and for clearly indicating the fundamental difference between Aquinas and Bonaventure in their approaches to the problem of creation and eternity.[70]

To complete Van Steenberghen's survey of studies on our subject, we must mention an article that appeared in the same volume as Van Steenberghen's study and follows it immediately. Its author, Father Antonius Coccia, discusses the doctrine of the eternity of the world on the basis of Bonaventure's *Commentary on the Sentences* and *Collationes in Hexaëmeron,* with occasional references to other works by the Seraphic Doctor.[71] Coccia shows his sympathy for Bonaventure's position and points out, among other things, the modern aspect of Bonaventure's theory in that it seems to have the support of contemporary science.

Having traced the recent developments in the controversy about the eternity of the world, Van Steenberghen approaches the subject himself and makes a brief analysis of the question from the *Sentences,* where Bonaventure's theory is presented. As a result of his analysis, he concludes that the reasons advanced by the Seraphic Doctor for the rejection of an eternal world can be reduced to two basic arguments. The first is based on the notion of *creatio ex nihilo* and corresponds to the sixth *ratio* brought forth by Bonaventure against the opposing theory and developed further

---

[69]See *art. cit.,* pp. 262–65, for Van Steenberghen's criticism of Tavard's position.
[70]*Ibid.,* p. 265.
[71]Cf. Antonius Coccia, O.F.M. Conv., "De aeternitate mundi apud S. Bonaventuram et recentiores," in *S. Bonaventura, 1274–1974,* III, 279–306.

in the actual solution of the problem at issue. The second argument is based on the notion of the infinite and the Aristotelian principles derived from it. It corresponds to the five *rationes in oppositum* which, in Bonaventure's arrangement, precede the argument from the notion of creation. Van Steenberghen rejects the first argument and endorses the second. For convenience sake, we shall first mention his points of agreement with Bonaventure's view and then discuss his objections to the argument based on the notion of *creatio ex nihilo*.

Van Steenberghen rightly observes that all Bonaventure's *rationes* against the theory of an eternal world rest on a datum that is granted by his opponents, namely, that an eternal world in the past implies an infinite series of events already accomplished. For if the series were finite, there would be a first term and hence a beginning of the world. After mentioning the five arguments from Bonaventure's text, Van Steenberghen observes further that although these arguments do not have exactly the same value today as in Bonaventure's time when Aristotle's physical theory of the world was commonly accepted, still their basic reasoning is sound; it shows very clearly the absurd consequences that would follow if the notion of an eternal world were accepted. In Van Steenberghen's view, the underlying theme of Bonaventure's arguments is that "in the quantitative order, the infinite is the ideal limit toward which an *indefinite* series of additional units *tends* but which it will never reach. Otherwise stated, in the real order it is impossible to have an infinite in act."[72]

Van Steenberghen is so convinced of the truth of his thesis grounded in the nature of discrete quantity, that he cannot see how a philosopher, or any person of judgement, could refuse to accept it. And yet, he remarks, there are those who persist in maintaining the possibility of an eternal world in a desperate fight whose history would be both interesting and amusing. In their attempt to defend an indefensible thesis, they display such "intellectual acrobatics," that one wonders how strong a role their imagination plays. Père Sertillanges' hypothesis of an infinite number is a case in point.[73] We may add that the hypothesis in question is a logical consequence of the theory of an eternal world, unless Thomas' distinction between number and multitude is accepted. But this, as previously noted, amounts to saying that an infinite series of past events, each one limited and fully determinate, would be numberless and indeterminate. The contradiction involved in this position is not difficult to see.

---

[72]Van Steenberghen, *art. cit.*, in *S. Bonaventura, 1274–1974*, p. 273.

[73]*L'idée de création*, p. 35. For Van Steenberghen's discussion of Bonaventure's argument based on the notion of the infinite cf. *art. cit.*, in *S. Bonaventura, 1274–1974*, pp. 271-76.

While Van Steenberghen accepts Bonaventure's argument against an eternal world based on the notion of the infinite, he criticizes the argument from creation *ex nihilo* and declares it worthless. The reason for its rejection is basically the same as that given by St. Thomas. The notion of creation *ex nihilo* does not imply a temporal priority of *nihilum* over being but only a sequence in nature, on the grounds that a created being, if left to itself, would be nothing, since all its reality comes to it from its cause. Thus the expression *factum ex nihilo* means simply *factum non ex aliquo*, i.e., made from no pre-existing subject. Hence creation *ex nihilo* does not necessarily involve a beginning of existence, as Bonaventure claims. Hence also Bonaventure's interpretation of *ex nihilo* as meaning *post nihilum* is incorrect, since no time is possible prior to creation.[74]

VI. APPRAISAL OF VAN STEENBERGHEN'S VIEW

A discussion of Van Steenberghen's position here outlined would entail a repetition of much that we have already said in this chapter in connection with Bonaventure's sixth argument from the *Sentences* and in our final comment on the controversy at issue. We shall, therefore, confine ourselves to Van Steenberghen's criticism of Bonaventure's argument.

In the first place, it must be made clear that whenever Bonaventure uses the expression *post nihilum* in reference to creation, he does not in any way imply a sequence in time between nothing and being, but only a sequence in origin and, more specifically, the beginning of existence from no pre-existing being, the *nunc primo esse*.[75] This point is not made clear by Van Steenberghen. He seems in fact to insinuate that Bonaventure's notion of creation *ex nihilo* involves a temporal succession, as though an imaginary time existed before creation and apart from the world.[76]

Secondly, to say that the formula *ex nihilo* has strictly speaking a negative meaning, in the sense that creation presupposes no pre-existing subject, is of course very true, and Bonaventure would agree with it. But what about creation itself or the actual emergence into existence of a being from nothing as the result of the creative act of God? Is this also a merely negative notion? We submit that once creation is conceived as a produc-

---

[74] See Van Steenberghen, *art. cit.*, pp. 268-71, for his criticism of Bonaventure on Thomistic grounds.

[75] See references in notes 48, 49, 50 and 55 above.

[76] *Art. cit.*, p. 270: "Aussi lorsque Bonaventure déclare, en réponse à Avicenne, que l'acte créateur est un acte de volonté et que, dès lors, Dieu peut vouloir éternellement que le monde commence d'exister *à tel moment du temps,* il imagine un temps indépendant de l'existence du monde, ce qui revient à introduire la durée temporelle dans l'éternité divine." See also his comment on p. 269: "Commentons: cette interprétation du mot *ex* revient à dire que *ex nihilo* signifie tout bonnement *post nihilum.*"

tion of being *ex nihilo,* it is far from clear that an instantaneous action is not involved whereby the being in question begins to exist. Just as through annihilation, which is possible at each moment of a created being's existence, a being would cease instantaneously to exist, so by creation a being does actually begin to exist. This is what Bonaventure had in mind when, toward the end of his life, he wrote: "Wise men agree that something cannot be made from nothing and be from eternity. For just as when something falls into nothing it necessarily ceases to exist, so when something is made from nothing, it begins to exist."[77]

One more question must be raised in connection with Van Steenberghen's concluding remarks. While acknowledging that Bonaventure has established the impossibility of an eternal world by furnishing the elements of a decisive proof *ab absurdo* against the hypothesis of an eternal past, Van Steenberghen affirms that Bonaventure was able to do so only by showing the contradiction of an infinite in act, not by his doctrine of *creatio ex nihilo.*[78] As a matter of fact, Van Steenberghen holds, his way of understanding creation *ex nihilo* would have somewhat compromised the solidity of his position.[79]

If this is the case, then the argument for the impossibility of an eternal creation which was foremost in Bonaventure's mind, would not only be useless but also damaging to his thesis. The only way to prove the temporal nature of the world is to be found, according to Van Steenberghen, in the essential dynamism of the substances of which the world is composed: a dynamism that is manifested in a continuous process of evolution that must have had a beginning and can be measured by time.[80]

We do not intend to contest Van Steenberghen's view, which is certainly worth considering. However, we must point out that his position restricts the concept of temporal creation by applying it exclusively to the present world or any other world similar to it. In the hypothesis, which is at least conceivable, that a different kind of world, let us say a static world, were created by God and kept in that state for the entire length of its existence, the theory of an eternal creation could be accepted. Such a view contradicts not only the mind of Bonaventure, who taught that no being whatsoever could possibly be created from eternity, but also seems to make an accidental property the basis for a being's temporal existence. Motion or change is in effect not an absolute requirement for a contingent being, whose only essential characteristics seem to be its continuous de-

---

[77]Cf. *In Hexaëmeron.* collatio IV, no. 13; vol. V, 351.
[78]*Art. cit.,* p. 276.
[79]*Ibid.,* p. 278.
[80]*Ibid.,* p. 276.

pendence on the cause of its existence and its successive duration. Nevertheless, we agree with Van Steenberghen's other conclusion that, given the dynamic nature of a world like the present one, it is easier to argue for a beginning of its evolutionary process and of its temporal creation.[81]

In conclusion, the question of whether or not the world could have been created from eternity remains one of the most difficult and perplexing issues in the entire field of philosophy. Strong arguments exist on both sides of the question, which should make one very cautious before committing himself either to the position of Aquinas or to that of Bonaventure. The fact that the problem under consideration involves an element of mystery that is proper to all God's acts and operations, such as the act of creation, should make one even more cautious in accepting either of the proposed solutions as a definitive one.

BIBLIOGRAPHY

Anderson, James. *The Cause of Being.* St. Louis: Herder, 1952.

Aristotle. *The Basic Works.* 10th printing. Edited and with an Introduction by Richard McKeon. New York: Random House, 1941.

Augustine, St. *De civitate Dei.* Migne, PL 41.

Bigi, Vincenzo C. "La dottrina della temporalità e del tempo in San Bonaventura," *Antonianum,* 39 (1964), 437-88; 40 (1965), 96-151.

Bonansea, Bernardino M. "The Impossibility of Creation from Eternity according to St. Bonaventure," *Proceedings of the American Catholic Philosophical Association,* 48 (1974), 121-35.

————. "The Question of an Eternal World in the Teaching of St. Bonaventure," *Franciscan Studies,* 34 (1974), 7-33.

Bonaventure, St. *Opera omnia.* 10 vols. Quaracchi: Typographia Collegii S. Bonaventurae, 1882-1902.

Carosi, Paolo. "La serie infinita di cause efficienti subordinate," *Divus Thomas,* 46 (1943), 29-77; 159-75.

Coccia, Antonius, O.F.M.Conv. "De aeternitate mundi apud S. Bonaventuram et recentiores." In *S. Bonaventura, 1274-1974,* vol. III, pp. 279-306. Grottaferrata (Rome): Collegio S. Bonaventura, 1973.

Fleischmann, Hildebrand, O.S.B. "De processu in infinitum in causis efficientibus," *Ephemerides theologicae Lovanienses,* 3 (1926), 5-28.

Gierens, M., S.J. *Controversia de aeternitate mundi.* "Textus et Documenta." Rome: Universitas Gregoriana, 1933.

Gilson, Etienne. *La philosophie de saint Bonaventure.* 2d ed. rev. Paris: Vrin, 1943. English edition: *The Philosophy of St. Bonaventure.* Trans. by Dom Illtyd Trethowan. London: Sheed and Ward, 1940. Very important work for the study of St. Bonaventure's thought.

---

[81]*Ibid.,* p. 277. For an explanation of how science favors the theory of a temporal origin of the world and, at least indirectly, the doctrine of creation in time, see next chapter.

_____. *The Christian Philosophy of St. Thomas Aquinas.* Trans. by L. K. Shook, C.S.B. New York: Random House, 1956.

Hontheim, Josephus, S.J. *Institutiones theodicaeae naturalis.* Freiburg i. Br.: Herder, 1893.

Maimonides, Moses. *The Guide for the Perplexed.* 2d ed. rev. Trans. by M. Friedländer. New York: Dover Publications, 1956.

Matthew of Aquasparta. *Quaestiones disputatae,* ed. by E. Longpré, *Archives d'histoire doctrinale et littéraire du Moyen Age,* I (1926), 293-308.

Périer, P. M. "A propos du nombre infini," *Revue pratique d'apologétique,* 27 (1919), 739-57.

Pinard, H. "Création," *Dictionnaire de théologie catholique,* III, 2, cols. 2174-2180.

Pius M. a Mondreganes, O.M.Cap. "De impossibilitate aeternae mundi creationis ad mentem S. Bonaventurae," *Collectanea Franciscana,* 5 (1935), 529-70.

Ratzinger, Joseph. *Die Geschichtstheologie des heiligen Bonaventura.* Munich: Schnell und Steiner, 1959.

Sertillanges, A. D., O.P. "La preuve de l'existence de Dieu et l'éternité du monde," *Revue thomiste,* 5 (Nov., 1897), 453-68; 609-626; 746-62.

_____. *L'idée de création et ses retentissements en philosophie.* Paris: Aubier, 1945.

Sharp, D. E. *Franciscan Philosophy at Oxford in the Thirteenth Century.* London: Oxford University Press, 1930.

Tavard, Georges H. "On a Misreading of St. Bonaventure's Doctrine of Creation," *Downside Review,* 69 (1951), 276-88.

Thomas Aquinas, St. *Summa theologiae.* 4 vols. Ed. by P. Caramello. Turin-Rome: Marietti, 1948-1950.

_____. *Summa contra gentiles.* Editio Leonina Manualis. Turin-Rome: Marietti, 1946.

_____. *In VIII libros Physicorum Aristotelis expositio.* Ed. by M. Maggiolo, O.P. Turin-Rome: Marietti, 1954.

_____. "De potentia." In *Quaestiones disputatae,* vol. II, pp. 7-276. Ed by R. M. Spiazzi, O.P. Turin-Rome: Marietti, 1949.

_____. "De aeternitate mundi contra murmurantes." In *Opuscula philosophica,* pp. 105-108. Ed. by Raymundus M. Spiazzi, O.P. Turin-Rome: Marietti, 1954.

Thomas Aquinas, St., Siger of Brabant, and Bonaventure, St. *On the Eternity of the World.* Trans. by Cyril Vollert, Lottie H. Kendzierski, and Paul M. Byrne. Milwaukee, Wis.: Marquette University Press, 1964.

Thomas of York. *Sapientiale,* ed. by E. Longpré, *Archives d'histoire doctrinale et littéraire du Moyen Age,* I (1926), 273-93.

Van Steenberghen, Fernand. "Saint Bonaventure contre l'éternité du monde." In *S. Bonaventura, 1274-1974,* vol. III, pp. 259-78. Grottaferrata (Rome): Collegio S. Bonaventura, 1973.

_____. *Hidden God.* Trans. by Theodore Crowley, O.F.M. St. Louis, Mo.: Herder, 1966.

_____. *Ontology.* Trans. by Martin J. Flynn. New York: Wagner, 1952.

_____. *La philosophie au XIIIe siècle.* Louvain: Publications Universitaires, 1966.

_____. "La controversie sur l'éternité du monde au XIIIe siècle," *Bulletin de la Classe des Lettres* (de l'Académie Royale de Belgique), 1972. Pp. 243-63.

CHAPTER IX

SCIENCE AND CREATION*

Will scientists ever be able to produce factual evidence against the doctrine of creation? This question is likely to arise in the minds of many well educated persons who lack sound philosophical and theological training. They may observe with bewilderment and awe the gigantic strides that science is making in its march toward the exploration of the secrets of the universe. Fear may enter their minds that the growing wealth of scientific discoveries in the fields of physics, astronomy, and astrophysics may some day lead scholars to discard the doctrine of creation as a theory that has been surpassed and is no longer acceptable. But this would be tantamount to saying that a conflict is possible between science and religion, reason and faith. We intend to show in this chapter that fear of such a conflict is absolutely groundless. We shall do so in separate steps, the first of which is the exact definition of the notion of creation; and the second, the explanation of the true relationship between science and theology—natural or revealed—as far as the creationist theory is concerned.

I. MEANING OF CREATION

Creation may be defined as the production of something from absolutely nothing that is pre-existent. Every production is of course the production of something that as such did not exist before. But in creation we have a more basic and radical kind of production, inasmuch as something is made from no pre-existent substance, element, or principle whatsoever that might serve as a material cause for the new being that comes into existence. Creation is the production of a thing in its totality, or, to give a more profound philosophical definition, creation is the production of a being precisely as a being. For a better grasp of the meaning of creation a few observations are in order.

When we say that in creation a being is produced from absolutely nothing that is pre-existent, we do not mean that prior to the existence of the thing created, or to the sum-total of created things that make up the universe, there was an absolute nothingness, and then, all of a sudden and

*This chapter appeared originally in a slightly different form in *Science and Religion,* ed. by John Clover Monsma (New York: Putnam, 1962), under the title "A Prime Instance Where Science Needs Religion." We are pleased to report that Roy J. Gibbons, science editor of the *Chicago Tribune,* has singled out our essay for special consideration in his review of the book above mentioned (Jan. 28, 1962).

in some inexplicable way, beings emerged into existence. This is a false notion that makes creation even more mysterious than it is in reality. Furthermore, this notion is in direct contradiction to one of the most fundamental principles of reason, namely, that for every effect there must be an adequate cause. If this is true in the order of change or becoming, it is much more so in the existential order, where the emergence into existence of being itself is to be explained.

Creation demands by its very nature a pre-existing efficient cause. Moreover, this cause can only be a being endowed with infinite power, for only such a being can bridge the gap between nonexistence and existence. If we sometimes speak of man as creator, as in the case of a poet or artist, we use the term "creator" analogically. Strictly speaking, man does not create. Even in his greatest productions he makes use of pre-existing material, such as canvas, a block of marble, or even words and ideas that are possible and meaningful only in terms of some pre-existing reality.

This affords us an opportunity to clarify the specific type of production that is proper to creation. Contrary to popular belief, creation is not a process involving change or becoming. As a matter of fact, it is not a process at all. The notion of creation as a succession in which an actual being replaces the same being conceived as nonexisting is erroneous. No succession is possible where there is nothing to be succeeded, but only the emergence into existence of an entirely new being. This is a most important point that must be kept in mind if one is to pass judgment, as we shall presently do, on the scientist's competence in discussing creation.

Just as creation cannot be thought of in terms of change or becoming, so all spatial or temporal imagery should be removed from its notion. It is a fact of common experience that when we think of creation we are likely to imagine an infinitely extended space into which the world is placed by the creative act of God. Philosophically speaking, this is a wrong way of understanding creation, for no space is conceivable apart from the universe of created things. All spatial determinations are in fact relative to the existing world. Moreover, the world as a whole does not occupy a place, since there is no other material being to which it could be related.

Likewise, we usually imagine the world as coming into existence at a certain moment of time, as if before creation took place there would have been a time in which God alone existed. Imaginative representations of this kind are wrong on several counts.

First, there was no time before creation, for time is the measure of motion in a changeable being, and before creation there was no such being. Time, like space, is relative to creation. An infinite duration apart from changeable beings is a fiction similar to that of an infinite vacuum. Hence, to use an expression of St. Augustine, already referred to in the preceding chapter, the world was created, not in time, but *with* time. That is why it is meaningless to ask at what precise instant the world was created, or whether creation could have been anticipated or postponed. The world could have existed longer than it actually has, but could not have been created except in the first moment of time, since world and time are coextensive.

Secondly, in creating the world God did not, as it were, come out of an eternal rest or inactivity, for his creative act is identical, and therefore coeternal, with his essence. This identity is due to God's absolute simplicity, an attribute that belongs to God on account of his supreme perfection. Accordingly, there was no time—we have already shown that time is coextensive with the world—in which God was not Creator. To quote St. Augustine again, "If there was no time before heaven and earth, why do they ask what you [God] did then? There was no 'then' where there was no time.... At no time, therefore, did you do nothing, since you have made time itself."[1]

Thirdly, to say that *before* creation there was nothing, or that creation was *after* nothing, is not correct. The reason is that *nothing,* as we have previously stated, cannot be the term of any succession, and succession is a necessary element in the notion of time. Hence it is wrong to speak of creation as though it implied a temporal succession from nothingness into being.

On the basis of the foregoing considerations, we are now able to define creation both from the point of view of God and from that of creatures. As far as God is concerned, creation is the eternal act by which the divine will decrees the existence of the world. This is also called active creation. From the viewpoint of creatures, creation is the relation of total dependence that they have to God in regard to their very being. This is called passive creation. Thus the essence of creation, as far as creatures are concerned, consists in a relation of absolute dependence on the Creator. Otherwise stated, "creation is in reality nothing else than a certain relation to God with newness of existing."[2]

As can readily be seen, the doctrine of creation from nothing is not easy to understand. Furthermore, it is questionable whether human reason would ever have attained to this doctrine without the aid of revelation. Apparently neither Plato nor Aristotle, nor any other philosopher prior to the Judeo-Christian revelation, was able to conceive the notion of creation in the sense that has just been explained. This should not surprise

---

[1]Cf. St. Augustine, *The Confessions.* Bk. XI, chap. 13, no. 15; chap. 14, no. 17.

[2]Cf. St. Thomas Aquinas, *De potentia,* q. 3, a. 3. For a discussion and evaluation of Aquinas' concept of creation see Section IV of the preceding chapter.

anyone who has but a little knowledge of the history of philosophy. Indeed, even after the Christian revelation there are still many philosophers who refuse to accept the doctrine of creation from nothing on the ground that it is absurd and contradictory. It is not our concern here to show that the creationist theory, far from being contradictory, is the only reasonable solution to the problem of the origin of things. Such proof exceeds the limits of this essay. Instead, we shall turn to positive science and examine its claim to solve the problem at issue. More specifically, we shall consider whether a scientist, speaking in the name of physical science alone, can really expect to unveil the "mystery" of the origin of the cosmos, and whether his verdict could ever be interpreted as a refutation of the doctrine of creation.

II. POSITIVE SCIENCE AND CREATION

Positive science, as is well known, is that branch of knowledge which is concerned with phenomena and their immediate causes. Some of its specific disciplines are physics, chemistry, biology, astronomy, astrophysics, and radio astronomy. The only method used in positive science is the empirical or experimental method, and its instruments include the most disparate devices, from the sun-dial to the most refined microscope and the radiotelescope. What does not fall within the realm of sensible experience is not an empirical datum and cannot be the object of empirical investigation. Thus understood, positive science has definite limits which the scientist himself implicitly admits, inasmuch as his criterion for the evaluation of a scientific theory is the amount of empirical evidence that goes to support it. Obviously, this is not an arbitrary limitation, but one that is imposed by the very nature of positive science and the rigorous method that the scientist sets for himself in his inquiry.

Keeping this in mind, we shall be in a position to evaluate the statements of those who object to the doctrine of creation on the ground that it is unscientific, unnecessary, and contrary to reason. These are statements that reflect an attitude prevalent among many scientists, as well as among many others who are the unfortunate victims of a purely positivistic approach to reality. Hence they deserve most careful consideration.

It is our contention that the doctrine of creation is completely beyond the reach of positive science, and that any rejection of it in the name of science is inconsistent and fallacious.

As previously stated, creation is the production of something from no pre-existent matter or element; it is the emergence into existence of a being that previously did not exist except as an idea in the mind of God. It is clear, then, that when a scientist applies his technique to the study of the entire cosmos or any part of it, he already has before himself the effect of creation, not creation itself, or the creative act, which is a purely spiritual act of the same nature as the author of creation. Not being a process, creation admits of no successive phases or moments which could form the basis for a scientific investigation.

It is true that the entire material universe did not have to be created in one single moment, since neither reason nor revelation tells us that God must create all things at one time. In fact, according to traditional Christian teaching, a soul is created each time a human being comes into existence. On purely rational grounds, therefore, the "steady-state" theory of a continuous creation of matter has a degree of probability equal to the theory of an evolving universe, or "big bang" theory, according to which all matter was created in one single event. As has been observed, "by spreading out creation in time and space, there is no reduction in the mystery, since multiplication of the occasions of creation as contrasted with the single unique event leaves it open to exactly the same objections [from the purely scientific viewpoint] as the latter."[3] The need for an explanation of the sudden appearance of matter out of nothing remains basically the same in both cosmological theories, even though revelation, as well as scientific evidence, seems to favor the theory of an evolving universe. The existence of the universe is what is to be explained, and this is not a scientific but a philosophical problem. Science may tell us *what* the world is once the world has been made, but not *how* it came to be, since this is not a problem whose answer is subject to empirical verification.

To hold, as some scientists speaking as philosophers are wont to do, that matter is eternal and needs no creator, is not to solve the problem of existence but rather to confuse the issue. An eternal universe—if it is possible at all,[4] and this is not the business of science to decide—is no more self-explanatory than a universe existing in time. The problem is not one of duration, which is a mere accidental feature of created realities, but one of *being*. To use a popular analogy, just as ten thousand idiots will never combine to form a wise man, so also, no matter how far in the past we extend the existence of the cosmos, we will always have to face the same basic difficulty: How is it possible for the world to exist? That existence is not part of its nature is evidenced by the fact that without any contradiction one can conceive the world as nonexisting. An eternal universe is therefore an eternally insufficient being which demands an eternal cause for its existence.

---

[3]Dr. Milton K. Munitz, "Creation and the 'New' Cosmology," in *The British Journal for the Philosophy of Science*, V (1954), 34. Quoted by E. L. Mascall in *Christian Theology and Natural Science* (London and New York: Longmans, Green and Co., 1957), p. 157.

[4]See the preceding chapter for a discussion of this question.

Furthermore, a matter that evolves into life, and even to the high level of intellective and conscious life, by blind mechanical forces and independently of any extrinsic agent, as the upholders of materialistic evolutionism teach, must be a very refined and mysterious matter indeed! Yet, those very philosophers and scientists who reject as "gratuitous" the doctrine of creation, are not at all embarassed to proclaim the absurdity of a self-existent and self-evolving matter, as though matter were a kind of demigod, if not God himself.[5]

Let us make it clear that we are not opposed to the theory of evolution, the validity and extent of which depend on the amount of scientific evidence that goes to support it. Our contention is that evolution is not self-explanatory and that it demands an adequate cause. That cause cannot be matter, which is itself in need of an explanation and is subject to the laws of evolution. It must therefore be a superior and supremely intelligent being which is above matter and its laws and, in the last analysis, the creative cause of all existing things. This is of course the teaching of divine revelation and, as we have seen in the foregoing chapters of this volume, of sound philosophy as well. The attacks of science against it are absolutely groundless.

Granted that physical scientists can pose no threat to the doctrine of creation, which is purely a philosophical and theological issue, can we say that scientific discoveries are completely irrelevant to the problem of the origin of things? To put it more bluntly, can we say that physical scientists know nothing of creation and that their findings have no bearing whatsoever on the creationist theory? To hold this view is not to do justice to science. Moreover, it is to introduce an unjustifiable dichotomy between science and religion, as well as between science and philosophy. There is no reason for such a dichotomy because both science and religion are concerned with truth, and truth is one. With regard specifically to the doctrine of creation, it must be said that not only is there no conflict between science and religion, but science is actually favorable to the creationist theory.

Indeed, the second law of thermodynamics, better known as the law of entropy, states that the amount of useful energy in the universe is constantly diminishing. This situation is due to a continuous flow of heat from warmer to colder bodies, without any possibility of a spontaneous

---

[5]Etienne Gilson writes in this connection: "A world which has lost the Christian God cannot but resemble a world which had not yet found him. Just like the world of Thales and of Plato, our own modern world is 'full of gods.' There are blind Evolution, clear-sighted Orthogenesis, benevolent Progress, and others which it is more advisable not to mention by name." *God and Philosophy* (New Haven: Yale University Press, 1941), p. 136.

reversal of the process. Thus the time will inevitably come when all energy will be equally diffused throughout the entire universe in the form of potential—as opposed to actual or kinetic—energy. This energy will never become useful again because of the uniformity of temperature among the bodies; for it is only when heat passes from a body of higher temperature to one of lower temperature that work is done. As a result, not only life but all movement will be impossible. This shows that actual energy and movement do not necessarily belong to matter. If they did, the movement of cosmic matter could never come to a standstill.

Now, if actual or kinetic energy does not belong to matter necessarily and yet, on the other hand, cannot produce itself, it is logical to conclude that it is imparted to matter by an external agent. Likewise, if movement has to come to an end, it must also have had a beginning. Otherwise the amount of useful energy, which is necessarily limited by its nature, would have long been exhausted, and no activity would be possible anywhere in the world at this moment. Physical science, then, seems to support the theory of a limited duration of the world, and consequently of the world's dependence on an external cause, a cause that philosophy and theology prove to be God.

It is true that science has not yet established whether the law of entropy is valid for the entire universe, since much of the cosmos remains to be explored. There is, however, a strong presumption that the physical laws which hold throughout the large portion of the universe known to us are equally valid in other parts that are still unknown but have, in all probability, the same basic nature and characteristics. Here is one area in which astrophysics and radio astronomy may make an important contribution to our scientific knowledge, even though the present writer cannot share the excessive optimism of a well-known scientist who stated that radio astronomy is "man's latest hope to probe the mystery of the origin of the cosmos."[6]

With the aid of experts in other newly developed physical sciences, radio astronomers may rightly expect to add many achievements to those already realized in the comparatively short history of their science. It is not unlikely that in his unrestrained yet legitimate ambition to unlock the secrets of the universe, man will reach out with more and more refined instruments into the vast dimensions of space and learn the exact magnitude of the world we live in. He may even be able to give a fairly accurate account of the multiphase process that led to the formation of our planet, the stars, and the giant galaxies that make up the universe. All these data

---

[6]A. C. B. Lovell, "Adventures of the Mind: Listening to the Universe," *The Saturday Evening Post* (Oct. 15, 1960), p. 40.

and scientific achievements will no doubt constitute an invaluable source of information for a philosopher and theologian in their explanation of the doctrine of creation. But physical science alone will never be able to solve the problem of the birth of the universe, simply because, it is worth repeating, the problem of existence is not a scientific, but a metaphysical and theological problem.

We may rightly conclude, then, that the doctrine of creation has nothing to fear from science. As Cardinal Newman said, "Nature and grace, reason and revelation come from the same divine Author, whose works cannot contradict each other."[7] One of the most formidable temptations of contemporary scientists is that of erecting a proud citadel, a modern tower of Babel, as a challenge of human intelligence to the sovereignty of the Creator. But "happy is the man," we can say with the late Pope Pius XII, "who can read in the stars the message that they contain, a message of power commensurate with Him who has written it, worthy of rewarding the seeker for his tenacity and his skill, but inviting him also to recognize the One who gives truth and life, and makes His dwelling in the hearts of those who adore Him and love Him."[8]

BIBLIOGRAPHY

Augustine, St. The Confessions. Translated, with an Introduction and Notes, by John K. Ryan. Garden City, N.Y.: Doubleday "Image Books," 1960.

Bonansea, Bernardine. "A Prime Instance Where Science Needs Religion." In Science and Religion, pp. 93-102. Ed. by John Clover Monsma. New York: Putnam's Sons, 1962.

Gilson, Etienne. God and Philosophy. New Haven: Yale University Press, 1941.

Lovell, A. C. B. "Adventures of the Mind: Listening to the Universe," The Saturday Evening Post, 233 (Oct. 15, 1960), 40-41 + .

Mascall, E. L. Christian Theology and Natural Science. London and New York: Longmans, Green and Co., 1957.

Munitz, Milton K. "Creation and the 'New' Cosmology," The British Journal for the Philosophy of Science, V (1954), 32-46.

Newman, Cardinal John Henry. The Idea of a University. New ed. London and New York: Longmans, Green and Co., 1947.

Pius XII, Pope. "The Heavens and the Glory of God," The Pope Speaks, IV (1957), 161-64.

Thomas Aquinas, St. "De potentia." In Quaestiones disputatae, vol. II, pp. 7-276. Ed. by R. M. Spiazzi, O.P. Turin-Rome: Marietti, 1949.

[7]John Henry Cardinal Newman, The Idea of a University (new ed.; London and New York: Longmans, Green and Co., 1947), p. 194.

[8]From the Address of Pope Pius XII to an Astronomical Conference sponsored by the Pontifical Academy of Science, May 20, 1957. Cf. "The Heavens and the Glory of God," The Pope Speaks, IV, 164.

CONCLUSION

In concluding this study, we would like to summarize the results of our inquiry and make a few final remarks.

This work began with an analysis of the principal atheistic philosophies in modern and contemporary times in an attempt to see whether their systematic denial of God poses a real challenge to traditional theism. The study of individual philosophers showed that, while none of them has been able to offer a real proof of the nonexistence of God, they have either refused to take the question of God's existence seriously, as in the case of Nietzsche, or they have adopted a negative attitude toward God even before trying to work out their philosophical theory. When Karl Marx wrote that "communism begins from the outset with atheism"[1] and that "only through the annulment of this mediation [i.e., God]...does positive humanism come into being,"[2] he set a pattern of thought not only for his direct followers, the dialectical materialists, but for other atheistic philosophers as well. We saw this clearly in the case of Sartre, whose existentialism is, in his own words, "nothing else but an attempt to draw the full conclusions from a consistently atheistic position."[3] Feuerbach's humanistic atheism was likewise shown to be the logical outcome of a purely subjectivistic concept of God and religion, while Camus' exaggerated notion of evil in the world and the apparent absurdity of human life were indicated as the primary cause of his revolt against God.

Our study has thus revealed that, because of the weaknesses and inherent contradictions of the systems discussed, none of them poses a serious threat to theism. There are, undoubtedly, positive elements in most atheistic philosophies, which a complete objective study could not afford to overlook; but the nature and purpose of this work have precluded any further expansion of the limits of our inquiry.

As we moved from the negative to the positive side of the problem of God's existence, we re-examined some of the basic theistic arguments with a view to exploring their probative value. The first two arguments, which originated with two of the greatest Christian thinkers, Augustine and Anselm, were submitted to a thorough investigation from the viewpoint of their literary context and the philosophical background of their proponents. In both cases the arguments were followed through their historical development, and the positions of both defenders and op-

[1] See "Economic and Philosophic Manuscripts of 1844," in *The Marx-Engels Reader*, ed. Robert C. Tucker (New York: W. W. Norton and Company, 1972), p. 71.

[2] *Ibid.*, p. 98.

[3] See "Existentialism Is a Humanism," in Kaufmann, *Existentialism from Dostoevsky to Sartre*, p. 310.

ponents were carefully stated and evaluated. The study has convinced us that the arguments in question are two pieces of profound metaphysical reasoning that are not only a credit to their authors but greatly enhance our understanding of God as the source of all truth and intelligibility and as the most perfect conceivable Being.

But the classic metaphysical arguments for God's existence remain the five ways of St. Thomas and Duns Scotus' comprehensive theistic proof. To these we have devoted a considerable amount of effort, first, by making Charlier's presentation of the five ways available to the English-speaking reader without sacrificing any of its contents or even its stylistic form; and, secondly, by presenting Scotus' proof in all its complexity, faithfully adhering to its original text and setting it within the general context of his philosophy. The chapters covering Aquinas' and Scotus' proofs are meant to answer the needs of those readers who are not altogether satisfied with the way the proofs are presented in scholastic manuals and look for a thorough and adequate presentation that meets all the requirements of strict metaphysical reasoning.

As a sequel to the classic theistic arguments, Blondel's original approach to God was next presented in all its essential and characteristic elements. Blondel's attempt to reach God by the method of immanence may prove valuable especially to those persons who, following a trend in philosophy initiated by Descartes and developed by subsequent rationalists and idealists, prefer to argue to God from the analysis of the self and its inner needs and aspirations rather than from the study of the external world.

In the closing chapter of the second part of this volume an attempt was made to clarify the notion of a theistic proof by freeing it of many persisting misconceptions. The section of the chapter dealing with contemporary atheistic trends may have seemed somewhat redundant, as it came after an extensive treatment of atheism in this same study. It was felt, however, that the section should be kept intact in its place because it contains observations and insights that are not found in our previous treatment of the philosophies concerned. The concluding section of the chapter dealt with those trends of philosophy that make all rational approach to God impossible. In it, the positions of Comte, Hume, Kant, and other modern agnostics were briefly stated and criticized, while special attention was given to the recent philosophical movement known as logical positivism.

The last, and by far the shortest, part of the volume was concerned with the important issue of the relation of God to the world and, specifically, with the doctrine of creation. Once the creationist theory has been firmly established on grounds that would have been too long to discuss, the way to an all-powerful and creating God becomes wide open. Our certitude of God's existence is, if we may speak thus, confirmed by the findings of positive science, which tend to support the contention that the world had a beginning, and by St. Bonaventure's philosophical theory of the impossibility of an eternal world.

By way of conclusion, we wish to reaffirm our conviction that, contrary to a widespread belief among contemporary philosophers, the existence of God is not only an object of faith but also a solidly established philosophical truth. In our approach to the problem under consideration, a special effort has been made to develop the *metaphysical* arguments for the existence of God, including those whose value is somewhat controverted. Evidently, these are not the easiest arguments to understand, since metaphysics is, by its very nature, the most profound and involved of all sciences. We insist, however, that these arguments, and especially those developed by Aquinas and Scotus, are objectively valid because they draw their strength from the application to reality of the most fundamental principles of knowledge. The fact that many people, including some of the best known philosophers, fail to see their value is due, in our opinion, not so much to the nature of the arguments, as to a conception of philosophy, and of human knowledge in particular, that makes difficult, if not altogether impossible, any rational approach to God.

APPENDIX

A SIMPLIFIED VERSION OF THE THEISTIC PROOF

The reader who has followed us in the discussion of the arguments for the existence of God, has no doubt realized the difficulty and complexity of the subject. While his efforts in going through the intricacies of each argument may have proved to be extremely rewarding, still he may wish that a more simple proof could be worked out which would include all the basic elements of the classic theistic arguments, especially those of St. Thomas and Duns Scotus, and yet lack none of the features that make those arguments so effective as rational demonstrations of God's existence.

Whatever the reader's reaction to the preceding discussion, this writer feels that an attempt to simplify the theistic proof by focusing attention on its essential elements rather than its secondary points may be a welcome novelty, if one can speak of novelty in this area of study. This is what we propose to do in this brief appendix.

Our formulation of the theistic proof consists in arguing to God by a sequence of inferential judgments that take as their starting point the most fundamental facts of our experience, namely, our own existence, the existence of the world, or that of any being whatsoever. It may be called a comprehensive proof because it includes in its logical development the best of the traditional theistic arguments which St. Thomas condensed in his famous five ways, as well as some of the elements of Duns Scotus' extensive and complicated proof.

The advantages of this proof over the traditional approach to God are: first, it discards all those elements of the five ways that reflect an outdated physics and are either scientifically or philosophically questionable; secondly, it proceeds systematically from something that is most evident to what may be directly inferred from it and leads gradually but inescapably to a theistic affirmation; thirdly, it is a simple and yet complete proof that avoids the intricacies of the Scotistic proof and the inadequacies of the five ways when taken apart from the rest of Aquinas' writings; finally, the dialectic of the proof is such that it leaves no room for misunderstanding or ambiguity and should appeal to twentieth-century thinkers who are not subject to antimetaphysical biases. The proof rests, in fact, on the ontological validity of the first principles of knowledge and reality, such as the principles of contradiction, sufficient reason, and causality, without which no rational ascent to God is possible. The justification of these principles amounts to the justification of philosophy itself, at least as this has been traditionally conceived, and is beyond the scope of this essay.

The proof involves several steps in an ascending order, each one leading closer to the summit of the ladder which is the means of our dialectical ascent to God. No effort will be spared in ascertaining the solidity of each rung of the ladder before the next step is taken. This may demand the stressing of notions that are familiar to philsophically trained minds but are nevertheless indispensable for a thorough understanding of the proof by those who are not used to dialectical reasoning. The proof is meant not only for the unbeliever who has never been able to convince himself of the rational nature of classical theism, but also for the believer who is genuinely interested in acquiring a rational justification of his belief in a Supreme Being.

It goes without saying that logical positivists—to mention the proponents of only one large contemporary philosophical movement—who dismiss in principle all statements about God as meaningless, will never be convinced by the logic of our proof, or of any other theistic proof for that matter. They simply refuse to be led into a metaphysical discussion by shielding themselves behind the principle that only sense data are the object of knowledge. Since God cannot be the object of sense perception without losing his nature of a spiritual substance and ceasing to be God, then no "meaningful" statement about him is possible. This is the price that a philosopher has to pay for demolishing the very foundation on which sound philosophical thinking is supposed to rest, namely, the objective validity of the first principles of knowledge and reality of classical philosophy. The same observations hold true with regard to those analysts who reject metaphysics altogether and reduce philosophy to a mere critique of language. Linguistic analysis, it must be emphasized, can be a very useful tool in the hands of a philosopher, but it is a mistake to consider it a substitute for philosophy.

While our proof has no appeal to the logical positivist, the analyst, or any other person with a similar cast of mind, it may be helpful to the man who looks for a simple and yet logical way of arguing to God without being encumbered with too many metaphysical subtleties which, useful as they may be, are not absolutely necessary for an understanding of the proof. The proof is self-explanatory.

1. *Something exists.* This is an evident fact of our experience, and as such it needs no demonstration. A demonstration is always in terms of something that is better known, and nothing is better known to me than the fact of my own existence or that of the world around me. This is so true that any attempt to demonstrate my own existence already assumes what I propose to prove.

The position of the sceptic who doubts the truth of his own existence is self-defeating; for to doubt is to think and to think is to exist. Thought itself is a reality, or, to be more exact, the representation of a reality. It is impossible to think of nothing; to think is to think of something. Hence even an idea can serve as a starting point for our ascent to God, just as anything in the material order, whether it be a grain of sand, an atom, or even an electron, can be used to verify the premise that something exists.

2. *If something exists, something has always existed.* It is a fundamental principle of philosophy, as well as of common sense, that *ex nihilo nihil fit*—from nothing nothing comes. One can give only what he has within himself or what is within his power to give. If at any moment in the past no being was in existence, even today there would be nothing in existence. The sudden emergence of something into existence from absolute nothingness—and by this we mean the negation of any being whatsoever—is an evident absurdity. For this reason even an outright materialist, who denies the existence of God, is forced to admit an eternal self-existent matter.

The only other alternatives that have been advanced to escape the logical necessity of an eternally existing being (which cannot be purely material for reasons that will be made clear later) are either that the world came into existence by chance or that it brought itself into existence. Neither of these alternatives is acceptable. Chance is but the meeting of conflicting series of causes which can act only inasmuch as they exist. To make chance responsible for the coming into existence of the very first being is not to explain existence but to avoid the issue.

The alternative of a being that causes itself to come into existence is equally absurd and contradictory. Causality is an act, and in order to act a being must exist. That, incidentally, is the reason why we speak of God, not as *causa sui,* the cause of his own existence, but rather as *ratio sui,* the reason for his own existence.

All things considered, the statement that if something exists, there has never been a time—if we can speak of time in relation to eternity—in which something did not exist, rests on solid grounds.

3. *If something has always existed, its existence is either by itself or by another.* Existence is an act that is at once simple and unique. It is simple because it is not a process in which there is a gradual development, as it were, from nothing into being. A process, by its very nature, implies a series of acts or operations conducing to an end, or a change that takes place within a being already existing. The act of existing is neither of these. Between nothing and being there is no room for a transitional development; the gap is absolute. Something either exists or does not ex-

ist. When we speak of something as coming into existence, such as a work of art, a plant, or a brute animal, we mean only that a being gradually takes shape under the agency of certain causes working on elements or materials previously existing. It is never the sudden emergence into existence of a being that did not exist before in any way. What really happens is that there is a change within a being already existing, or what in philosophy is called becoming. Far from being identified with the act of existing, becoming always presupposes existence.

Because of its simple and unique nature, existence cannot be the product of two different agents, each one contributing a part to the emergent being. Hence, to maintain that a being can exist both by itself and by another, as though it were the product of a combined action of two agents, is contradictory. Moreover, a self-existent being cannot depend on any cause for its existence, just as a being that exists through the causality of another cannot be self-existent. The two types of being are mutually exclusive, and so the disjunction contained in our statement is perfect.

The possibility, to say the least, of an eternally self-existent being is the object of our immediate discussion. Whether a being that does not possess within itself the reason for its own existence could have existed from all eternity is not agreed upon by those philosophers who have discussed the problem. The present writer is inclined toward denying such a possibility. But the question is irrelevant to this discussion, which is concerned, not with the possibility of an eternally dependent being, but rather with the necessity of an eternally independent and therefore self-existent being. This is what we propose to prove in the following paragraph.

4. *Whether a being exists by itself or by another, we must admit a first self-existent being which is both necessary and eternal.* To prove the truth of this assertion, which is the central point of our discussion, we must first show that a being that depends on another for its existence cannot be fully explained except by its relation to a necessary being. In fact, a being that depends on another for its existence is called a contingent being, a term derived from the Latin verb *contingere* —to happen. If a contingent being does actually exist, as is the case with all beings which do exist but at one time did not exist, then its existence is due not to itself but to the causality of an extrinsic agent. To state it more clearly, a contingent being is one which of its nature is indifferent to existence and nonexistence. If it happens to exist, it is not because its nature demands it (otherwise it could not fail to exist), but because another being has brought it into existence.

The number of contingent beings and the length of their span of existence are irrelevant to our point. Even if contingent beings did exist from all eternity and in an infinite quantity, were that possible, their existence would still remain unexplained as long as the causality of an extrinsic agent is denied. The reason, it is worth repeating, is that existence is not part of their nature and its explanation must be sought outside of it. This explanation can be found only in a being that is not contingent—otherwise we would have to face the same problem—but necessary, i.e., a being whose nature it is to exist and cannot even be conceived without contradiction as nonexistent.

A necessary being is therefore self-existent and eternal. It is self-existent, for that is precisely the meaning of a being whose nature it is to exist; it is eternal, for a being that begins to exist or ceases to exist is not necessary but contingent. Is such a being also the first being in the order of existence? If by "first" we mean that a necessary being must precede a contingent being at least by a priority of nature, if not of time, then the answer can be only in the affirmative, and the reasons are those mentioned above. A contingent being can in fact be understood only through a necessary being, and not vice versa. But if by "first" we mean that a necessary being must have absolute priority over all other conceivable beings, then the answer depends on whether it is possible to have a plurality of necessary beings—in which case the question could again be raised as to which of them is first—or whether a necessary being must also be unique, i.e., one alone. This second alternative is the only one defensible on strictly philosophical grounds.

A necessary being, as previously stated, is a being whose nature it is to exist. Now existence is a simple perfection, or a perfection the concept of which implies no imperfection or limitation whatsoever. Hence a being that exists by intrinsic necessity must possess existence to the fullest possible degree. It must exhaust, as it were, within itself the entire range of existence, for it *is* existence, and whatever belongs to existence belongs to it. This, incidentally, is the reason why a contingent being is so dependent on a necessary being that it shares in its existence rather than having an existence of its own in the strict sense of the term.

It may be objected that the existence we have just described remains a purely mental concept until it has been proved that the being in question does actually exist and possesses existence to a supreme degree. The answer is that our mind has arrived at that concept of existence from the consideration of actually existing things and not from purely logical concepts. It is true that the dialectical process takes place in our mind and follows strictly logical rules, but that is precisely how a philosopher must work. He can reason and argue only through concepts in his mind. But when such concepts are grounded in the reality of actually existing things, they acquire a real, ontological value. Hence to argue to the unlimited existence of a unique necessary being from the limited existence of contingent beings of our experience is to do, not logic but metaphysics. More precisely, it is to offer a logical explanation of a metaphysical problem, the problem of the one and the many.

There is another way of proving that there can be only one necessary being. It consists in showing that the existence of two or more necessary beings involves a contradiction. Indeed, if there were two necessary beings, then the reason for their distinct existence would be either something essential or something that is purely accidental. If it is something essential, then each being lacks a perfection that is necessary for the existence of the other, and so neither one is necessary in the full sense of the term, since necessity admits of no possibility of being otherwise. If the reason for their distinct existence is something purely accidental, then each being is necessary and contingent at one and the same time. It is necessary, for this is precisely what the nature of that being is supposed to be; it is contingent, for it possesses a perfection or reality that is not absolutely required for its intrinsic constitution and yet is a necessary prerequisite for its separate existence. In either case, the contradiction is evident. The conclusion must therefore be accepted that there is a first self-existent being which is both necessary and eternal.

It may be added as a corollary to this analysis that this same being is also transcendent and unique. It not only ranks above all other beings but it constitutes a category of its own that makes it absolutely distinct from all others.

5. *A self-existent being is infinitely perfect and the cause of all other beings.* This statement represents the culmination of our proof for the existence of God and at the same time affords us some knowledge of the divine nature. Strictly speaking, the theistic proof has already been completed in the preceding paragraph where reasons have been given for the need of admitting a first self-existent being which is necessary, transcendent, and unique. However, to grasp fully the meaning of the proof, one must further determine the nature of such a being and establish more definitely its relationship to the world.

A self-existent being is infinitely perfect because no limitation can be placed on it either by itself or by another. Not by itself, because the reason for its own existence cannot be the reason for its limitation in existence, and existence, as has been shown, is a pure perfection. Better, existence is the source and sum-total of all perfections. To exist means to be in act, to have the fullness of being; only nonbeing must be excluded from it, and nonbeing is no cause of limitation because it is nothing.

Nor can a self-existent being be limited by another being, for all other beings are contingent, and as such they depend on a necessary and therefore self-existent being for their own existence. Furthermore, a self-existent being, as previously stated, is also the first in the order of existence. This is an additional reason why it cannot possibly be limited by a being that comes after it; the opposite is rather true. Hence, since a self-existent being can be limited neither by itself nor by another, we must conclude that it is infinite and contains within itself all pure perfections to the utmost degree. Such perfections include life, intelligence, and love, to mention only the most obvious. Were it not so, it could be conceived as being in potentiality to those perfections and would not be fully in act, that is, pure act, as the notion of existence indicates. This becomes even more clear from the fact that such perfections are found in creatures, which derive their entire being from the first cause, as the following consideration will show.

A being that exists in virtue of its nature and is therefore uncaused, first, and infinite, must also be the efficient, final, and exemplary cause of all other beings. It must be their efficient cause, for, since none of them can exist of itself, the only reason why they are actual rather than merely potential must be that a being whose nature it is to be has brought them into existence. This same being must likewise be their final cause, for every agent acts for an end and a first being can have only itself as an end, or else it would depend on something that is its own effect. Finally, since no effect is possible without an idea in the mind of the agent that serves as a pattern and exemplar according to which the effect is made, and since such a pattern cannot, in the case of a necessary being, be derived from something outside itself, the first and self-existent being must also be the exemplary cause of all beings that come into existence.

Our dialectic has thus led us step by step from a fact of immediate evidence to the acknowledgment of a Supreme Being, which alone can afford a rational explanation of our own existence and the existence of the world in which we live. Since this Supreme Being has all the characteristics that traditional and classic theism ascribes to God, it must be concluded that God exists.

Needless to say, the proof here proposed is not meant to be a substitute for the proofs of classic and traditional philosophy, since none of its elements are really new. What is new is its formulation, which follows a different pattern from that of the Thomistic and Scotistic proofs, in an effort to achieve the same goal they reach, but by a more simplified line of reasoning. There is no denying the fact that the proof could be embellished with additional elements that would make it more complete and self-sufficient, but then it would lose its intended simplicity and conciseness. The proof is, at any rate, an extended piece of metaphysical reasoning, and no matter how hard one may try to simplify it, it still shares the difficulty inherent in all metaphysical thought, the most profound and yet the most rewarding of all intellectual pursuits.

INDEX

This Index includes only the names and authors mentioned in the text or footnotes—the latter being indicated by an "n" appended to the page number—except for those authors whose name or works appear only in the Bibliography and the editors or translators of certain works listed in the Bibliography under their name.